HEALER *of* SOULS

Other books referencing Father Peter Mary Rookey, O.S.M.:

Do You Believe Jesus Can Heal You? by Margaret M. Trosclair, S.O.S.M.
Father Peter Rookey: Man of Miracles by Heather Parsons
Father Peter Rookey: A Laborer of the Harvest in the Lord's Vineyard by Barbara Wojtowicz
The Living Christ by Harold Fickett

HEALER *of* SOULS

FATHER PETER MARY ROOKEY AND THE
INTERNATIONAL COMPASSION MINISTRY

Kathleen E. Quasey

Library of Congress Control Number:		2007902835
ISBN:	Hardcover	978-1-4257-6669-6
	Softcover	978-1-4257-6667-2

Book design by Kelley Witzemann
Book cover photography by John Sundlof

Nihil Obstat
Reverend Anthony J. Brankin, S.T.L.
Censor Deputatus
November 23, 2005

Imprimatur
Reverend George J. Rassas
Vicar General Archdiocese of Chicago
November 29, 2005

The *Nihil Obstat* and *Imprimatur* are official declarations that a book is free of doctrinal and moral error. No implication is contained therein that those who have granted the *Nihil Obstat* and *Imprimatur* agree with the content, opinions, or statements expressed. Nor do they assume legal responsibility associated with publication.

Healer of Souls: Father Peter Mary Rookey and the International Compassion Ministry

First edition 2008

The Scripture quotations contained herein are from the *The Holy Bible*, revised by Bishop Richard Challoner, A.D. 1749-1752, Douay-Rheims Version, 1989, Tan Books and Publishers Inc., Rockford, Illinois 61105.

This book was printed in the United States of America.

To order additional copies of this book, contact:
Xlibris Corporation
1-888-795-4274
www.Xlibris.com
Orders@Xlibris.com
36258

For my Fathers:
Richard L. Quasey,
Rev. Peter Mary Rookey, O.S.M., and
Rev. Robert T. Sears, S.J., Ph.D.

With men this is impossible : but with God all things are possible.
Jesus Christ (Mt 19:26)

The Miracle Prayer

Lord Jesus, I come before You just as I am. I am sorry for my sins, I repent of my sins, please forgive me. In Your Name I forgive all others for what they have done against me. I renounce Satan, the evil spirits and all their works. I give You my entire self, Lord Jesus, now and forever. I invite You into my life, Jesus. I accept You as my Lord, God, and Saviour. Heal me, change me, strengthen me in body, soul and spirit.

Come, Lord Jesus, cover me with Your Precious Blood, and fill me with Your Holy Spirit. I Love You, Lord Jesus. I Praise You, Jesus. I Thank You, Jesus. I shall follow You every day of my life. Amen.

Mary, my Mother, Queen of Peace. St. Peregrine, the Cancer Saint, all you Angels and Saints, please help me. Amen.

Say this prayer faithfully, no matter how you feel. When you come to the point where you sincerely mean each word, with all your heart, something good spiritually will happen to you. You will experience Jesus, and He will change your whole life in a very special way. You will see.[1]

Notes

[1]   Peter Mary Rookey, O.S.M., *The Miracle Prayer,* Imprimatur, Francisco Maria Aguilera Gonzalez, Auxiliary Bishop of Mexico (Chicago, IL: Servite Fathers, 1993).

Fig. 1.   *The Risen Christ,* stained glass window, St. Ignatius Parish, Chicago, Illinois, 2006.

Contents

Preface

Father Peter Mary Rookey, O.S.M., is often referred to as *the healing priest*. Thousands of healings of body, mind, and spirit have been reported worldwide. Witness letters, some with medical consensus, have been submitted as evidence of the Healing Power of God. Daily, the International Compassion Ministry's phone lines are jammed with prayer requests. In many countries, people have stood in line for hours to attend Father Rookey's Masses and healing services. Inspired by the Holy Spirit, he compassionately has ministered to thousands from morning to night.

While there has been much discussion about the effects of Father Rookey's God-given Gift for Healing, little is known about the man. Like masters of any art, the greatest are those who make the difficult seem effortless. Those who observe their work often are mesmerized by what they are seeing when the seemingly impossible becomes possible.

Unwaveringly, Father Rookey simply believes what Jesus said, *Amen, amen I say to you, he that believeth in me, the works that I do, he also shall do; and greater than these shall he do. Because I go to the Father : and whatsoever you shall ask the Father in my name, that I will do : that the Father may be glorified in the Son* (Jn 14:12-13). Father Rookey prayerfully intercedes to Christ with apparent manifestations of His Love.

In the years 2002-2005, through a series of interviews with Father Rookey and the staff of the International Compassion Ministry, God's Grace was given to learn more about Father Rookey's way of faith. Before each session, we celebrated Mass. Following Mass, Father Rookey would invoke the Holy Spirit before beginning the interviews. At three o'clock, we would break to say the *Chaplet of Divine Mercy* and then return for another hour of interviews. The following insights into Father Rookey's background, perspectives, and teachings provide a context for the reported healings of thousands worldwide.

What began as a simple inspiration to document Father's life changed into a discussion about the experience of souls as they journey toward God. In effect, there are three main sections: The first regards Father Rookey's soul's journey, his constant "Yes" to God; the second pertains to spiritual questions of a gradually deepening nature; and the third presents a collection of witness letters testifying to healings of body, mind, and spirit.

As different subjects arose, it became necessary to study the works of the Founding Fathers; St. Thomas Aquinas; the magnificent pioneering work on memory and reconciliation by Pope Benedict XVI, then Cardinal Joseph Ratzinger and President of the International Theological Commission; the beautiful encyclicals of Pope John Paul II; as well as the research of spiritual directors and international psychologists, psychiatrists, and medical doctors in the area of prenatal and perinatal development.

Only minor edits have been made to the original recordings. However, some sections were reorganized to ensure a smoother flow of the material and subjects. Supplemental information to the main text is provided for greater clarity or for the presentation of witness letters and prayers.

The editorial capitalization of divine pronouns and attributes is used as a reflection of Father Rookey's deep reverence for the Father, the Son, and the Holy Spirit, and to emphasize the superior nature of these Divine Persons. Capitalization is also used to honor the Angels and the Saints who are important members of the Mystical Body of Christ. The Douay-Rheims version of the *Bible* is quoted because of its poetic, traditional language. Photographs have been selected with a preference for those that best capture the personality of the subjects and support the text. Images of both the living and dead are included since the Church sees both as a vibrant and vital part of our Community of Saints.

It is our hope that these words will touch the souls of those who read them. Through God's Grace, we pray this work will provide illumination for their spiritual journey home by increasing knowledge and trust in the Loving Power of God.

Acknowledgments

Thanks be to God for permitting this work to be fulfilled. The decision to document Father Rookey's ministry unexpectedly marked the beginning of a spiritual journey of many years. It was a great privilege to pray and talk with him. He generously set aside time for interviews and reviewed each part of the manuscript. Each interview began with a general theme and questions. However, due to inspiration and Father's spontaneous, joyful participation and appreciation for detail, typically each discussion would lead us on another delightful path of discovery. It was this aspect of the process that uncovered the deepest spiritual revelations.

Rev. Robert T. Sears, S.J., Ph.D., my spiritual director, time and again, provided expert resources, guidance, and keen insight as the manuscript unfolded. His original work in the healing of family systems became critical as we addressed the most sensitive aspects of praying for the healing of the spiritual family. I am deeply grateful for his prayers, kindness, encouragement, and faith in responding to the promptings of the Holy Spirit.

Due to the nature of the manuscript, it was important to submit the work for formal review by the Archdiocese of Chicago. Rev. Jeffrey Grob, Associate Vicar for Canonical Services, faithfully facilitated communications with Rev. Anthony J. Brankin, S.T.L., Censor Deputatus. Rev. Grob's direction to persevere in researching some of the more complex subjects of spiritual healing and doctrine led to the important refinement of thought and expression.

Rev. Brankin was the ideal censor for this work. His precise examination of words, thoughts, and intentions and persistence for clarification, raised the nature of the process and the quality of the end result. His insightful questions inspired the exploration of many wonderful writings by leading theologians, past and present, as well as secular research studies.

There were several others who assisted with the content, presentation, and research, notably †Rev. Burns Seeley, S.S.C.J.; Rev. John H. Hampsch, C.M.F.; Andrew Miles, O.S.B.; Lea and Alan Embree; Mary (Kay) Geary; David Murray; and Liz Murray. Important testimonies were provided by Tony Brown; Doug Carson; Vicki Gutierrez; †Jim Hrechko; Elson Legendre; Br. Chris Moran, O.S.M.; Bill Mea; Joe Molloy; Sabina Reyes; Maureen Sheridan Scott; Margaret Trosclair, O.S.S.M.; Barbara Wojtowicz; and Bernie Verweil. Sr. Mary Caran Hart, S.S.N.D., diligently edited numerous witness letters incorporated into this work.

The Archdiocese of Chicago Office of Communications and Media Relations; Rev. Richard Bulwith, Our Lady of Lourdes Parish; Rev. Christopher Krymski, O.S.M., Pastor, and Rev. Frank Falco, O.S.M., Associate Pastor, the Basilica of Our Lady of Sorrows and National Shrine; Rev. C. Frank Phillips, C.R., Pastor, St. John Cantius Parish; and Rev. Joseph M. Jackson, Ph.D., Pastor, St. Ignatius Church, generously permitted photographs of sacred art.

Barbara Wojtowicz also provided copyediting services and discussed the fine points of editorial manuscript development. Her understanding of Father's ministry proved invaluable and her time was a Gift of the Heart. Nora Lloyd assisted with proofreading and the selection of photographs, many of which were kindly provided by Robert Benson and John Sundlof.

Friends and family members provided support throughout the development process, especially my beloved father, Richard L. Quasey, may he rest in peace; my mother, Mary C. Quasey, who contributed editorially; Linda Jane Gentry; Zina Long; and Mary Johnson. Their steadfast love, prayers, insight, and encouragement will always be remembered.

The staff of the International Compassion Ministry must also be acknowledged for their extraordinary faith and prayers for this project. Their patient compassion and love in ministering to the thousands of people who call the office is an outstanding manifestation of Christ's Presence among us.

Kathleen E. Quasey
October 15, 2006

Those Who Believe

On the second floor of a brown brick executive office building in the far south suburbs of Chicago is the suite of the International Compassion Ministry. In many ways, the office appears ordinary with phones being answered, white filing cabinets lining the walls, stacks of paper here and there, and several administrative desks.

But in one of the offices is a small chapel with a handmade wooden altar flanked by framed prints of the Blessed Mother and Jesus revealing their Hearts. The basic instruments of the Mass: a chalice, paten, two candles, towels, and water are placed on a simple white altar cloth. Behind the altar is a crucifix, while below is an image of Jesus with soft, compassionate eyes. Binders, stuffed with prayer intentions, lean against the foot of the altar.

A wooden tabernacle from a Servite seminary and a large statue of St. Peregrine the Cancer Saint are in one corner. Across the room on a pedestal are statues of the Blessed Mother, St. Joseph, and a large St. Michael the Archangel. A small photograph of Father Rookey rests against St. Michael next to a St. Padre Pio prayer card. Other photographs of Pope John Paul II and Cardinal Francis George are displayed too. A large contemporary painting of the Blessed Mother is across from the altar. Opposite a wall of windows is a pewter relief of the *Last Supper*.

But this is no ordinary place, for amazing spiritual work is carried out day after day, year after year, by a small team of

Fig. 2.   *Father Peter Mary Rookey, O.S.M.*, International Compassion Ministry, Olympia Fields, Illinois, 2005.

dedicated people whose lives have been forever changed by their relationship with Father Peter Mary Rookey. All of them are deeply devoted to loving Christ, His Blessed Mother, the Angels, and the Saints. Together they form a powerful spiritual force that has brought healing to thousands of souls throughout the world through their prayers for intercession.

In the west corner of the space is Father Rookey's office. A black bench is against a wall; file cabinets stacked with materials are against another. If carefully placed, a coffee mug can balance on the window ledge. Sunlight often spills in on two sides of the room, while evergreen trees tower outside. On occasion, a flock of Canadian geese wing by, pursuing their instinctive journeys. It is in this space that Father Peter Mary Rookey spends most of his time facing a desk, where he talks on the phone, praying intently with person after person who calls for his intercession. On any given day, continuous calls stream in ranging from a woman on the South Side of Chicago asking for prayers for her errant son, to a sad voice seeking relief from depression in County Mayo, Ireland, to a healing plea from faraway New Zealand.

At eighty-nine years of age and of medium build, Father Rookey is graced with robust energy, wry humor, a gentle demeanor, and endless optimism. When challenged by disturbing news, his docile nature typically prevails. Always hospitable and ready with a quick joke, his timing perfected by tips provided over the years by his late friend and comedian, Bob Hope, he offers coffee, cookies, or whatever is on hand. He fasts on coffee with honey throughout the day, having a meal only in the evening, because he believes that combining fasting with prayer increases the power of intercession. For Father Rookey, daily fasting is part of his job.

Occasionally, the sternness of his years as an administrator will slice through when he will be very precise and insistent in his direction. Despite his overall amiable nature, Father Rookey is a serious, dedicated priest, a powerful healer of spiritual, physical, and mental disorders. He is a master of spiritual discipline in balance with the loving, compassionate side of Jesus, yet ready to forcefully strike evil and imperfection. Father Rookey is a true spiritual warrior dedicated to Christ.

Fig. 3.   *Father Peter Mary Rookey Preparing for Mass I,* International Compassion Ministry, Olympia Fields, Illinois, 2005.

Every day at noon, Mass is said in the small chapel. At three o'clock, the office staff gathers again to recite the *Chaplet of Divine Mercy*. With patience, devotion, and simplicity, they respond with prayers and love to those who call on them for healing of body, mind, and spirit.

Through the intercession of Father Rookey and his staff to the Power of Jesus, the Blessed Mother, and the Saints, many prayers are answered. Miraculous, spontaneous healings, gradual conversions, and deliverance from evil spirits have been reported from people of all ethnic backgrounds, economic stations, professions, and spiritual denominations. Besides the daily spiritual work, this small group extends their ministry by providing a monthly newsletter to a 40,000-person mailing list, answering letters asking for prayers or those reporting healings, and by arranging Masses and healing services throughout the world. At these Masses and healing services, throngs of people come to receive the Sacrament of Reconciliation, recite the *Rosary*, participate in the Mass, and to be blessed by Father Rookey's healing hands that hold the relics of the seven founding Servite Saints and those of St. Peregrine, St. Philip Benizi, St. Juliana, and St. Anthony Pucci.

For these precious eighty-nine-year-old hands of Father Rookey have been graced to act as God's Instruments with the power to: . . . *Heal the sick that are therein, and say to them : The kingdom of God is come nigh unto you* (Lk 10:9). For many of those years, his miraculous hands have been used to teach, write books, and to carry out the customary duties of a priest. But for some of those years, these blessed hands have been holy instruments directly transmitting the Power of Christ, thereby healing those who have been fortunate to feel His Grace. Called by people from all continents, Father Rookey, through the Power of Christ, has ministered to those brought to him: . . . *Preaching the gospel of the kingdom : and healing all manner of sickness and every infirmity, among the people* (Mt 4:23), through Masses and healing services.

Those who encounter Father Rookey for the first time often have mixed reactions. Disbelieving muscular young men have been seen falling suddenly to the ground, knocked out cold by

Fig. 4.   *Touched by the Spirit*, Our Lady of Sorrows Basilica, 2002.

the gentle spiritual touch of these gnarled hands, only to rise minutes later dazed by their first spiritual encounter. Others stiffen at his touch and remain unaffected.

More welcoming people, from children to adults, slump in a semiconscious state in what is called *resting in the Spirit*. In this condition, some cry uncontrollably, others weep gently, while many others exhibit a serene expression. Others feel called to stand in proxy for a loved one or for a special request. In this manner, long-distance healings are reported with those who have been prayed for frequently making significant changes in their lives or experiencing freedom from disease. Regardless of the initial purpose, for most, this is a time of deep spiritual healing through the Grace of God.

For anyone who has witnessed the thousands of people who have been touched by these hands, it is undeniable that the sacred is present at these Masses and healing services. The supernatural Power of God works in concert with Father Rookey, using him as His Instrument to bring healing to those who humbly seek His Assistance: *He hath done all things well; he hath made both the deaf to hear, and the dumb to speak* (Mk 7:37); all in the name of Our Lord.

What is remarkable about Father Rookey's approach is that it is deeply grounded in the core teachings of the Catholic faith and insists on complete participation in these teachings to facilitate one's healing. For those who have lived their lives in an easy-lifestyle culture, especially in the United States, this insistence may seem to be ultratraditional while, in fact, it is consistent with current Church teachings.

He sees no alternative, for it is clear to Father Rookey that the Divine and Eternal Laws must be obeyed, for any departure from them will result in suffering. His goal is to guide souls into alignment with Divine Will. Father Rookey persists in encouraging full and regular Confession, daily prayer, and daily Mass attendance, if possible, as well as frequent fasting accompanied by hours of deep prayer. He understands that people must of their own free will conform their lives to live in accordance with God's Laws if they are to receive God's Blessings and Peace. Father Rookey, through his own humble and patient demeanor, provides a living example of how to live a holy life.

He encourages a simple, spiritual lifestyle that is an alternative to today's materialism, rationalism, careerism, and individualism. By shedding these artificial man-made values and replacing them with Christ's innate Generosity, constant Caring, and Divine Love, we begin to be healed ourselves and can help heal those around us. This process of value exchange and spiritual development usually takes time because it is a subtle, intricate process that requires unraveling entrenched behaviors and orientations. To succeed, we need Divine Assistance.

Father Rookey lives in a state of prayerfulness. Just as any other professional who has developed skills over a lifetime, Father Rookey, like other priests and religious, has spent much of his lifetime learning God's Ways. For Father Rookey, this life path has been deeply satisfying, while at times challenging, for it is no simple goal to commit one's entire life to vows of poverty, chastity, and obedience. But through Christ's Intercession, it is possible. The presence of the supernatural Power of God is evident in Father Rookey's life. Indeed, it is his belief in the power of the supernatural that permits him to act as an intercessor for those who have not lived a life equally committed to fulfilling God's Law.

Father Rookey seems to be in this world but not of it. From his practice of rising early in the morning to recite the *Divine Office* and to offer Mass, leading Mass again at noon, followed by the recitation of the *Chaplet of Divine Mercy* in the mid-afternoon, through evening prayer and rosaries sprinkled in-between, Father Rookey lives immersed in prayer. Highly sensitive to spiritual forces, he lives between worlds, pulling souls to the path of enlightenment, healing, and peace, all the while confronting those forces that interfere with a soul's union with God.

In a secular age when many people disdainfully dismiss the supernatural Power of God and the teachings of the Catholic Church but readily accept the power of the supernatural as portrayed on Hollywood screens, Father Rookey provides a countercultural perspective that is based on over two thousand years of Church teachings. *They to whom he was not spoken of, shall see, and they that have not heard shall understand* (Rom 15:21); individual by individual, Father Rookey brings the power of the supernatural to each soul. At Father Rookey's Masses, miracles often occur and more miraculous seeds are planted in the hearts of those who attend, seeds that often bear fruit in the months or years later.

For Father Rookey, the greatest healings are not the visible physical healings but the invisible spiritual healings where transitioning souls come to know the beauty of Christ's Teachings and begin to understand God's Will in an entirely different way. These inner healings are manifested in deep emotional, psychological, and spiritual changes that draw a soul's will into conformity with the Will of God and His Divine Laws. Often in the process, a soul turns away from the material world to lead a spiritual life. The transformation of a soul from one that is disbelieving, cynical, and self-centered to one that magnifies faith, hope, and love is truly one of the most spectacular achievements possible to humankind.

The Mass and Healing Service

Partaking in one of Father Rookey's Masses and healing services is to enter into communion with not only those present but also with those Saints, ancestors, and Holy Ones who have lived before. The over one hundred-year-old Basilica of Our Lady of Sorrows on Chicago's impoverished West Side is Father Rookey's spiritual home and the place of large Masses held every First Saturday of the month. Here, among boarded up Victorian-era gray-stone homes, wind-swept streets, and sporadically placed storefronts offering the most basic of services, is one of the most beautiful churches in the world.

Outside, the basilica appears almost neglected. With its white paint peeling in places, this huge edifice fits in with the rest of the neighborhood. In back, a lone security guard watches over cars parked in two steel-wire fenced lots. But inside this holy building, the faithful prayers and motions of generations have been absorbed into its walls and gently worn into its marble floor. In the 1940s, 70,000 people a week jammed its pews and wound around the blocks to pray for peace in the world. They made private offerings and intentions at each of the side-altars that line the long walls, each dedicated to a Saint, the Blessed Mother, or the Sacred Heart of Jesus.

Today, candles still flicker steadfastly emitting the faith and hope of those who light them. Flowers are placed in

Fig. 5.   *Altar*, Our Lady of Sorrows Basilica, Chicago, Illinois, 2006.

simple glasses, carefully presented in vases, or are strewn on the various altars in appreciation for a prayer answered, or as an act of love. Sixty feet above, a fabulous gold floret ceiling spans eighty-feet across. Hues of rose, blue, and purple rise in a color spectrum in between the medallions. The walls are covered in painstakingly painted symbols and repeating rhythmic embellishments, while large-scale paintings of the Servite Saints, Saint Juliana, the Blessed Mother, and historic religious events cover others. The magnificent two-tiered white altar is embellished with watching Angels and a depiction of the *Last Supper*, with a gold-encased tabernacle in the middle and a gold crucifix high above. This is truly a holy place—a place where miracles happen.

Father Rookey's Masses and healing services follow an order no matter where in the world they occur. The process is essential to healing and includes the *Sacrament of Confession*, saying the *Rosary*, participating in the Mass, and hearing witnesses, all followed by the laying on of hands using the relics of the Seven Servite Saints.

The Sacrament of Reconciliation

On a First Saturday, people begin to arrive around ten o'clock in the morning to get in line to participate in the *Sacrament of Reconciliation*. Many have come prepared by fasting and praying beforehand. They know from experience that the *Sacrament of Confession* together with fasting and praying helps open their hearts to the Healing Powers of Christ. Long lines of penitents extend from three dark-wood confessionals that serve as spiritual offices of the priests. Another space is provided for those who prefer face-to-face Confession as a sacred method of spiritual cleansing.

An important condition of the healing process is accepting personal responsibility for transgressions and having the courage to face oneself in the Presence of God. The *Sacrament of Reconciliation* opens a person's heart through the most

Fig. 6.   *Barrel-Vaulted Ceiling,* Our Lady of Sorrows Basilica, Chicago, Illinois, 2006. Over a thousand ornate, gold-leafed panels adorn the nave.

desired qualities of humility and docility: an acknowledgment of our weakness as human beings to live in accordance with God's Law and a willingness to be guided to a higher level of spiritual development. Through this Sacrament, a soul recognizes specific failures, discovers the lies that permeate its interior wounds, and discerns spiritual truths. The sincerity of the penitent is paramount to receiving the Grace of Mercy.

ᢉᢉᢉᢉᢉᢉᢉᢉᢉᢉᢉᢉᢉᢉᢉᢉᢉᢉᢉᢉᢉᢉᢉᢉᢉᢉᢉᢉᢉᢉᢉᢉᢉᢉᢉᢉᢉᢉ

The Sacrament of Reconciliation

Choosing to participate in the Sacrament of Reconciliation *is to join the community of people who constantly choose to perfect their spiritual lives, moment by moment, day by day. Engaging regularly in this Sacrament enables a soul to constantly refine its spiritual life to become closer to God. Over time, as a soul embarks on a spiritual path, it begins to discern the wisdom of constantly seeking the balance of God's Peace. As human beings, it is natural that we often fail in our quest. But as a soul becomes more aware of its faults and the areas of weakness unique to its nature, it is better able to master them and to undertake ways to strengthen its character. This Sacrament helps a soul develop a heightened sensitivity to the subtle inclinations of its heart and mind, and to persevere, with the assistance of Divine Grace, throughout its life to ultimately attain a higher level of spiritual development and a closer union with God.*

Priests are trained in psychological and spiritual counseling so they can respond sensitively to questions regarding life directions, challenges, and spiritual progress. Through spiritual Grace, the priest opens himself to God as a spiritual intercessor. He is bound by his vows not to reveal the content of confessions, because the words that transpire between priest and penitent are sacred. In this holy crucible, a soul is guided toward Communion by the Light of God.

The Grace of Forgiveness is necessary for healing. A soul who desires deep spiritual healing may first need to carefully remember and forgive people and themselves for negative behaviors that have affected one's life leaving memory wounds. Bonds of trauma; fear; strong emotions, particularly anger and jealousy; unsacred sexual unions; greed; and dysfunctional relationships can bind a soul to the past making it spiritually stagnant while experiencing recurrent pain. Unresolved family histories of physical, mental, and emotional abuse; addictions; divorce; miscarriage; abortion; materialism; careerism; and relationship control issues, among other sources of suffering, can lead to chaotic periods of life and sinful behavior. In this state, a soul often continues to hurt itself and others.

Father Rookey knows these unhealed injuries can lead to long-term, unhealthy, unproductive, life patterns and unstable personalities. Extreme symptoms of under- or overworking, emotional distancing or rage, the inability to trust, relationship manipulation, lifestyles that repeat the original dysfunctional pattern, and similar expressions may manifest. Through injury to body, mind, and spirit, additional negative spiritual forces can enter, multiply, and eventually dominate one's life.

Satanic forces also can enter through active participation in occult practices (including voodoo; curses; the secret rituals of gangs and fraternal organizations, especially Freemasonry; Wicca; magick; New Age spiritualism; and Satanic masses; as well as more common participation with Tarot Cards; Ouija boards; horoscopes; séances; and palm readings). Any medium that suspends a soul's control over its will to another spiritual force, organization, or human being is dangerous. Many times, those who participate in these activities, even for entertainment only, do not realize that the spiritual forces, once entered, can stay and grow within passing down negative effects for generations.

In a secular culture that encourages personal control, the spiritual act of giving up control of one's

will and life to God is a difficult surrender. Many who readily give over their wills to negative behavior, people, or organizations will not align their wills with God, the Source of their creation, Who loves them and is the True Source of all abundance and healing.

In the Catholic faith, maintaining one's free will is paramount for being free to do the Will of God or to separate oneself from God, if that is what the soul desires, even if it leads to suffering. How a soul chooses to employ its will is part of each soul's sacred life journey.

Confession is a proven method for stopping damaging behaviors, words, and thoughts and redirecting one's soul to healthier ways of living. For all these reasons, the Sacrament of Reconciliation *is essential to beginning the healing process. It is through this Sacrament that an individual recognizes and thereby begins to separate oneself from negative behaviors and pledges to recommit one's life, of its own free will, to beneficial behavior for God, oneself, and others.*

As one of God's many creatures, we are powerless without His Sustenance. But all too often, preoccupied by worldly concerns, we ignore His Presence until general discouragement, depression, illness, relationship destruction, or other events overwhelm us and we cry for help. By remaining separated from God, it is not possible to be in a right relationship with Him. Father Rookey helps heal this separation in a practical, determined, spiritual manner.

He teaches that we first must ask God to help us before healing can manifest. We need to open the doors of our hearts to invite in God's Presence because God always upholds our right to free will and will not enter our lives unless invited.

When a soul makes the formal decision to invite God into its life, it is important that it is properly prepared for the

Fig. 7. *Confessional,* Our Lady of Sorrows Basilica, Chicago, Illinois, 2006.

encounter of His Holy Presence. Frequently, when a person approaches Father Rookey for a healing he will tell him/her to "Go to Confession, first." The *Sacrament of Confession* is an especially important rite because it is the first step in exploring and identifying sources of disturbance. It is an agent for preparing and opening the heart and will to encounter the Healing Presence of God. Many people who have not gone to Confession for decades, through the encouragement of Father Rookey, will find the courage to seek out a priest who will hear and heal them through Christ's Compassion. Through this Sacrament, a soul cleanses itself so it can be presented in its most pure state to Our Lord.

Act of Contrition

O my God,
I am heartily sorry for having offended Thee,
And I detest all my sins,
because of Thy just punishments,
But most of all because
they offend Thee, my God,
Who is All Good
and deserving of all my love.

I firmly resolve,
with the help of Thy Grace,
To sin no more
and to avoid
the near occasions of sin.

Amen

Saying the Rosary

While people are going to Confession, others fill out prayer requests for specific intentions and drop them in a basket as Father Rookey leads the congregation in the Servite *Rosary*. The Servites, or Servants of Mary, is the religious Order Father Rookey joined and in which he became a priest. The Blessed Mother is the inspiration for his spiritual name, Father Peter *Mary* Rookey, taken as a sign of devotion to her.

In the Servite version of the *Rosary*, the *Seven Sorrows of Mary* are remembered. As the *Rosary* is being recited, the basilica becomes filled with people, many of whom have traveled long distances, sometimes from overseas, to participate. They represent various ethnic and professional backgrounds, and even different faith traditions. Women dressed in the latest fashions, to the disheveled homeless, to laborers and suburbanites in jeans and jackets can be seen among the crowd. Usually among the hundreds of kneeling people are those who speak a range of languages.

Father Rookey leads the *Rosary* incorporating a different language for each *Our Father* and *Hail Mary* of the decade. As the voices rise and fall in the traditional waves of the prayer chant, people become absorbed in their meditations and prayer intentions. There is a feeling of becoming part of an ancient continuum of people throughout the ages who have petitioned God in this manner. Word by word, prayer by prayer, intentions are offered up, gently persisting, gently pleading to be heard and answered.

Father Rookey always petitions the Blessed Mother first, asking for her intercession to Christ. For according to Father Rookey, "Christ came into the world through His Mother, Mary, and it is through her that we are favorably presented to Christ." It is believed that saying the *Rosary* over and over will wear down the hardest hearts, like water against stones, and that prayers eventually will be answered, or the problem solved in the Ways of God.

The Holy Rosary of The Blessed Virgin Mary

A contemplative prayer meditation, the Holy Rosary *of the Virgin Mary represents an offering of a prayer crown of mystical roses to the Blessed Mother. In the Catholic Tradition, it is thought that Jesus, like any good son, listens to the pleas of His Mother, Mary, Our Lady of Light, who illuminates Heaven and earth with her wisdom. Mental meditations include the Joyful, Luminous, Sorrowful, and Glorious Mysteries of the Catholic faith that trace the birth, transformation, mission, crucifixion, and Resurrection of Jesus and the experiences of His Blessed Mother. Each Mystery, designated by a series of prayer beads called a decade, is encapsulated by vocal prayers. Each decade is introduced by the* Our Father, *followed by ten* Hail Marys, *and concludes with the* Glory Be. *Depending on the local custom, small prayers of petition can be added.*

The Rosary *evolved over time. The monastic Psalter, based on the recitation of one-hundred-fifty Psalms, was adapted to a simpler version for the laity. One hundred fifty* Pater Nosters, *or* Our Fathers, *were counted on prayer beads. Others favored the Angel Gabriel's address to Mary:* Hail, full of grace, the Lord is with thee: blessed art thou among women *(Lk 1:28), recited in a series of fifty, a hundred, or a* Psalter *of one hundred fifty. Gradually, phrases were attached to the* Psalms *and the prayers of Jesus and Mary. Eventually, the* Psalms *were omitted and the phrases referring to the life of Jesus and Mary from her joyful Annunciation to His glorious Resurrection became grouped into the mysteries. Reflections on the Sorrowful Mysteries were added in the fourteenth century.*

Fig. 8.   *Annunciation,* stained glass window, St. Ignatius Parish, Chicago, Illinois, 2006.

St. Elizabeth's exclamation: Blessed art thou among women, and blessed is the fruit of your womb *(Lk 1:42), was combined with Angel Gabriel's address in a prayer known as the* Hail Mary. *Originally noted in the liturgies of St. James of Antioch and St. Mark of Alexandria, the current form emerged in the sixteenth century. The petition to the Holy Trinity:* Glory be to the Father, to the Son, and to the Holy Spirit, *was formed into the prayer of the* Glory Be *and recited at the end of each decade.*

According to legend, in 1214, the Blessed Mother appeared to St. Dominic in Toulouse, France, during a time of great cultural revolt against God and the rise of the Albigensians. St. Louis Mary De Montfort, the acclaimed Extraordinary Preacher of the Rosary, *in his book* The Secret of the Rosary *said that the Blessed Mother spoke to St. Dominic, who had been severely fasting, praying, and offering penances for the conversion of sinners:* I want you to know that, in this kind of warfare, the battering ram has always been the *Angelic Psalter,* which is the foundation stone of the *New Testament.* Therefore, if you want to reach these hardened souls and win them over to God, preach my *Psalter.*[1]

St. Louis recognized that our entire perfection consists in being conformed, united, and consecrated to Jesus Christ. The simplicity of the Rosary *offers a way to embark on a path of holiness over time by molding our wills to conform with the Will of Our Father and softening our hearts to be remade into the image of Christ. In 1521, another Dominican, Alberto da Castello, wrote a book* The Rosary of the Glorious Virgin, *using the term* Rosary *for the first time. By the end of the sixteenth century, the fifteen Joyful, Sorrowful, and Glorious Mysteries were established with the tradition remaining until 2002 when Pope John Paul II, citing the* Rosary *as his favorite prayer meditation, added the Mysteries of Light, the Luminous Mysteries, for contemplation.*[2]

In many families, treasured rosary beads are handed down through the generations with love. Said alone or in a group, creating a prayer weaving of special intentions to be offered up with each decade, the Rosary *offers a welcome respite from the world and precious time for communication with Our Lord and His Blessed Mother. For centuries, lay people, religious, Saints, and Popes have depended on the* Rosary *as a core meditation practice for the perfection of souls and as a method of plaintive personal petition and spiritual support in times of trial.*

Saying the Rosary *helps further open our hearts by reflecting on the great challenges of God to humankind. Character-deepening spiritual qualities are strengthened by saying the Rosary, including submitting our will to the Will of God with humility; having the courage to persevere through life's most serious challenges; denying self-interests for the benefit of others; remaining firmly committed to life vocations, including those of work, marriage, and religious service; responding to one's calling by developing Spiritual Gifts; and believing in the miraculous intercession of Christ and His Blessed Mother.*[3]

Our Father,
Who art in Heaven,
Hallowed be Thy Name!
Thy Kingdom come,
Thy Will be done,
On earth as it is in Heaven.

Give us, this day, our daily bread,
And forgive us our trespasses,
As we forgive those
Who trespass against us.

And lead us not into temptation,
But deliver us from evil. Amen.

Hail Mary, full of Grace, the Lord is with thee!
Blessed art thou among women,
and blessed is the fruit of thy womb, Jesus.
Holy Mary, Mother of God,
pray for us sinners,
now and at the hour of our death. Amen

Glory be to the Father,
and to the Son,
and to the Holy Spirit.
As it was in the beginning,
is now and ever shall be,
world without end. Amen.

Oh, my Jesus, forgive us our sins.
Save us from the fires of Hell.
Lead all souls to Heaven,
especially those
who are most in need of Thy Mercy.

Sacred Heart of Jesus,
pray for us!

Mary, Immaculate Queen,
triumph and reign!

Ave Maria!

To observe Father Rookey say the *Rosary* is a special experience. Energetic and sporting tousled gray hair and a beard, Father Rookey wears the Blessed Mother's black widow's habit of the Servite fathers; a long rosary with large black beads sways at his side. He paces back and forth in front of the altar, sometimes raising his voice to a sharp pitch as he calls out the mysteries, amplified by Scripture, after years now deeply

Fig. 9.   *Rosary Meditation II: Father Peter Mary Rookey, O.S.M.,* Chicago, Illinois, 2005.

impressed in his memory. He carefully emphasizes certain words to convey an understanding of the profound importance of each one and sometimes links the mysteries to an important issue of today—"Abortion today, makes Herod look like a *rookie!*"

Proficient in several languages, as he leads the *Rosary*, Father Rookey asks for people who speak different languages to stand and lead a decade as a symbol of the universal Church. Often, he intersperses gentle humor into his dialog while he begins his personal steep spiritual ascent leading to Mass. As the *Rosary* progresses, sounds of Polish, Irish, Spanish, French, German, and Caribbean Island languages permeate the air with the responding chorus following in English. Slowly, an informal unity descends upon the prayerful congregation. Those who may be saying the *Rosary* for the first time listen carefully to those who have been saying it for years, gradually joining in as the prayer sequence becomes familiar.

Sometimes during the *Rosary*, the *fragrance of roses* wafts throughout the basilica. The fragrance can be very strong, then suddenly disappear. Other times it is light and barely perceptible. For those who first smell the fragrance, they may think it is someone's perfume. By attending these services repeatedly and smelling the fragrance, it becomes clear this is not an ordinary occurrence, but one of the many, unexplainable Blessings of God.

Toward the end of the *Rosary*, Father Rookey will ask who has smelled the fragrance of roses. Hesitating hands go up in the crowd while others look around disappointed. Father Rookey will say, "Cheer up! More of you might smell the fragrance during Mass. We've even heard of cars being filled with the fragrance on the way home!" In these gentle ways, Father Rookey makes people feel that they are all part of it and that they can have hope in experiencing God's Presence, too. In some way, somehow, by belonging to this prayerful group, they begin to believe, even if in a small way, that it is possible that a human being can begin to talk to God and that He will hear them.

Participating in the Mass

When Mass begins, Father Rookey comes up in the procession waving to those he recognizes and sometimes taking time to briefly touch someone. People who are in wheelchairs, or who are severely ill, sit in the front pews or off to the side of the altar. On any given Saturday, these areas are filled to capacity and spill over along the side aisle. In these chairs and pews are young people who have been paralyzed, jaundiced babies with cancer, those who in appearance look well but who may have a life-threatening disease, others with shaved heads from operations or deformities of many kinds, and the elderly with a host of impairing conditions. Others suffer from depression, financial distress, self-rejection, and addictions. Truly, it is a tiny sea of suffering.

The Mass is the most powerful form of prayer and source of healing known to humankind and acts as a method of intercession for positive change anywhere in this world, or in the spiritual world. For Father Rookey, saying Mass is a privileged encounter with Christ.

He begins with the *Penitential Rite* and then proceeds through the *Liturgy of the Mass* singing the *Kyrie Eleison*, in a voice that quavers and is moving in its penitential quality. Through the readings and the Gospel, Father Rookey is actively engaged, reciting the Gospel of the day from memory.

Sometimes in his homily, he will report on a recent message from Our Lady of Medjugorje, or share information about a particular Saint, or about the Pope's requests. Then Father Rookey turns and the congregation stands to face the Blessed Mother and recite the *Miracle Prayer*.

The Miracle Prayer

Lord Jesus, I come before You just as I am. I am sorry for my sins, I repent of my sins, please forgive me. In Your Name I forgive all others for what they have done against me. I renounce Satan, the evil spirits and all their works. I give You my entire self, Lord Jesus, now and forever. I invite You into my life, Jesus. I accept You as my Lord, God, and Saviour. Heal me, change me, strengthen me in body, soul, and spirit.

Come, Lord Jesus, cover me with Your Precious Blood, and fill me with Your Holy Spirit. I Love You, Lord Jesus. I Praise You, Jesus. I Thank You, Jesus. I shall follow You every day of my life. Amen.

> *Mary, my Mother, Queen of Peace. St. Peregrine,*
> *the Cancer Saint, all you Angels and Saints, please*
> *help me. Amen.*[4]

࿐ ࿐

After the *Miracle Prayer*, prayer requests are shared among the congregation, so that everyone can pray for one another. Prior to distribution, the congregation raises their arms and hands to bless the basket of prayers while Father Rookey reads seven petitions out loud. Usually he takes one of the petitions, especially if it regards a couple asking for intercession for a baby or for a child who is ill, to pray for himself. "Jesus," Father Rookey often says, "loves children more than anybody." Many women have said they have become pregnant after Father Rookey has prayed for their request for a child, with some bringing their newborns to the basilica to thank God and to show appreciation to Father Rookey for his intercession.

ɕɕɕɕɕɕɕɕɕɕɕɕɕɕɕɕɕɕɕɕɕɕɕɕɕɕɕɕɕɕɕɕɕɕ

Dear Father Rookey:

Thank you for all of your prayers over the past three years for me and my family members. My two babies are so special and are here by the Grace of God and because of your healing hands. My little girl is twenty months old. I want you to know that she kisses every crucifix and Cross she can get her sweet hands on. She kisses my statue of the Blessed Mother and any and all pictures of Jesus' Mommy. I asked her to kiss the crucifix on my Rosary one time, and it just took off. She has always been our little angel for whom we have thanked God—our angel that the doctors said we may not have. Because of your precious Gift of Healing, we have this angel.

Thank you again.

Georgia, September 2002

࿐ ࿐

Eucharistic Celebration

For Father Rookey, the *Eucharistic Celebration* is the ultimate intercession with Christ. Christ interceded for us and continues to intercede for us by transcending man-made time, geography, and spiritual dimensions through this most intimate Sacrament, which permits us to receive the Healing Power of His Body, Mind, and Spirit—to become one with Him in *common-union*. Jesus, at the same time that He was being betrayed and preparations were being made for His death, presciently gave us the Gift of Himself in the form of the Eucharist to Heal, Purify, and Protect our souls for generations to come. Through His supernatural Intercession manifested by His deliberate Self-Sacrifice, He empowers us to turn away from the culture of death, or evil (E-V-I-L), to embrace its opposite, the culture of life, to live (L-I-V-E), for His Resurrection conquered the power of death and affirmed the transcendent power of everlasting life.

In the *Eucharistic Celebration*, Father Rookey is absorbed in the Mystery of Christ's Body and Blood becoming present in the Host and wine. He says that Christ allows him to see His Face in the Eucharist. Usually several other people have the same experience. Many people come forward to receive Communion carrying their prayers in their hearts. Other people offer special intentions for those in need of healing of body, mind, and spirit or to assist the souls of the deceased and for their intentions, because the *Eucharistic Celebration* unites all the souls of the living and the dead in Christ's Healing Love. In this Divine Sacrament, the Medicine of God, there is tremendous power. As hundreds of people receive the *Sacrament of the Eucharist*, the power of prayer and God's Healing Presence can be felt reaching beyond the constraints of man-made time and space, seeping into the hearts and souls of those in need of His Grace.

During Mass, the fragrance of roses is usually present somewhere in the basilica. At some of Father Rookey's services, bleeding and sweating crucifixes have been reported. It is truly amazing the number of times that supernatural influences are felt and seen over several Masses. Many people say they have seen the Blessed Virgin Mary appear carrying the infant Jesus in the painting of St. Juliana. She seems to appear every First Saturday at Our Lady of Sorrows to those blessed enough to see her. Even among those people who do not come frequently to the Mass, many have said they have seen her there.

All of these occurrences are perceived by Father Rookey to be blessings and signs that the Blessed Virgin and Christ are reaching out to us through our different senses of sight, smell, taste, touch, and hearing. He remains undisturbed by these blessings, referring to similar occurrences that have happened since the time of Christ. Over and over again, Father Rookey encourages and cajoles, gently assisting us in taking the first step in opening our minds, bodies, and spirits to the Healing Power of God.

ɞ ɞ

Father Rookey frequently speaks about Sacred Hosts that have been miraculously transformed into flesh and blood. Incidents have been reported throughout Christian history, even today. One of Father's favorite occurrences happened in the eighth century, in Lanciano, Italy, when a priest was strongly tempted to doubt Jesus' Real Presence. During the Mass, at the Consecration, the Sacred Host changed into a circle of flesh. The consecrated wine turned into bright red blood, coagulating into five small clots, different in form and shape. Four studies showed that the flesh is cardiac muscle flesh, both flesh and blood are type AB positive, the proteins in the blood are like those in normal fresh blood, and both are visible after 1200 years. Many similar incidences have been reported through the centuries throughout the world. More recently, four consecrated Hosts have been spotted with human blood in separate Masses celebrated at the home of the silent soul, Audrey Santo in the years

Fig. 10. *Bleeding Consecrated Eucharistic Host,* Convent of St. Augustine, Los Teques, Venezuela, 2006. This Host began to bleed during a Mass at the apparition site in Betania, Venezuela, on the Feast of the Immaculate Conception, December 8, 1991. The Department of Legal Medicine of the judicial police of Venezuela tested the blood and found it to be of human origin. (Source: Michael H. Brown and Drew J. Mariani, *The Bridge to Heaven: Interviews with Maria Esperanza of Betania,* Marian Communications, Ltd., Lima, PA, 1993.)

1992, 1995, and 1996, according to Father Thomas P. McCarthy, C.S.V., who was a concelebrant at the 1996 Mass celebrated by Father George Joyce. These occurrences are under investigation by the Church.

This is my body, which is given for you. Do this for a commemoration of me. This is the chalice, the new testament in my blood, which shall be shed for you *(Lk 22:19-20). These miracles of the* Eucharistic Celebration *are accepted as part of the history of the Catholic Church as are the power of relics to heal and protect. Christ, the Blessed Mother, the Angels, and the Saints want to intercede for us; they only are waiting patiently for us to ask for their help. These signs of their presence are to encourage us to have faith in the power of prayer and in the potential of God to heal us in body, mind, and spirit.*

Participating in the Adoration of the Eucharist *offers a special* Communion *with Christ when the consecrated Host is present in a monstrance on the altar. In these intimate, sacred hours of private adoration, it is possible to place one's many burdens before the Lord and listen for His response. Like other devoted religious, Father Rookey frequently prays before Our Lord for hours to fill up his spirit with the Presence of Christ. And, Jesus, full of loving generosity, never fails to refresh his spirit or minister to his pleas.*[5]

Jesus, I trust in You!

The Healing Service

After the Mass, those who have experienced healings provide testimony and express gratitude to God. These witnesses provide encouragement to others in the congregation who may be feeling overwhelmed by their suffering. For example, if a person who has brain cancer hears of the healing of a person with brain cancer, he/she may feel more hopeful about his/her situation and is able to increase his/her faith and trust in God's Mercy.

Dear Father Rookey,

A neurosurgeon from New York gave the following witness:

I am married with a young family and have a successful practice. A while ago, I began to experience visual impairment. I was diagnosed with inoperable brain cancer. I heard about Father Rookey's healing services through a friend, went to one, and was blessed by him. A short time later, x-rays revealed no trace of the cancer. I went from a feeling of despair to delight.

During the blessing, a friend took a picture, which revealed, in addition to the doctor and Father Rookey, a circle of light above a chalice seemingly suspended above and to the left of Father. This picture was passed around the church for all to see, and all were in awe.

I wondered about the picture, and then the reason for it came to me. If there was ever a time you didn't quite get something, you may have heard someone say, "What's the matter, do I have to draw you a picture?" Christ, in the picture, was revealed in the Blessed Sacrament and was saying to all in that church, "Receive Me and I will rescue

*you when you are in despair." The same holds true
now.*

Now, I see perfectly.

July, 2003

ƊƊƊƊƊƊƊƊƊƊƊƊƊƊƊƊƊƊƊƊƊƊƊƊƊƊƊƊƊƊƊ

It is often through the patient acceptance of suffering that we and those who love us experience the first deep spiritual healing prior to physical healing. However, Father Rookey is careful to emphasize that we must accept whatever God has in store for us. Not everyone is healed in the way he/she requests but may be healed in another way through his/her suffering for the benefit of their soul.

ꞔꞔꞔꞔꞔꞔꞔꞔꞔꞔꞔꞔꞔꞔꞔꞔꞔꞔꞔꞔꞔꞔꞔꞔꞔꞔꞔꞔꞔ

Sacrificial Suffering

In the Catholic faith, suffering is considered to be a Mystery of human life experience; all suffering is permitted by God, the Creator of Creation. Suffering is thought of as a purifier of the spirit, an agent for strengthening the soul, and, frequently, as a means of intercession and atonement for others, including past, present, and future generations. It was through God's Suffering in the Divine Person of Jesus Christ that the victory over death and the forgiveness of sins was secured for all generations.

Through His continued Intercession, especially during the Mass, we are healed and our spiritual lives renewed. Like His Suffering, human suffering can be used to transmute good out of the greatest evil. Frequently, through suffering, aspects of one's soul are healed or others close to us, by witnessing our suffering, are brought to a point of spiritual healing. Many of the great Saints and mystics experienced excruciating suffering while their spiritual lives grew in holiness. Suffering, when approached with interior surrender and when treated with sensitivity and respect for the forces that manifest in the disturbance of body, mind, and spirit, can ultimately lead to the curing of these illnesses, spiritual enlightenment, and union with God.

After Mass, arms and hands are raised to pray for the concelebrating priests and the *catchers:* men and women who hold people as they fall back into their arms to rest in the Spirit, or who minister to those who are experiencing spiritual difficulty. The song *Spirit of the Living God* is sung at this blessing time. The catchers then begin to line up the immense crowd shoulder to shoulder around both tiers of the altar. People in wheelchairs and the severely ill are blessed first.

Father Rookey takes his reliquary Cross, a crucifix containing the bones of the Seven Holy Servite Founders, St. Philip Benizi, St. Juliana, and St. Peregrine the Cancer Saint, and begins the laying on of hands. He uses St. Peregrine's oil for anointing. His face is very concentrated just as when he is celebrating the Eucharist. At this time, he says the Force of God works through him as a healing agent. Many have reported the feeling of a light electrical vibration when Father Rookey blesses them. Others have felt spontaneous warmth throughout their heads and bodies.

As Father Rookey constantly prays, he may rub the arms or legs of someone in a wheelchair. Usually one or two people will find the strength to get up and push their wheelchairs out of the church themselves. Of course, when this happens, there is applause and many tears. The rest of the congregation continues to pray the *Rosary* during this time, led by members of the International Compassion Ministry. Hymns are sung in between decades. All the while, Father Rookey continues to bless, and the catchers continue to lay down those who are able to experience resting in the Spirit, until there are lines of people standing in between those who have prolonged resting experiences.

Because God knows us as individuals, each person has a different reaction to the blessing. Some people may rest in the Spirit for a minute or two, while others may rest in the Spirit for a half hour or more. The Holy Spirit provides each person with what he needs emotionally, physically, mentally, and spiritually. Those who are standing in proxy for another person may hold a picture or possession of that person and may say a few words to Father Rookey about their prayer intention. Others who have a special prayer may share it with Father Rookey or remain silent. Most people pray quietly until their turn comes so that they are focused on their intention when Father Rookey blesses them.

He moves very quickly along the line without rest, ministering at times to over a thousand people. Another priest holds the Eucharist in a gold chalice, following him closely. Sometimes, it is possible to feel the Power of the Eucharist and Father Rookey from a distance. The force can make bodies sway backward before they are touched. As Father Rookey approaches, sometimes a whole line of people will crumple to the ground, one after the other.

The line of people waiting to be blessed extends along the aisles of the basilica. Ushers help control the crowds so that Father Rookey is not rushed upon. In time, Father Rookey blesses every person in the church as requested. As he works the lines of souls, he breaks into a sweat but continues unceasingly for hours. The people in the pews continue to kneel or sit and recite the *Rosary* and other prayers in a sustained litany. Sometimes healings take place in the pews when people begin to spontaneously cry in what is known as the *Gift of Tears*. When this occurs, a deep inner healing is taking place and these individuals are treated with gentleness and respect.

For those who have served with Father in the International Compassion Ministry, they are in awe of what they have been privileged to see. Many have witnessed first-hand a blind person seeing for the first time, once paralyzed limbs moving, the expressions of tears and serenity, and occasionally, the tortured faces of the possessed. They, like Father Rookey, are humbled by what they have seen and the Power of God to heal. They are humbled, too, by the deep faith and sincerity of those who come

Fig. 11.　*Servite Reliquary Crucifix* (containing the relics of the Seven Holy Founders, St. Philip Benizi, St. Juliana, and St. Peregrine, the Cancer Saint), Chicago, Illinois, 2005.

seeking Christ's Help—those precious, vulnerable souls who have reached the critical stage of inviting God into their lives.

And, unfortunately, they have seen the hardened faces of those who refuse to believe and the skeptical looks of those who will not accept the unexplainable Presence of the supernatural in this world. There is a sense of compassion for these inquisitive, logical, sometimes mocking souls who are not yet ready to take the leap of faith. God may choose to work with these souls in a different way. Often, just being at a Mass and healing service will initiate a long process of healing that will manifest in months or years to come.

The Ultimate Spiritual Coach

Until recently, Father Rookey would leave a four-hour Mass and healing service in Chicago to minister to another congregation in St. Louis, Missouri, on the same day. He is a tireless worker who feels the call to bring Christ's Message of Peace, Joy, Beauty, Patience, Compassion, and Mercy into the world to as many people as possible as quickly as possible. Wherever he is called to say Mass, whether it is in Ireland, Mexico, the Philippines, or somewhere else in the United States, the people are essentially the same, bringing the same suffering and desires for healing to God through the Mass and healing services. For example, in Mexico City at Our Lady of Guadalupe, Father Rookey said Mass and blessed people from eleven o'clock in the morning until six o'clock in the evening. People stood in lines ten deep to feel the Touch of the Holy Spirit. Truly, Christ has blessed Father Rookey with a calling to heal with his hands.

After his last Mass and healing service, Father Rookey delights in sharing a meal and a glass of wine and dessert with friends, discussing everything from world events to personal spiritual developments and queries. Indeed, Father Rookey seems to be most vibrant around the altar of Our Lord, or that of a family-style restaurant, or in a modest kitchen. He loves to trade a joke, or, if a piano is available, he is quick to play and join in a favorite tune.

Father Rookey is challenged as much as any human being in his daily life. Sometimes he will grow slightly impatient if there is too much concern expressed about what he is eating or insistent reminders of a doctor's instructions. Frequently, his hearing aids will emit a piercing sound and need to be adjusted in mid-sentence. He'll allow his Scotchness to vent if the price is outrageously high for travel. And, he ruefully wills his Catholic-knees to the floor, time and time again, despite the challenges of age. The rare earthiness of his humor may come as a surprise, too, but in all these instances we are reminded that Father Rookey, despite his gifts, is only human, faced with many of the foibles that challenge all of us.

Always, there is a sense that he is observing his own reactions. Soon he meets each challenge in a steady concerted manner built on years of self-discipline. This is where his spiritual nature rises and assumes its place as a guiding force. At these times, we are reminded of just how difficult the spiritual journey can be moment by moment, for all of us are human and subject to the reactions of our natures as creatures of God.

Father Rookey lives spontaneously and is unfazed by disrupted schedules, time, distance, or unexpected complications. He places full trust in the Blessed Mother to work out all logistics. One Sunday before Mass, he said, "Are you going to come with us to St. Paul [Minnesota] today?" A mere eight-hour journey!

When traveling with Father Rookey, ordinary time dissolves into *Rosary Time*—the number of decades or rounds it takes to get from here to there. Father Rookey often leads the Mysteries, while others chant the succession of *Our Father*s, *Hail Mary*s, *Glory Be*s and *Oh My Jesus*. Quick touches by Father restore lapses in concentration. Even during regular conversation, Father Rookey frequently threads tiny white beads through his fingers in constant contemplation—as if engaging in a parallel spiritual dialog. When stopping for breaks, Father can often be found wandering onto patches of grass islands at gas stations, or walking the aisles of the convenience stores continuing his meditation.

Unburdened by possessions, Father Rookey carries what he needs in a thin plastic grocery bag. It is not that proper luggage hasn't been given to him time and time again, but people will find when they try to give anything to Father Rookey that he quickly gives it to someone else. Father participates in a spiritual gift-economy. When a gift is received, he perceives its essence and acknowledges the intent of the bestower with gratitude, but quickly turns over the gift to another person. A gift received soon becomes a gift given adding momentum to the love intended and extending the blessings of the initiator of the gift beyond himself to others. Contrary to our materialistic world, Father Rookey's goal is to not own anything in fulfillment of his vow of poverty. His only possession is a well-traveled black leather satchel. The heavy bag contains treasured letters, books, recent articles of the Pope, messages from Our Lady of Medjugorje, and an assortment of other items dear to Father Rookey.

When on airplanes, Father Rookey can be found pacing the aisles saying the *Rosary*. On one occasion, Father Rookey was in a small plane in the Midwest when a terrible storm erupted pitching the plane up and down. Father Rookey was saying the *Rosary* as usual. Someone noticed that when he lifted his hands up, the plane went up and when his hands were down, the plane went down. A few of the passengers assisted in holding his praying hands up for the remainder of the journey that ended in a safe landing, and—no doubt—marked the beginning of conversion for a few disbelieving souls!

My sister and brother-in-law had gone on a couple of pilgrimages with Barbara and Bob Smith from Petowski, MI. Barbara called Mike (my brother-in-law) and asked him to help her set up a conference at Boyne Mountain, Michigan, with his cousin. The parish priest was very supportive. So, Mike and Eddie went out the Tuesday before the conference and helped set up the entire resort area. There were five thousand adults and about three thousand kids and teens. This event is yearly, but that was the first year it had gotten so big. They had to set up the stages, chapels, get statues from the local parish, etc. They also had to transport the speakers from the airport.

Well, my sister, my niece, and a couple from our prayer group took a flight from San Francisco early Friday morning, which stopped at O'Hare in Chicago for a transfer to Traverse City and then on to Pelston. After we left Chicago in the small commuter plane, we were told there was a storm we were going to be flying into. I am not sure how many were in the plane but it was one of those that had one stewardess and one aisle with two seats on each side. I was sitting next to a priest and my sister was across the aisle with my niece in back of me. The other couple was seated near the back of the plane—not too far away.

We didn't have much difficulty with the storm at all and arrived at Traverse City on time and layed over for ten minutes. We took off and immediately were told to keep our seatbelts on because it was going to be bumpy. I have been in turbulence before but NOT like this. The stewardess had just started pouring cokes and coffee in back of the pilot's cabin when we gained altitude to avoid the storm. She never got any further pouring anything, and that which she had poured spilled out anyway.

We first tried to climb above the storm quickly. That didn't work. It was about four o'clock in the afternoon. We could see all the lightening out the windows. The pilot said they had stopped all landing back at Traverse City, so we had to go on to Pelston. We would climb about five hundred feet straight up, and be hit by the storm, and drop the same amount of altitude. The first couple of times this happened, we all just sat very still. Finally, the priest next to me asked me if I would pray with him since we had already introduced ourselves and our destination was the same—he was one of the speakers. We held hands and prayed quietly together. I looked over at my sister, and she had her eyes closed and rosary beads in hand.

This sudden dropping and immediate climbing continued. We were bounced around like a puff from a dandelion. Next thing I knew, Father Rookey, who was sitting in the back of the plane, started saying the Rosary out loud and everyone prayed—Catholics and non-Catholics. When he kept his arms raised with the rosary beads, we could gain altitude, but when he lowered them, our plane fell. Two people next to him supported his arms through the next twenty minutes and we were able to land safely. It turned out that we

were the last plane in from Chicago that night as the storm was so severe. Our friends who sat near Father Rookey verified that when he had his hands raised in prayer was the only time we were able to fly straight or gain altitude. The pilots said they had never flown without control before. The funny thing was that the stewardess said she was Baptist and learned the Rosary *that afternoon too.*

When we debarked, there was one last flight from New York via Detroit and those passengers were all bleeding, etc., from things falling out of overhead compartments. Their journey was not as traumatic, nor were they tossed more than two times or so.

My brother-in-law and his cousin met us at the airport in a van, and we shoved in all our luggage as well as Father Harbinger of HLI (he must be 6'6"), and two other priests, and the five of us.

Of course, many other miracles happened that weekend like crying statues, the spinning sun, and the Door of Heaven with Our Lady visible in the Heavens, etc.

On our flight back from Pelston, we had the same stewardess. She took one look at us and said that if we had another flight like that one a few days before, she would have to become Catholic. We told her she could say the Rosary *without becoming Catholic.*

Maureen Sheridan Scott
Michigan 2000

(Reprinted with permission of Maureen Sheridan Scott)

Fig. 12. *Father Peter Mary Rookey Preparing for Mass II,* Our Lady of Sorrows Basilica, Friars' Chapel, 2005.

Back in his office, Father Rookey is often interrupted by someone who has traveled long hours to talk with him or yet another phone call requesting a blessing. Usually, Father patiently takes the requests and stops to pray, unless he and his staff are in the middle of reciting the *Chaplet of Divine Mercy*, when he'll pick up the phone during his praying and pacing and say, "We're praying the Divine Chaplet for you, can you call back later?" He never misses an opportunity to seize the moment to bring a person closer to Christ, or Christ to the person who has asked for help. He responds to his Master's Call no matter how tired and regardless of his immediate circumstance.

This harvesting of souls is a constant process that Father Rookey has developed into a fine art. Father Rookey has seen the evolution of a soul thousands of times and is familiar with the nuanced opening of the interior heart. For it is the gradual softening of hearts that allows the Love of God to take root leading to the long-term healing of body, mind, and spirit—the great *triple healing*. Each step is a brave moment, and is received with dignity, love, and encouragement. For it is no small matter for a soul to release itself from its negative attachments, addictions, long-held resentments, control, anger, ridicule, and criticism to the free-flowing, abundant nourishment of the Love of Christ. Indeed, it is the greatest of human victories.

For Father Rookey, watching the rebirth of a soul is an endlessly fascinating and joyful experience. He is the ultimate coach, gently assisting with his soft humor that shifts perspectives and providing kernels of truth just at the moment when a soul is ready to listen and learn. One soon realizes that Father Rookey is very precise in his direction. He may make a comment and in the days or months ahead one will understand what he meant. He may tell a person something about his past or his family that had not been shared with him. His perceptiveness and Gift of Knowledge he respects as sacred Graces from God, always holding in confidence those insights into a soul while revealing to the soul hidden places in need of healing.

It is this underlying keen intelligence of Father Rookey that is especially fascinating to observe. He values the condition of the soul above all knowledge, social position, talents, and wealth. He knows that these exterior sources of prestige often double as agents that inhibit the interior development of a soul to its fullest capacity by masking the presence of disturbed, hidden soul wounds in need of Compassion and Grace. Through healing of these undesirable traits, a soul becomes more beautiful in the Eyes of God, a process Father Rookey refers to as a *beauty treatment*.

He accepts all who come to him. Wherever he goes, someone usually recognizes him, stopping to remind him of a certain person whom he has blessed along the way, or to ask him for a prayer. While it is mostly the ordinary faithful who reach out to him, the powerful of our day, from celebrities to sports stars, to gangsters, to academics and theologians, seek him out, too. No matter the station in life, what is important to Father Rookey is a soul's ability to consistently forgive and to express compassion, love, humility, faith, hope, and joy throughout the challenges and sufferings of life. He remains balanced in his direction, always quick to admonish us to "do good to those who hurt you," to accept suffering for the healing of others, or to improve a weakness in ourselves. Accepting this orientation, one realizes that we are all participating in this miraculous journey of the human spirit that has continued throughout the ages.

In his private life, Father Rookey seeks out moments of solitude, whether it is walking along the sidewalk near the train tracks late at night close to his priory, reciting the *Rosary*, or performing the *Stations of the Cross* alone in Our Lady of Sorrows Basilica. In these precious hours, one can only wonder what transpires between Father Rookey and Our Lady and Our Lord, Jesus Christ. Once he said, "It only takes one person to hold the Church up." In these powerful, concentrated prayer sessions, surely Christ and Our Lady hear Father Rookey's prayers and put miracles in motion, healing souls worldwide.

Father Rookey has boundless energy and a zest for continuing his healing ministry not just in Chicago or the United States but throughout the world. He feels that Christ has asked him to continue to spread His Good News of healing, light, and love. For it is the healing of souls that is his mission, and through the Power of Christ thousands of people have returned to Our Lord.

Notes

1   St. Louis Mary De Montfort, *The Secret of the Rosary*, translated by Mary Barbour, T.O.P., Nihil Obstat, Gulielmus F. Hughes, S.T.L., Censor Librorum, Imprimatur +Thomas Edmundus Molloy, S.T.D., Archiepiscopus-Episcopus Brooklyniensis, 1954 (New York, NY: Montfort Publications, 1995), p. 18.

2   "I myself have often encouraged the frequent recitation of the Rosary. From my youthful years this prayer has held an important place in my spiritual life. I was powerfully reminded of this during my recent visit to Poland, and in particular at the Shrine of Kalwaria. The Rosary has accompanied me in moments of joy and in moments of difficulty. To it I have entrusted any number of concerns; in it I have always found comfort. Twenty-four years ago, on 29 October 1978, scarcely two weeks after my election to the See of Peter, I frankly admitted: 'The Rosary is my favourite prayer. A marvellous prayer! Marvellous in its simplicity and its depth [. . .].'" From: Pope John Paul II, *Apostolic Letter: ROSARIUM VIRGINIS MARIAE of the Supreme Pontiff John Paul II to the Bishops, Clergy and Faithful of the Most Holy Rosary* (Citta del Vaticano: Libreria Editrice Vaticana, 2002), Sec. "The Popes and the Rosary."

3   Michael O'Carroll, C.S. Sp, *Theotokos: A Theological Encyclopedia of the Blessed Virgin Mary* (Wilmington, DE: Michael Glazier, Inc., 1983), p. 313-314; St. Louis De Montfort, *The Secret of the Rosary*; Pope John Paul II, *Apostolic Letter: ROSARIUM VIRGINIS MARIAE.*

4   Rev. Peter Mary, O.S.M., *The Miracle Prayer.*

5   "[The analysis was conducted by Professor Doctor Odoardo Linoli, university professor-at-large in anatomy and pathological histology, and in the chemistry and clinical microscopy, head physician of the united hospitals of Arezzo and Doctor Ruggero Bertelli, professor emeritus of normal human anatomy at the University of Sienna. The conclusions were presented on March 4, 1971 'in detailed medical and scientific terminology to a prestigious assembly, including ecclesiastical officials, the provincials and superiors of the Friars Minor Conventual, and representatives of religious houses in the city as well as civil, judicial, political and military authorities, representatives of the medical staffs of the city hospitals, various religious of the city and a number of the city's residents.' An authentic copy of the conclusion was presented to Pope Paul VI in a private audience.] As a result of the histological (microscopic) studies, the following facts were ascertained and documented: The flesh was identified as striated muscular tissue of the myocardium

(heart wall), having no trace whatsoever of any materials or agents used for the preservation of flesh. Both the flesh and the sample of blood were found to be of human origin, emphatically excluding the possibility that it was from an animal species. The blood and the flesh were found to belong to the same blood type AB. The blood of the Eucharistic miracle was found to contain the following minerals: chlorides, phosphorus, magnesium, potassium, sodium in lesser degree, and a greater quantity of calcium. Proteins in the clotted blood were found to be normally fractionated, with the same percentage ratio as those found in normal fresh blood." From: Joan Carroll Cruz, *Eucharistic Miracles and Eucharistic Phenomena in the Lives of the Saints,* Nihil Obstat, Rev. John H. Miller, C.SC., Censor Librorum, Imprimatur+Philip M. Hannan, Archbishop of New Orleans (Rockford, Illinois: Tan Books and Publishers, Inc., 1986): Chap. 1, p. 3-7; Fr. Thomas P. McCarthy, C.S.V., with Cynthia Nicolosi, *Forever a Priest* (Oak Lawn, IL: CMJ Marian Publishers, Il, 2004).

God Calls

How did it happen that a soul born into the heartland of the United States was transformed to have an extraordinary love for God? What Graces were at work, what conditions made it possible for a small voice to say "Yes" to an unknown lifetime journey of studying, embracing, and sharing a blazing love for God? For all creatures of God, a soul's development is a process, changing as it is confronted with the challenges of life through its own suffering and by responding to the suffering of others. How each soul chooses to respond, moves one closer to or further from the Presence of God. For Father Rookey, it was the direct experience of suffering at a young age that led to the conscious opening of his soul to God—to his first "Yes."

Father Rookey first responded to God's Call as a child. Born in 1916 and christened Peter Joseph Byron, Father Rookey was raised in a devout Irish-Catholic family in Superior, Wisconsin, one of thirteen children born to Anthony Daniel Rookey and Johanna McGarry. Johanna McGarry was content with her life and wanted to die as she was born: as a poor

Fig. 13. *Soul Fire*, Chicago, Illinois, 2006.

woman with an order of God and family in her life. She knew the hard work involved in raising a large family, as she was one of twenty children raised on a family farm in Stillwater, Minnesota.

In those days, in a small town, families had single-digit phone numbers. The Rookey family had a hauling business advertised as *Call 9*, because one of the nine Rookey boys would be sure to be of service. Industrious, practical, prayerful, and with a good sense of humor, the Rookeys survived well enough, part of a minority Irish population in a town where Germans, Norwegians, Danes, Swedes, and Finns immigrated years before.

One Fourth of July, as a young boy, Father Rookey was playing with his brother lighting firecrackers and racing back and forth to see them burst upward in all their glory. They lit another one. The boys, huddling in the darkness, looked for the expected burst of light. When none came, Byron rushed over to re-light it. In a horrifying moment, it exploded in his face. One can only imagine the heartbreak of the family when the doctor told them he thought Byron's sight was gone forever. Now with twelve other children to attend to and a business to run, Johanna had to watch over her blind son. For young Byron, this was a time of shock and dismay. Fervently, he made a promise to God that would change his life: if his sight would be restored, he would become a priest.

With a firm trust in God, Johanna led the Rookey family in prayer, praying the *Rosary* every night on their knees for almost a year. Miraculously, reversing the medical prognosis, their prayers were answered. Over a period of time, Byron began to see again. Remaining true to his promise, he began his quest to become a priest. Having heard great stories about the beautiful Masses at Our Lady of Sorrows Basilica, at the age of thirteen, young Byron entered the Servite seminary, Mater Dolorosa (Mother of Sorrows), Servite school in Hillside, Illinois, just outside Chicago.

The Servite Order began with a group of seven wealthy merchants who lived in the thirteenth century in Florence, Italy. They suddenly turned away from business to form a religious community for the service of Mary, the Mother of Jesus. Where before they had been involved in pursuing great wealth and were influential in the highest political circles of their day, after what can only be described as a spiritual conversion, they changed their lives. The Virgin Mary appeared to all of them at the same time, and these competitive men found themselves turning away even from their families to live together, thereby founding the Servite Order. Far from the small town of Superior and suddenly separated from his warm family life, like these men, little did young Byron Rookey know what God had in store for him and for multitudes of souls.

On May 17, 1941, Father Peter Mary Rookey was ordained. Seven years later, he was to embark on a mission that would prove to be a life-changing event for him and thousands of others.

Can you tell us where you were born and about your family background?

I was born in Superior, Wisconsin, on October 12th, 1916, during World War I. On the lighter side, my brother always jokingly asked, "Where was the war when you broke out?" *(laughs)* We lived in a house that has since been destroyed. The property was built on by *Superior Telegram*, as it's called. The company was known for the *Superior Paper*, a newspaper. The original house, where I was born, has been destroyed, but where I was reared that house is still there on Ogden Avenue in Superior. When I travel on Ogden Avenue in Chicago, I think of that.

By the way, when you go by on Ogden Avenue, there's a big line of churches here in Chicago. One after the other, non-Catholic churches. One of them is named St. Mary's Baptist Church. The front is beautiful. It wasn't built as a church. It's a remade building. It's unusual because our non-Catholic Christians don't believe in a devotion to Mary. It's the first time I've ever heard of that.

So I was born on Ogden Avenue in Superior, Wisconsin. One of thirteen children, I was five from the bottom! *(laughs)* Nine boys and four girls, they all survived.

What were your names?

Byron was one of my baptismal names. They used to call me Byron. In the seminary, they called me Peter.

Your mother's last name was McGarry?

Yes, Joan, or Johanna, McGarry from Stillwater, Minnesota. The state prison is there. The standard joke was that my dad had to come and bail her out! James McGarry was her father's name; her mother's family name was Byron. She was supposedly related to Lord Byron who wrote all of the poetry. He was a handsome guy—ran after the ladies a bit. She was also of Irish ancestry. She came from St. Louis and James McGarry came from County Limerick in Ireland. They had twenty children. Four of the young ones died; sixteen survived. They lived in Stillwater in the days when the now well-known Venerable Solanus Casey was a streetcar conductor. The Caseys lived across the river in Hudson, Wisconsin, on a farm, also.

What did they raise on the farm?

Oh, the usual—potatoes, wheat, food for the cows—that sort of thing.

Did you go to work on the farm in the summer?

The farm had gone by the time I grew up. They had both gone to Heaven. A sister, one of the McGarrys, married a Raleigh across the river in Wisconsin in Somerset, which is just across from the city. They had a big farm, and we were allowed to go down from Superior, the boys and the girls, just two at a time if we were good. We were allowed to go down and visit them "x" number of weeks. The sister's name was Katherine, and she married this man by the name of Jack Raleigh. They had a family of about five or six. They started a famous restaurant in Somerset called *Jack Raleigh's*. He and his wife became nationally famous. Before Mrs. Raleigh died, she was ushered into the National Museum of Restaurateurs. Sometimes they invited us to the restaurant.

Your family had a hauling business?

My dad was a logger in the early days. He probably logged on the river near the Twin cities. That's how he met my mother. Then he started hauling oil for Standard Oil. He had a horse and oil wagon, and he decided to go into business and started to haul coal. Coal was a cheap commodity up there because the ships would bring the coal from the mines and drop it in Superior on the port. They would pick it up at the port and deliver it to the homes. Coal was a great source of energy and heat. It was a great business then.

Later, he got into the moving industry and started the so-called *Rookey Transfer*. Since he had nine boys, it was very interesting as he had plenty of brawn to carry out the moving business. We developed a big warehouse, eventually, by the waterfront of Lake Superior. The *moving and storage,* as they called it. We later adopted the United Van Lines name and became a franchise of the national United Van Lines. That's how we ended up. Of course, that's all gone. My brothers all died who were running it.

Did you work on the trucks?

Oh yes, before I went to the seminary. During the summer holidays, I would help out, too.

You were quite young?

Oh yes, in my teens.

Was your mother a very religious person? Did she have a great faith?

Oh yes, she did. We were at Sunday Mass every Sunday and prayed the *Rosary* at night very often.

And your father, was he a very religious person?

Oh yes, he was an upright man. He was a kind of Joseph. They were a very normal couple. They enjoyed the dancing, and so on. They were not off on cloud-nine.

How did you select the Servite Order when you became a priest? Did you research different Orders?

No, I came into the Order, like I'm sure many—if not most—of us, through a person of the holy Servites. We had a very holy man named Father McDermott in Superior, Wisconsin, who was pastor of St. Patrick's, and then I had a very good friend by the name of John O'Brien. He's the one who eventually got me into the Servite Order. The O'Briens and the Rookeys were very close. There were very few Irish in Superior. Almost everyone was of the northern peoples, Swedes, Norwegians, Finns, and Danes. The Irish stuck together quite a bit because there weren't too many of us.

O'Brien preceded us a year at Hillside Seminary here in Chicago; it was called Mater Dolorosa Seminary in those days, Mother of Sorrows Seminary. He came back with great stories of the seminary in Chicago. He had glowing accounts of Our Lady of Sorrows Basilica and how certain Mass servers had to go up behind the altar and light the candles. I think all of these things added up to my coming. We had about a dozen from Superior at one time in the seminary.

How old were you when he came back?

I was thirteen. I was just finishing eighth grade.

When Father O'Brien came and told you about the seminary, did you initiate your entry?

The eventual Father O'Brien. He was just a student then. He took the name of Gregory. His name was John O'Brien. But at any rate, yes. He was able to interest quite a number of Superiorites in the seminary. Of course, it was just a high school level—most of them came out. That was par for the course in those days—start out with a big class and end up with a trickle. I guess they weren't convinced enough to really go on. It was just a kind of passing notion with some of them.

Did you experience the loss of your eyesight before that, too?

Oh yes. I was only a young lad. I can't remember how old I was. I try to forget all that. *(laughs)* I had an idea, for some reason or another, that I should keep that a dark secret—the early years. I didn't like to refer to it.

Why?

For some reason or other. I don't know. Eventually, I thought it would lift people up to know that prayer brings miracles.

Can you describe what happened?

It's described in the books already.

But you had a firecracker?

A big firecracker. My young brother, Bernard, and I had tried to light it. I blew on it to make it go, and it blew up in my face. That's how I lost my eyesight.

You were blind for about a year?

Probably less, because I don't recall missing a year of school.

Do you remember not seeing and what that was like?

Oh! *(laughs)* It wasn't pleasant, I'll tell you, being in the dark. The Lord gave me this experience, so I can relate to people who are blind. It seems as a result of that many people have received their sight in the healing ministry.

When you were blind, did your mother have your family pray the Rosary?

Yes. It was mostly prayer that did it, because the doctors couldn't do much with me.

Did you believe when you were that little that God would heal you?

Oh, of course. I think that my priestly vocation entered in there, too. When you are down, you promise the moon! *(laughs)* I think I promised at that time that I would give myself to the Lord and become a priest, if possible.

So you came down to Chicago to go to the seminary out on the far West Side?

Yes, Hillside, where the big cemetery is. Mount Carmel was the original one, and they developed next to it Mary Queen of Heaven.

A priest from Ladysmith, Wisconsin, drove us down the first time. A bunch, about a half a dozen of us, started in my class from Superior. There were other Superiorites already in the seminary.

Were these people you knew from home?

Oh yes. I knew some of them. They were classmates in grade school. One name I remember is McCumber; another was a Pat Macnamee . . . John O'Brien, of course, was in the class ahead of us. Another man in his class was a Flaherty, who ended up being very active in the cathedral up there. He came out and married—he was back in latter days. He was an extraordinary Communion man who helped in the cathedral up there.

Did you first become associated with Our Lady of Sorrows when you were at Hillside?

Oh yes. They used to have us come in for funerals or for special occasions. It was very impressive and beautiful, the basilica. All of our brothers went there to sing the Mass for our seminary at Hillside.

It is amazing that you returned there after sixty-plus years of being a priest.

Yes. I got ordained there in 1941. May 17th.

Is it your home, in a way, Our Lady of Sorrows Basilica?

Yes, eventually. The Lord blessed that church so powerfully.

You have had a life-long affinity, too, for gangsters since Chicago was such a hot spot at the time.

Yes. That was in 1930 when I entered into the seminary. That was the big gangster era. I think it was that same year, or was it 1929, or 1930, that the terrible massacre, the St. Valentine's Day Massacre, occurred on the South Side here? I was down

Fig. 14. *Father Peter Mary Rookey, O.S.M.,* Our Lady of Sorrows Basilica, Chicago, Illinois, 2005.

there in those days. I would often as not go by the grave of Al Capone. It's in Mt. Carmel out here. I spent many years in Mater Dolorosa Seminary. That's the old Latin for Mother of Sorrows, which is the great charism of the Servite Order.

Another little smile . . . the Irish ladies, when I told them I was out at the seminary, they would say, "Oh, you are out at the *cemetery*!" And I would say, "No, I'm out at the *seminary*." The cemetery was the biggest industry in Hillside. It still is a big one with the restaurants for the funerals and all that sort of thing—workers for the graves, the mausoleum, and so on.

You mentioned that you started out with a large class, but you stayed it through. Did you have some kind of revelation? What happened to make you decide to stay?

Oh, I guess the Lord just touched me, and one night I told my mother I felt that I'd like to become a priest. She was delighted, of course. I'm sure she was praying for somebody, that one of those nine boys, would be a priest.

What age were you at that time?

I was just in eighth grade.

When you went to Hillside, you stayed through while some of your classmates left.

Oh, I was tempted though, by homesickness and all, to leave. But there was a very good priest, Father Coughlin, a very saintly man. He was an assistant to the rector, and he encouraged and helped me a great deal.

It must have been hard when you had so many brothers and sisters and your mother and father.

Yes.

How often did you go home?

We got home at Christmas and in summer at that stage. Once you entered the spiritual year, you didn't get home. After high school is the spiritual novitiate. That's par for the course of any spiritual order. You have a spiritual year that can be extended another year. Then you make your first vows, if you are willing, for three years, and that can be extended, also. If you're finally accepted, you take your final vows.

The first year, do they want you to stay away from your family so you can make a decision if you want to follow what God wants you to do, while experiencing how it is to live continuously in a God-focused community?

That's right.

Then you make a decision to go for three more years, as an extended time. During that time, can you come home?

Well yes, you are easily dispensed of your temporary vows.

But as far as just visiting your family, over the next three years, did you visit your family?

No, you don't go home. In those days, you didn't anyway. Things have changed and have loosened up tremendously. It's not all good, I think.

ೞೞೞೞೞೞೞೞೞೞೞೞೞೞೞೞೞೞೞೞೞೞೞೞೞೞೞೞೞೞೞೞೞೞ

Bernie Verwiel first met Father Rookey as a seminarian. He came to work for Father Rookey and the International Compassion Ministry later in his life. He provided the following testimony:

I entered Mater Dolorosa seminary at the age of fourteen. Father Rookey was two years ahead of me. He was a junior, and I was a freshman, so that's a long time ago. He was always, for all the years I've known him in the seminary, for about ten years, outstanding. Almost everybody in the seminary is ordinary like everybody else, but Father Rookey was about the only person in the seminary who was unusual—his attitude toward everybody and his charity toward everybody. In a seminary, there's a great deal of cliques. They're hard to avoid. Father Rookey was never in a clique. All I can say is that there was nothing extraordinary—he was just a wonderful person, and everyone admired him. But he was certainly outstanding.

When did you encounter his Gift of Healing?

I never knew about his gift. I left the seminary around 1944 and entered the army, so I was part of the war effort. I never heard about his Gift of Healing until several years after I had returned from the army. It must have been twenty years after I left the seminary, in about 1962, that I resumed my friendship with Father Rookey. Somebody in the Servite Order finally recognized his Gift of Healing and invited him back to Our Lady of Sorrows where he was given the role that he now has as the head of the International Compassion Ministry. After my wife died in Florida, I moved back to Chicago in September in 1995, and, shortly after that, the following year, 1996, March or April, I joined the staff here, and I've been working here ever since as a volunteer.

What most impresses you about Father Rookey?

The most impressive thing is his down-to-earth attitude, his humility, his sense of humor—he has a great sense of humor. And his attitude that I'm just another person no better than you are. Some people act like, hey, this guy is a wealthy guy; he must be very important. And many times he does act important. But Father Rookey doesn't have that flair, that I'm a very important person. He doesn't have that—and that's very important.

During the next three years, were you a novice at Hillside?

No, we had a novitiate in Milwaukee. We did our so-called philosophy course up there. After those four years, we had four years of theology.

That's where you learned Latin?

Oh no. The Latin you started right at Hillside. Right in the first year of high school. We had Latin every year, deeper and deeper, and more difficult authors. We took the train in to Loyola University in Chicago to take courses, so we could have a degree, but we resided at Hillside. That was the trouble with the seminaries. Most of them anyway. They were not university recognized. You came out with a wonderful education but no parchment to show for it. The Orders and the dioceses would have to send their seminarians on the side to a university to take courses so they could get a degree. Then at least you'd have a Bachelor of Arts or Bachelor of Science when you were ordained.

Where did you learn how to play the piano?

I learned that at the seminary, too.

When you were growing up, had you been anywhere outside of Milwaukee, except for going shortly into Minnesota or into Chicago?

No, we didn't travel. After finishing in Milwaukee, I was sent back to Hillside and finished my theology studies there.

What books did you read in the seminary that were most helpful in your spiritual development?

Thinking back . . . the *Bible*, of course, and the history of our roots, the seven merchant men of Florence way back in 1233, the history of our Servite Order, in other words. I studied the popular Saints like St. Thérèse, the Little Flower. And, our own Servite Saints, St. Peregrine, St. Philip Benizi—he's not a popular saint like St. Francis of Assisi. St. Francis has always impressed me. And St. Anthony and the popular Saints—their books and their lives, I should say.

What other books did you read?

The *Confessions of St. Augustine* made a big impression upon me and *The Lives of the Saints*. Especially in the seminary days, I was interested in the boy seminarian Saints like St. Stanislaus Kostka, who was a Jesuit seminarian. He died before he was ordained. And St. Aloysius Gonzaga, a Spanish Saint. They both died. I visited their rooms in the Roman College in Rome, where they studied and eventually died while they were students. They were very important to me as a student, because I was one of them as a seminarian.

And, more recently, the *Poem of the Man~God,* written by a secular-Servite, Maria Valtorta.[1] She wrote this five-volume theme about the life of Christ. It's not poetry; it's prose. She wrote quite a number of other religious works. She was a mystic from Viareggio, which was about thirty-five miles west of Florence on the Mediterranean seaport, rather more like a fishing sort of town.

What impressed you most about the Servite Founders?

I think the love they had for each other stands out for me. They, incidentally, came from opposing political camps. Something like in our country we have the big parties—the Democrats and the Republicans. In those days, the Pope, Martin IV, was a civil potentate, besides being a religious head of the Church.

They had what they called the Papal States that took in a lot of central Italy. There was a fight going on at this time, and Our Lady appeared to the Seven Founders on August 15th, 1233, and invited them to come apart and begin the Order together. She brought them together, because, as I often say jokingly, three and a half of them belonged to the party of the emperor and three and half belonged to the party of the Pope! They were divided because of the battle going on between the emperor and the Pope at this time.

They got to love each other and "bury the hatchet" as the Indians would say here in America. So well, in fact, that the history of the origin of the Servite Order says that, later on in their lives, they found it very difficult to be apart from each other for any length of time, which is a terrific show of God's Grace, how they got to love each other so, so much. And then there were personal aspects of their biographies.

Wasn't St. Peregrine part of a gang that attacked one of them because of the political issues?

St. Peregrine, he was, yes, anti-Pope for his town, Forli. He came from the City of Forli, which was above Florence and east of

Fig. 15.   *Seven Holy Founders,* altar, Our Lady of Sorrows Basilica, Chicago, Illinois, 2006. The Blessed Mother appeals to the Seven Holy Founders to become her *Servants.* The Servite Order was established in 1233 in Florence, Italy, under the patronage of Our Lady of Sorrows. Mural by Richard Schmid (1956), featuring Pope Pius XII crowning the church as a basilica.

it. St. Philip Benizi was invited by the Pope to go and preach peace to Forli that was rebellious against him.

He arrived with a companion Servite in the square of the city and began to preach peace. Peregrine was part of, if not a leader, part of a Burgund group of young people who attacked him verbally and even physically. St. Philip took it very peaceful, as we say in John Wayne's language, "real peaceful like," and departed in peace. His attitude and his reaction to this violent attack impressed this young Peregrine so much that he eventually was touched, ran out after St. Philip and his companion, and asked for pardon.

Eventually, he became a Servite. I believe he was part of the community in Sienna for some years, then he moved back to his native town where he really made his name. There's another great book—his life. He was known for his very great love for the poor. Providing food and whatever—helping the poor. It was the poor who flocked to his funeral from all over.

That's not too well known about Peregrine. He's known as the Cancer Saint because the Lord healed his cancerous leg that probably came from his great penance. He wanted to stand so far as possible always. That probably had something to do with the cancerous leg he had, which was healed instantly, as we know.

He wanted to stand?

He wanted to stand—as a penance. That was one of his great penances, to stand.

For hours?

Oh, 'til he dropped sort of thing.

The lives of the founding Servite fathers are very applicable to today, even though the Order was founded hundreds of years ago.

Fig. 16. *The Miraculous Cure of St. Peregrine, O.S.M.*, painting by Gregorio Lazzarini (1665-1740), Venice, Italy, Our Lady of Sorrows Basilica, Chicago, Illinois, 2006. St. Peregrine Laziosi (1265-1345) had a cancerous leg that was miraculously cured when he prayed before the altar and had a vision of Christ the night before his leg was to be amputated.

Yes. The Order was founded in the early years of the thirteenth century when a man named Bonajuncta and his companions, who were merchants in Florence, Italy, left their professions to retire outside of the city in a life of poverty and penance.

It's interesting that some of them were cloth merchants. They must have been very powerful because of the cloth trade.

The cloth trade was a big thing in Florence. The Florentine people were well dressed. Florence was the art mecca; some people called it the Art Mecca of the World. All of these great people like Michelangelo, I mention only one, and so many artists were there, and their works.

The silk trade routes were running through there, too. It was truly a high-fashion city.

Yes. I engaged a wonderful artist in Rome to paint the picture of the Seven Founders and Our Lady appearing to them, according to the tradition. Their anniversary is coming up in several weeks, the 15th of August, the Assumption of Our Lady in 1233, when she was supposed to have appeared to them.

They belonged to a group called the *Laudesi*, a strong confraternity, which in Italian means the Praisers of Our Lady. They met in a small chapel adjoining the present cathedral. This is a marvelous structure, by the way, very artistic, and it has different colored marbles on the outside. It has a remarkable, very attractive architecture. There is a bronze plaque attesting to the chapel that stood there next to the cathedral. That's where Our Lady appeared to them.

These were very wealthy, very powerful men, living in one of the most fashionable cities in Europe at the time. For them to have seen Our Lady and then to have decided to take a vow of poverty must have seemed to have been a very radical idea to their friends and families.

Yes. And some of them were married. They had to make their arrangements with their families. Being people of means, they

Fig. 17. *The Sacred Host: Father Peter Mary Rookey, O.S.M.*, International Compassion Ministry, Olympia Fields, Illinois, 2006.

probably were able to arrange to have their families taken care of. We don't know much about their families, but we know some of them were married.

How was it that they could do this when they were married?

They were mature people. They must have worked it out with their families. Even some of the Apostles were married. Peter, for example. In the *Poem of the Man~God*, according to Maria Valtorta's visions, it says that Peter and his wife were not able to have children, but he was given a young boy so he could be a spiritual parent.[2] Not much is said about the others being married.

There are a lot of questions today about the Church's position that doesn't permit married priests.

The tradition of a celibate priesthood goes way back, before the beginning of the Church.

Of course, Jesus wasn't married.

Yes. Even Joseph was a Nazirite. That was a sect that lived apart from people, grew their hair long, and were celibate. They were also vegetarians, if I'm not mistaken. They led a very modest sort of life. This is brought out by Maria Valtorta's visions in the *Poem of the Man~God*, in the part on Our Lady, in the beginning book telling about her marriage with Joseph, and how they finally got to talk with each other. Like Joseph, Mary, of course, was a virgin. Just as she asked Angel Gabriel, How can this be done that I have a child, I know not man? Joseph asked Mary, Why don't I just go on as I am, a Nazirite, and you, a virgin?[3]

The idea of celibacy is found in many faith traditions. In the Catholic Church, part of the idea is that a priest is giving his all to God and he should not be conflicted in regard to his priorities. Practically, a parish priest needs to be at church every Saturday and Sunday, and during the week for weddings and funerals, and then there are the feast days, and the long holy seasons. The Church is his first obligation, because he has taken a sacred vow to serve God. His family needs must come second to the needs of his parishioners—his spiritual family.

Yes. I'll never forget Cardinal William F. Baum for whom I worked for three years in the Ozarks. He was yanked from there to become archbishop and cardinal of Washington and then over to Rome. He headed up a big congregation there. He was a very intelligent man, a very beautiful, soft, soft-spoken man. He was raised as an ecumenicist, also.

For one of our priest gatherings in the Ozarks, in the Diocese of Springfield Cape Girado, Missouri, he invited an Episcopalian bishop to address us about the question of celibacy. This bishop, an archbishop of the Episcopalian Church, said, Don't think that having a married clergy is going to solve all your clerical problems. He had his daughter, or his daughter-in-law, with him. She was telling about how her husband, a priest, was divided so much between the family and the church vestry, the people who assist in the church similar to our parish council. They call it the vestry. It was quite a struggle. This was brought out by this archbishop in his talk.

Think of all the endless obligations with little time for private prayer. It must be hard for a priest who has a child, who needs to do something on Saturday afternoon, and he has a commitment to administer the Sacraments. He must always be disappointing someone, while—at the same time—not being able to take care of his own spiritual needs, so he can effectively help others.

Yes. The Church will always hold up virginity and celibacy as an ideal. Of course for religious there is no question. They take the vows of poverty, chastity, and obedience. There would be no change there for religious priests. We couldn't have a wife and children in the monastery! *(laughs)*

The Church has constantly held up celibacy for her clergy as a sign that it can be done. I often use as an example, you are a man and you have an awful time with purity, sins against the flesh, let's put it that way—it covers a multitude of sins. "Oh, I see a blond or brunette that I just can't resist, sort of thing. Oh? I'm doing it, so can you." You don't need to speak too much about the possibility. Or, maybe you're married, and it's adultery you are committing. Or, you are single. Whatever. Sins against the flesh that you just can't overcome. "Oh, no? You have your parish priests living a celibate life—a life of purity." The Church wants that sign to be there just to know that it can be done.

Even the Romans with their pagan practices recognized this. In the Roman Forum, the ruins of the Temple of Vesta were dedicated to the goddess, Vesta. Part of their worship was that they kept a flame in front of the temple. It was the job of the Vestal Virgins to keep it lit. They were very revered by the pagan Romans. They kept their virginity and were put on a pedestal by the pagan Romans. That was their big deal, the goddess Vesta. She was supposed to have been a virgin. She wasn't anything anyway. She was an un-god as all of them are.

Even non-Christian persons hold celibacy up as a more perfect way. That is what the Church has done through the centuries. Mary offered herself to the temple. That's why she told Gabriel, *How shall this be done, because I know not man?* (Lk 1:34). Joachim and Anna, according to tradition, had given her to the temple, because they told God if they ever had a child she would be offered to the Lord. Just like the mother of Samson. Her husband had two wives, and the other wife was always putting her down because she was sterile. She suffered a lot because it was a curse not to have children.

It's not like that today!

(*laughs*) She promised the Lord. She was crying before the high altar, and the high priest, his name was Eli, I think, overheard her. He blessed her. She went home, and she conceived, finally. She had promised the Lord she would bring the child to the service of the temple.

Is this thinking along the lines of offering firstfruits, whether it's the fruit of the womb, the fruit of the field, or our wages today? In Ireland, it was often the firstborn son who became the priest. That was a sacred way of living.

That's right. The firstborn was always special. In Jerusalem, they wanted the first lamb of a sheep to be offered in the temple. They didn't want imperfect animals to be offered; only the best for the Lord.

That is a great humility.

Yes. This will always be. The Holy Father, Pope John Paul II, presented this in his great encyclical on the priesthood he came out with a few years ago. It will be always. That is why the Church has always upheld it, although the Eastern Rites have swallowed that—they have a married clergy. But they still have a tinge, a taste of it, in that if I get married, I can't become a bishop. *(laughs)* There is still the reverence for celibacy, even in their way of practice.

Can we talk about the role of a priest? There is the idea that priests are called to the art of guiding and healing souls.

That's certainly, I would say, the outstanding work of a priest.

It's not just ministering to the ordinary concerns of a community, but it is the idea of providing spiritual direction.

Very much so. The basic virtue of priesthood is carrying out the *Sacrifice of the Mass* and giving the Sacraments.

As a form of intercession for the people?

Yes.

In order to do that properly, it takes a lot of time for personal prayer and engaging in long periods of fasting on occasion. Is that true?

Oh, definitely. If anybody is called to prayer and fasting, it's the priest. I find in the International Compassion Ministry that nothing happens unless I pray and fast.

It is essential to the process.

Yes. One of the reasons I fast all day is because, very often, we have healing services in the evening. I feel very uncomfortable praying for people on a full stomach. I just feel very uncomfortable doing that. I like to be prepared. Before I carry out the services, normally we have prayed all the *Divine Office* for the day, and then we have the *Scriptural Rosary*, the *Seven Dolors*, the *Seven Sorrows of Our Lady* that is read with the Scripture, before the laying on of hands. There is prayer preparation and then the Mass. I like to have a Mass because that is the Power, the Healing Power. At Communion time, we say, *My Lord, I am not worthy . . . but only say the word and I SHALL BE HEALED. (laughs)* The Eucharist heals.

When you are going to have Mass, it takes hours of preparation for you to prepare for that moment?

Right. Oh, yes.

Like an athlete working out, you are conditioning and preparing yourself mentally and spiritually.

Yes. The Archbishop of Milan, St. Charles Balmero, in one of his talks to the priests in the breviary for his feast day, he says, You say, I'm so distracted at Mass. But what were you doing *before* the Mass? Chattering? Distracting yourself?

Which is another reason why it's hard to be married and do the Mass properly.

Yes. A priest should pray before a Mass, recollecting his thoughts.

In the morning, don't you say prayers and do a physical work out?

Many prayers. I pray all of the *Divine Office* and then do some physical exercise, also.

What kind of physical exercise do you do?

Push-ups.

How many push-ups do you do?

I never count.

A couple of hundred?

At least. I do a lot of walking too.

Is it true that you stand on your head when you say the Psalms?

Oh, yes.

For how long?

Maybe five minutes.

You take care of your own body, mind, and spirit?

Yes. The Lord created them. I find I only do it because it makes me more fit for the spiritual; it makes the body work for the soul.

Do you consider the idea of the function of a priest as a spiritual warrior who is representing the authority of the Church?

Definitely. Just a simple example, when a prayer group cannot cast out the demon when someone is being attacked or possessed, it takes the Sacrament of the Orders, the priest, to finally give the fatal blow to the demon to get him out.

You're operating against this oppositional force to God. Are priests our frontline spiritual men?

I've never heard it put that way—but it sounds good. It sounds right. *(laughs)*

It seems, that's the job. They are our spiritual warriors, the ones who defend us from harm.

Well, the fact that a priest is called to dispense the Sacraments that are the bulwark against evil, it is obvious.

The Sacrament of Confession is so important.

Oh yes. Every one of the Sacraments has its importance. It is so fundamental; the *Sacrament of Reconciliation*, we call it now, is so basic to our healing. We recommend you go to Confession at the healing services. We usually have Confession during the praying of the *Seven Sorrows Rosary*, before the Mass.

The process of confession is referred to as a light version of an exorcism; it helps protect that person, is that correct?

That's correct.

At the end of the confession, a priest blesses the person to protect him/her from spiritual harm so he/she does not sin again. It isn't just the person confessing, it's the priest providing spiritual protection, right?

We can believe Jesus when He gave the keys to Peter: *Whose sins you shall forgive, they are forgiven them; and whose sins you shall retain, they are retained.* (Jn 20:23). Since Jesus came to save not only the people of His time but for all time in every nation, it is obvious that power was given through Peter upon all His chosen priests. Otherwise, we would not be able to partake in that great Gift of God's Absolution.

And the meaning of being chosen that priests are trained in body, mind, and spirit to act as intercessors?

Correct.

They have to be set aside from the general population.

Right. Part of the training includes courses in *moral* theology.

The Servite Founders chose to set themselves apart to do the Work of God. Wasn't Florence like America is today? America is wealthy and powerful, and Italy, at that time, was extremely powerful commercially. It was in a culture that celebrated affluence that the Servites turned from serving the wealthy and powerful to serving the people.

Yes, good point—to start living like Christ lived. I was just reading the *Poem of the Man~God.* According to Maria Valtorta, Our Lord told her about three men who approached Him. One man said to Him, Well, I'll go wherever You lead me; I want to be a disciple. And, where do You live? And so on. Jesus answered him, Even the birds build their nests, but the Son of Man has no place to lay his head, so if you want to lead a life like that be my guest.[4] The Servite Founders did follow that. They had a nice life evidently, but vowed to embrace poverty and live without anything of their own, and share the little they would have with each other and with the community that sprang up from their example. It was a complete break from their affluent past.

Fig. 18. *Seeking the Sacred: Father Peter Mary Rookey, O.S.M.,* Pilgrimage to the Holy Land, 2005.

They were like St. Francis of Assisi. He chose a similar direction.

Yes, St. Francis of Assisi. Assisi is not too far from Florence. He also was from an affluent family. According to the story, his father brought him to court, and the bishop was the judge. The Church and the government were very closely allied in those days, and it wasn't unusual for a bishop to also be a judge. His father brought him to court because he was giving away so much of his family's goods. According to the story, St. Francis took off all his clothes and said, Here, now I'll be like Jesus. I'll have nothing. That's how he started. That became the Franciscans' great sign: their poverty, their great poverty.

That's not exactly conducive to married life! They couldn't expect their families to make that kind of sacrifice.

Yes. That was the beginning. They took up in a residence that was given by the bishop, who was very close and open to them. His name was Ardingo, and he spiritually helped them with direction and everything. He gave them a church. All of them became priests and clerics, except one who was Alexis, whose last name was Falconieri, which translates: *people who work with falcons. (laughs)* Falconieri. His niece was St. Juliana Falconieri, and she started the Servite nuns. Her house is right on the square near the cathedral.

Falcons were also affiliated with the nobility because they were sport hunting birds.

Yes. He died at the tender age of one hundred ten years old, St. Alexis. They were canonized altogether as the *Seven Confessors,* as they called them. The Saints are roughly divided into Apostles, Martyrs, Confessors, Virgins, and Nonclerics—widows or married people. They were the first ones canonized as a group of confessors all together. They wanted their bones to be united. That was an interesting thing.

Wasn't St. Philip Benizi known for healing lepers and converting prostitutes?

Yes, correct, also.

And he manifested food for people whenever they were poor?

The painting in our general headquarters in the dining room, the refectory, as they call them, the whole back wall of the refectory, depicts St. Philip and the *Miracle of the Loaves*. This poor, very poor community of Servites was without food. When he was visiting them, and as he prayed, there was a knock on the door, and there came people with baskets of food for the community.

Notes

[1] Maria Valtorta, *The Poem of the Man~God*, Vol. 1-5, translated from the Italian by Nicandro Picozzi, M.A., D.D., revised by Patrick McLaughlin, M.A. (Valtortiano srl, Isola de Liri (FR) Italy: Centro Editoriale, Valtoriano, 1990). Note: In 1993, Joseph Cardinal Ratzinger, Prefect for the Congregation of the Divine Faith (CDF) wrote to the Most. Rev. Raymond J. Boland, D.D., Bishop of Birmingham Alabama, to notify the publisher of *The Poem of the Man~God*, Caritas of Birmingham, of the CDF's request that the publisher comply with the most recent decision of the Holy See and its preference for method of notification in regard to the work: (Prot. N. 144/58 i), dated April 17, 1993: "it might be clearly indicated from the very first page that the 'visions' and 'dictations' referred to in it are simply the literary forms used by the author to narrate in her own way the life of Jesus. They cannot be considered supernatural in origin." Ref: *http://www.bardstown.com/~brchrys/Chrchval.html.*

[2] "You will have the boy." From: Valtorta, *The Poem of the Man~God*, The Second Year of Public Life, Sec. 199: "Jesus Goes to the Lepers of Siloam and Ben Hinnom, The Power of Mary's Word," Vol. 2, p. 307-309.

[3] "[Joseph] But I was not expecting to be the chosen one as I am a Naz[i]rite and I have obeyed because it is an order of the Priest, not because I wish to get married . . . [Mary] Since My childhood I have consecrated Myself to the Lord. I know this is not the custom in Israel. But I heard a voice requesting My virginity as a sacrifice of love for the coming of the Messiah . . . [Joseph] I will join my sacrifice to Yours and we shall love the Eternal Father so much with our chastity that He will send His Saviour to the world earlier, and will allow us to see His Light shining in the world. Come, Mary. Let us go before His

House and take an oath that we shall love each other as the angels do." From: Valtorta, *The Poem of the Man~God*, The Hidden Life, Sec. 12: "Joseph is Appointed Husband of the Virgin," Vol. 1, pp. 65-66.

4   "Foxes have holes and the birds of the air have nests, but the Son of Man has no where to lay His head. The world is My home, wherever there are spirits to be taught, distress to be relieved, sinners to be redeemed." From: Valtorta, *The Poem of the Man~God*, The Second Year of Public Life, Sec. 178: "Jesus Meets Three Men Who Want to Follow Him," Vol. 2, p. 191-192.

The Journey Continues

As a soul progresses in its development, spiritual guidance is often provided through persons who are more experienced in the Ways of God. For Father Rookey, the gifted Father James Mary Keane was an important influence. As an engaging teacher, Catholic publisher and broadcaster, founder of the Servite Orders in Ireland and Australia, leader of massive devotional Novenas, and an exceptional priest, Father Keane was a role model, and, with others, laid a firm foundation for the developing Rookey-priest. As God would have it, Father Keane wove in and out of Father Rookey's life as a source of inspiration, leading the way as significant spiritual milestones were reached.

Fig. 19.   *Servite Mosaic Emblem,* altar, Our Lady of Sorrows Basilica, Chicago, Illinois, 2006. The seven lilies in the crown of the emblem symbolize the Seven Holy Servite Founders and the Seven Sorrows of Mary. The shape and letters together represent the Order of the Servants of Mary. The circular shape symbolizes the "O" in "Order." The "S" represents "Servants." The "M" represents "Mary," the mother of Christ.

Were you also influenced by a contemporary Servite, the Very Reverend James Mary Keane?

He was the *master,* as they call them, at Hillside when I was in high school. He knew me very well.

He started a Novena *that was very powerful worldwide during World War II.*

Yes, he's the famous man. He's the one who started it. He was *cursed with versatility!* A professor at Loyola told about a British great who had so many talents he didn't know which to develop. He was cursed with versatility! Certainly, Father James Mary Keane had many talents. He was a very holy priest. He initiated a lot of Marian things. He started a Marian magazine called the *Age of Mary,* and he had a television program on WGN [a local Chicago station] called *Behold Thy Mother,* which was very popular; it was a weekly program. He had prayers and a talk on Our Lady.

This booklet, Queen of Martyrs—Pray for Us, *was it all written by Father Keane?*

It was compiled.

Several million copies were made. Amazing!

This was the *Novena* that drew over seventy thousand to Our Lady of Sorrows Basilica, every Friday for years.

Was it during the war years?

It started in 1937. The *Novenas* were popular for many years after that. St. Thérèse, St. Jude, St. Anne, the Miraculous Medal—all of the *Novenas,* the *Novena Epoch.* We still have *Novenas,* but they aren't the big deals they used to be.

A lot of people don't know what they are.

Yes. *Novena.* What's that?! Reminds me of the old guy—just to break up our solemn discussion here—this guy was in the building trades and went to Confession. And he told the priest, "I see these odd pieces of lumber around, and I can't resist throwing them into my rig, and taking them home, and building stuff with them. So, I guess I'm guilty of stealing." The priest said, "Did you ever think of making a *Novena*?" And, he said, "No. But Father, if you have the plans, I have the lumber!" *(laughs)* That bears out your statement, *Novena*? What's that?! *(laughs)*.

Novena

A Novena, *a very ancient tradition, is a nine-day prayer devotion offered for special intentions. Often* Novenas *are used to prepare for a Saint's or Church feast day such as St. Anne's feast day, Christmas, Corpus Christi, or in honor of the Blessed Mother and the Archangels.* Novenas *offer the petitioner a sustained period of time for prayer, fasting, and receiving the spiritual benefit of attending nine consecutive days of Masses. Commemorating and assisting the souls of the departed; asking for intercession for diseases of the body, mind, and spirit; discernment for important life challenges; successful resolution of family problems; and similar intentions for others are all part of the collective outpouring of souls to the Will of Christ and the intercession of His Blessed Mother, the Angels, and the Saints, through the ritual of* Novenas.

Besides the nine days of a Novena, *symbolically the number nine is reflected in the nine months Christ was carried in His Mother's womb, the ninth hour of His crucifixion when He released Himself to His Father, and the nine days of prayer He requested from His Apostles in preparation for receiving the Holy Spirit. The apostolic hour of None, the praise of God in nine* Psalms, *and the nine proclamations of the* Kyrie *in every Mass also reinforce the use of nine, a number one less than the perfection of ten, a number associated with God. While a* Novena *can be made at anytime as a private devotion, often there is comfort in participating with friends and family throughout a*

nine-day public devotion. Sacred music, processions, and a celebratory feast at the conclusion of a public Novena *help encourage the virtue of perseverance and instill confidence that a soul's prayers will be heard and answered for its benefit through God's Mercy.*

On Friday, January 8, 1937, Father Rookey's mentor, the Very Reverend James Mary Keane, O.S.M., established a Perpetual Novena in honor of Our Sorrowful Mother. *According to the Very Reverend Keane:*

"The first Novena *consisted of the* Via Matris, *six prayers culled from the ancient Servite Manual, two hymns to Our Blessed Mother, the* Memorare, *and* Benediction of the Most Blessed Sacrament. *On March 22 of the same year, the Cardinal Archbishop gave his Imprimatur for the publication of the* Novena *prayer book. One year after his Eminence granted the Imprimatur, 73,000 people were making the Novena at 38 services each Friday in Our Lady of Sorrows Church. This phenomenal weekly attendance at one church constituted a world record.*

Reverend Norbert E. O'Connell, Pastor of St. Cecilia's Church, Chicago, was the first priest in the world to follow the Servites in this successful work. On January 14, 1938, the Novena *was inaugurated in his church. Twelve years later it had been established in more than 2,000 churches throughout the world. This included 125 churches in the Archdiocese of Chicago alone, 49 Cathedrals in the Western Hemisphere, 76 dioceses in the United States, 11 dioceses in Canada, various dioceses in Old Mexico, China, England, Italy, Panama, India, British West Indies, Brazil, Colombia, Peru, Australia, Ireland, Cuba, Uganda and Swaziland in Africa.*

The attendance had mounted to over 1,000,000 persons each Friday; the number of weekly services to more than 2,000. Besides the Braille edition for the

Fig. 20. *Pietà,* original sculpture by Michelangelo Buonarroti (1499); marble reproduction carved in Pietrasanta, Italy, by Spartaco Palla, Our Lady of Sorrows Basilica, Chicago, Illinois, 2005. The *Pietà* shrine attracted tens of thousands of pilgrims during the Novena Epoch, circa World War II.

> *blind, the* Novena *prayer book is now published in 22 foreign languages—French, Spanish, Italian, German, Belgian, Gaelic, Bohemian, Slovak, Slovenian, Lithuanian, Polish, Hungarian, Roumanian, Croatian, Chinese, Malayalam, Tamil, Bengali, Calcutta, Portuguese, Kankany, and Zulu."*[1]

Over 70,000 people coming!

Quite a production there. It was filling people in cathedrals all over every Friday, drawing to this one church alone all those thousands.

It was incredible.

A spiritual phenomenon. That's why I make this *Via Matris.*

The Seven Sorrows. *Are the* Via Matris *and the* Seven Sorrows *the same thing?*

Yes. Then there is the *Servite Rosary.*

In the Servite Rosary, the Seven Sorrows *are in place of the five decades on a traditional* Rosary?

Yes. Instead of ten *Hail Marys,* there are seven *Hail Marys.* There are seven mysteries, too.

You were ordained a priest of the Servite Order on May 17, 1941, at Our Lady of Sorrows Basilica.

Fig. 21 and 22. *Our Lady of Sorrows,* altar and statue, Our Lady of Sorrows Basilica, Chicago, Illinois, 2006. Our Lady's Seven Sorrows include the *Prophecy of Simeon,* the *Flight into Egypt, the Loss of Jesus in the Temple, Meeting Jesus Carrying His Cross,* the *Crucifixion, Receiving the Dead Body of Jesus,* and the *Closing of the Tomb.*

At Our Lady of Sorrows Basilica, by Archbishop John O'Brien of Chicago.

He was an archbishop?

Well, he was an honorary *arch*-bishop. They often gave those titles for outstanding service.

He was a great role model for you, His Eminence John O'Brien.

He was a very simple man. He served Mass at our Servite church, the Assumption, downtown, when he was a young lad. He was always very close to the Servites.

He must have been pleased to ordain you.

There were seven of us.

Once you were ordained, where did you go?

I went back up to Milwaukee. I was assigned up there as the assistant to the novice master, Father Hugh Mary Bryers. He was from Chicago, also. Then I was yanked from there to Portland, Oregon, to do some parish work out there in 1943.

How long did you stay there?

Four years.

Did you assist a pastor?

Yes. Part of the hatching of the Servite Order in Benburb, Ireland, was done in Portland that year because Father Keane was stationed at the grotto there at that time.

Now, Father Keane, why did he have it in his mind to go to Benburb?

Because of his Irish ancestry. His people were from Galway.

Why did he go to the North where there was so much trouble?

The reason he went to the North was because it was the only diocese that was open to having us. At that time, in the 1940s, Ireland didn't need any priests. They had so many vocations. One of the greatest shipments from Ireland were priests and brothers and sisters to all over the world. That was one of their great exports. *(laughs)* Now, they are hurting terribly. The seminaries are closing. But at that time, no bishop wanted more religious—they were filled up! *(laughs)* They didn't want any new foundations. Father Keane went to this bishop and that bishop trying to get in.

What happened, it was an Act of God, I guess. There was a very enterprising young priest called Father Peter Moore from a town called Moy. Sounds Chinese: M-O-Y. He was a very, I guess you'd say, almost a prophetic young fellow, just a young curate, a handsome young fellow. He was the assistant. They call them a *C.C.* over there, the *Catholic Curate*, and the *Parish Priest* is called a *P.P.* He heard about this estate of the O'Neills going to auction. The O'Neill clan was the great clan of the North.

The O'Neill clan produced many great heroes and leaders. Owen Roe O'Neill had his castle in Benburb that is roughly half way between the City of Armagh in County Armagh, and Dungannon, County Tyrone. Owen Roe O'Neill, by the way, won his notoriety in history at the *Battle of Benburb*, as it was called, during June 5th, 1946, when he won this battle against superior English and Scottish forces. We have his speech before the battle, and the last words of his short speech were, Let your password be *Sancta Maria*; Holy Mary. Now the Servants of Mary, the Servites, are there. The castle, incidentally, had been in the hands of the Orangemen [an anti-Catholic organization] for several centuries.

At the turn of the last century, 1902 or so, a big whiskey baron, Bruce, from Belfast, built this huge home, monstrosity, or whatever you'd want to call it, on the castle grounds. A red brick three-story thing with stables adjoining it for the horses and buggies and places for the servants above the stables. It's all laid out. There were big glass houses above the castle grounds where they grew their crops. The Black Water River flows through the grounds by the ruins of the O'Neill castle. In fact, to this day, some portions of it are still inhabited in the castle with this big building in front of it.

Bruce built that in the old days when workers were cheap, giving them three squares a day and a place to stay besides. He built this huge—what became an unmanageable—big place. He had to have people to keep it up. The property had become a white elephant. Nobody could afford it. He passed away, and the property went through several hands, and was put on the auction block.

Peter Moore heard about it being on the auction block. He had a bright idea and got a hold of some wealthy people; people with a few pounds like the Collins and Senator Sean Lennon who was the only Catholic in the Dail, the government of the Six Counties of the North. He was from Armagh, too. He knew all about Benburb and the O'Neill Castle. They talked to the cardinal, John Dalton of the Armagh Archdiocese, which, incidentally, was the original diocese of St. Patrick who started the Church in Ireland.

He talked them into buying the place for the archdiocese and the Parish of Moy with the approach, Some religious order will come along and want this place, and we'll turn over a few pounds. Which was fine, you know. So the archdiocese bought the place. Peter Moore was able to manage this big, big deal. A little simple assistant pastor. He went around to the so-called houses that were on the corners of this property, and he said, Don't worry, we're not going to do anything against you. You can continue as long as you want—because those houses were part of the *ancient domain,* as they call it.

Residential houses?

At the *gates.* They were called *gate houses,* at the various gates in the wall. Father Peter Moore put his brother, from the South of the Six Counties, and a Protestant minister in the crowd at the auction, and they were the ones who bought the place. The Orangemen didn't realize it was going back into Catholic hands, and when they realized it, it was discussed up in the Dail that is Northern Ireland's government up near Belfast where they have their headquarters; Stormont, they call it. Stormont Castle.

That's a wonderful story.

Yes, it was a historic moment. Father Keane came in 1947. Father Keane, after going from this diocese to the next diocese, he eventually came up there. A bishop told him, I think the cardinal might have something for you, because he had formerly been the assistant bishop in Armagh. Father Keane made tracks to talk to him, and, Oh yes, we have something I think you might like. They brought him out and showed him this big monstrosity and all. That was the beginning.

He must have been thrilled.

He started negotiations, and we had to have the Servites back here in Chicago buy it because that was an American province.

What was the purpose of the mission?

Well, to spread the Order. Ireland was always great with vocations. It was fertile ground. We promoted our African missions, especially, because the Irish were always great for missionaries. And, in fact, most of our Irish vocations went to the missions.

Did they have a high school?

No, in Ireland we didn't receive them until they had finished their college [similar to an American high school]. They entered into the spiritual year of the novitiate. They became novices when they entered. Accepted, they would make their simple vows for three years.

After your assignment in Portland, Oregon, where did they send you?

Then I did a year as assistant to the so-called master, or rector, at Hillside again and taught high school seminarians. I was a spiritual man for them. That was the prelude to my leaving for Ireland in August, 1948, to establish the Order there with James Mary Keane.

They brought you over there because you had had several years of training novices, is that right?

Father Keane was the spark plug of the whole thing, and he invited me to be part of the foundation.

You must have been good with the priests coming into the Order.

Well, he thought so! *(laughs)*

It must have been easy to go with him to Ireland.

He invited me. I never would have gone. He invited me to help set up in Ireland. There were seven of us unholy, uncanonized fathers, Servites, in Ireland.

What did you do to establish the Order?

He started off before we officially opened. We were cleaning up this big estate because it hadn't been used for some time, the big grounds and all.

What were you trying to accomplish there?

Father Keane and I spoke about this at our beautiful shrine to Our Sorrowful Mother in Portland, Oregon, the year before we left, which was in 1947. To give you a little smile between the lines, *Our object, all sublime, we hoped to achieve in time;* that's a quote from Gilbert and Sullivan's *Mikado* about the Lord High Executioner. *(laughs)*

Our objective, all sublime, was to create an ideal Servants of Mary community: praying; fasting; celebrating the feasts of the Church, especially those of our Order; healing; writing; preaching; and so on, making it an ideal community for the whole Order. We certainly tried to do that in a prayerful way. We not only prayed the *Divine Office* every day in community, but also we prayed the various hours of the day. We tried to carry out the Liturgy as perfectly as possible. We sang the Liturgy, and sang, what they called in the old days, the High Mass, parts of the Mass every morning and parts of the *Divine Office* on feast days and on Sundays. All of this was to build up the spiritual life, in as perfect a way as possible, for these young aspirants to the Order, to give them a very solid spiritual foundation. For example, we began to not only pray the *Divine Office*, but also the little *Office of Our Lady*, every day.

This was all in Latin with Gregorian Chanting?

Yes. Father Gregory O'Brien to whom I owe my vocation as a Servite; he's gone to Heaven now. He was one of the seven that began Benburb.

Oh, he came over too. How nice!

Yes.

You trained the novices, and you also did services for the public?

Yes. We had to make the Order known. We did everything. We helped the parishes, we preached missions, edited books *(laughs)*, placed newspaper articles, press—did everything to make the Servites known.

In time, did they start to have spiritual retreats as part of their services?

Yes, eventually, we did have retreats there, too. But I would go out to the parishes and preach the mission, and so on. Or another thing, we went to the colleges and talked up the Order at the colleges in Ireland. We invited anybody who wanted to become a religious.

Prayer for Vocations

Mary, humble servant of God Most High,
the Son to whom you gave birth has made you the servant
of humanity.

Your life was a humble and generous service.

You were servant of the Word,
when the angel announced to you the divine plan of salvation.

You were servant of the Son,
giving him life and remaining open to his mystery.

You were servant of Redemption,
standing courageously at the foot of the Cross,

Fig. 23. *Crozier*, Ordination Mass at the Cathedral of Caracas, Caracas, Venezuela, 2006.

close to the Suffering Servant and Lamb,
who was sacrificing himself for love of us.

You were servant of the Church,
on the day of Pentecost, and with your intercession
you continue to generate her in every believer,
even in these our difficult and troubled times.

Let the young people of the third millennium look to you,
young daughter of Israel, who have known the agitation of
a young heart when faced with the plan of the Eternal God.

Make them able to accept the invitation of your Son,
to give their lives wholly for the glory of God.

Make them understand that to serve God satisfies the heart,
and that only in the service of God and of his kingdom
do we realize ourselves in accordance with the divine plan,
and life becomes a hymn of glory to the Most Holy Trinity.

Amen.

His Holiness Pope John Paul II
From the Vatican, 16 October 2002

Notes

[1] Very Reverend James Mary Keane, O.S.M., editor, *Queen of Martyrs: Pray for Us* (Chicago, Illinois: Servite Fathers, 1987).

The Catholic Encyclopedia: An International Work of Reference on the Constitution, Doctrine, Discipline and History of the Catholic Church, 15 Vol., edited by Charles G. Herbermann~Edward A. Pace~Conde B. Pallen~Thomas J. Shahan and John J. Wynn, Nihil Obstat, Remy Lafort, S.T.D., Censor, Imprimatur+John Cardinal Farley, Archbishop of New York (New York, NY: *Catholic Encyclopedia*, imprint, Robert Appleton Company, 1907-1912; New York, NY: Encyclopedia Press, Inc., 1913; online edition: New Advent Inc., 2003): *www.newadvent.org*.

Joseph Hilgers, *Novenas, Ad honorem Sanctae Dei Genetricis, Rosarii sacratissimi Reginae,* transcribed by Herman R. Holbrook, *Catholic Encyclopedia* (New York, NY: Robert Appleton Company, 1911), Vol. XI, *http://www.newadvent.org/cathen/11141b.htm.*

The Gift of Healing

All souls are blessed with Spiritual Gifts and natural talents that are entrusted to the free will of the soul to develop for the benefit of God and community. As a soul nurtures its Spiritual Gifts, God reveals Himself through additional Spiritual Gifts that are able to manifest because of the continued development of the soul. As Father Rookey chose to follow the path to maturity of his faith and character, even working his body many times to the point of physical exhaustion, the Holy Spirit began to respond by working through the instrument of his person, extending the Spiritual Gifts already bestowed. It was as an extension of Father Rookey's actions of blessing people with the relics of the Servite Saints, in the name of God, that spontaneous healings began to be reported.

Other Gifts of the Spirit manifested, including the powerful gift of assisting a soul toward conversion from the service of self to the service and love of God. Many other gifts followed as Father Rookey immersed himself in the practical work of God, day by day and

Fig. 24. *From the Remains of St. Philip Benizi, O.S.M.*, relic, Friars' Chapel, Our Lady of Sorrows Basilica, Chicago, Illinois, 2006. Father Rookey used a relic of St. Philip Benizi when he began his healing ministry in Benburb, Ireland, and received the Gift of Healing. St. Philip Benizi was known as a man of miracles and a promoter of Servite vocations.

year by year. As always, spiritual mentors, those who come into our lives to help us press open our hearts ever wider to receive greater spiritual understanding, were present to encourage him and to help him understand the Ways of Our Lord.

🐦🐦🐦🐦🐦🐦🐦🐦🐦🐦🐦🐦🐦🐦🐦🐦🐦🐦🐦🐦🐦🐦🐦🐦🐦🐦🐦🐦

How did the healing services begin?

I always say the story begins from the first days we were over there. I arrived in August of 1948. The way it started was, very simply, I prayed for the people who came to the priory for a blessing. You know, the locals.

They just came to the door?

Yes. We had daily Mass, and they were able to come to assist at daily Mass. There were very few Catholics in Benburb. We are talking about the NORTH of Ireland where the Catholics were put down, especially in that little place. It was an Orange stronghold. But eventually, the Orangemen gradually moved away because of all the Catholic pressure there. It is mostly Catholic now. The Orangemen are very anti-Catholic. They were always talking about the Catholic minority. They wanted to get rid of the Catholic minority out of those six counties. Now the Catholic minority, according to the latest statistics, has become a Catholic majority. I think mostly because the Catholics are having children and non-Catholics not so many.

People would come to the door and ask for a blessing?

Yes, so I'd bless them. Some of them came back and said they were healed of some malady or another. That started the people coming. I was blessing them with our Servite Saints' relics: The Seven Holy Founders, St Philip Benizi, St. Juliana, and St. Peregrine the Cancer Saint, especially. Pretty soon busloads of people were arriving, and we had to have services outdoors. We had to have the services normally on weekends. That's when people were free.

Did you have them on Saturdays in the day?

In the day. Yes, Saturdays and Sundays usually.

Did they come mostly from the North of Ireland, or did you get them from the South?

All over.

You must have put the Servites on the map.

That helped, too. Yes. It got in the papers and all.

Was one of the first healings that of a woman who was born blind?

As a little girl. Yes, her parents brought her. She was put *live* on various television programs in the South and in the North of Ireland.

She was born blind and had her sight restored.

It seemed the Lord blessed this endeavor in creating a model community with all the praying, and so on, by permitting these miracles.

He appreciated the intention of perfection.

Right. It also helped spread the Order through the miracles. Just as Jesus spread His Word through His Miracles, it made people come to hear Him.

He helped the Order in this way?

Yes, in starting the Order.

Just as you do now. It's the healing that brings people to Christ.

Definitely, definitely. The signs are powerful. In the Gospel today, the people saw Jesus cast this demon out from this man in the synagogue in Capernaum. They were aghast with this fellow, *What word is this, for with authority and power he commandeth the unclean spirits, and they go out?* (Lk 4:36).

He makes Himself known when He wants to.

Exactly.

ᒉᒉᒉᒉᒉᒉᒉᒉᒉᒉᒉᒉᒉᒉᒉᒉᒉᒉᒉᒉᒉᒉᒉᒉᒉᒉᒉᒉᒉᒉᒉᒉᒉᒉᒉᒉᒉ

Dear Father Rookey:

About 1948 or '49, my husband tells me a story about his young brother when he was about seven or eight years old. My husband's family lived in Armagh, about seven miles from the Benburb Priory. This young brother had a murmur in his heart, and his mother, Rose, had heard about the young priest (yourself) who had the Gift of Healing. So as there was no other way to get to Benburb except by bicycle, off they went. But at every hill, young Tommy had to get off the bicycle and pant up the hill.

Anyway, they arrived at the priory, and you, Father, prayed over Tommy. After that, Tommy got onto his bicycle and rode like the devil home not stopping once. His mother could not keep up with him and could not believe what she saw. And Tommy, to this day, never looked behind him.

Praise God.

N. Ireland 2003

ᒉᒉᒉᒉᒉᒉᒉᒉᒉᒉᒉᒉᒉᒉᒉᒉᒉᒉᒉᒉᒉᒉᒉᒉᒉᒉᒉᒉᒉᒉᒉᒉᒉ

What did Father James Mary Keane think?

He was delighted, anything that would make us known. He didn't last too long. He was elected assistant general of the Servite Order, so he went to Rome. Later, he helped establish the Servite Order in Australia. We had the big celebration in Benburb on June 5, 1949. We officially opened, and we had a big celebration there on the grounds. The usual—singers, swingers *(laughs)*, all kinds of things, a big crowd. It was very well attended. Eamonn DeValera, the famous hero of Ireland, came. He had become president and *taoiseach,* as they call the prime minister. Costello, was the prime minister. They came up over the border. He still had a price on his head, Eamonn DeValera, but nothing happened.

But he came for the opening celebration. That was nice.

Yes—with his bodyguards! *(laughs)* And then the cardinal archbishop, from whom we had bought the property, he came out, and he ordained. He started with four priests and three deacons in their last year of theology. He ordained them that day, too. That was part of the celebration. We had a banquet, of course, with all that.

Did you convert any of the Orangemen while you were up there?

Well, yes, we . . . I didn't convert them, the Lord did, of course. But we did have one man, who was a famous convert, Dr. Richard J. Hunter, a very outstanding man. He was born of a doctor-father and grandfather, born off the coast of Africa, the West Coast of Africa. I guess they were missionary doctors. He studied and became a doctor, too. He was also a scientist in the medical world. His great thrust was children, before they were born . . . embryology. In fact, he invented some procedures in embryology. He was invited by Johns Hopkins University to lecture up and down North and South America; he was that good, he was that well known.

He came to America in the twenties when we had Prohibition. He was full of fun. He had a lot of stories about going into a drug store in New York. The big Irish cops would hear his accent and say, "Oh, you're from Ireland?" They'd tell him, "Anything you want to drink, here's my number!" Prohibition corrupted the police force. It was a taking of the right away from the people. You can't take their right to drink away. The problem is they abuse it, but you can't take it away from them. They made it a capital offense to have whiskey! *(laughs)* Jesus, of course, drank wine, so it can't be all that bad, and He instituted the *Sacrament of the Eucharist* under the form of bread and wine.

Anyway, he had a lot of stories like that from when he was over here. The way we met was one of our novices, a little lay brother novice, came out of the Order. He was from a town called Portglenone of County Antrim, one of the Six Counties of the North. He left the Servites and went home. This Dr. Hunter, after his terrific career, ended up for ten years as secretary of Queens University in Belfast. All the students loved him and called him Dickey. His name was Richard, Dickey, Hunter.

Not only that, he was very interested in lion taming! *(laughs)* He would go over to Europe and view these acts, and, if he liked one, he would bring the act over for the circus every year. He put on the *Hunter Circus.* That is still going on, by the way. The descendents have continued it. He was the founder of the zoological society of Belfast, also. He had a lot of stories.

For example, they had an alligator, and they'd write it up in the papers that the zoo was open. It told about this big alligator they had in the water, and they made a big deal for Easter. It was an outing to go to the zoo for the children. The poor alligator up and died on Good Friday! *(laughs)* You know, alligators don't move too much. At lunchtime, they closed up for lunch. He had the attendants just turn the alligator around. When the kids came back, he said, Oh, he moved! *(laughs)* Saved the day for Easter, you know.

They left him there dead until Easter?!

Well, they kept him. Easter was the big weekend. After that, I guess, they had to get rid of him. Anyway *(laughs)*, he had a lot of stories because he not only directed the circus but he was also a lion tamer. He had a lot of stories about being caught in the cage, and all that stuff. He was a very interesting character, just a little 5' 5." Full of good jolly and humor.

Anyway, I was telling you about this little novice whose name was John Birt. In fact, I just talked to his relatives. He's now in Phoenix, Arizona. He, eventually, became a pilot, or an official, I don't know which, in the United Airlines. He's retired now, a very lovely guy. We felt terrible when he left. He started working for this Dr. Hunter, who had retired in Portglenone. He had an estate there and lived as a gentleman. He had a few pounds. He took John Birt on as a general man of affairs. John Birt drove him around and did his errands.

But he was an Orangeman?

Yes, he was an Orangeman.

But he hired a Catholic?

(laughs) Yes. He took a shine to him, I guess. But anyway, John kept telling him all about Benburb, and he got excited. I think he already had a tendency to change, to become a Catholic. I was invited to give an eight-day retreat for the Trappists in Our Lady of Bethlehem Abbey, there at Portglenone. I didn't know what the Trappists needed a retreat for—they are always on retreat! *(laughs)* But the abbot kept after me to do this ministry. At the end of the retreat, I wanted to visit the Birts because they were very dear to us and to all the Servites. So I dropped in on them. Mrs. Birt said right away, Oh, she said, John's been working for Dr. Richard Hunter; he would like nothing more than to be invited to Benburb. We called him up, and he said, I'll be right over! *(laughs)* He was so excited! *(laughs)*

He came over, and we *shot-the-bull* a little bit, and talked. We invited him up. He came for some weeks at a time—came up about three or four times. We were happy to have him; he was such a joy. Put some life in the place! I shouldn't say that, but anyway, it was a joy to have him. We threw big tomes at him. For example, there was a Canon Smith from England who had come out with an expose of the Catholic faith. He ate that up. He was very brilliant. He ate that up in no time, and other works, including the *Catechism*. Finally, he was ready at Easter. I invited the cardinal to baptize him because he was so prominent, very well known. Oh, he said, you fellows, as he prepared himself for the baptism. As his tears mixed with the water in the baptismal font, he said, I'm going to lose all my Orange friends . . . my Orange friends, I'm going to lose them, or something like that.

Oh . . . How old was he?

He was already retired.

Still, it must have been a big sacrifice for him!

Oh yes. I kept corresponding with him from Rome. I left Benburb after five years, after I was elected assistant general of the Servite Order. We kept corresponding. We would visit the houses in Ireland. We would get together when I got over there until he died. A very interesting man, I'll never forget him.

Besides the ministry, you had healing services, and all the people kept on coming.

Yes. After Father Keane left, they made me the prior because I was about the only one they had to put in there. *(laughs)* The other young priests were just ordained, no experience, you know. They couldn't . . . it would be difficult to make them a superior. We had our philosophy courses there, too. We had to get professors for that. We had an international professor staff. Most were Servites. One man was from Hungary that was under communism. He escaped from Hungary, went to Rome, and he was teaching at our university in Rome. Father Keane got him as part of the staff. Then there was another Italian professor, a very brilliant fellow, too. And they got a lay man professor, a man from the University of Louvain, Jean Van Haelen. Our young priests were teachers, also. That was our staff.

I had to carry on meetings in Latin because I had not studied in Italy. I didn't know Italian at that stage. I learned it when I got to Italy. We had an Italian, Hungarian . . . but they all understood Latin. The man from Louvain as well. The others had studied through Latin. We used to carry on our meetings in Latin instead of trying to translate into these different languages and waste time. That was interesting. We all had spoken Latin in the seminary. The professor asked the questions in Latin, and we responded in Latin. We were trained in it.

Did you visit Rome during that time?

Yes. Once I came over from Ireland, just in the quick. I had a short time off. I was in Italy on my way back to Ireland just in time for the canonization of Maria Goretti. Pope Pius XII canonized her. It was an exceptional canonization in that her mother was present and also her assassin. She was a little farmer girl from a town near Anzio, Italy.

Our military forces entered that Mediterranean port town to capture Rome from the Nazis, in 1945, I believe. She was attacked by a would-be lover, a farmer boy, and she resisted. She was only fifteen or so, and she was brought to the hospital in this town, and died.

Fig. 25. *Filled with Laughter, Father Peter Mary Rookey, O.S.M.,* International Compassion Ministry, Olympia Fields, Illinois, *2004.*

When did that happen?

I think it was in the teens, in the last century, as I recall—1915 or so.

During World War I?

Yes, she was canonized by Pope Pius XII in 1950 in July.

How many years were you at Benburb?

Five years.

You were the prior of Benburb, and then you were assigned to Rome, but you were still having all of the healings happening?

Well, I was elected assistant general of the Servite Order in Rome and left Ireland in the summer, in June of 1953. They had a General Chapter of the Order that occurs every six years. I was sent a telegram by the general of that time, who had just been elected. His name was Alphonse Monta, *little mountain,* and that's the way he was built. *(laughs)* Little Mountain. A very powerful little guy, a wonderful man. I was told to come, bag and baggage, not to return.

გგგგგგგგგგგგგგგგგგგგგგგგგგგგგგგგგგგგგგგ

> *I first met Father Rookey in September 1949 when I joined the Servite Order at Benburb Priory, Ireland, that had recently been founded by the legendary Father James Keane. All of us newcomers expected all the priests to be devout holy men, and indeed they were, but there was something special about Fr. Rookey who became our master of novices. He seemed to have a mystic aura with an intensity of prayer and deportment about him, interspersed with moments of subtle humor.*
>
> *Now the Benburb priory, in those days, had no heating; and in the cold wet winter of northern Ireland, the internal temperature never seemed to rise*

above the freezing point. To our amazement, we found out that as a penance Father Rookey slept with one blanket only on his bed and had no pillow! Ouch!

Father Peter always had a great sense of humor and a seemingly inexhaustible supply of jokes. I have a clear memory of him saying, "I beg your pocket book," when I thought he had misheard me. I can remember the people who came to Benburb Priory to see the new Order, even though it was some eight hundred years old. The curious came, and some were sick, but as well as a warm welcome, Father Rookey would pray over them and touch them with the relics of the Servite Saints, especially St. Philip Benizi. Although we were not given any information, rumors of cures filtered through, especially of a blind child given the Gift of Sight after a blessing by Father Rookey.

Every Sunday, the buses arrived with ever increasing numbers, and then suddenly it all stopped, as we understood it, by the request of Cardinal Dalton of Armagh. My own feeling in later years tended toward unworthy thoughts that complaints were lodged by parish priests whose Sunday collection plates were affected by their parishioners going to Benburb. I remember Father Peter collapsing during Mass, exhausted from fasting and lack of sleep. But he had no concern about his own state, but humbly asked forgiveness of anyone he might have offended. I left a few years later, deciding that Pater Familias *was more suitable for me than the priesthood.*

I lost touch with Father Peter for many years. But here in Australia, some ten years ago, my daughter rang me to say Father Rookey was in Melbourne conducting healing Masses. Somewhere, I must have told her about this saintly priest in such terms that she remembered his name. I rushed to Melbourne and introduced myself after Mass. He gave me a great welcome, and, with his usual humor and play on words, said he had not recognized me as I had been a whipper-snapper when we last met, but he had been "fully manured" at that time. I have kept in touch since and was greatly honored when he and Brother Jim stayed with us when we had a Healing Mass here (Lakes Entrance, Australia) a few years ago.

Doug Carson, former-Novice, Order of the Servants of Mary, Benburb, Ireland

🐦🐦🐦🐦🐦🐦🐦🐦🐦🐦🐦🐦🐦🐦🐦🐦🐦🐦🐦🐦🐦🐦🐦🐦🐦🐦

In the Service of Souls

It was time for Father Rookey to begin another phase of his spiritual journey. While in Rome, he lived amidst the great tradition of the Catholic Church, learning more about the sacred arts, the music, language, and Liturgy used to praise God, of the great sacrifices of the Martyrs, and the works of the Saints. And, Father Rookey was asked by Reverend James Mary Keane to research and to write about the mystic St. Maria of Agreda. While performing the practical work of teaching and administration in Rome, Germany, and Belgium, Father Rookey met with St. Padre Pio and Teresa Neumann of Konnersreuth. These contemporary holy people developed mystical, intimate relationships with Christ that manifested in His bleeding Wounds of the Cross on their persons with their heads, hands, feet, and sides suffering as He suffered.

Father Rookey's faith and humility increased as he witnessed, over and over again, the limitless supernatural Power and Love of God for all of His Creation. He became more and more deeply affected by Christ's Suffering and offered to bring back to Him the most distant of souls.

Fig. 26. *Crucifix*, St. John Cantius Parish, Chicago, Illinois, 2006.

You went to Rome.

I went to Rome. That was the end of that. I arrived in Rome on June the 28th. The next morning was the Feast of the Apostles Peter and Paul. That is a big day in Rome where they were martyred—St. Peter's great feast. Our first priest from Benburb, our new foundation in Ireland, was ordained that day. I happened to arrive just in time to witness his ordination.

The Dominican Church is nearby the big pagan temple. *All the gods*, it is called. The Pantheon, it's called. In Greek, *pan* is *all*; *theos* is *god* . . . theology, theocratic. The words come from that. And *pas—pasa pan* is a positive comparative and the superlative of the adjective *all* in Greek: *pas, pasa, pan* . . . masculine, feminine, and neuter, I guess you'd call it. The Pope, eventually, dedicated it to *All the Saints* instead of all the false gods.

It was a very historic moment for this old sinner. Here I had had him as one of my first novices. He was ordained rather shortly because he had already finished his philosophy course, and all he had left was the spiritual year and four years of theology that he did in Rome at our Servite Marian University.

What was his name?

His name was Thomas Carroll. It's quite a frequent Irish name. Our promoters in Atlanta City for the ICM (International Compassion Ministry) are Thomas and Karen Carroll. They have a very beautiful family. There are a lot of Carrolls. Our present English-speaking assistant to the general is Patrick Carroll.

When you were in the North of Ireland, there was a lot of persecution of Catholics going on, right?

Yes.

Were you ever personally accosted?

By the Orangemen?

Yes.

Well, I was stopped in the car two times.

What happened?

I was greeted with a gun both times: once by the Orangemen and once by the British military.

What did they want?

They wanted to make sure I wasn't doing anything *(laughs)*, against the Six Counties, I guess. They just wanted to check.

They pulled you over?

Yes. The first time, I remember, I was with our general, Father Alphonse Mary Monta. We had been visiting some of the families of our seminarians who were in our university in Rome, the Marianum. We wanted to bring word from their parents back to Rome. We were coming back from Belfast to Benburb. It was about ten o'clock at night. We were flashed down. They said there was a roadblock ahead, which was not unusual in those days. This was about 1954, I would say.

We were stopped at the roadblock, and this man came up with a gun in his hand. He asked me for my driver's license. I still had an Irish driver's license. I had it in my briefcase behind the driver's seat. I said, "OK," and I reached back to get it out of my briefcase, and he put this gun right to my head. He thought I was reaching back to pick up a rifle, or something maybe. *(laughs)* I reassured him. They finally let us go through. I told him I was a former prior in Benburb, and all that.

Then another time, I was stopped at a checkpoint, also. They pointed guns at you to make sure you'd be sure to stop and be checked. *(laughs)*

They wanted to know if you were carrying information or weapons?

Yes. Exactly. They'd search the car. The second time, it was the regular army, the British soldiers.

Were a lot of the Catholics near Benburb harassed, also?

Oh yes. Of course they were.

What were your duties in Rome?

Well, administrative. I was the spokesman for the English-speaking part of the Order. It would be too concentrated to get into, but, in general, taking care of all of the correspondence in English from the various parts of the Order, then accompanying the general to various countries, making visitations to the Servite houses, helping with the Chapters of the Provinces of the Order. Those are the annual meetings of a particular province. And, our own frequent meetings of the Council, as it's called, of the Council Members, deciding on questions pertaining to the Order. I did six years there going around visiting the houses with the general, hither and yon, on various continents and countries.

Did you learn Italian just by being in Rome?

When you have to eat and drink, you learn it fast! *(laughs)* Some of the priests taught me. I had some classes, and, of course, reading the papers. Italian is so close to the Latin, so knowing the Latin was helpful.

Did you visit St. Padre Pio when you were there?

Yes. It was during those years in Rome that I went down to visit Padre Pio, several times.

You were interested in his ministry?

Well, I went down to meet a holy man. I did, on one occasion, go down there to ask his advice. I was striving to bring the Servite Order up to Sweden. We had never penetrated that far in Europe in the northern part. I was trying to advance the Order, and I had the general's ear on that. He, in fact, went up to Sweden with me one time. But I could not convince the English and American provincials in it. I can understand why—because it's a very closed sort of mission. I think part of the problem is the very geographic situation up there. It's the cloistered part of Europe. It's been separated by the waters over the centuries. The Lutheran faith took over up there, and they lost the faith in the Church. Now, they are nominally Lutheran, not practicing, just like France is supposed to be so Catholic, and yet the practice is comparatively poor in this very Catholic country that has produced so many Saints.

I asked St. Padre Pio's counsel about that. And, his answer was, "Do everything under obedience." He practiced what he preached, as we know. At one point, a bishop obtained from Rome a suspension of Padre Pio for ten years! He was not allowed to do anything but celebrate spiritually, not to dispense the Sacraments including Confession, which was his big mission, and was only allowed to celebrate private Mass.

I have to thank his namesake, Father Pius. He called himself Pius, so as not to be confused with Padre Pio. He used the full Latin name PIUS—Pius, instead of Pio, the Italian. Father Pius was the American secretary for the English-speaking community of the Capuchins there. He allowed me, on one of my visits, to celebrate in the chapel where Padre Pio celebrated. They allowed me—after the Mass in which I participated—to come back to the sacristy. Two big husky Capuchins protected Padre Pio, especially from the ladies who wanted to kiss his hands. That hurt his hands because he had the wounds in his hands and his side, so he'd utter a few epithets! *(laughs)* It hurt him when they touched him, and he'd yell out a little bit.

I followed them into the sacristy, devested, came out, and they let me go over to the altar where he had celebrated. It just had the candles and the crucifix, the bare essentials, water and wine, and towels that I had brought myself. As I approached the altar, I perceived, for the very first time, this marvelous fragrance of the Saints, of Our Lord, and Our Blessed Lady. That was the first time I perceived the fragrance. Now, that's common—it happens every time we have a Mass. It usually starts during the *Seven Sorrows Rosary* we have before the Mass everywhere. Invariably, quite a number of people smell the fragrance.

That reminds me of . . . I want to show you a little antiphon of the *Psalms* in the *Office of Our Blessed Lady*. Well, I can just explain it to you. I pray a little *Office of Our Lady* every day for vocations because—according to the Ancients of the Order—if we are faithful praying the *Office*, we will never lack vocations, so I have been faithful to that. The second *Psalm* of the *Office*, a second antiphon, "Sicut myrra . . . 'Holy Mother of God, you give forth a fragrance as of myrrh.'" It seems this idea of fragrance has always been associated with the Saints, with the Presence of the Lord and Our Lady. I've visited San Giovanni Rotondo a number of times since he died, after his death in 1968.

What struck you the most about Padre Pio?

Oh, I think his great devotion. To be near him was holy—it was to feel very privileged to be near him, to see his great devotion at Mass. He would go into ecstasy sometimes at Mass. That's why they never allowed him to celebrate a public Mass, or very rarely, apart from those ten years when he was suspended, because they never knew when he was going to finish. After a public Mass, you might have another Mass coming up, or something.

He celebrated Mass on the St. Francis side, on the right side in the church in San Giovanni Rotondo. But it wasn't in the sense of having a Sunday Mass that was formerly scheduled. He always celebrated at five o'clock in the morning. You had to be at the church at 4:30 a.m. to try to get in. They were already gathered at the doors. *(laughs)* They opened the doors at 4:30 a.m.

Ready to go.

Yes, it was just an ordinary daily Mass.

Would he go into ecstasy at that hour?

Yes. In those days, you did not have concelebration. Each priest celebrated Mass by himself. I just assisted. The last time I went down there, he was still alive. The Hopes, the Bob Hope family, were in Italy, and I drove them around Europe, then they ended up in Rome. Mrs. Dolores Hope and her sister, Mildred Malatesta, wanted to visit him. Malatesta is a very interesting name. It means *a headache!* In Italian. *(laughs)* She married a *malatesta*.

Was he a headache?!

(laughs) No, he was a very nice man. They wanted to go down there, so I brought them down, and we were able to see Father Pio. I assisted at his Mass at the side altar of St. Francis there.

What else did you do when you were in Rome? Was this the time you wrote the book Shepherd of Souls: The Virtuous Life of Saint Anthony Pucci, *about a Servite priest?*

Yes.

Who was the Pope at that time?

It was Pius XII. Then John XXIII followed him. It was John XXIII who eventually canonized Servite St. Anthony Maria Pucci, *Shepherd of Souls* as he's called, as a model for the participating members of the Council. That was at the opening session of Vatican II. It was quite a beautiful moment for this simple little forty-five-year-old pastor in Viareggio. Incidentally, Viareggio was where Maria Valtorta wrote all those wonderful works, especially the *Poem of the Man~God.*

Was she living when you were there in Rome? Was she writing?

Yes, she was living.

Did you meet her?

I didn't know about her too much at that time. I never got to meet her personally, I'm sorry to say. She's of a more recent vintage. She died in 1968. She wrote during World War II. She suffered the pains of the damned. She suffered terribly in her later years. But that's the way of the Lord.

Did you also continue your music studies there?

Yes, I just went a year, and then I got too busy. I went to one yearly session. The end of that year was very beautiful because I went to the *Institute of Sacred Music.* It was founded by another canonized saint, St. Pius X. In 1954, as part of the Marian year, Venerable, or I should say, Pope Pius XII canonized his predecessor Pius X, the Pope from 1903 to 1914. His name was Pius the 10th, and he reigned for only eleven years, as I recall. He was a reformer of Church music and Liturgy. He wrote a *motu proprio* about the Liturgy and sacred music, especially the Gregorian Chant. He wanted to upstage the Gregorian Chant—and *polyphony,* as it is called. That means *many voices, poly phonos,* from Greek—many voices music—whereas the chant is just the one voice.

I had been teaching the Gregorian Chant here and in Ireland, at the seminary especially. I taught nuns and others as well. Of course, the Liturgy, I taught that, also. But on the side, I attended this Institute of Sacred Music; in Italian: Istituto de la Musica

Sacra, Via della Scrofa in Rome. It's opposite the entrance to St. Augustine Church. St. Augustine is a Saint for whom I always had a great regard. Pope Pius XII had the canonization in the summer after our year of study there, the scholastic year. He authorized a delegation of seven of us who attended this musical college to sing the Mass for the canonization of Pius X. That was a great moment for us in Rome.

The Sistine Choir sang what's known as the *Common* of the Mass, the parts of the Mass that are generally used in the Mass. We sang the *Proper* of the Mass, the text *proper* to the particular Saint, the particular feast. These parts vary from day-to-day, whereas the *Common* includes the *Kyrie* and the *Lord Have Mercy*. Then if there was a *Gloria* in the Mass, the *Gloria*, and the *Creed* if there was a *Creed* decreed. *(laughs)* The *Creed* and the *Gloria* are not in every Mass. They're just in feast day Masses. Then the *Holy, Holy, Sanctus*, and the *Lamb of God*—those are known as the *Common*. The Sistine Choir sang that, and our little group sang what is known as the *Proper*. The *Entrance, Introit*, they call it. Then the response after the reading, the *Alleluia*, its *Verse*, then the *Offertory Antiphon*, they called it, then the *Communion Hymn*. Those were the *Proper* parts of the Mass we sang.

It must have been a great day.

Yes. It was a great moment.

Fig. 27.   *Father Peter Mary Rookey Playing the Organ,* organ loft, Our Lady of Sorrows Basilica, Chicago, Illinois, 2006. Installed in 1902, the four-manual Lyon and Healy organ is one of the oldest still in operation. Father Rookey played the organ for Latin Masses and Gregorian chant.

Fig. 28.   *St. Cecilia: Patron Saint of Musicians, Poets, and Singers,* stained glass window, Our Lady of Sorrows Basilica, Chicago, Illinois, 2006. While being married against her wishes, St. Cecilia was singing *Psalms* in heart in praise of Jesus. Her husband and brother-in-law converted and were later martyred because they gave proper burials to Christian martyrs. St. Cecilia was arrested for burying them and ordered to sacrifice to false gods, which she refused to do. She was suffocated and beheaded in turn, circa 117.

Do you have a degree in Gregorian Chant?

Well, I guess. I studied sacred music.

They gave you a degree in sacred music?

Yes, they gave me a degree, unworthy as I was. *(laughs)*

You know how to play the organ?

Yes. We had to take exams, of course. Playing and singing.

Did you provide material for the Age of Mary *for Father Keane, too?*

Yes. I wrote for his magazine. One of the editions was on the *Mystical City of God,* about a Spanish mystic, a Franciscan nun, Maria of Agreda. I think she is a Venerable. They asked me to write about her when they were making this edition on Maria of Agreda's work and her life in the *Age of Mary.* The article was reproduced later in the biography of the *Life of Maria of Agreda.*

She has come to more of the limelight in late years because she is supposed to have had the Gift of Bilocation. The Spanish missionaries in Mexico and the South, Southwest came upon some Indians who knew the faith, and they asked who instructed them, and it was Maria of Agreda, because they gave a description that fitted her.

The missionaries were Spanish—Franciscans. They tell about Blessed Junipero Serra, the famous one who founded so many missions. He's been called a Blessed, if not canonized. He boasted in one of his letters that he carried two books with him on his travels around: the *Bible* and *The Mystical City of God* by Maria of Agreda, the beautiful life of Mary by this mystic. It was shortly after her death that they were exploring over here. They were pretty dedicated to Maria of Agreda.

The Mystical City of God, her great work, was put on the *Index of Prohibited Books* two times. *(laughs)* A very close friend of Father Keane, a graduate of Notre Dame, was a very dedicated man. In fact, Father Keane let him edit the various editions of the *Age of Mary.* You wanted to do something with her, so why don't you dedicate a few editions to Mary and talk about her? And they did. He wrote to me in Rome and asked me if I would research the book. A lot of people said, "Oh, I wouldn't read that, it's on the *Index*, you know!" While researching, I found all these things in libraries and in the archives of the Vatican library. I looked this all up, and, yes, it was on the *Index*, but it was completely cleared.

The Index was a way to ban books?

Yes, by the big theologians in Rome and in the Sorbonne, the famous university in Paris. They were sitting on their sore buns and judging this work! Due to their efforts, it was put on the *Index* two times. Innocent the XI was a secular Servite and was received in the very place where I lived while in Rome on the Via San Marcello. His family name was Odescalchi, a big name. His family's palace, they were very wealthy, was a block long and half a block wide. I could almost reach out and touch the building, it was just so narrow! They called it the Via San Marcello, but it was more like an alley! *(laughs)* He was beatified in 1955 by Pope Pius XII. He was laid out in a glass coffin under the second altar on the right as you enter St. Peter's. The first altar is the *Pieta*, the Michelangelo sculpture. He was the one who put his hand over the condemnation by the *Index* people and said, *Hos libros ab omnibus impune legi possunt:* These books can be read with impunity by all. That's a *canonical sentence*.

The Knights of Columbus of Fort Wayne, Indiana, recently asked me to write the introduction to the new edition of her biography because a good part of the book is what I wrote. Their Council is named after Solanus Casey, who was from Superior, by the way. The Caseys and the Rookeys knew each other. He was a streetcar conductor. He was an Irishman, an O'Casey, like *"Casey at the Bat"!* [A famous poem written by Ernest Thayer]. He studied at St. Francis in Milwaukee when he found out he had a vocation. He was in his late twenties. I think twenty-six to twenty-eight years old. Later, he became a Capuchin priest. This Solanus Casey read the *Mystical City of God,* by the mystic Maria Agreda, every day on his knees. He thought the world of that work. The Knights of Columbus saw this book and noted that I was in it. That's how I got into the act.

After Rome, where were you called to serve?

After Rome, they asked me to conduct the International Servite College at the University of Louvain in Belgium. The

University of Louvain was given its charter way back in the Middle Ages. It's a very ancient, very old Catholic University, where, incidentally, Archbishop Fulton Sheen graduated with highest honors. In fact, in the early books he came out with, he very proudly put after his name *Egregie du Louvain,* which meant he graduated with high honors and would be eligible to be a professor there at Louvain University.

I did that for three years. I was the prior and general man for this college that had young men on their way to the priesthood studying theology at the university. It was about half and half young priests and young theologians studying. They were from various countries, so we used French as our language. That was the language they were taking courses in at that university. It was a two-language university: Flemish and French. We adopted French, and we had our liturgies, and I gave my talks in French.

I was also associated at that time with the American College. They called these residences *colleges,* but the students went to the university. They had certain religious courses in the college, also. I remember one time when the spiritual director had to leave, they asked me to take over in his place for a short time. I was confessor over there. The men used to come to our college for counseling.

In fact, there's a lovely priest up in Oshkosh, Wisconsin, now, who was a student then in the American College. His name is Father Vander Kreek, William Vander Kreek. He was one of the people we helped. He's in the Green Bay diocese. There were various dioceses who sent the men whom they wanted to go on to study to Louvain. Father William has a parish up there. Recently, he got into the headlines because he helped a young lady who was in prison. He raised the $50,000 bail so she could be free until her trial.

After your assignment at the University of Louvain, where were you called?

I was there for three years. That was from 1959 to 1962. Then I came back to Chicago. In 1962, I was established at Our Lady of Sorrows as assistant pastor for just nine months. At that time, it was quite a Hispanic parish. I helped in the parish there with Father Brissette, who was, incidentally, from Marrinette, Wisconsin. It rhymes with his name: Father Clarence Brissette from Marrinette. *(laughs)*

Then the general, Father Alphonse Mary Monta, ordered me to help the Servites in Germany. I went back to Europe for almost five years. From 1963, I guess it was until 1968, about five years, I was in Germany—four and a half to five years.

What did you do in Germany for those years?

I did seminary work for the first year in Bavaria, in what is called in German a *Wahlfahrtsort,* which means a place of pilgrimage. We took care of the pilgrims who came there as well. We had a seminary in this place called Weinlinden, about forty kilometers south of Munich, München.

Irish-wise, by the way, München was one of the many places that the Irish monks dotted Europe with their monasteries. From those monasteries, cities grew. Munich was one of those. It's interesting that the flag of the capitol of Bavaria has a München. *München* means a little monk. *Chen* is a diminutive, an additive to words. Like *mädchen* is a little girl, a little maid. Mädchen, for example. *(laughs)* So München. Maybe you saw, or maybe you were too young to see, the Olympics in Munich way back in the 1960s or 1970s. The 1970s, I think. The flag was displayed. The flag has a monk with his arms outstretched. That's *München*—the little monk! *(laughs)* The flag to this day for Munich is a monk with arms outstretched.

It is a very Catholic area.

Bavaria has always been considered quite Catholic. While visiting Bavaria, I was able, in 1950, to meet an outstanding person in Teresa of Konnersreuth. She was a mystic with the Wounds of Jesus. You've probably read about her. Teresa Neumann of Konnersreuth, a little, tiny town above Munich.

Teresa, in fact, used to come to our cloistered nuns' place in Munich, the Servite nuns there, to pray. She had many phenomena surrounding her. For one thing, it's a well-established fact, she lived only on the Eucharist from the time she was a young girl. A mädchen! She neither ate nor drank. She lived only on the Eucharist, the little Host. She was a *living tabernacle,* a fact they discovered because the Host stayed in her mouth from one Communion to the next. As she received the new Communion, the previous Host disappeared.

She suffered the Passion on Fridays normally, unless it was a feast day—Sacred Heart, or whatever, or during the Easter Time, a joyful time. But she suffered the Passion with Jesus in ecstasy. Like St. Padre Pio, she bled from the Wounds of Christ—the Wounds of the Crown of Thorns—hands, feet, and side. Even under ecstasy, she spoke Aramaic, the language of the time of Jesus. That's what He spoke. It's a corruption of Hebrew. Something like our Italian and Latin—Spanish and Latin. She was unschooled. She had only a minor type of education. The Lord used this very simple little farm girl. After the Passion on Friday, she was up and at 'em on Saturday morning with the farm work. She kept the church, swept it, kept it in flowers, cleaned the altar cloths, and so on.

She was not a nun?

No. She was just a simple girl. She was examined, maybe more examined, than any other mystic. If you are interested, I was made a member of a group that's called the Konnersreuth Circle, which is based in Haugen, Germany. Through a man who was born next door to Konnersreuth and knew her cousins very well, we were made part of this circle that promotes Teresa's canonization. He lives in New Jersey, here in the States. If anyone deserves to be canonized, she certainly does.

Did you see her in ecstasy?

No. I wasn't there in ecstasy time.

But did you meet with her?

Yes. But in 1950, I had not yet been in Germany. I was stationed in Rome at the time, so I didn't know German to be able to speak with her. It was later that I went to Sprachinstitut, an institute to learn German. It's called Walchensee, which is a very good course. Anyway, that was my work there.

The rest of the time, I was in western Germany in the Rhineland. I was in Düsseldorf and in another town where we had a beautiful parish and monastery called Gelsenkirchen-Buer . . . it is easier to say B-U-E-R—Buer. But the full title is a double-city, Gelsenkirchen-Buer, Diocese of Essen.

What did you do there?

Parish work.

You now speak how many languages?

Latin. I taught Greek. I was in the French part of Europe for a number of years; then Germany, five years; Italy, six years. I had to learn all those languages. El Español is coming up. It's very necessary in our country. I wish I had been in Spain to learn it very well.

God's Gift of Peace

Sometimes, God changes our lives very quickly. A soul that is relatively comfortable and thriving can be confronted with long years of challenge. As creatures limited by human perception, it can be difficult to understand what seems to us to be the mysterious Ways of God. In these prolonged periods, a soul is probed, tested, refined, and strengthened to become an even more powerful instrument. Submitting our will to the control of God for a lifetime can be a difficult trial, or it can be experienced more easily through graceful interior surrender. Through the twists and turns of service, the soul becomes more pliable to the whims of the Spirit and learns to discern the steady undercurrent of God's Hand in its life. For Father Rookey, there were many years of detours where his most evident spiritual gift of direct healing was not used, but other gifts were required. Aligning his will with the Will of God brought him yet another gift—the Gift of Peace.

Fig. 29.   *Our Lady of Sorrows Altar,* Temple of Jerusalem, Pilgrimage to the Holy Land, 2005. Father Rookey celebrated a private Mass on the Feast of Our Lady of Sorrows.

Where were you assigned after Germany?

One day, our provincial, Father Terence Mary O'Connor, arrived from Rome. He was the provincial here in Chicago. He had just visited our general in Rome who was also an American at the time, Father Loftus, whom, incidentally, I taught when he first entered the Order out here at Hillside. *(laughs)* I taught him from 1946 to 1947, his first year in the Order.

And here he was the general in Rome!

He entered the Order when I was assistant out there at the seminary in Hillside, outside of Chicago. *(laughs)* He knew that I knew he was an aspirant in the Order, and here he was a general. *(laughs)* General Father Joseph Loftus! Father Terence O'Connor had just come back from asking Father Loftus if he could get the Rookey-priest back to America.

Had you wanted to come back?

I just did whatever I was told. Oh no, I don't want you to think I'm holy or anything, but I felt that God would bless me best if I just went along with wherever I was assigned. I think that's where your peace is. The thing about going only wherever *you* want to go is you can only blame yourself after! *(laughs)* It was a kind of philosophic thing, too, besides theological. But anyway, he came through Düsseldorf and I met him at the train station, and, as we were coming back to the car, he said, I just got permission from Father Joe Loftus for you to come back to the States. I dropped his suitcase and said, Would you say that again?! *(laughs)* He told me then. But there was a hitch to it. He said, We need a missionary in the Ozarks. *(laughs)*

Oh. Kind of a big hitch.

(laughs) So from all this worldwide sort of life, as I jokingly say, I was condemned to the Ozarks. *(laughs)*

Why did they want you to go there?

They needed a man down there, that's all. The priest had left who was working there, and they needed another priest, and I filled the slot. *(laughs)* I did sixteen and a half years in the missions in Missouri: the Diocese of Springfield, Cape Girardo it's called. It takes pretty much the whole of the south part of Missouri. It is a widespread diocese with very few Catholics, comparatively speaking, and lots of territory. I did sixteen and a half years; as I jokingly say, "Sixteen and a half years, fourteen minutes, and fifteen seconds down there—and enjoyed every minute of it!" *(laughs)*

When they sent you to the Ozarks, they must have forgotten you were there.

They just left me. I didn't make any waves. I was enjoying it so, they didn't realize that—I was enjoying it! *(laughs)*

What did you do down there?

Oh, we had a lot of churches and a mission.

It was like your adventure up to Sweden where you wanted to establish a mission.

There were four or five churches, but it was over two-hundred miles around those churches.

You offered Masses?

Masses, confessions, everything. When they were hatched, matched, and dispatched. Baptized, married, and buried. *(laughs)*

What do you remember the most about it?

Oh, I don't know. I had very dear friends who made the stay a little easier. I did get permission to get updated. I asked the same Father Terence O'Connor, who was provincial, if I could go to the university and get another degree. Shortly after I got there, in 1968, I started this degree. I did it slowly. I did it in theology and language, and I got a Masters degree.

At which university?

At the University of St. Louis, which is a Jesuit university, just like the University of Detroit is a Jesuit university; Marquette in Milwaukee; Loyola, here in Chicago. I was honored there by them putting me on the staff of their *Theology Digest*. That's a publication of the university, which I feel very humbled about. I didn't even realize they were doing it, and I found my name on the editorial page. *(laughs)*

They must have wanted your help because you did that kind of publication work in Ireland.

It was just because I was doing theology courses.

Did you write for this publication?

We did some odds and ends. I knew German. They needed a German man, a German-speaking person. That was part of it.

You brought the Continent to them!

(laughs) Well, I don't know, I didn't do too much. I didn't deserve it, let's put it that way. It was during my time in the Ozarks, by the way, when Bob Hope's daughter Linda Hope went to the University of St. Louis, and she was honored. I knew the head of the university there. A very beautiful man. He was very close to the Hopes. He even had Linda as part of the Board of Directors. She was very intelligent.

Have you been friends of the Hope family for a long time?

Since 1947 . . . I've known them a long time. I met them through Father James Mary Keane in Oregon. They were very close. Eventually, I was invited to come and stay with them many times. On a lighter side, like the Irish lady who wanted to be blessed for *very close veins,* Father Keane and the Hopes were very close. *(laughs)* Recently, they gave $50,000 to our grotto in Portland. The National Sanctuary of Our Sorrowful Mother is its official title. It was for a new building for pilgrims. They were supposed to have a bronze plaque put up on that building. They wanted it in honor of Father James Mary Keane and . . . [me], but I never saw it out there. I was out there two times in the last two years, and I never saw any . . . *(laughs)*

That was very kind of them. When you were in Missouri, you were doing parish work, and then you also worked at the university. You had a job working with the editors and went to school. What else were you doing there?

I also brought people to Europe during those days, just as kind of a vacation sort of thing because I knew the languages over there and had traveled those countries so much. I had been in Europe almost twenty years—from 1948 until 1968, I was overseas.

Did you host pilgrimages?

Yes and no. Some of them were pilgrimages, and some of them were just tourist trips. I even brought a bunch to Hawaii one time, and we went to Ireland a few times and traveled the Ring of Kerry. The most ambitious one was Ireland, France, Italy, Spain, and Portugal where we hit the shrines. Ireland, and then Lourdes in France, then to Rome and to the shrines there. Then we went to Spain and then over to Portugal, to Fatima.

Did you go to Jerusalem?

The first pilgrimage I did to Jerusalem was when I was in Rome those six years, around 1955. I was invited to give a mission to our armed forces in Turkey. That was during Lent. I fell in with a man who worked for the U.S. government. He was not directly in the military, but he was a finance-educated man who was helping with official work that way. A very beautiful man and very holy, from across the line here in Indiana. I still speak with his family. He died rather young. But he said, Why don't we go over, we're so close here in Turkey. Why don't we go over to the Holy Land for Holy Week? Which we did. We went to Jerusalem from Istanbul. That is Turkish for Constantinople. They changed the name to Istanbul—and that's no bull! We did a Holy Week there in the Holy Land.

At that time, the Jews had not conquered Jerusalem. They just had David's Tomb in the corner of the city. In those days, you went through the Arab part. They would like you to show your baptismal certificate for passage. That meant that you were not circumcised, so you were not Jewish. *(laughs)* And then you went through the Arab part. Finally, we went to the Mandelbaum Gate by taxi, and the taxi man left us off. We picked up our suitcases and went through a no-man's land to the Jewish part.

You had the guns of the Arabs behind you and the guns of the Jews in front of you. *(laughs)* But they wanted tourists, so unless you were suspect, or whatever, they wouldn't shoot you. But it was a little shaky. I had never been in a situation like that before. Then we went around the Jewish conquered part of the Holy Land. That was my first time. Since then, I've brought people there a half a dozen times at least. I've never been in the Holy Land when there has been peace. It's always been a shaky sort of thing.

You were busy in the Ozarks.

Yes, it was very busy. We had all these churches, you know, driving some distances. And then you had to clean the lavatories and sweep the churches sometimes.

There was no general help?

You were general flunky. Whenever we could, we would get people to do it. Sometimes they were lax, lax about the whole thing. When you had to have Sunday Mass, you had to clean it up before. But in general, the people were very good.

Then you came back to Our Lady of Sorrows?

In 1984, finally, the provincial, Father Augustine Kulbis, invited me to meet him. He invited me to come back to Chicago and begin the healing services again.

How did he know you did the healing services?

He knew from way back. I had him as a student in Rome in the 1950s. He was a theology student then. He studied also in Benburb, and he heard about it over there.

But what prompted him to call you?

Actually, it all kind of fell together. I had begun a little secular Servite community. We had taken over an Ursuline school in the Arcadia Valley where we had our main house, and where

I had taken care of the nuns. But they had closed the school. The nuns were getting older, and so on—the old story. This big, huge girls school, Ursuline Academy, it's called, was vacant. The nuns living there were retirees, and they couldn't take care of things too well.

They had a beautiful big chapel that was like a church. That actually was the church for many decades, before we built our own churches there. Here this place was all up in the air. We made a deal with them, for this little group that we started, that we would take care of the grounds and the buildings in exchange for rent. We signed a little agreement at the altar. And I had a manager. He was a very responsible businessman, a builder of houses, a manager of houses. He was very good. He had moved down there from the city like so many people. He thought the world of these nuns. He was very thick with them, the nuns.

We had that for three years. This mother superior with whom we had made the deal, she wanted to give us the whole place; but, shortly after we made our agreement, another superior was elected, and she couldn't wait until we got out of there. She had just the opposite feelings about this community.

We had a little factory and everything to support. You see, one of the things that prompted us to start this community was the economic depression. The big employers down there in Ironton, Missouri, were the iron mines for which the Confederates and Unionists fought, by the way, in the town right next to it. There were three lead mines, also. The lead industry went down the sewer because of all the hue and cry on lead poisoning. The big buyers of paint, gasoline—there used to be lead in gasoline and other things—all collapsed because of the hue and cry against lead. They had to close, except one—St. Joe Lead. They were international, so they could continue. All that employment went down the stream. It became very depressed financially. We were trying to give work to people.

What did they make?

They made furniture. We started out with outdoor furniture. We had unskilled labor, and it was easy to make. Anyway, the contract came to an end. The Ursulines didn't want to renew because the superior had talked to the major superior. We had to sell out everything. We had an auction for all of our things and were able to cover expenses that way, and even gave a big fat check to the Province of Servites.

How many people did you have working?

Oh, it wasn't big. I think we had about a dozen people in the community. Some stayed, and some came and went. Some stayed a couple of days, and then they would go home and then come back. I had a beautiful young man, who eventually became a priest, as a lay leader. It was a lay community. I just wanted to be their spiritual man. We had Mass, prayed the *Divine Office,* and so on.

When we had to close shop, it was at that point that Father Augustus Kulbis, a Lithuanian, a South Side Chicago name, a fine man, contacted me. He did a wonderful job as provincial. He was provincial a few terms, just a very level-headed sort of man. I came back to Chicago and took up residence at Our Lady of Sorrows. But I really didn't get under way until about 1986, even though I left down there in August of 1984.

At this point, Our Lady of Sorrows was undergoing a complete renovation, the monastery and the church, because there had been a fire. The race riots had taken place at this time. This was during the 1960s and 1970s, and even in the 1980s. It was still very much of a war zone sort of place. The church had been abused terribly and the monastery, too. Nobody wanted to live on the West Side because it was too dangerous.

The Order went through a period of discernment at that time—what should we do with this beautiful big church that was so well-known with all those seventy-thousand people coming every Friday over the years and now abandoned because nobody dared to go out that way? And, the monastery, what will we do with it? They went through a period of discernment, and, thank God, they finally decided, No, we're going to bring it all back up. That's why it is there today. They were going through that, so they had no place for me to stay at the moment. I didn't really get going with this until about 1986.

Father Augustine Kulbis invited you back specifically to do the healing services?

Yes. In fact, he wanted me to be the head of the basilica, have a bronze plaque on my door and all this stuff. I said, "I don't want any of that, please. I don't want to get in trouble with the prior and the pastor. All these hats! *(laughs)* I just want to do the work—the healing."

When did you become a Knight of the Holy Sepulcher?

That was when I was in Missouri already. I believe 1984, if I'm not mistaken. We were received locally. The Pope was our great leader, and he authorized anyone to come into the Knights.

At sixty-eight years of age, you were knighted and you received permission to start the healing services again?

Yes, from the provincial, Father Provincial Augustine Mary Kulbis.

Did he give you a letter?

Yes. He gave me a formal *obedience,* as they call it. It took awhile to get the services started again.

You hadn't done any healing services since Ireland?

No. I hadn't done any healing services from 1953, when I left Ireland, until almost the life of Our Lord, thirty-three years later. They had asked me to do all these other things in the intervening years.

So you ended up doing the healing services. How were they received?

What started it was the Ambassadors of Mary, which, by the way, was founded by Father Keane. They had a Mass on Saturdays, confessions, and so on, called the *Power of Prayer.* About one-hundred-fifty to two-hundred people would come to this First Saturday Mass of the month. I asked the leader man and his wife, who drove quite a way from Iowa. They drove all the way to run this every First Saturday. He was a businessman, organized. I asked him if it would be O.K. to have some services after their Mass. That was the beginning of the return of the services.

You used the relics again and the blessing?

Yes. The same as I did in Benburb.

And people started coming back again.

After Father Augustus Kulbis finished his term of office, the next man, who has gone to Heaven, he didn't buy this at all. He condemned me to Cabrini Green [a public housing project known for gang violence]. He told me to close the office. We had an office in the monastery in back where all those rooms are. And I had a secretary. It was under the provincial set up. He told me to fire the secretary and close the office. But Father Charles Mary Brennan, who was the pastor down at St. Dominick's in Cabrini Green, said, We'll have it here. Of course, who's going to come down there? No parking! Sacrifice their cars and their lives! *(laughs)* It was *Cabrini Green! (laughs)* Anyway, the faithful few continued. We had almost as many there as we did at Our Lady of Sorrows in those faltering first services.

Did you get many people from Cabrini Green?

Oh, there were very few Catholics. But people came from quite a way around. A lot of healings took place this time. The word got out, and they braved going down there for the services.

One of the funny parts, I don't know if I mentioned this, you'll find it in Heather Parsons' book *Man of Miracles.* I believe she mentions how she hailed a taxi man one time when she came to visit. She was over here from Ireland. The taxi man said, Lady, you better get another taxi; I'm not going down there. He left her out off at a compromising place, some ways away from the place. She had to walk through this maze to find us. We had services there for three years then, during the term of this new provincial. But then they closed St. Dominick's Church because of no parishioners.

I was moved to Seven Holy Founders Church in Calumet Park, south of Chicago. But that was only for about seven months. We had some services there during our stay. It was at that time, Jim Hrechko, who was to become our business manager, started coming to help us half a day a week down in Cabrini. He'd come down on the train, and I'd come pick him up and take him back. He was such a businessman and all. I told him our predicament, and I said that I didn't want to move again.

He kept coming then to Seven Holy Founders in Calumet Park, helping very well. He helped me move when I eventually moved out of there. I said, "I don't want to move all this office stuff again. Let's get a stationary place." We went over about ten options, and then Betty Pesavento invited us here to offices in Olympia Fields, Illinois. She was the manager at that time, and she brought us into the meeting room and gave such an offer Jim could hardly reject.

Jim Hrechko works as the business manager of the International Compassion Ministry; he shared his thoughts about the ministry:

I've been with Father for the most part of fifteen years. I came to know who Father was through the Infant Jesus of Prague prayer group in Flossmoor, Illinois. The prayer group holds a Mass and healing service every First Monday of the month. Father was in the early stages of his healing ministry, and, if he didn't have anything going on that particular Monday, he would show up at the Infant Jesus of Prague. Problems developed with my middle son, which occasioned the need, one time, to ask my son to see either a doctor or talk to a priest.

He indicated that he would talk to a priest, whereupon I located Father's phone number through the prayer group, got a hold of Father, and arranged for an interview. Father was at St. Dominick's in Chicago. And when I went upstairs to tell my son that the interview was set up, he said he wasn't going because he had changed his mind. The following Monday was the First Monday of the month. I went to the prayer group, and Father Rookey was there and doing the laying on of hands. During the Sign of Peace, I

walked up to Father and introduced myself to him, since he didn't know who I was when I called for my son. He said to me, "Our Lady, Queen of Peace, sends you her peace." This was the beginning of a friendship that eventually led to my volunteering for him in his office at St. Dominick's in Chicago one day a week.

When St. Dominick's was being closed, Father Rookey had to move and find a new location, and his new location was in Calumet Park in Seven Holy Founders. Seven Holy Founders did not have any office space or secretary space to continue ministry operations from there requiring him to seek new quarters. Closed convents, etc., were investigated, and we were offered an opportunity to come to this location, since one of Father's supporters was the office manager for this building, and we, in turn, came to look at it.

The price was right. And with Father remaining in Berwyn, eventually, there was a need for someone to maintain the office. Since I live about two and a half to three miles from this location, I indicated that I would come to the office on a daily basis, on one condition. (laughs) I told Father if I came to the office, and he would allow me to run the office, that I would have to have complete control. He indicated, Fine. Be my guest. So, here I am. I make all his travel arrangements, his appointments; I do the accounting, recording of Mass requests, payment of the bills, and so on.

Instead of working one day a week, you're working five, right? And weekends?

Yes. (laughs) That's right. And, sometimes weekends. I usually come to the office on Saturdays, too, after

Fig. 30. *Jim Hrechko,* International Compassion Ministry, Olympia Fields, Illinois, 2006.

I attend Mass, but really to check the answering machine to see if there are any critical calls.

So much for retirement!

Yes! (laughs) I'm retired!

You are giving your retirement years up to do this. What impresses you the most about the ministry?

When you talk about retirement, retirement is not the end of a person's being. It continues. There's a richness in this work, a satisfying richness, a fulfillment. When I think of retirement, I don't think of life as stopping. I think it just goes on to another path. For me, it's been a beautiful path.

What is it about this ministry that is particularly special to you? How have you changed by being involved?

Well, I still continue to believe that nothing is impossible with God. I've seen too many instances where this has been fulfilled. My problem with my son has not been resolved, with his illness, but with God, nothing is impossible. Being with the ministry has allowed me to cope and to look forward—whatever God wills, we accept.

Is it mental illness?

Yes. Brought on by drug addiction. Not only drug addiction, alcoholism, etc. Just this morning, I read in the Tribune *where a teenager in Arlington Heights died because of a heroin overdose. He was seventeen years old. The drug problem is so tragic. In this particular case, it ended up in the teenager's death. But at one point in time, early in my son's drug problem, in entering a treatment program, he had to answer a questionnaire that indicated a list of drugs. A person had to check off those drugs he had used. My son told me there were only about two that he had never used. That's sad. But I think it was the drug usage that eventually caused his mental illness. The drugs fried his brain in that sense; we just continue. Father is a man of great faith and extreme humility. He has a profound love of people. If he sees, he never recognizes, or will acknowledge, any human fault or deficiency. Father really believes that we are all God's Children, and he never recognizes the failure.*

It makes us better to know him; he makes us want to become better.

Yes, indeed.

When did you name it the International Compassion Ministry?

Oh, I started that right from the beginning. We began on a small scale with evenings at St. Dominick's in Cabrini Green, then at the Seven Holy Fathers. Then we started at other churches, too, all around. We were doing that from our office. We were getting invitations. I was going to St. Louis every First Saturday. When we finished here in Chicago, I would drive down. We only had a few people, so I was able to drive down there in time for the evening. I was having services all around all this time.

Did you do any overseas services?

Oh, I had maybe taken a group once in awhile. When we took up over here, we began getting requests from all over; then it started worldwide.

But who gave you permission to have healing services again at Our Lady of Sorrows?

It was under the new provincial.

But the man who was there before, who shut you down—what happened to him?

He only lasted three years and was put out. Then there was the next man. Father John Mary Huels was his name. Jim and I went and spoke with him and a finance man, Father Luke Mary Stano. He made out another kind of contract with the Province. That's how it developed.

How many people are on your mailing list now?

Since we stopped publication of the newsletter for some time, we've lost a few thousand. I think we are down to about 40,000 now, if I'm not mistaken. We were almost 50,000.

You were giving Masses and healing services all over the world—the Philippines, Mexico, Europe, and all over the United States?

Yes.

Over these years, what is it that you find the most meaningful about your ministry?

Oh, I think, basically, the fact that, obviously, it's what God wants me to do. Our peace only comes when our will is one with the Father's Will. Otherwise, we never have *peace*. We'll always be disturbed. I think that's where it is.

If I didn't feel this was what God wanted me to do, I wouldn't do it, because I wouldn't want to be going against what He had planned for me. But with the tremendous signs He gives with the healings, it seems quite obvious this is what He wants of me—to expend myself helping people spiritually and even physically. That's really, I think, what stands out in this ministry. The marvelous works He performs have been a great source of support in our lives. As I often quote His Words, If you don't believe My Words, believe My Works.[1] He's continually backing up His Words with His Works.

Father Rookey came several times to St. Domatilla. And single-handed, he prayed over people. They fell, and they were healed. In Sligo town, it's been a few years, outside of Benburb, Ireland, I spent two years from 1994 to 1996. Because my mother was old, I requested to go back, so I could be close to her.

And I remember Father Rookey. There were 8,000 people at a church in Sligo. He prayed over each one. And when he was leaving, it was on Radio Eireann, the radio man said, "Father Rookey, you must be exhausted!" Father Rookey said, "On the contrary, I feel exuberant." So, that's the Spirit. He was seventy-seven years old, and he could say that. If the Spirit wasn't in him, he couldn't have done what he did.

Brother Chris Moran, O.S.M.

Didn't Jesus say that the Apostles would go out and do more than even He had done?

Oh yes, exactly. I feel all priests are called to preach the Gospel and allow Jesus to back up His *Good News* with His *Good Works*, but maybe not in the heavy sense that He has called some of us.

Now, I just wrote the foreword to the re-release of the book on one of our Servite parish priests, Father St. Anthony Maria Pucci, who was a parish priest for forty-five years in Viareggio, Italy. Some remarkable miracles were worked through him. That's what they used for his canonization process. But actually, his main work was as a parish priest and reaching out to the poor in the parish, and through his life, and through his word, helping them to follow Christ. I feel all priests are called to that.

Not only priests but certain lay people as well. A good example is a man down in Florida who was coming to our services. Now he's duplicating those services, and he's being invited by parishes to pray the *Seven Sorrows Rosary* with the

Scripture, as we always do before the services, and give a little talk, followed by the laying on of hands. He is just a lay person, so he cannot celebrate Mass, but he's carrying on. Many others are doing the same.

The Lord at His Ascension—before He went back up to the Right Hand of the Father, Ascension Day—He said, Those who believe these signs will follow . . . in My Name they will cast out demons, the sick upon whom they lay their hands will recover[2] . . . those who believe. That's kind of a blanket sort of word, as far as I can see. I think it's quite obvious that He has chosen ordinary, what we consider ordinary, people to work His Works. I think this account you are writing up is a kind of miracle. *(laughs)* How you've been so inspired in the energy and motivation to do it. I think that's so inspiring.

Oh, I'm just stubborn. (laughs) That's all. When I get on a track . . . It has nothing to do with . . . (laughs)

(laughs) The Lord said it a different way . . . *He who perseveres to the end, he will be saved.*[3]

He needs to save me . . . from myself! But in your own life, how have you persevered through this journey where you could begin your healing services again? You have this unique Gift of Healing you felt was your calling, and yet you were sent to do so many other things. You were recognized by the Order for your gifts of administration; training novices; teaching languages, sacred music, and Liturgy; daily pastoral care; providing spiritual direction; providing hospitality for pilgrims; and for leading pilgrimages. You don't know how many people you have healed indirectly because you have trained many, many priests to go out to do the service of God. But how do you feel about it now, in that these other jobs weren't exactly what you felt called to do?

Fig. 31. *The Beatification of Anthony Pucci, O.S.M.,* painting by Michelangelo Bedini for the beatification ceremony at St. Peter's Basilica in Rome, 1952; façade windows by the Clinton Glass Company, Chicago, Our Lady of Sorrows Basilica, Chicago, Illinois, 2006. The Russian brass sanctuary lamp, shimmering with metallic passion flowers, was a gift by a doctor in thanksgiving for the healing of his daughter through the intercession of Rev. Thomas Moreschini, O.S.M.

The basic thinking is from Jesus: I didn't come to do My Will, but the Will of My Father.[4] In religious life, it has always been, from way back, the vow of obedience. Doing the Will of God. And, for you who have become a religious, the will of your superior. Unless, like if your mother and father told you to commit murder, obviously, that would not be the Will of God. But normally, God is expressed in your superiors.

The word obedience *today seems restrictive. But obedience enables a person to receive the Graces of God. Perhaps the person above them knows better for that person, in a particular stage of their life, what they need. Maybe we aren't so smart sometimes about what's best for us.*

In a sense it is a release. But of course it can be a painful release—like this is right now. All those years . . . but you're at peace, and that's where it is.

Notes

1   *Do you not believe, that I am in the Father, and the Father in me? The words that I speak to you, I speak not of myself. But the Father who abideth in me, he doth the works. Believe you not that I am in the Father, and the Father in me? Otherwise believe for the very works sake* (Jn 14:10-12), The Holy Bible, Douay Rheims Version, revised by Bishop Richard Challoner, A.D. 1749-1752, Imprimatur +J. Cardinal Gibbons, Archbishop of Baltimore (Rockford, Illinois: Tan Books and Publishers, Inc.,1971), hereafter cited as "Douay."

2   *. . . And these signs shall follow them that believe: they shall speak with new tongues . . . they shall lay their hands upon the sick, and they shall recover* (Mk 16:17-18), Douay.

3   *He that shall persevere to the end, he shall be saved* (Mt 24:13), Douay.

4   *Because I came down from Heaven, not to do my own will, but the will of him that sent me* (Jn 6:38), Douay.

Fig. 32.   *Pietà and Father Peter Mary Rookey,* original sculpture by Michelangelo Buonarroti (1499); marble reproduction carved in Pietrasanta, Italy, by Spartaco Palla, Our Lady of Sorrows Basilica, Chicago, Illinois, 2005.

The Power of Saints and Relics

The Catholic Church has an ancient tradition of honoring heroic men and women of all ages, backgrounds, and talents for dedicating their lives to the service of God. While some are born to be Saints, others become holy as they progress in their journey toward God.[1] Other great Saints were previously great sinners who had lived destructively but who chose to dramatically turn their lives around to serve God and His People with equal passion.[2] These Holy Ones are celebrated on feast days and are often called on to assist us with our various challenges. Christ's Mother, the Blessed Virgin Mary, is called upon in a similar way because her life was a tremendous example of how to endure personal suffering for the benefit of the greater good.

Articles of clothing and parts of the bodies of Saints, called relics, are believed to act as healing agents and are venerated in the Liturgy of the Church. Guardian Angels, too, are invoked for protection and assistance within the Church Tradition.

The supernatural presence of Angels and Saints is accepted as a part of the natural human experience.

Fig. 33. *Scelig Mhichíl (Skellig Michael),* Kerry, Ireland, 2005. Ireland's westernmost sacred site predating the sixth century Christian monastic settlement that is part of the St. Michael/Apollo axis of sacred places.

Shrines are found all over the world, where Saints lived, or are buried, or where Jesus, the Blessed Mother, and Angels have appeared, or where other miracles have occurred. These holy places are visited to petition for special intentions or as a personal pilgrimage of love, thanksgiving, and devotion.

As one becomes closer to God, manifestations of supernatural forces are discerned more frequently and recognized as signs of God's Love for us. Father Rookey is quick to point out incidences of God's Beauty and Mercy in our lives, for God is the Creator of all Creation, and He is with us always, in all that is seen and unseen.

🐦🐦🐦🐦🐦🐦🐦🐦🐦🐦🐦🐦🐦🐦🐦🐦🐦🐦🐦🐦🐦🐦🐦🐦🐦

Ireland is known as The Land of Saints and Scholars. *St. Patrick fostered the Catholic faith in Ireland during the fifth century, in part, by lighting a fire in opposition to the druid Beltaine fire ritual. The lighting of what became known as the Paschal Fire was later incorporated into the Church's Easter Vigil services. As a result of St. Patrick's mission, many of the druids became monks. Some of the best of Irish society's sons and daughters also responded to St. Patrick's mission by becoming the abbots and abbesses of the new Catholic monasteries on land given by the local chieftains. Many more Saints were formed, particularly in the early years of the Church in Ireland.*

Yes, he built the Church in Ireland on the monastic system. In fact, the monks of Ireland dotted Europe with monasteries during the Dark Ages and saved the culture that way. Those monasteries were, very often, the beginnings of what now are big cities, like Münster in the western part of Germany. *Münster*—that means *monastery* in German. The city was begun as a monastery. And, in Italy, many of the places in Italy started as monasteries. St. Gallien in Switzerland is named after an Irish monk, St. Gaul. They spell it G-a-l-l-i-e-n. That city was started as a monastery, like the City of St. Paul was too.

St. Oliver Plunkett was a great Catholic Martyr of Ireland.

St. Oliver Plunkett was the archbishop. He was canonized in 1975. I had a healing Mass on the 25th Anniversary of his canonization in Chicago at Gaelic Park.

About three years ago, when I was in England, a chaplain in a big monastery in Wales went after our promoters, Bernard Ellis and Martin Duggan. He kept after them because he wanted to have services in the prison they ministered to nearby. He was a monk in Downside Abbey, this great historic abbey. The church of the abbey would put many a cathedral to shame. It is a huge, big, place in Wales. He was the chaplain in the penitentiary there. He wanted services for the prisoners. Bernard and Martin finally caved in, and we drove down.

First, we went to the monastery, and some of the monks wanted a blessing. And lo and behold, Oliver Plunkett-wise, they brought us up into this huge church and to Oliver Plunkett's monument. He's encased in a big coffin of stone. It was such a surprise because he was the Archbishop of Armagh and here he is in a tomb in Wales, in Downside Abbey. They told us the story of how he got there. He had visited before his martyrdom. The British government had a price on his head. But he visited the monks, and, as he was departing, he said, You've been so kind to me, can I do anything for you? And one of the monks said, Yes, you can give us your body. He probably figured he'd end up a Martyr. He was a prominent man, and the British were after him. He signed a donation document for his body to the abbey.

His head is kept in St. Peter's Church in Drogheda, Ireland. It's on the Boyne River that flows into the Irish Sea. I've often gone by and seen his head that is in a glass box like a reliquary. But his body is in Downside, Abbey.

I had a dear friend, Father Thomas O'Fee, who succeeded Cardinal John Dalton as the Archbishop of Armagh. When St. Oliver's canonization was coming up, and the cause was coming to a crucial moment, Father Thomas O'Fee went to the monks of Downside Abbey asking for the body to put into the cathedral of Armagh. The monks went into the archives and found the donation statement signed by St. Oliver Plunkett himself, donating his body to them.

He was sentenced to be hung, drawn, and quartered.

That was very common, hung, drawn, and quartered.

Have there been miracles affiliated with his relics?

There must have been because that's part of the process of canonization. They say, by the way, that St. Peregrine was the first one who went through the canonization process. But before that, "You're a holy son of a gun," of popular acclaim; then, "You're a Saint!" But eventually, the Church wanted to make it a little more official. Maybe some of the people named Saints weren't so saintly! *(laughs)* They started this process. First you're venerable, then blessed, then canonized.

St. Oliver Plunkett—Bishop and Martyr: A Patron Saint for Peace and Reconciliation

St. Oliver Plunkett was a peacemaker, consummate diplomat, and soldier for the Church, skills he developed partly as a necessity of his heritage. Born on All Saints Day, November 1, 1625, in County Meath, Ireland, of renowned Anglo-Irish descent, he was friendly with many influential Protestants despite the severe persecution of Catholics of the era. His positive relations with Protestant officials enabled him to intervene frequently on behalf of Irish-Catholics. Fluent in four languages, St. Oliver studied in Rome for twenty-three years. He was elected Archbishop of Armagh and Primate of All Ireland and then was ordered by Pope Clement IX back to colonial Ireland. Due to the horrific effects of massacres, famine, and disease brought about by Cromwell's war in Ireland, the Irish population had been reduced by at least fifty percent.[3] For the first few months of St. Oliver's return, due to bigotry, he did not appear in public unless disguised as an army captain. To maintain this posture, he would frequent taverns, join in song, and even kiss a bar-maid or two, as was the custom.

There were few priests, for many had been killed or sold into slavery as part of the lucrative Irish slave trade. The Church organizational structure had been shaken. *Among the priests who remained were several factions of which there was a minority who dressed like the laity and lived with them, and who had no authority to whom they were bound to report. There were many incidences of poor conduct, but just as important to St. Oliver, there was evidence that many had lost the art of guiding souls. As a result, St. Oliver embarked on a period of reform, although he wryly informed Rome,* the spirit was willing, but the cash was weak.[4]

He improved clerical standards and restored clerical discipline, but not without raising resentment, too. He invited the Jesuits to re-establish Catholic schools that had been absent for twenty years. The schools trained a new generation of young, devout priests and aspiring lay leaders, and even attracted Protestants. He negotiated on behalf of the Irish resistance and mediated in a noted dispute between the Dominicans and Franciscans, but, in the process, incurred great criticism and a few life-long enemies. By his own records, he personally confirmed 48,655 Irish-Catholics in the forests and rugged areas throughout Ireland, ministered to others who had been spiritually neglected, and assisted those suffering from the ravages of yet another famine.

In 1673, the persecution of Irish-Catholics escalated again due to the rising strength in England of the Protestant Parliament against the Catholic Court. All regular Catholic clergy, bishops, and vicar-generals were ordered banished from Ireland and to register at the sea-ports. Catholic schools and religious houses were closed. In a defining moment, St. Oliver refused to report for deportation and went into hiding. The British government sent spies to track down the resisting clergy. While the storm soon passed, it was a prelude of worse to come.

Five years later, Titus Oates, a disturbed man, was expelled from a Jesuit school because he was deemed unfit to proceed with his novitiate. Before he left, he went to an altar and said, I am bidding farewell to Jesus.[5] *He then proceeded to concoct the Popish Plot alleging that the Pope was raising an army of 40,000 strong in Ireland that would invade England and proscribe the Protestant religion. The charge was ludicrous considering the dissolute state of the Irish-Catholic people and the extent of British military control. Protestant political operatives, most notably Lord Shaftesbury, praised Oates naming him the* Savior of the Nation. *For three years, a frenzied hysteria was let loose throughout England and Ireland. As before, by government order, Catholic priests were hunted down and imprisoned. Many were executed.*

Again, St. Oliver went into hiding using the disguise of a gentleman with the name of Mr. Meleady. The Privy Council ordered his arrest to question him about an allegation that he was assisting the French in planning an invasion of Ireland. In 1679, he was imprisoned in Dublin Castle. He was brought to trial in Dundalk, but the prosecution's two key witnesses—a former clergyman, who was dismissed by the primate, and a Franciscan, with a long-standing resentment of St. Oliver—failed to testify. The trial was moved to Dublin to be tried by an all-Protestant jury, but Lord Shaftesbury soon realized that even an all-Protestant jury would not convict the innocent man.

St. Oliver was transported to Newgate prison in London where, from October 1680 to May of 1681, he was held in solitary confinement in leg irons. He fasted three to four days a week, entering a deep state of prayer. On May 3, 1681, St. Oliver was informed of the charges against him. He was declined his request for a delay of trial so that his witnesses could be brought over from Ireland. The trial took place on June 8, 1681. The corrupt proceedings included key testimonies by three priests, and, when concluded, the jury came back in fifteen minutes.

St. Oliver was convicted of high treason for propagating the Catholic faith. He was sentenced to death by Lord Pemberton:

You must go hence to the place from whence you came, that is Newgate. And from thence you shall be drawn through the City of London to Tyburn; there you shall be hanged by the neck but cut down before you are dead, your bowels taken out and burnt before your face, your head shall be cut off, and your body divided into four quarters to be disposed of as his majesty pleases.[6]

In addition to the Earl of Essex, a supporter of Shaftesbury, at the Pope's request, the governments of Spain, Austria, and France, urged King Charles II to reprieve the sentence. But the king dared not grant him pardon due to the fervor of the day.

With thanks to God, St. Oliver accepted the white crown of martyrdom. In his final words, he, like Christ, forgave all who had a role in bringing about his death, asked forgiveness from all whom he may have moved to murderous anger, and blessed the King of England. He was executed on July 1, 1681. With his death, the fury of the Popish Plot era was quenched. The Earl of Shaftesbury was imprisoned the next morning.

On Father Rookey's 59th birthday, October 12th, 1975, Oliver Plunkett was canonized by Pope Paul VI at a Mass assisted by Cardinal Karol Wojtyla of Krakow, who was invited by peace advocate and Primate of All Ireland, Cardinal William Conway. Like his predecessor St. Oliver, Cardinal Conway presided over a politically volatile and violent time in Irish history, The Troubles, notably marked by the horrific Bloody Sunday massacre. His Eminence remarked, "Violence can make the road to justice much longer and leave it strewn with innocent lives."[7] On September 29, 1979, Pope John Paul II (Cardinal Wojtyla) visited Drogheda and again remembered St. Oliver Plunkett's legacy of justice, forgiveness, and peace. He, too, appealed to those advocating for violence to have the courage to embrace Christ's path of forgiveness and love, saying, "On

my knees, I beg you to turn from violence."[8]
*In the Archdiocese of Armagh, St. Oliver Plunkett
is recognized as the Patron Saint of Peace and
Reconciliation. He is similarly honored by others
throughout the world.*[9]

🐦🐦🐦🐦🐦🐦🐦🐦🐦🐦🐦🐦🐦🐦🐦🐦🐦🐦🐦🐦🐦🐦🐦🐦🐦🐦🐦🐦🐦🐦

*The relics and the tombs of the Saints were considered to be powerful
both for their healing properties and the money attached to the
process—the offerings of the people. During the Reformation, Henry
VIII went to great effort to destroy the shrines that held the relics
of the Saints. To disperse their power, he ordered that the bones of
some of the Saints be dug up and strewn so they could never be put
together again. Monastic holdings were dissolved and sold. He also
approved the destruction of the beautiful jeweled religious items
that were created in honor of God. Many people don't understand
the role of relics in the Church. You use relics as a healing agent.
Can you tell us more about the power and the tradition of the use
of relics?*

The relics of the Saints were mentioned even in the *Old
Testament*. The first thing that comes to mind is Elijah when he
had Elisha following him for some time. The Lord told him to
take on Elisha as his assistant to carry on after he passed on.
When Elijah came to the Jordan River, he took his cloak and
held it over the river. It parted just like it had for the Israelites
and the Red Sea. He and Elisha passed over onto dry land to
the other side.

Eventually, he said to Elisha, Now, I'm leaving, do you
have some desire? Elisha said, I want a double portion of your
spirit.[10] And, Elijah said, Well, that is very difficult, but if you
see me going up into Heaven, then you will know that you
have it.[11] He was brought up to Heaven in a burning chariot,
and his cloak came off, and Elisha obtained his cloak. He held
the cloak over the Jordan, and it parted just as it had for Elijah,
and he went over onto dry ground again.

On a personal note, when I was stationed at St. Dominic's in
Cabrini Green in Chicago *(laughs)*, I was carrying on a low-key
ministry, and we received a telephone call when Sister Mary

Caran was our secretary. Sister Mary Caran Hart, S.S.N.D., helps us with the ministry. She edits the miracles and the witness letters we receive and puts them out every month in the newsletter.

Sister Mary Caran and I received a telephone call from this lady. According to this woman's private revelation, she said, The Lord has given me a special gift to tell certain people the names of their Guardian Angels. Then she said, I was given notice to telephone you and tell you the name of your Guardian Angel. The name of your Guardian Angel is *Chariot of Fire*! Elijah. *Chariot of Fire*. *(laughs)* I told Jim Hrechko, who works here. He was sitting at the kitchen table having his coffee in the morning, and when he spoke the name *Chariot of Fire*, he rested in the Spirit. I'm going to have him tell you about that.

JIM HRECHKO: Well, before having breakfast, I say Grace. The most recent time was about two weeks ago, when, after Grace, I would ask the Blessed Mother and the Servite Saints to intercede for Father Rookey. One day, I decided to add St. Michael the Archangel and Chariot of Fire to intercede for Father.

Did you rest in the Spirit?

JIM HRECHKO: Well, that one time. I just kind of sat there with my breakfast letting my eggs get cold! *(laughs)* Yes, anytime I invoke his Guardian Angel the Spirit stirs within me.

FATHER ROOKEY: She was asking about the power of the relics and the Saints and Elijah's cloak. Elisha inherited Elijah's spirit after he left. Elisha took his cloak and said, Dear God in Israel, or words to that effect, and the Jordan parted, and he went across onto dry land. That was the relic of Elijah's cloak. That was one of the first relics in the *Old Testament*.[12]

As a practical example, when I first came back to this ministry in 1986, I was invited to come to one of the biggest hospitals in Chicago, the Presbyterian Hospital—now the Rush University Medical Center. It's here on the Eisenhower Expressway. The occasion was a young Italian father of a family, I guess he was about thirty years old, who was dying of cancer of the marrow of the bone. His dutiful wife was sitting beside him. I went in and prayed with them both.

He had his arms under the covers and was in a comatose state. I blessed the wife with the reliquary crucifix containing the relics of St. Peregrine the Cancer Saint, the Seven Founders and all, speaking about relics.

There is a part of each one of them in the crucifix you use?

Yes, in this reliquary crucifix. I blessed her because he was in a coma. I was preparing to leave when she said, Father, would you mind placing the crucifix in Frank's hand? I said, No. She said, Because when you placed it on my head an electric shock went through my body from the top of my head to my toes. She took Frank's hand from under the covers and I placed it in his hand. And, whoof! He came out of the coma and started uttering indiscernible words at first. A day or two later, I came back, and they had arranged with the chaplain to have a Mass in his room. That was around Thursday, and he was sitting up taking part in the Mass, very alert. That was an example of the power of the presence of the Saints and the relics.

Did he recover?

He recovered for a month or so. But it seems that the Lord called him back really for the family's sake, because they were all nonaccepting of his sickness and his approaching death. He spoke to all of the family very gently and said, You know, I'm ready to go, and all this, and reassured them in every way, and united them, then he went to Heaven. It looks like the Lord brought him back for the family's sake. His father, mother, brothers, and sisters were still living. That was a beautiful miracle that the Lord worked through the relics of His Saints.

ଔ ଔ

Dear Father Rookey,

Recently, we attended a Medjugorje conference in Pittsburgh, Pennsylvania. While we were at the

Fig. 34.   *Servite Reliquary Crucifix and Father Peter Mary Rookey, O.S.M.,* Chicago, Illinois, 2005.

conference, I met a gentleman who had been away from the Church for twenty-three years. He suggested that I take this Miracle Prayer *card and pray it for the rest of my life.*

Since I have a sister who has been away from the Church for about twenty-five years, I asked this gentleman what made him want to return to the Church. He said he lives near Our Lady of Snows Shrine in Illinois, and he didn't know what made him go to the shrine with his family one day. Upon entering the shrine, he met a priest who said, "Welcome," and extended his hand for a handshake. When they shook hands, he felt a shock go through his hand and entire body. The priest turned out to be you, Father Rookey. He said from that moment on, he cannot get enough of praying, reading Catholic books, the Church, and Sacraments.

Pennsylvania, 1999

♪♪♪♪♪♪♪♪♪♪♪♪♪♪♪♪♪♪♪♪♪♪♪♪♪♪♪♪♪

No other religion has Saints like the Catholic Church.

They have Saints, I guess, or holy people, but they don't normally pray to them to ask for their intercession.

Some religions think the Catholics, when they pray to Saints, are committing idolatry because of the statues and paintings, but that isn't quite what we are doing.

I think we could claim the same for you who have a picture of your mother on your desk, or your wife, or husband, and so on. They simply remind us. It is not a case of falling down and worshipping. The *Catholic Catechism* refers to the holiness of Saints. Holiness.

If our loved ones pass on, we do feel their presence because we believe their souls live after death and are with us. These holy people are named Saints because they had special gifts, and we identify with them. Just like different artists have special talents, or, for example, different musicians. Every person has a different talent, a different gift. These Saints had special talents for healing, service, and assistance, or were renown in their profession. We name them, for example, the Patron Saint of the Arts, or the Patron Saint of Carpenters.

Yes. That's true. The *Catholic Catechism* speaks of the Communion of Saints. It says:

"The Church is a "communion of saints." This expression refers to the "holy things" (sancta), above all the Eucharist, by which "the unity of believers, who form one body in Christ, is both represented and brought about" (LG3);

The term "communion of saints" refers also to the communion of "holy persons" (sancti) in Christ who "died for all," so that what each one does or suffers in and for Christ bears fruit for all;"

We believe in the communion of all the faithful of Christ, those who are pilgrims on earth, the dead who are being purified, and the blessed in heaven, all together forming one Church; and we believe that in this communion, the merciful love of God and his saints is always [attentive] to our prayers" (Paul VI, CPG § 30).[13]

These weren't just talented people. They were talented people because of their dedication to Christ. That's what distinguished them.

Right. What you are saying is backed up by Paul's word, in Corinthians 1:12-13, where he speaks of the Gifts of the Holy Spirit: To one is given the Gift of Prophecy, to another the Interpretation of the Prophesies, to another the Gift of Tongues, to another the Gift of Healing, and so on, and so on.[14] That's what the Saints had. The Lord bestowed them with special gifts. St. Paul had, among other things, the Gift of Preaching.

St. Philomena is known as the Patron Saint for Mental Illness.

Yes.

St. Bridget is recognized as a healer of people and animals and is the Patron Saint of Poets and Craftsmen and the Protector of Households.

She is a great Saint. She was the founder and the abbess of the monastery of Kildare. St. Joseph is the Patron Saint of the Family.

Also, it is believed that he is the Patron Saint of the Dying because he died in the arms of Jesus and Mary. He is invoked for those who are passing on. Pius XII created the *Feast of Joseph the Worker* in the time of the Communist hey-day back in the 1950s. He set up the *Feast* of *Joseph the Worker* as a model. My little one-liner about Jesus and Joseph is that they were carpenters . . . so they were always looking for joiners! Especially, Jesus.

Saints are also affiliated with the different Orders in the Church, too. St. Peregrine the Cancer Saint is from your Order, the Servite Order.

Yes. That's right. St. Peregrine is recognized as the cancer patron for cancer sufferers.

There is also a tradition in Catholic families to name their children after Saints.

Of course. Our Lady in Medjugorje, in our day, just last year, remarked about the Saints in one of her messages she has given out since 1981. She's been giving out a special message on the 25th of every month. I believe it was on the *Feast of Peter and Paul* that she mentioned how we should invoke our name Saints for protection because we were given that name with a special Grace.

Even in the *Old Testament*, great value was given to giving the newly born a proper name. One of the great stories is of the birth of John the Baptist. He was going to be given the name of one of the family.[15] Zachary was the father. Because he had doubted the Angel's word that he and his wife would be having a child in advanced years, he was struck dumb until the time John the Baptist was born.[16] When John was born, they came to the old man. They were still wondering what they would name him. The Angel had told Zachary, John is his name![17] No one in the family had that name.[18] Great store was always put on the naming of the child. Today in our befuddled world, it is such a mockery to give children names of horses, anything.

Fig. 35.   *Relic of St. Peregrine, O.S.M., The Cancer Saint,* St. Peregrine Shrine, Our Lady of Sorrows Basilica, Chicago, Illinois, 2006.

Movie stars.

Nonsensical names. To have a person live through his life without a meaningful name! I was very fortunately named Peter Joseph—and also Paul for my confirmation name. I call on those Saints, as Our Lady reminds us to do. I call on my namesake Peter, my first name, very often in my prayers.

The Saint gives an identity to the child with the custom of feast days and celebrations.

Yes. Very often, people follow an ancient tradition in the Church and call the child after the feast day.

On the day that the child was born?

Yes, the day that the child was born is seemingly important because the Saint associated with the day is considered to be a special patron and protector of the child. The Hispanics often use the days of the Mysteries, also. For example, you hear the name Lourdes, Our Lady of Lourdes, because the child was born on February 11th, the day Our Lady appeared at Lourdes. Or, for example, they were born on the 15th of August, so they are called Assunta, if they are Italian, for the day of the Mystery of the Assumption of the Blessed Virgin Mary. It wasn't just the name of the person of the Saint, but also, the Mystery of the day in the case it is a Mystery that is being celebrated.

Sabina Reyes works in the office of the International Compassion Ministry, answering the many calls that come in every day. Sabina shared her story of how she came to work for Father Rookey:
I first got to know about Father Rookey in the early 1990s when somebody told me about this healing

Fig. 36. *Mass: Sabina Reyes and Father Peter Mary Rookey, O.S.M.,* International Compassion Ministry, Olympia Fields, Illinois, 2005.

service where people were falling down. I had never heard of a Catholic priest blessing people and of people being slain in the spirit. I heard he had a very powerful ministry and service. I decided to go. The very first time that I went, I could just feel the energy in all of the church, and I was deeply, deeply moved. In fact, the first day I was there, I saw up in the mural of St. Juliana the image of the Blessed Mother holding the Baby Jesus in her arms, which just brought me to tears, and I knew this was a holy place. That was the beginning of my relationship with the International Compassion Ministry, or should I say, with my love of Father Rookey, because I just felt his holiness and his goodness.

I started going to every First Saturday Mass—that was about 1992-1993. I would see people helping around the church, and I said, "If I were a helper, I could get closer to Father and know him better." I love to help, and I have always been a volunteer all my life. I started volunteering, and then, eventually, came to the office to start helping here, too. It was an awesome Grace, as far as I was concerned, to be here in his company.

I started coming to the office in 1996, and, I must say, at first I was very intimidated by the telephones. I did not want to answer the phone. I just didn't feel I would know what to say to people. But as time went by, slowly, little by little, I started answering the telephone. I started enjoying doing that, but, at the same time, I was also working up until the year 2001 as a youth minister in my church, and I

Fig. 37.   *Saint Joan of Arc,* Our Lady's Chapel, St. Ignatius Parish, Chicago, Illinois, 2006. At the age of seventeen, inspired by visions of St. Michael, St. Catherine, and St. Margaret, Joan D'Arc led troops into battle (1429-1430) to defend the throne of the French king, Charles VII, from English domination. She was captured, imprisoned, sold to the English, ordered to be burned alive as a heretic, exonerated postmortem, and canonized. She is the Patron Saint of France, captives, soldiers, martyrs, and rape victims.

couldn't put in too much time over here. I left that job in 2001; actually, the youth ministry was shut down in my church. Then I started coming here on a regular basis. I could feel this was such a Grace to be able to talk with people, to hear their problems, to know their sorrows and their joy. The people who were suffering with terminal illness, etc., and to still hear the joy in their voices because of their faith was uplifting for me. I started to yearn to be here on a regular basis, but I knew that I couldn't stay here if I weren't offered a job.

I started to pray about it, "I could be here for a while, but, if they'll offer me a job, then I could stay forever." The amazing thing was I was offered a job, and my first paycheck came on the feast day of St. Sabina! (laughs) I laughed and I smiled. It was a great Grace that He had said "Yes" to my prayer and had permitted me the Grace to be here and in the light of Father's Grace.

When he comes in, the office is just filled with his energy, his goodness. He is a model for us. A great lesson is to be learned in observing how God works in the lives of people who give over to His Will and are obedient to His Will. Father is eighty-nine years old, and he has the energy of a sixty-year-old man. He has the joy of a youngster, of a child. He's so positive when he comes into the office, and he says, "OK, you kids, that's what we're here for"—to pray and to do all this work.

When I look at him, he inspires me to do the Will of God and to be joyful at what I am doing. I must say, that at times, it gets difficult to continue to answer the phone. My neck gets stiff and my ears get sore, but when I look at him, I say, "He's going through the same thing, and, if he can do it at the age of eighty-nine, I can do it too." And I say, "For love of you, Lord, I continue to do this even when my neck is stiff and I'm just tired." I continue to do it, and every time I do that I offer it up, and I'm

> *renewed. I'm sure I learned that from Father. I'm
> sure because that's what he does. When he's tired, he
> takes a little catnap, then he's back again, and he's
> renewed. I see it happening. I see it happening in
> small ways for me and in big ways for Father. He's
> a great inspiration. For me, he's a model, a model of
> God's Grace. God's Love among us is right here in
> Father Rookey.*

We name people after Angels, too.

Yes, the Angels. Now, that's another help to explain to our non-Catholic Christians about the veneration of the Saints and Angels. In the *Old Testament*, the Jewish Chosen People accepted the veneration of the Angels. Angels figure in the salvation history pretty strongly. So it isn't only a Catholic sort of acceptance. It goes back to the time of the Children of the Promise, the Chosen People. It is corroborated in the Scriptures.

The name becomes a supernatural affiliation of the child from the beginning?

Yes.

For accessing the supernatural world.

Who can complain about that?!

In the Catholic Tradition, Guardian Angels were often used beneficially by the Saints.

Yes. The recent canonization of St. Padre Pio brought that to our attention. He was always sending his Guardian Angel to persons who asked for prayers, favors, healings, and so on. It's in his biography that he often sent his Guardian Angel to them to bring news of their healing.

Guardian Angel Prayer

Angel of God, My Guardian Dear
to whom God's Love commits me here.
Ever this day be at my side
to light and guard and rule and guide.

Amen.

If someone is named after a Holy Person or an Angel, it makes them aware from the beginning that there is a supernatural power that can help protect them and their family, too.

Yes, like an outstanding hero in our country, it gives them something to imitate. We imitate, venerate, and praise ordinary heroes. The Saints are all heroes, especially those who gave Christ to their fellow man.

When we study the Saints, who are human beings, we learn how they developed a spiritual character within themselves. It helps the child understand that there is a virtuous way of life to which they should aspire.

Yes.

It is the same with the Virgin Mary. Many people who are not Catholic do not understand our veneration of the Blessed Lady.

Yes. Well, the answer to that is that we cannot honor Mary more than God has already honored her. We hesitate to say we shouldn't honor her, but look how God has honored her for us. We can't outdo God in honoring her. How much more should we honor her? God has shown us the way. Again, if you read

Fig. 38. *Guardian Angel*, foyer, St. John Cantius Parish, Chicago, Illinois, 2006.

in the *Poem of the Man~God* by Maria Valtorta, according to her visions, Jesus speaks of His Mother, speaks so poetically of her always, My Mother! Oh, My Mother![19] So even He can't easily find the words to describe her sometimes.

Is it one of Christ's Gifts to us that women were elevated in society because of His Mother, Mary?

Yes. Women followed Jesus and the disciples and did chores for them. I suppose they washed their clothes or prepared meals for them, bought supplies, and helped them in every way. They were giving to Jesus who associated very much with women. He wanted them to be part of His Ministry. I read that in the *Poem of the Man-God*. In the Scriptures, it is not brought out too much.

There are many miracles affiliated with Mary.

Of course. Speaking of Holy Thursday and these holy days, one regards Our Lady and the rising of Jesus on Easter. Jesus had spoken, preaching to the people, to the scribes, and to the pharisees who had asked for a sign. He gave the sign of the man in the desert, and the sign of feeding the people, and making the sea come back and drown the Egyptians who were following them. Jesus said, The first generation asks for a sign, but no sign will be given to it except the sign of Jonah the Prophet. Like Jonah was in the belly of the whale for three days and three nights, so shall the Son of man rise.[20]

According to the visions of Maria Valtorta, He mentions this in the *Poem of the Man~God*. He had spoken of this, and He explains, I was not in the tomb three days and three nights. That time was shortened by the prayers of my Mother to the Father. I rose before time on Easter Sunday morning.[21]

It is one of our prayers to ask her to intercede for us and to end our suffering?

Yes. And in the devotion to Mary, one of the best known prayers is the prayer of St. Bernard, the *Memorare*:

Fig. 39. *Blessed Mother and the Infant Jesus,* Our Lady's Chapel, St. Ignatius Parish, Chicago, IL, 2006.

Remember, O most gracious Virgin Mary
that never was it known that anyone
who fled to thy protection,
implored thy help
or sought thy intercession
was left unaided.

Inspired by this confidence,
I fly unto thee,
O Virgin of virgins, my Mother.

To thee I come, before thee I stand,
sinful and sorrowful.
O Mother of the Word Incarnate,
despise not my petition,
but in thy mercy,
hear and answer me.

O clement, oh loving,
O sweet Virgin Mary!
Pray for us,
O Holy Mother of God,
that we may be made worthy
of the promises of Christ.

So, *never was it known.* We want to ask for her intercession. Those are powerful words.

In regard to the Saints and the Blessed Mother, God wants us to ask for their intercession because they are leaders of our spiritual community.

Yes. I think, humanly speaking, the Lord said to Adam that it is not good for man to be alone, so He created Eve. It is well known in the spiritual world that they were re-created—the new Adam, Christ, and the new Eve, Mary.

According to the ancient teaching of the Church, Jesus, through the Cross, gave us His Mother to be our mother. *Woman, behold thy son* (Jn 19:26). He told St. John, *Behold thy mother* (Jn 19:27). The Scripture places a lot of emphasis on the fact that Jesus used the word *woman* like God used for Eve because she was taken from the rib of man—she was a *wo-man (laughs),* is the idea.

He used that word *woman* when He performed His first miracle in Cana in Galilee, also. Mary went to Him and said, *They have no wine* (Jn 2:3). And He said, *Woman, what concern is that to me and thee? My hour has not yet come* (Jn 2:4). Here He was, and now His Time had come, and He used *woman*. He changed the water into wine, at her request, before His Time. That is another powerful example of how strong Mary's intercession is—how highly honored she is by God.

Many of the beautiful traditions of making pilgrimages to the shrines of the Saints and holy places, having blessed crucifixes and statues of Patron Saints in our homes, having priests bless our dwelling places, celebrating feast days, having numerous Masses said for the dead and indulgences, making atonement for the sins of our ancestors, and praying Novenas for special intentions have been diminished with the advancement of secular humanism. The opportunity to live in a sacred manner that recognizes the constant interface between the living and the dead, our ancestors, has been pushed aside in our modern world, but it still exists.

Of course. We experience it through prayer and a holy way of living. Luther was opposed to praying for the dead. Luther threw out seven books of the *Bible* and violently dismissed over a thousand years of Catholic teaching, which was based on even more ancient traditions of recognizing the dead as a living part of our spiritual family. He especially rejected the book of 2 Maccabees that encourages us to pray for the dead. Opposition to praying for the dead grew throughout the Reformation. Shrines and churches were destroyed and pillaged, the bones of the Saints were unearthed and strewn here and there. It was a terrible time for the Church.

During the Reformation, there was a persecution of the Catholic Church for its devotion to the dead, the supernatural Power of God, and the Communion of Saints. A great debate arose regarding the written evidence in the Bible to support these beloved Church traditions. The book of Tobit with its miraculous

healings; the book of the great woman leader, Judith; several chapters of another legendary woman, Esther; the books of 1 Maccabees and especially 2 Maccabees, where we are encouraged to pray for the dead; the exquisite instructions of Wisdom and Ecclesiasticus; as well as sixty-six verses of the third chapter of David called the Songs of the Three Children; *and the story of the redemptive Power of God in the book of Baruch were all removed from Protestant bibles due to contention regarding the source of the original writings.*

The texts of the Bible *developed over time. The Old Testament, consisting of sections of the Law, written by Moses, the Prophets, and the Writings, was handed down through oral tradition until it was formally assembled into an official written canon over many years from 430 BC through 100 BC. These transcriptions were in Hebrew. At about the same time, other sacred works were formally composed in Greek and were favored by the Hellenistic Jews due to more mystical, expansive teachings.*

In the very early years of the Church, after the Dispersion of the Jews, the Palestinian Jews settled abroad with many losing the use of the Hebrew language. This also occurred among a colony of Jews who settled in Alexandria, Egypt, who, out of necessity, learned the Greek language. About seventy scholars, or Septuagint *(meaning* seventy *in Latin), translated the books of the Hebrew* Bible *into Greek for the Greek-speaking Jews of Alexandria. These scholars*

Fig. 40.   *Reliquary of St. Ambrose, Father and Doctor of the Church,* St. John Cantius Parish, Chicago, Illinois, 2006. A lawyer and consular governor of Milan during the time of the Arian heresy, St. Ambrose was named bishop and devested his worldly goods. An advocate for the poor, proponent of virginity, renowned theologian, indefatigable scholar, author, and orator of popular acclaim, St. Ambrose strongly defended the Church. St. Augustine was attracted by his theological discourse and, eventually, was baptized by St. Ambrose. St. Ambrose died in 387.

combined the beautiful Greek compositions of the books of Wisdom and 2 Maccabees with the Hebrew texts into one catalogue. The union of the Hebrew and Hellenistic compositions created a powerful new perspective of Christian law and spirit.

It is thought that the books of Tobias and Judith were originally written in Aramaic, but they could also have been written in Hebrew—while the books of Baruch, Esther, and 1 Maccabees were probably written in Hebrew originally. The books of Wisdom and Ecclesiasticus were written in Greek. The Greek texts belonged to the Library of Alexandria as far back as the third century BC. Although there was contention between the Alexandrian and Jerusalem scholars, the Greek texts were eventually so highly regarded that these editions were used to correct another version of the Hebrew texts that were written much later in the sixth century AD. This Greek version of the Old Testament, known as the Bible of the Jews of the Dispersion, was used by Christ, His Disciples, and the Evangelists.

Pope Damasus' synod, convoked in 382 AD, and the 405 AD Canon of Innocent I confirmed the catalogue of books in the Bible. Both catalogues contain all the deuterocanonicals cited above without any distinction and are identical with the Catalogue of Trent issued by a Council that met three different times, headed by three different Popes between 1545 and 1564 to address the issues that led to the Protestant Reformation. Eventually, Pope Pius IV, in 1564, reconfirmed the decrees of the other Popes that the Catholic Bible consists of all of the books and writings as authorized in the early formation centuries of the Church. The ancient practices of praying for the purification of the souls of the dead, as well as almsgiving and securing indulgences and works of atonement on their behalf, were affirmed as part of the living and written tradition of the Catholic Church.[22]

It is an ancient thought that we are part of the eternal Communion of Saints: that our lives are lived in conjunction with those who went before and those who will come after us. One day, we will be reunited with them. This gives tremendous meaning to our lives.

We are all part of the Mystical Body of Christ, now and for eternity. It's a powerful and beautiful way of life.

Dear Father Rookey,

Everyday my husband would light your blessed candle and recite your prayer. I know that we don't always get healed physically, but we do get healed spiritually.

My husband had a tumor in his kidney, and it spread rapidly to his bones. Our Lord saw he was in great pain and took him away from us to be with Him in Heaven. I had gone to bed and prayed, "Lord, if I am the one that is keeping him, I release him into your care." After, I heard a voice singing "How Great Thou Art." I went to his room, there was a peaceful look on his face. I told my daughter that I thought daddy just died.

A few years back, I met a wonderful black lady in the hospital, and everyday she would get up and sing "How Great Thou Art," and I do believe it was that person singing.

Another beautiful thing happened. My daughter, who had been married for twelve years, asked her father, a few days before he died, to ask God to give her a baby. He said, "Sure." My husband died on May 3rd; the doctor told her she conceived on May 6th. Both she and her husband are happy.

Illinois, June 2001

Notes

1   Rev. Desmond Forristal, *Oliver Plunkett in his own words*, Nihil Obstat, Kevin Kennedy, D.D. Imprimatur+Dermot, Archbishop of Dublin (Dublin, Ireland: Veritas Publications, 1975), p.105.

2   Ibid.

3   "Why is the memory of Oliver Cromwell such an emotionally charged aspect of Irish folk culture? A. The population of Ireland was reduced between 1641-1652, from 1,448,000 to 616,000, mostly the result of starvation and disease related to Cromwell's activities; B. No other European conflict of the same period was characterized by such devastating effects on population; C. Irish Catholics were cleared to west of the Shannon River. 1. Were told to go "To Hell or Connaught"—meaning to die and go to Hell, or move as directed to west of the Shannon by May 1, 1654; 2. About 100,000 were sold into slavery in Jamaica, Barbados, etc.; 3. Most land was taken out of Irish Catholic hands; D. The Protestant minority now controlled three-fourths of the Irish land. 1. A new class was created, the "Protestant ascendancy;" 2. But a Protestant community was not created; E. Cromwell is remembered, but others such as Sir Walter Raleigh, Sir Humphrey Gilbert were also devastating characters in Irish history." From: Seamus P. Metress, Ph.D., *Outlines in Irish History: Eight Hundred Years of Struggle* (Detroit, Michigan: Connolly Books,1995), p. 27-28.

4   Forristal, *Oliver Plunkett in his own words*, p. 38.

5   Ibid., p. 68.

6   Frank Donnelly, *Until the Storm Passes: St. Oliver Plunkett, the Archbishop of Armagh Who Refused to Go Away* (Drogheda, Ireland: St. Peter's Roman Catholic Church, 2000), p.10.

7   "Profile: Cardinal William Conway," *BBC News World Edition*, Friday, December 20, 2002, *http://news.bbc.co.uk/2/hi/uk_news/ northern_ireland/2594079.stm*.

8   His Holiness John Paul II, *The Pope in Ireland: Addresses and Homilies*, "Address of Pope John Paul II at Drogheda, 29 September, 1979" (Dublin, Ireland: Veritas Publications/Catholic Communications Office, 1979), p.19.

9   Forristal, *Oliver Plunkett in his own words*, p.105; Frank Donnelly, *Until the Storm Passes: St. Oliver Plunkett, the Archbishop of Armagh Who Refused to Go Away* (Drogheda, Ireland: St. Peter's Church, 2000); Metress, Ph.D., *Outlines in Irish History: Eight Hundred Years of Struggle*; His Holiness Paul VI, *Homily of the Holy Father Paul VI*, "Canonization of Oliver Plunkett" (Citta del Vaticano: Libreria Editrice Vaticana 1975);

http://www.vatican.va/holy_father/paul_vi/homilies/1975/documents/hf_p-vi_hom_19751012_en.html; Malcolm Brennan, "English Martyrs," *The Angelus,* December, Vol. I, Number 12 (1978), *http://www.angeluspress. org/angelus/1978_December/Saint_Oliver_Plunkett.htm;* "Profile: Cardinal William Conway," *BBC News World Edition;* Francis Cardinal Patrick Moran, *Blessed Oliver Plunkett,* transcribed by Marie Jutras, *Catholic Encyclopedia* (New York, NY: Robert Appleton Company, 1911), Vol. XII, *http://www.newadvent.org/cathen/12169b.htm;* Don Mullan, *Eyewitness Bloody Sunday: The Truth* (Dublin, Ireland: Merlin Publishing, 2002), *www.merlinwolfhound.com.*

Dermot P.J. Walsh, *Bloody Sunday and the Rule of Law in Northern Ireland* (Dublin, Ireland, Gill & MacMillan, 2000).

"Oliver Plunkett," *Patron Saint Index, http://www.catholic-forum. com/saints/sainto13.htm;* "Saints & Angels, St. Oliver Plunkett," *Catholic Online, http://www.catholic.org/saints/saint.php?saint_id=372;* "Praying for Peace," *An Phoblacht Republican News,* Thursday, 22 April, 1999, *http://republican-news.org/archive/1999/April22/22lett.html;* "Lord, we ask your blessing upon the people of Ireland, And upon Irish people throughout the world; We pray especially for peace in Northern Ireland, and reconciliation among its communities. May they reach out across ancient divisions, In trust, friendship, and forgiveness," Cathedral Tour: Chapel of St. Patrick and the Saints of Ireland, "Westminster Cathedral, *http://www.westminstercathedral. org.uk/art/art_chsp.html.*

10 *And when they were gone over, Elias said to Eliseus: Ask what thou wilt have me to do for thee, before I be taken away from thee. And Eliseus said: I beseech thee that in me may be thy double spirit* (4 Kings 2:9), Douay.

11 *And he answered : Thou hast asked a hard thing : nevertheless if thou see me when I am taken from thee, thou shalt have what thou hast asked : but if thou see me not, thou shalt not have it* (4 Kings 2:10), Douay.

12 *And he struck the waters with the mantle of Elias, that had fallen from him, and they were not divided. And he said : Where is now the God of Elias? And he struck the waters, and they were divided, hither and thither, and Eliseus passed over* (4 Kings 2:14), Douay.

13 *Catechism of the Catholic Church,* 2nd ed., Interdicasterial Commission for the Catechism of the Catholic Church, Imprimi Potest+Joseph Cardinal Ratzinger (Citta del Vaticano: Libreria Editrice, 1997): The Profession of Faith, Part II., "The Communion of the Church of Heaven and Earth," Sec. 960-962, p. 250.

14 *To each is given the manifestation of the Spirit for the common good. To one is given through the Spirit the utterance of wisdom, and to another the utterance of knowledge according to the same Spirit, to another faith by*

the same Spirit, to another gifts of healing by the one Spirit, to another the
working of miracles, to another prophecy . . . (1 Cor 12:7-10), Douay.

[15]   *And it came to pass, that on the eighth day they came to circumcise the*
child, and they called him by his father's name Zachary. And his mother
answering, said : Not so; but he shall be called John (Luke 1:59-60), Douay.

[16]   *And behold, thou shalt be dumb, and shalt not be able to speak until the*
day wherein these things shall come to pass, because thou hast not believed
my words, which shall be fulfilled in their time (Luke 1:20), Douay.

[17]   *But the angel said to him: Fear not, Zachary, for thy prayer is heard; and*
thy wife Elizabeth shall bear thee a son, and thou shalt call his name John
(Luke 1:13), Douay.

[18]   *And they said to her : there is none of thy kindred that is called by this name*
(Luke 1:61), Douay.

[19]   *"My Mother! Oh, My Mother!"* From: Valtorta, *The Poem of the*
Man~God, The Passion, Sec. 599: "The Agony and the Arrest at
Gethsemane," Vol. 5, p. 533.

[20]   *An evil and adulterous generation seeketh a sign : and a sign shall not be*
given it, but the sign of Jonas the prophet. For as Jonas was in the whale's
belly three days and three nights : so shall the Son of man be in the heart
of the earth three days and three nights (Mt 12:39-40), Douay.

[21]   "With regard to hours, they were thirty-eight instead of seventy-two,
in which My Body had remained lifeless. With regard to the days, it
should have been the evening of the third day to say that I had been
in the sepulchre three days. But Mary anticipated the miracle. As
when Her prayers She opened the Heavens a few years in advance of
the predetermined time, to give the world its Salvation, so now She
obtains some hours in advance to give comfort to Her dying heart.
And I, as the beginning of dawn on the third day, descended like the
sun and with My brightness broke human seals . . . "From: Valtorta,
The Poem of the Man~God, The Glorification, Sec: 616: "Comment on
the Resurrection," Vol. 5, p. 712.

[22]   George J. Reid, *Canon of the Old Testament*, translated by Ernie
Stefanick, *Catholic Encyclopedia* (New York, NY: Robert Appleton
Company, 1908), Vol. III, *http://www.newadvent.org/cathen/03267a.*
htm; The Right Reverend Henry G. Graham, *Where We Got the Bible:*
Our Debt to the Catholic Church, Imprimatur+Johannes Ritchie, Vicar
General, Glasguae 1911 (Rockford, IL: Tan Books, 1977); Erwin R.
Goodenough, *The Church in the Roman Empire* (New York, NY: Henry
Holt Company, 1931); Rev. Burns Seeley, S.S.J.C., St. John Cantius,
Chicago, Illinois, 2005.

Praise, Invoke, and Petition

When Father Rookey is asked to intercede for others, he follows a method of prayer that is based on ancient Catholic Tradition. When praying, he is engaged and alert and acts in a manner as if Christ were manifest before him. There is a feeling of deep respect and formality, no matter what the circumstances. First, Father Rookey uses familiar words and prayers and then petitions for a specific intent. With years of living a life intertwined with prayer, Father Rookey also has a graceful ease to his tone as he implores Christ, the Holy Spirit, the Blessed Mother, the Angels, and the Saints to answer his requests. At these moments, one senses that They are listening to one of Their favorite sons. Perhaps They are as accustomed to hearing his prayers as he is to praying to Them.

When someone asks you to pray for them, how do you pray?

I usually follow the way the Church prays. That is, put praise as number one. Just as when we approach any great person for

Fig. 41.   *Intercession: Eucharistic Celebration and Father Peter Mary Rookey, O.S.M.*, International Compassion Ministry, Olympia Fields, Illinois, 2005.

a favor, we normally compliment them. I ask a million from you, for example, because you've always been so generous with your blessings God has given you, and so on. I build you up first. That's been the way the Church approaches God.

You notice there are compliments in the prayers of the great ones like Judith,[1] in the *Old Testament*, who saved her people from destruction. Or Moses, when people departed from the Lord in their worship, or complained in the desert that they weren't getting enough to eat, or that they had no water. Moses prayed in a complimentary way. For example, you brought us out to the Promised Land through the desert for the people to perish for want of water and food? What will the Gentiles and the Nations say? You brought them into the desert to die? *(laughs)* He moves the Lord to grant his request. You are so great![2]

That's in the *Psalms* of David. Many of the *Psalms*, or songs, are songs of praise. *O Praise the Lord, all ye nations!* (Ps 116:1), for example, is the beginning of one of the *Psalms*. We, in the *New Testament*, repeat so often the *Glory be to the Father, and to the Son, and to the Holy Spirit.* That is a basic prayer. Also, the *Lord's Prayer.* Jesus teaches us. First, we praise God. The first part of the prayer is, *Our Father, Who art in Heaven, hallowed be Thy Name.* Then after praising the Lord, we ask Him, *Give us this day our daily bread and forgive us our trespasses.*

It is praise for Him, but it is humility for us.

Yes. We bow down in adoration and humility before the Lord, and then we give our petitions. Jesus reminds us that even before we pray, the Father knows our needs. But He loves to have us voice those needs as children, as His Children. Just as a mother knows the needs of a little child before he asks, but still she loves to hear him say, "Mommy, can I have a piece of toast?" Or, "Can I have something to eat or drink?" This is the way we approach the Lord, with praise. That's the way I approach the Lord.

When I pray for people on the phone, for example, I normally begin: *Glory be to the Father, the Son, and the Holy Spirit.* And then I use another song of praise: *Glory to God in the Highest, Peace to People of goodwill. We PRAISE You; we give You GLORY. We THANK You for Your goodness. Lord Jesus Christ, Our Lord, You ALONE are the Holy One, You alone are the Lord, You alone are the Most High, Jesus Christ, with the Holy Spirit in Glory of God the Father.*

A hymn of praise. And then I ask Jesus. I remind Him of His Words, "Jesus, You said, ask the Father anything in My Name and He will grant it.[3] We only ask, Lord." I remind Him also of His Words: Ask, and you shall receive; seek, and you shall find; knock, and it shall be open to you.[4] Very often I remind Him of His Words, Heaven and earth will pass away, but My Word will never pass.[5] "Please make Your Word come to pass now, Lord." And then I ask Him for the person being prayed over, if he can be healed of his cancer, or whatever petition we have. In our days, cancer seems to be the plague of our time. We call cancer by many other names, but, basically, it's about the same thing.

Do you use the relics when you are praying with people over the phone?

Also.

You basically do what you would do if they were in front of you except you don't touch them?

Right, right. God's Power is not limited. It goes out over the waters, the mountains.

ɢ ɢ

Father Rookey receives calls for prayers of healing continuously at his office. He carefully listens to each request then begins to pray for the specific intention. Depending on the request, he selects the appropriate prayers. Following is an example of how Father Rookey prays over the phone.

Father Rookey's Phone Prayer

Glory to You, Father, Son, and Holy Spirit,
    now and forever.
Lord, let His Face shine upon us and be gracious to us,
Lord, look kindly upon us and grant us His Peace;
Jesus, You alone are the Holy One;

You alone are the Lord;
You alone are the Most High,
Jesus Christ, with the Holy Spirit
and the Glory of God the Father. Amen.

Glory to You, Father, Son, and Holy Spirit.
Mary, conceived without original sin,
pray for us to have recourse to you.

St. Michael, the Archangel, please drive far
from us all evil spirits constantly attacking us,
cast them into Hell by the Power of God.
Thank you.

St. Peregrine and all the Angels and Saints,
please come to our aid.

(Father Rookey asks for the requested healing)

The Blessing of Almighty God,
the Father, the Son, and the Holy Spirit,

(Father Rookey blesses with holy water and relics)

descend upon us,
bringing us healing and peace,
now and forever.

Spirit of the Living God,
fall afresh on us.
Melt us, mold us, fill us, use us,
heal us, deliver us.
Spirit of the Living God, fall afresh on us.

Be healed in the Name of Jesus, now,
and be filled with His Holy Spirit.
Let us continue being united together
with our daily rosaries.
And together, we shall overcome.

Fig. 42.   *Phone Prayer: Father Peter Mary Rookey, O.S.M.,* International Compassion Ministry, Olympia Fields, Illinois, 2005.

Please drop us a line and tell us how things are going,
and we will answer your letter.

God love you, dear.

𝄞𝄞𝄞𝄞𝄞𝄞𝄞𝄞𝄞𝄞𝄞𝄞𝄞𝄞𝄞𝄞𝄞𝄞𝄞𝄞𝄞𝄞𝄞𝄞𝄞𝄞𝄞𝄞

Then you pray to the Blessed Mother? We believe a mother often has
a softer heart. We can go to her for compassion and understanding.
And, Jesus, a good son, will respond to the authority of His Mother's
requests.

Yes. After I praise the Lord, then I ask our Blessed Mother Mary.
I remind her of her word. Hers was a command to Jesus as it
was in Cana, Galilee, where He changed the water into wine
before His Time sort of thing. And the Saints, for example, St.
Peregrine, if it's a case where people are asking for healing of
cancer, I ask for the powerful intercession of St. Peregrine. Many
miracles have been attributed to him, millions of miracles. For
almost seven-hundred years, we have been invoking him. He
died in the fourteenth century.

That's what I tell people, "Let us continue our prayers."
I invoke the Holy Spirit first and ask Him to enlighten them
and to let His Healing Spirit come upon us. And then, I invite
them to continue their prayers, especially through the *Rosary*,
the powerful prayer of the *Rosary*. Basically it's only the *Lord's*
Prayer and the words of the *Bible*, the *Hail Mary*, the words of
Gabriel, the Angel, and Elizabeth, her cousin.

Every month, Our Lady has been telling us how powerful
it is to pray the *Rosary*. I've seen that and experienced it
so abundantly. For example, if somebody is in a bad state
and under the influence of Satan, we gather around and
pray a decade or two of the *Rosary*, and they will come out
of it. I've seen that so often. Then I'll say, "Let us pray our
rosaries together, and together we shall overcome, as the
Afro-Americans sing so beautifully, 'We Shall Overcome.'"
That is more or less how I pray with people, if there is time. If
we are not rushed, I often pray with them the prayer the Lord
gave us through Myrna Nazzour [a stigmatist and visionary].
We have copies of this.

Our Lady to Myrna Nazzour

Pray for God's Will to be done to you, and say:

Beloved Jesus,
Grant that I rest in You above all things,
Above all creatures,
Above all Your Angels,
Above all praise,
Above all rejoicing and exultation,
Above all glory and honor,
Above Heavenly Hosts,
For You alone are the Most High,
You alone are the Almighty
And good above all things.
May You come to me and relieve me,
And release me from my chains,
And grant me freedom
Because without You, my joy is not complete,
Without You, my table is empty.
Only then will I come to say:
Here I am, because You have invited me.

February 21, 1983, Damascus, Syria

This is the prayer of Myrna Nazzour, a Syrian woman. Has Our Lady been appearing to her?

Yes. I believe that's the prayer I prayed with Mrs. O'Donnell from County Mayo, Ireland, who had a terrible abdominal problem. She'd been operated on ten times, had very little bowel left, had pains in her abdomen constantly, and could not go to the lavatory normally. Her stomach would swell up and be very painful, and that would be a sign that she would have to go back to the hospital. She had only a bit of her bowel left, and they didn't think it would do any good, and it didn't. She called on the phone, this was in October, 2002, and said the next morning after the blessing, she began experiencing again the swelling of her abdomen and pains.

She was going to take her medicine, but she said she remembered those words I told her, "Be healed in the name of Jesus." That really struck her, and she pulled her hand back from taking the medicine she usually took for this trouble. She was going to go back to the hospital the next day, but in the morning, lo and behold, her abdominal swelling went down, and she *felt like a million*, to use an odd expression. No more pain. She got up, which was something she hadn't done in a long time, dressed herself, cleaned up, went to Mass and told everyone, all and sundry, who would hear her, including the priests and the bishop and her doctors. I used this prayer when I prayed over her that time. That was over the Atlantic Ocean!

A long distance call!

Long distance! *(laughs)*

Prayer works long distance. There are no limitations for God!

We have her wonderful witness letter on file.

Dear Father Rookey,

I am writing to you to praise and thank God for the Gift of Healing I received after you blessed me over the phone. My healing was immediate and very apparent, and in thanksgiving to Our Lord and Our Lady and for the good of the Church, I have told my story to anyone who has asked me, including giving my testimony on a bus while on a pilgrimage.

I had had ten operations over a number of years on my abdomen, mostly for adhesions and bowel obstructions. I had been hospitalized nine times this year. I was unable to continue with my studies or even do normal housework and cooking. I had four opinions by surgeons and specialists. There was nothing they could do for me. They were waiting for my bowel to block-off completely, and I was told that they did not know whether after the next operation I would have enough bowel left to live. I was also suffering from a bad reaction to medication the night you blessed me. My parish priest had anointed me the previous week.

After you blessed me, I didn't feel anything different at first, but I felt hopeful. I told my husband, "That was the strangest blessing I've ever had, but I think I've been healed." When you told me, "Be healed," it was like a command. I honestly didn't think I had enough faith to be healed, but you sounded so sure. When I went to bed, my stomach started to rumble and make lots of very loud noises. It seemed to be getting bigger. I was supposed to take medication as soon as this starts, and I got up to get it, but I remembered what you had said, "Be healed!" I thought, "No, I won't take it because he told me to be healed." I got back into bed and the noises continued. I was very nervous waiting for the pains to start, but they never came. Instead, slowly and gently, I began to pass air. I felt movement inside me almost like the movement I felt when I carried my children.

It went on for hours. I fell asleep, and—at one point during the night—I awoke and it was still going on. At 5:00 a.m., I woke up and was able to move my bowels normally, without pain. That morning, I was able to get dressed and go to Mass myself. My color had changed overnight, and I had energy. Everyone I met noticed the change because it was so dramatic. Since then, I can eat anything I want. I have had no abdominal pain. My bowel is working normally for the first time in years. I have not had to take medication for that problem since that night. I've told our priests and the bishop, two of the many doctors who have seen me for this problem, and all of them believe me and are delighted.

I am praying for you. I thank God every day, many times over, for the new life I am living. May God bless and keep you always.

Ireland, November 2002

When you are laying on hands, are you constantly praying to Jesus?

Oh yes, I'm constantly praying. He does it all. I don't want any credit. I'm just a big sinner. I'm getting thinner and thinner!

You're like the relay. When you lay on hands, do you feel an energy go through you too?

Sometimes.

How do you think of those people who don't make the transition of serving God before they die? They pass on, but they haven't been reconciled.

You have to give them into God's Hands. You never know, they may have had a last moment Good Thief sort of conversion.

That would be between that person and God?

Yes, and Our Lady. According to the visions of Maria Valtorta, in the *Poem of the Man~God,* to show you the power of Our Lady, Our Lord, after giving Maria Valtorta the picture of Gethsemane, praying, sweating blood, and all that, He said an Angel came down to comfort Him. It was Mary who obtained that Angel from the Father for Him.[6]

Bill Mea assists Father Rookey and the International Compassion Ministry. He has witnessed many miracles at the healing services from the blind recovering sight to the lame walking. Bill shared the following insights about Father's healing gift and praying:

BILL MEA: *I don't know where I heard it, just the other day, but the Father, the Son, and the Holy Spirit cannot refuse her. They cannot refuse her. Do we ever need to make friends with Mary!*

Fig. 43.   *Blessed Mother,* Italian wood-carved statue, Chicago, Illinois, 2006.

FATHER ROOKEY: *(laughs)*

Do you turn people over to Mary? You have Jesus working through you to reach other people, but do you also present other people to her?

FATHER ROOKEY: *The Lord came to us through Mary, and He wants us to go back to Him through Mary. It's as simple as that.*

BILL MEA: *He said, through one of the visionaries one time, "Everything, everything, everything," He said it three times, "goes through My Mother."*

FATHER ROOKEY: *That's what they say. All Graces come through Our Lady. The Author of Grace came to us through her, Jesus, the Author of Grace.*

When you pray, you ask for them?

FATHER ROOKEY: *I always get Our Lady.*

You ask for Mary?

FATHER ROOKEY: *Yes.*

🐦🐦🐦🐦🐦🐦🐦🐦🐦🐦🐦🐦🐦🐦🐦🐦🐦🐦🐦🐦🐦🐦🐦🐦🐦🐦🐦🐦🐦

Notes

1   *O God of the Heavens, creator of the waters, and Lord of the whole creation, hear me a poor wretch, making supplication to thee, and presuming of thy mercy. Remember, O Lord, thy covenant, and put thou words in my mouth, and strengthen the resolution in my heart, that thy house may continue in thy holiness : And all nations may acknowledge that thou art God, and there is no other besides thee (Jdt 9:16-19), Douay.*

2   *But Moses besought the Lord his God, saying: Why, O Lord, is thy indignation kindled against thy people, whom thou hast brought out of the land of Egypt, with great power, and with a mighty hand? Let not the Egyptians say, I beseech thee: He craftily brought them out, that he*

might kill them in the mountains, and destroy them from the earth: let thy anger cease, and be appeased upon the wickedness of thy people. Remember Abraham, Isaac, and Israel, thy servants, to whom thou sworest by thy own self, saying: I will multiply your seed as the stars of Heaven: and this whole land that I have spoken of, I will give to you seed, and you shall possess it for ever. And the Lord was appeased from doing the evil which he had spoken against his people (Ex 32:11-14), Douay.

3   *That whatsoever you shall ask of the Father in my name, he may give it you* (Jn 15:16), Douay.

4   *Ask, and it shall be given to you : seek, and you shall find : knock, and it shall be opened to you* (Mt 7:7), Douay.

5   *Heaven and earth shall pass, but my words shall not pass* (Mt 24:35), Douay.

6   "I was God Who had become Flesh. A Flesh, that being without stain, had the spiritual strength of dominating the flesh. And I do not refuse, on the contrary I implore the help of the Full of Grace, Who in that hour of expiation would have also found Heaven closed over Her head, that is true, but not to the extent that She should not succeed in detaching an angel from it, since She is the Queen of angels, to console Her Son. Oh! Not for Herself, poor Mother! She also has tasted the bitter abandonment by the Father, but by means of that suffering offered for Redemption, She obtained and made it possible for Me to overcome the anguish of the Garden of Olives and to bring the Passion to completion in all its multiform bitterness, each of which aimed at cleansing a form and a means of sin." From: Valtorta, *The Poem of the Man~God*, The Passion, Sec. 598: "The Passover Supper," Vol. 5, p. 518.

Pray, Pray, Pray

Besides the Mass, private prayer is the highest form of human expression for communicating with God. With or without words, through prayer, one's thoughts and feelings find union in calling out to God, or, in return, receiving His Grace. In our world of perpetual action, often when a soul enters the quiet of prayer it may seem uncomfortable at first. Then soon prayer may extend beyond formal prayer time as tumultuous waves of a soul's long-held feelings find a release with emotions tumbling forth for months on end. After holding back from God for so long, a soul's re-encounter can be similar to that of meeting an old friend where there is so much to tell, examine, and re-examine, but this time with His Perspective.

Eventually, when the emotional waves subside, serenity creeps in and times of prayer become times to cherish as gentle moments where the soul's most intimate thoughts and hopes can be shared and receive guidance. In these moments, a soul often petitions Jesus and His Mother for help with special intentions. These hours of spiritual nourishment alleviate suffering, replenish God's Graces, and fill the soul with renewed faith, kindness, quiet strength, and love.

Fig. 44.   *Father Peter Mary Rookey, O.S.M.*, Chicago, Illinois, 2005.

*Over time, by experiencing God's Presence
through the senses, a soul may choose to live in this
world in a different way, sometimes with new friends
and goals, and, with time for God. For Father Rookey,
prayer is as essential to his life as the air he breathes.
During many hours of the day, his breath is engaged
in prayer, silently or vocally reaching out to touch
the many souls who come to him, asking, "Father,
can you pray for me?"*

🐦🐦🐦🐦🐦🐦🐦🐦🐦🐦🐦🐦🐦🐦🐦🐦🐦🐦🐦🐦🐦🐦🐦🐦🐦🐦

How do you think of prayer in your life?

I think I hear Our Lady in Medjugorje again telling us to *pray,
pray, pray,* until prayer becomes a pleasure for us, a joy for
us; not something to be done, but rather something we look
forward to, as I do. Once people receive this turning around
to the Lord, this surrendering to God, the uniting of their will
to the Will of God, then they begin to find a joy in lifting up
their minds and hearts to God. Of course, Mass is the greatest
prayer. If possible, we enrich ourselves, help ourselves, with
this great, great Mystery of Love through daily Mass.

The *Lives of the Saints* are filled with this way of making
ourselves holy. Many people are lifted up by reading the *Lives
of the Saints.* Another great sanctifying help that God gives us
is His Holy Word, reading the *Bible* that God and His Church,
and Our Lady in her apparitions, and Our Lord are constantly
reminding us to do—hearing His Word. Faith comes through
hearing,[1] St. Paul tells us in his letter to the Romans. The
continual reading and meditating on the Word of the *Bible* is
very, very important.

How much time do you spend a day praying? What is your routine?

About two or three hours, at least, every day I pray. I've been
praying rounds of the *Rosary,* all the *Mysteries of the Rosary,* and,
of course, the *Seven Dolors* daily. Two and three times a day, I
go through all of the *Mysteries,* the *Sorrows of Our Lady.* The
Way of the Cross, a type of *Stations of the Cross,* has been a great
powerful prayer, also. As Servites, we pray the *Stations of Our*

Lady, as well, the *Seven Sorrows Stations,* which are also called the *Via Madres,* the *Way of the Mother.*

Do you read the newspapers or watch television?

Oh, just the headlines usually. I don't spend a lot of time with it. Or the TV either. I just don't have time. The former provincial asked me one time, Father Michael Guimon. You don't watch TV, he says. And, I said, "Déjà vu . . . it's all stuff I've seen." Déjà vu! *Déjà vu* is French for *already seen.*

Same news; different day.

Yes. Murders, you name it. Political talk. I do pray for all the people who are suffering in wars and from famine and AIDS. It isn't that I cut myself off from them and the cares of the world. I think it becomes a kind of addiction to be watching. Our Lady in Medjugorje mentions sometimes, especially to us Americans, to spend more time praying and less time before the television! *(laughs)*

Sometimes you say you see the Face of Jesus in the Eucharist. Can you please explain how it happens for you?

The Lord makes Himself visible, helps us through our senses. He lets many people in our healing Masses see Him in the Eucharist, in the Host, or else standing beside the celebrant at the Mass. They see our Blessed Lady at Our Lady of Sorrows Basilica on every First Saturday here in Chicago.

Dear Father Rookey,

I brought some relatives and friends to your healing service and told them how I had seen Jesus in the monstrance during the blessing. And one of them said to me, "I saw what you saw in the monstrance."

I was reading the hymn "Shine On Me" when I experienced a very strong perfume. I felt it all around me, down from over my head to my elbows. Then it was gone, as suddenly as it came. It was wonderful.

When I went to Mass Sunday morning, I could not sit comfortably, but, when I got home, I realized I had not had any discomfort traveling and no pain at all during your beautiful Mass. I had knelt not once, but three times during the Mass, not having knelt in church for about five years. I traveled home pain-free.

My friend did not rest in the Spirit, but she clearly had some experience when you laid your hands on her, as she said, "The force of the Power." My husband said his legs were shaking when you blessed him. Something truly wonderful happened to us last night.

England, May 2001

And there is the fragrance of roses?

The *fragrance of roses* has always been a sign of God's Presence or of the Saints. It happens at every healing Mass, or healing service, I should say. Some people take issue with calling it a healing Mass. It's better to say the Mass and healing service.

It's the old story. The example speaks volumes. Words are fine, but when we see a living example it impresses us much more because we are being nourished through our senses—seeing, hearing, smelling fragrance—all these things. As an example, as I jokingly often say, "Your actions speak so loudly I can hardly hear a word you are saying!" If actions don't go along with our words, we're not very effective preachers.

Spiritual directors are also a great help to us as God speaks through them. It is very hard to get a spiritual director today because of the shortage of priests. When we go to Confession, we always get a little direction there and that fills in a little bit. And praying with a group of people is a great help to us.

What is the function of a spiritual director in a person's life?

The direction is under the influence of the Holy Spirit, and it helps people choose their way through life. That's direction, trying to choose the right direction. In a smiling way, our bishop at home, Father Thomas—he's gone to Heaven—would often jokingly talk about this Jewish lady friend he had. When he became a bishop, she sent him a gift with a little note, and when he opened it up it was a gift of a pair of socks. And the note said, For two feet going in the right direction! That's what direction is: a spiritual director gives us a pair of socks so we walk in the right direction.

In the spiritual direction, it is always easy to go the wrong way. The devil is always at work throwing us this way and that. I remember a man in St. Louis, a very holy man, who was certainly misdirected because he was the breadwinner of the family and decided that he should give his life to prayer and spiritual reading and go to Mass every day. His wife was compelled to go out and look for a job to support the family. I don't know who his spiritual director was, or whether he had one, but that's an example of how we can go in the wrong direction.

There are examples of that all over. Some people leave the Church because, as one woman said, the people in the parish are not as friendly to her, so they go off to another persuasion. I often tell people like that, that maybe the priest got off on the wrong side of the bed one morning and didn't speak to them as softly as he might have. I ask, "They don't go to *church* anymore?!" In other words, I tell such people, "I'm not going to allow any person to steal the greatest treasure I have—my faith." You just have to pray for those people if you feel they have offended you in any way, or we feel they have offended us. Then we are the ones who are enriched because it makes us holier.

It is true in your Masses and in your general demeanor that the way you pray is very positive. It's not very critical. You are optimistic or you try to be.

Oh yes, *accentuate the positive*, they say. Bing Crosby had a song *Accentuate the Positive and Eliminate the Negative*. That was a song he used to sing—he was a crooner, you know.

Those are all ways. We started to talk about prayer groups. Our Lady, especially at Medjugorje, is encouraging us to form prayer groups. She is reflecting her Son's Words—as she always does—Where two or three are gathered, I am in your midst.[2] Praying together makes the prayer very powerful.

Is this a process for creating an atmosphere about oneself: changing affiliations sometimes from people who are not interested in spiritual development to those who are actively seeking to develop greater spiritual well-being?

Yes, these are ways to continue the healing process and to receive healing. Or if not an immediate healing, it increases, speeds up, the process of our healing that is taking time. When I was healed of blindness, it did not happen instantly; it was a process—praying, praying, praying.

That is what the Lord wants for us: to sanctify us through our praying. Only good can come from that. In the development of our Spiritual Gifts, we ask Him—in charismatic prayer groups—as well as the Holy Spirit. *Charismatic* is a word bantered about a good deal. It simply means the gifts, the *Gifts of the Spirit.*

Some people come to the healing services, and, as I lay hands upon them and ask the Holy Spirit to heal them, they burst into tongues. One of the Gifts of the Holy Spirit is tongues. They go down resting in the Spirit and exploding in the beautiful Gift of Tongues. Sometimes I pray over priests so they will go out for the laying on of hands. They go out to their parishes and begin healing services. That's how it goes.

There is a spiritual awakening of people as they go through the Mass and healing service. At Our Lady of Sorrows Basilica, where hundreds of people come from all over the United States and the world, the reactions are mixed. Some people who are very skeptical will sit back and watch, or they'll be critical and won't quite believe it. And then there are other people who encounter something like the smelling of the fragrance of roses and begin to consider the possibility of a renewed faith.

You often see people sit back there who see people fall down and rest in the Spirit and think, "That won't ever happen to me." Then they go up, and—all of a sudden—the Spirit takes over and makes them believers, and they rest in the Spirit and have a *rendezvous* with the Spirit.

Dear Father Rookey,

I have never felt anything like it. When you laid hands on me, I started to feel something happen. I didn't think anything was going to happen, so I tried to turn and go back to my seat. I tried to move, but my feet would not move. The next thing I realized, I was resting in the Spirit. I was crying and breathing so deeply. I felt so loved—more than anyone has loved me—and so protected, submissive, and peaceful. I hope you will come back soon. God bless you.

Illinois, May 2001

As you come through laying on hands, you encounter each individual at the services. It's really spectacular because you are faced with so many individual souls, all of them approaching you from a different experience base, or point of view, and you get many different manifestations of the Holy Spirit. Some people cry spontaneously.

The Gift of Tears—that's part of our healing process, too. That's one of the Gifts of the Spirit. Over the centuries in the monasteries, the monks had prayer at night time for the Gift of Tears. It is the greatest gift, Spirit-wise. You've heard me say more than once that some people cannot cry, so they end up like the ducks when they fly upside down—they quack up!

I had a lady in Ireland who came to me. She was a very hard-type of character. She never cried, she told me. But she came to the house where I was staying and wanted to go to Confession. She made a confession after many, many years. She received the Gift of Tears in the Sacrament of Reconciliation with the Lord. It was the first time she had cried, I don't know whether it was in her whole life, but certainly for many, many decades of her life. She was a middle-aged person as I recall.

Dear Father Rookey,

I attended your Healing Mass on July 11, 2000. From the moment I entered the church, I felt so different. I cannot find the right words to describe my emotions. I could not stop myself from crying and at first was very embarrassed.

You addressed us and said it was normal to cry as it was an outward sign of inner healing. I am not sure what you did to me to release my tears. My whole body was racked with sobs, which I could not control. For a long time, I could not stop crying, but eventually I became aware of my surroundings.

Whatever the outcome, I now know I can deal with life and that God is always with me. My own personal miracle took place, maybe not visible to other people, but it happened, and, as I said, it is still going on.

Michigan, December 2000

Tears are an indication of an internal healing?

That's where it is. The tears are often an outward sign of the inner Grace. That's why the Church describes the Sacraments as the outward sign of the inner, interior Grace.

For example, in the Sacrament of Baptism, again, God is perceived by sensible signs. Jesus gave us the water; He demonstrated it for us by allowing Himself to be baptized by His cousin, John the Baptist. The water washes. Also, in Confirmation and the Holy Orders, the Holy Spirit comes upon us through the sign of the imposition of the hands. That's why, as long as I'm able, I lay hands on each person, so that they can

Fig. 45.   *Jesus Christ Baptized by St. John the Baptist,* stained glass window, Our Lady of Sorrows Basilica, Chicago, Illinois, 2006.

experience resting in the Spirit. I don't like to deprive anyone of that wonderful privilege.

Is it true that God has blessed everyone, and each of us has a gift for healing, in one way or another, if we allow Him to work through us?

Yes. He gives the Gift of Healing even to lay people. There is a man in West Palm Beach, Florida, a man named Bob McCormick. He's about forty years of age. He's been coming to the services every year, and now he's carrying out services to parishes and prays over people and they are healed—in hospitals and other places. He carries out the services very much like we do with the Scripture, with the *Seven Dolors*, the *Seven Sorrows of Our Lady*, the *Rosary*, and then a talk. But he cannot concelebrate Mass, which is a great part of a healing service. One of the priests can do that for him. But he is carrying on, so he's received the Gift of Laying On of Hands.

Prophecy is another Gift of the Spirit. One of the wonderful Gifts of Prophecy I've seen in my own life. A lady came to us after the services. She came to me and said, In the *Consecration* of the Mass today, as you lifted the Host and the chalice, I was given three words for you. First word: *You have prostate cancer.* Second word: *Fear not* (that's a word repeated 365 times in the *Bible*, they say once for every day of the year), *My Precious Blood, which you receive, heals you.* And the third word: *These eyes will always see me,* because the Lord allows me to see Him in the Eucharist. That happened about ten years ago. Since then I have had to undergo examinations by physicians three different times, different years. They could never find prostate cancer. I guess she had the Gift of Prophecy.

Another event in my lifetime: after giving services, I think it was in Iowa, in August about five to six years ago, a lady wrote to me. She said, I never get any words from God, but, at the Mass and the healing service when you were here, the Lord gave me a word for you that you must take off a month and just fill up spiritually. Like Jesus told the Apostles, Come apart and rest awhile,[3] and pray. He was the best example of that; He would spend whole nights in prayer it seems.

I guess I didn't discern the word as I should have maybe. In any case, I ignored it. Some months later, I fell at Medjugorje and hurt my leg, and I had to take *two* months off to recover from the operation. *(laughs)* The Lord said, You didn't hear

Me? I'll let you know to do it. That was a prophetic word. I'm sure anyone among our readers and people could repeat things like that.

When you are traveling saying the Mass and offering healing services, you go from city to city and spend hours and hours with people you haven't met before or who are meeting you for the first time. Somehow they are drawn to you. When you are faced with all of those people and you begin the process of laying on of hands, it's almost like you are in a different zone yourself.

Well, it's Jesus doing the work. We are just the eyes, ears, nose, and throat of the Lord. He asked to come to us in this form, otherwise we couldn't experience Jesus. If an Angel appears to you, for example, he has to put on a human form. Gabriel had to come to Mary in a human form, otherwise she could not have perceived him. Angels don't need words because they are pure spirits. But they have to say words if we are going to perceive their presence. Everything has to come through our senses. In a lighter vein, that is why I tell people, "When Caesar Augustus called a census, Mary and Joseph came to Bethlehem and came to their senses!" *(laughs)*

It seems you get a great joy out of praying for people.

Well, it's kind of selfish because, when I pray for them, I'm praying for *meself! (laughs)* For deliverance! *(laughs)* I have nothing to lose, everything to gain.

Dear Father Rookey,

We still hear stories of your visit here last summer. Attached you will find a story that my seven-year-old son wrote about your visit. His home-school group had a writing contest in which they were to write about the action of the Holy Spirit in the Jubilee 2000. He won 2nd prize in his age division! The following are some excerpts from his story:

It was a three-hour drive to the airport to get Father Rookey and his friend. My mommy was kind of nervous about picking them up. I was a little bit nervous when Father's airplane landed. My sister and I held up signs for him that said, "Praised be Jesus Christ, now and forever." I felt a little better once we met him.

We drove to the church and prayed the Rosary on the way—for three-hours! I was hungry when we got there.

The next day, we went to church and there were a lot of sick people there. Father said Mass and laid his hands on all the people's heads. We left there and went to another church. On the way, we prayed the Rosary again. We sure prayed a lot with Father Rookey around!

A lot of people were healed after Father's visit. My mommy's back was healed by Father Rookey. My friend doesn't wear glasses anymore since Father Rookey prayed over her. Her mother fell down [resting] with the Holy Spirit, and her legs were healed. Since Father Rookey was here, I don't complain when we pray the Rosary anymore. I believe he helped me like prayer. The Blessed Mother told Francesco to pray more rosaries if he wanted to go to Heaven. I would like to go to Heaven some day too.

North Carolina, May 2001

ꙮꙮꙮꙮꙮꙮꙮꙮꙮꙮꙮꙮꙮꙮꙮꙮꙮꙮꙮꙮꙮꙮꙮꙮ

Notes

[1] *Faith then cometh by hearing; and hearing by the word of Christ* (Rom 10:17), Douay.

2   *Where two or three are gathered together in my name, there am I in the midst of them* (Mt 18:20), Douay.

3   *Come apart to a desert place, and rest a little* (Mk 6:31), Douay.

Giving Gifts to God

Each soul's life is a miraculous gift from God, for every soul has been graced with Spiritual Gifts to be developed in this world for the benefit of His Creation. Usually those talents that come most naturally to us, from the simple to the sophisticated, are recognized as God-given Gifts. Other Spiritual Gifts are bestowed later in life as the character of a soul matures.

As a soul moves closer to God, it often reflects on the strong motivations in this life to pursue earthly power, wealth, and sensuality. Attachment to worldly pursuits, benefiting primarily the self, can compete with a healthy attachment to God and cause a misuse or underdevelopment of Spiritual Gifts. Similarly, the inclination to use long-dormant gifts that are intrinsic to a soul's nature may become stronger as a soul becomes more disturbed when it lives away from the Will of God.

Recognizing the power of one's gifts for serving others for the benefit of God and His Creation often marks a turning point in the journey of a soul. The soul is released from personal attachment to these gifts and sees them instead as God-given Graces

Fig. 46.   *Our Lady of Czestochowa, the Black Madonna,* altar, St. John Cantius Parish, Chicago, Illinois, 2006.

> *destined to be shared for the greater good. By releasing attachment, the soul turns itself toward the Embrace and Care of God to be used as His Instrument to manifest goodness in the world. How a soul chooses to use its gifts determines how it responds to God's Call—what it sows and what it reaps.*
>
> *Father Rookey gave God the ultimate gift—the gift of his lifetime on earth.*

Some people choose to make a lifelong commitment to God, giving their entire lives to His service. Is this way of life a mystical marriage or union in the sense of a person directing their free will to join the Divine Will?

It depends on your calling. God calls you. As He Himself says, you have not called Me, I have called you. That is why they call it a vo-ca-tion.[1]

What was your experience?

Somehow the Lord put it in me to be a priest. It is a desire to give your life entirely to God. I also made one further step and became a religious with the three vows of poverty, chastity, and obedience.

Can we talk about each one of these vows: poverty, chastity, and obedience? Today, these precious gifts to God are not highly valued because our secular society is predominantly hedonistic, or pleasure seeking, materialistic, and individualistic. The emphasis is on satisfying our self-desires, our own appetites, instead of selflessly serving others, which, of course, is a greater challenge.

Our Holy Father, Pope John Paul II, as all the Popes have done down through the centuries, always upheld the beautiful custom of offering the priestly life of celibate ways, of priests giving themselves entirely to the service of the people. The

Fig. 47. *Father Peter Mary Rookey, O.S.M.,* Chicago, Illinois, 2005.

celibate life is a powerful example to those who are perhaps given to a life of sex.

These days, the gays are saying we have no choice—I have this tendency to be with people of the same sex, and I have no choice but to practice that lifestyle against God's Law. Which is not true because they have free will. This is not talking against the gays but explaining there is nothing wrong with having a tendency to a certain way of living or doing things, but it is wrong if the tendency is toward evil.

I may be heavily inclined to gambling. I have a wife and family perhaps, but I've become addicted to gambling, and I say, "I have no choice but to follow this." Or, if I'm addicted to drugs, "I can't help myself, I'm bent this way"; or, "I'm an alcoholic, I can't live without drink"—which is a denial of a basic point of view of philosophy, of a basic attribute of man. He has a will. He *can* will. Because man has a will, he can will good, or he can will evil. He cannot say, "I cannot." If he wills, God will supply strength to that will and help him overcome or stabilize that tendency, so he will not sin. Even perhaps as an alcoholic, he may be able to take a little libation once in a while, if he is able. That is usually very difficult, but some alcoholics are able to do that.

Or, if he's a married man, he can will to control his sexual life, if he's very much of an addict to sex, or—I should say—the misuse of sex, because sex is holy. God gave a wonderful gift to man. Your mother and my mother and father used sex or we wouldn't even be here. But many misuse it. I mean sex is not evil. But sex is misused. Just like drugs are not evil; alcohol is not evil. Everything God made is good, but it's our misuse of these wonderful gifts that make them evil for us.

But getting back to celibacy, the Pope wants to let that be a great help to those who are struggling with sex or the misuse of sex. They say, "I can't do it," but when you have a living pattern in front of you, you know it can be done.

I have before me a letter from a man who was a homosexual. I believe he came to our healing services as well, if I'm not mistaken. At least he sent me a tape of his conversion story. With prayer, he was able to come to terms with this tendency and make it normal according to God's Will, not to live with other men in a sexual way. He wants me to provide some words for the jacket of this book he's writing to give hope to gays that they can overcome these tendencies.

I remember a man in London. I showed you a newspaper article about the young man, the son of a top lord in the House of Lords, who was embarrassing his father because he was a very prominent man in the British government. He developed AIDS. He was living a unisex union with another man. He came to be blessed in the congregation line, and he told me before I blessed him that he wanted to be healed of AIDS. I did not know anything about him. The Lord seemed to give me a *word of knowledge,* as the saying is, and I told him point blank, "You must promise the Lord you will not continue this life of sodomy with your boyfriend any longer, and you will be healed." He was healed instantly. That was written up a number of times in the papers. Here you have a young man with his powerful tendency of homosexuality, and he promised the Lord not to continue this life, and he was healed instantly of his AIDS.

That goes for the other vows of obedience and poverty. Again, quoting the sovereign pontiffs, like John Paul II, it's a sign in our midst that it can be done. I can live with very little. And I can live also obeying a human superior who represents the Lord for me.

These things, all down through history, have been signs in our midst that it can be done. That is why the Church continues to encourage religious life and the vows of poverty, chastity, and obedience among her clergymen.

Those are some of the most fundamental elements, if we look at the reverse side of it, as far as Satan goes. Poverty, chastity, and obedience are the direct opposites of the worldly values of wealth, sex, and power.

Yes, those are the basics of our lives. We give our goods, we give the gift of our sexuality to the Lord, we give it back to him like St. Joseph, the Nazirite, and our Blessed Lady. Then the most intimate part of us, our will, bending our will to God through a human superior. More than that, you cannot give! Giving your everything to the Lord.

Choosing to live a religious life is counter to what we are encouraged to do most of our life.

Yes. When you are following what they are doing out there in the world, living a consumptive type of life, and taking more and more and more, and then you see somebody trying to live with less and less and less; it becomes a sign in our midst. It makes you think . . . *but with God, all things are possible* (Mt 19:26).

These are all signs in our midst. The Lord gives us these signs so we can be encouraged to live a little less luxuriously. For example, I'm a billionaire, but I can live without attachment to my goods. It's not a sin to be rich; it's a sin to become *attached* to my riches.

Jesus was a countercultural influence. Even the year in which He was born was the same year of the great tax census used by Caesar to extract money for tax purposes.

I hadn't thought about that; yes, a very good point. Well, I always thought of it in this way: he, Caesar Augustus, declared this census. Everybody knows that governments prepare censuses so they can gather taxes. *(laughs)*

Right!

(laughs)

Also, Jesus, in the temple, turned over the tables of the merchants.

Yes. That was for a different theme: about the *use* of wealth. Those people were not Romans; they were of the Jewish race and selling the sacrificial necessities for the pilgrims. The point you might want to make there is in regard to Mary Magdalene who washed His Feet and dried Them with her hair at a Pharisee's house, then poured very expensive spikenard over His Feet. Judas, who held the purse strings for the community of the Apostles and Jesus, complained loudly that this money could have been used for the poor. John says Judas objected not because he cared for the poor, but because he held the purse strings! *(laughs)* That could be a point for reflection. Jesus replied, She's doing it against my burial, for the poor you always have with you, but Me, you will not always have.[2]

There has been criticism, too, of the Church's investment in art and in beautiful sacred objects. At one time, the Church was the World's Patron of the Arts. The artists devoted their work to God and the celebration of God and His Creation. Art wasn't a selfish or individualistic pursuit or expression. It was to benefit the sacred community in praise of God.

The arts lift us up spiritually, unless the artist's intent is not a spiritual one. Obscene art, of course, is not art at all. It's pornography. It doesn't deserve the name of art. Real art lifts one up. Look how uplifting over the centuries it's been, for example, the *Pieta*, which represents the center, kind of the center, of the Servite charism with Mary holding Jesus after He was taken down from the Cross. In Italiano, it's known as the *Pieta*, which roughly translates as *pity, pity*. Then the magnificent Michelangelo's *Last Judgment* that forms the background for a very important event every time a Pope is elected, where the cardinals gather in the Sistine Chapel. He painted this at the request of Pope Paul III in 1536.

In a lighter vein, the *Last Judgment* shows Jesus, in the upper part of the painting, coming in judgment in great majesty in a cloud with the Angels of God, just as He told Caiphas during the Passion He was going to come. Then the center part of this big wall, floor to ceiling, painting shows Purgatory, and down in the bottom part of the painting depicts Hell. Michelangelo depicted a cardinal in Hell with whom he had had a rather serious disagreement! *(laughs)* He put him in the hot place! *(laughs)*

For all to see for centuries!

(laughs)

You are saying that it's not the money or the talent or even the perfume offered by Mary Magdalene, but the use of those things.

Yes.

Why is it so difficult to trust God completely? Is it our superego, the inflating of ourselves: a reluctance to acknowledge our weakness as creatures of God?

Yes, it is a complete dependence on God for everything. I guess that's where it is.

We talked about fear being an issue of evil versus good and doubting our capacity to exercise our free will and another being attachment to

material things, pleasure, or the opinion of others. Do we need to give up our fears and our attachments so we can consciously serve God?

Yes, that's what Jesus commanded. It's a complete giving of ourselves in order to serve God better. One of the earliest examples is the founder of monasticism in the Church, the Western Church anyway, St. Benedict. He had properties and he was living very well, and he had his sister, St. Scholastica.

He heard the Gospel at Mass of the rich young man who came to Jesus and said to him, What must I do to enter the Kingdom of Heaven?[3] Jesus said, Keep the commandments.[4] He said, I've kept them since my youth.[5] He was a fine young man, I guess. Jesus said, If you be perfect go sell all you have, and give to the poor, and come follow me.[6] He was a man of much wealth, so he went away sad.[7]

Jesus then gave a little sermon to His followers of how difficult it is for a rich man to enter Heaven. He used an example of a saying about the breach in the wall in the City of Jerusalem; they called it the *eye of the needle* because camels could just barely get through the breach in the wall. It is easier for a camel to pass through the eye of the needle than it is for a rich man to enter the Kingdom because he gets attached.

Notes

[1] *You have not chosen me : but I have chosen you; and have appointed you, that you should go, and should bring forth fruit; and your fruit should remain : That whatsoever you shall ask of the Father in my name, he may give it to you* (Jn 15:16), Douay.

[2] *Let her alone, that she may keep it against the day of my burial. For the poor you have always with you; but me you have not always* (Jn 12:7-8), Douay.

[3] . . . Good Master, *what shall I do that I may receive life everlasting?* (Mk 10:17), Douay.

[4] *And Jesus said to him, Why callest thou me good? None is good but one, that is* God. *Thou knowest the commandments* (Mk 10: 18-19), Douay.

Fig. 48. *Peace: Father Mary Rookey in Petra, Jordan,* Pilgrimage to the Holy Land, 2005.

5   *Do not commit adultery, do not kill, do not steal, bear not false witness, do no fraud, honour thy father and mother. But he answering, said to him : Master, all these things I have observed from my youth* (Mk 10:20), Douay.

6   *And Jesus looking on him, loved him, and said to him : One thing is wanting unto thee : go, sell whatsoever thou hast, and give to the poor, and thou shalt have treasure in Heaven; and come, follow me* (Mk 10: 21), Douay.

7   *Who being struck sad at that saying, went away sorrowful : for he had great possessions* (Mk 10:22), Douay.

Freely Aligning With God

කු

St. Augustine and St. Thomas Aquinas expressed the philosophic system that there is a natural permanent law that ensures the perpetuation of Creation. In simple terms, for example, the sun rises in the morning; the moon rises at night. The seasons come and go, and the creatures of the waters, air, and earth all live in habitats and in groups suited to their needs and in ways that sustain the continued existence of their species. Human beings live in communities of families, towns, and nations. These ways of living cannot be changed by humankind because the intrinsic conditions for life were created by God for the benefit of Creation. Conditions for perpetuating life are very precious and must be protected in order for life to continue as God intends. Each soul is an integral part of Creation; each thought, word, and action of the soul affects the rest of Creation. A soul needs to cooperate with Divine Law, or suffering will occur for itself and community. Each moment, a soul chooses to come closer to or further away from Divine Grace, from God's Laws and Love, bringing healing or suffering to community and self.

Fig. 49.   *Sun Shining Through Portal of a Bee-hive Monastic Hut, Scelig Mhichíl* (Skellig Michael), Kerry, Ireland, 2005. Established by the sixth century and named after St. Michael, hermits and monks inhabited this remote sacred settlement for over six hundred years.

The conditions favorable to sustaining life are known as the Natural Law; Natural Law is refined by the authority of Divine Law. For example, throughout all the ages and in all cultures, men and women have married. But marriage under Divine Law is recognized as a Sacrament, an eternal union of spirits, a higher level of relationship that manifests for the good of God and His Creation. When we go against the Divine Laws of God, sin and imbalance occur in ourselves, our relationships, and in the world.

Yes. It's written in the conscience of every person—even those who may not know Christ.[1] The Natural Law was written even in the hearts of the Romans. The centurion became a believer in Christ, *Indeed this man was the son of God* (Mk 15:39), he said under the Cross after the earthquake at the time of the death of Christ. That Natural Law is even in the hearts of those who do not know officially Christ's Church. The *super*natural law is built on it. It does not destroy the Natural Law, as St. Thomas Aquinas says so well, it perfects it.[2] Jesus said about the Law of Moses, I did not come to destroy the law, but to fulfill it.[3] Christianity is Christ's working with Divine Law through His Church. He came not to destroy the Natural Law, but to lift it up, sanctify it, to make it holy, make it worthy of eternal life.

People come to you requesting healing. Their lives are out of balance. Maybe they are at a turning point: they've worked for years and they sense something is wrong and that they are not living their lives in the way they should. They are in despair, suffering from symptoms of being despondent, or enduring the pain of physical or mental illness. What is the relationship between activating one's free will to request to be healed and the process of healing?

They are drawn to the healing process because of some problem: physical, mental, or spiritual. Once they turn to the Lord, just like the Good Thief on the cross, the Lord reaches out to them and brings them spiritual cleansing. He cleansed the *leprosy* of the Good Thief in a moment. That's all it takes. All it takes is an act of our will, and then all it takes again is an act of God's Will to cleanse us.

Fig. 50.   *Our Lady of Sorrows*, statue, Friars' Chapel, Our Lady of Sorrows Basilica, Chicago, Illinois, 2006.

For some people, it seems, it requires more of a process in which case the healing takes place over time. It takes time to heal wounds and to re-trace the path that led to one's separation from God, from following His Divine Laws.

That's the normal one. It has to be that first turning toward God. Then our whole life is a life of reconciliation where we are reconciled to God every day. That's why we continue to pray. At the beginning of Mass, we always turn to God to be reconciled before we enter into the Mystery of the Eucharist. We acknowledge our faults and receive His Mercy.

It's a constant perfecting process. Especially for people who have entrenched behaviors, attitudes, regrets, hurtful memories, long addictions, or struggles. We need to reassess our lives, figure out what we are doing, why we are doing it, and whether we should be doing something else that is more rewarding in God's Eyes.

Re-assessing our lives. That's all part of the process.

You teach a process that leads us away from our suffering by explaining the Sacraments and encouraging us to choose to take a path that will lead us closer to God, by aligning our will with God's Will, even if it is a struggle.

Basically, I tell them there is no other way of becoming great and turning ourselves into the image of God and of Christ, which we lost through the sin of Adam and Eve and through all the sins of the world since. There is no other way of bringing that image back except through struggle, trouble, challenge. There's no other way. We have to have challenges. If we didn't have ill health, we'd have to have the challenge of financial difficulties, or difficulties in our families, difficulties in relationships with other people, or difficulties in handling natural disasters. For example, our house has been wiped away by a flood, earthquake, or severe weather, by the ocean, or other disasters.

There is no other way to become great except through struggle. We have to come to handle these troubles and ways of

Fig. 51. *Crucifix,* Friars' Chapel, Our Lady of Sorrows Basilica, 2006. The hand-carved wooden crucifix was made in Mexico, circa 1750.

trying our strength. I often say that if everything were peaceful and nice in our lives, we would all be persons without backbone and without character, without any powerful personality. We'd be like butterflies. Always, the best example of those things is Our Lord. Look at all the difficulties He handled. Even His own extended family thought He was nuts, crazy, not in His right mind. And, the hierarchy of that time, the Pharisees were almost to the man, with the exception of Nicodemus, against Him. They were the real ruling spiritual junta. He was sentenced to death and suffered terribly before He died. Our Blessed Mother, Mary, the Mother of Sorrows, suffered with Him. There is no other way of becoming great.

A key turning point is not rejecting the struggle but accepting the struggle.

Yes. Accepting the struggle. I can walk away from it, but then it doesn't do me any good. I often think, in that context, of St. Monica, whose feast we had in August. She had a pagan husband who treated her like a pagan. In those days, women were not respected too much in a pagan sense. Today, she would have seen one of these signs that we see up on North Harlem Avenue here in Chicago, a great big billboard, "Divorce $250 and up." She could have thought, I'm not going to put up with this sort of thing. But, no, she stuck with her husband and prayed for him for forty years. He finally became a Christian. And her great son Augustine was a ne'er do well. He had a child out of wedlock and did all types of things, and yet he became one of the greatest lights in the Church.

ଔ ଔ

Dear Father Rookey,

I praise and thank Jesus and Mary every day for the countless blessings and special Graces that I have received throughout my life, some of which were bestowed upon me directly through you and the Miracle Prayer.

> *I am a witness to your healing of me from dear Jesus with the Holy Spirit! Not only was I physically healed of my nicotine and caffeine addictions, but I also received mental, emotional, and, especially, spiritual healings . . . the continuing day by day awesome and wondrous triple scoops of conversion of mind, heart, and soul!*
>
> *I now realize that all the moments and phases of joys, sorrows, sufferings, self-denial, and self-giving acts are God-given opportunities for me to draw closer to God.*
>
> *Illinois, July 2001*

What do evil and free will have to do with loving God?

Basically, evil is possible because God made us, as the psalmist says, in *Psalm 8*, He has made us a little less than Angels.[4] He has given us the faculty of free will, like the Angels, so we can give Him the highest form of love, a free love. The plant life and animal life can only give God the love that is put in them; they have no choice. It is not a free love. Or, like the parts of the universe: the sun, the moon, and the earth. These creatures of God can only give Him a very limited form of worship and love.

But to have the highest form of return on His investment sort of thing, He had to give us free will and took the chance that our free will would be misused. Lucifer and some of the Angels misused their free will, became proud, and rebelled against God, and so did man, through the temptation of Satan, the temptation of Adam and Eve, and all temptation since then. God receives from us the high form of love, the portion that comes from a free agent. To receive that kind of love, He also took the chance of that love being misused. That's why we have so much evil—the misuse by Satan and mankind of free will.

Today, personal control of our lives is encouraged. This seems to be related to what you are talking about regarding free will and liberation, surrendering ourselves to serve God so He can fulfill His Plans for us.

Well, Christ's answer to that is: . . . *You shall know the truth, and the truth will make you free* (Jn 8:32). That's liberation. That's *supreme* liberation: to know the Truth. Jesus gave us that Truth.

When we try to control our lives, are we interfering with our discovery of the Truth?

Correct.

He gives us a way of living that is unique for each of us. Is our control a way of denying our true selves? Is it a misdirection of our own growth?

If my direction is contrary to the One Who created me, then obviously, I'm not going to number one: have the Truth that would make me free, that's real liberation. And, number two: I would be confused by being independent of the Will of God. I came to do Thy Will, Jesus said.[5] He was perfect, and He said, I came not to do My own Will, but the Will of Him Who sent Me[6]

When we try to control, are we denying Christ the opportunity to reveal Himself to us?

Correct.

He has made us a certain way. Unless we follow His Will, we may not develop our gifts the way we are supposed to.

That's right. It's useless for me to strive to be an artist when I don't have that gift from the Lord, or to be a musician, or be a great demagogic sort of speaker, if the Lord hasn't given me that gift.

We need to live in concert with our natures.

Yes, so we can use the gifts He's given us. One of the great gifts that we don't realize is the Gift of Suffering. Some people are called to be victim souls. They suffer for their families, or they suffer for their country. This is a special vocation and a special gift. On the lighter side, I often tell people, "Cheer up. If you were well, instead of lying in bed or being harnessed to a wheelchair, you'd have to be working, and who wants to work?!" *(laughs)* That is an overlooked gift, the Gift of Suffering.

It is a Mystery in the Church, too, that suffering itself is a form of intercession.

Jesus, again, is the ideal there. Nobody suffered like Jesus, no man in history. And, no woman in history suffered like Mary.

Do you find that people come to you with depression and emotional disturbances because they are not doing what God wants them to do?

Very often, very often. *It's hard for you to kick against the goad* (Acts 9:"5), Jesus told Paul on his way to Damascus. It's hard to go against the Will of God. When Paul was persecuting the Christians, he was kicking against Jesus. Jesus said, Paul, Paul, why are you persecuting Me?[7] And Paul asked, Who are you?[8] It was Christ he was persecuting. Paul was persecuting Jesus because we are all members of His Body. In other words, for example, He said if we do good to somebody, then, when it comes to the Last Judgment, He's going to tell us, As often as you did it to the least of my brothers, you did it to Me.[9] He identifies Himself with us as members of His Body.

When Paul stopped persecuting people, he started on a spiritual path and, eventually, like St. Augustine, became a great Saint. But he was the one who had to freely align his will with God, to say "Yes" to God.

Yes. It's the same for everyone. We have to align our wills with the Will of God, then we can become great by doing His Will.

Notes

[1] "As to the common principles, the Natural Law, in its universal meaning, cannot in any way be blotted out from men's hearts." From: Anton C. Pegis, editor, *Basic Writings of St. Thomas Aquinas*, Vol. I and II, Nihil Obstat, Arthur J. Scanlan, S.T.D., Censor Librorum, Imprimatur+Francis J. Spellman, D.D., Archbishop, New York (New York, NY: Random House, 1945): Vol. II, Aquinas, ST II, Q, 94, ART. 6, The Natural Law, "Whether The Natural Law Can Be Abolished From The Heart of Man?" p.781.

2   "By the Natural Law the eternal law is participated proportionately to the capacity of human nature. But to his supernatural end man needs to be directed in a yet higher way. Hence the additional law given by God, whereby man shares more perfectly in the eternal law." From: Pegis, *Basic Writings of St. Thomas Aquinas*, Aquinas, ST II, Q, 91, ART. 4: "On the Various Kinds of Law, Whether there was any Need for a Divine Law," Vol. II, p.753.

3   *Do not think that I am come to destroy the law, or the prophets. I am not come to destroy, but to fulfill* (Mt. 5:17), Douay.

4   *Yet you have made them a little lower than God, and crowned them with glory and honor* (Ps 8:5), Douay.

5   *. . . because I seek not my own will, but the will of him that sent me* (Jn 5:30), Douay.

6   *Because I came down from Heaven, not to do my own will, but the will of him that sent me* (Jn 6:38), Douay.

7   *Saul, Saul, why persecutest thou me?* (Acts 22:7), Douay.

8   *And Saul asked, Who art thou, Lord?* (Acts 22:8), Douay.

9   *. . . as long as you did it to the one of these my least brethren, you did it to me* (Mt 25:40), Douay.

Turning Toward God

░░

As a soul becomes closer to God, there comes a time when it looks at itself and others through a new perspective guided by the Grace of God. Each soul is beautiful and gifted in the Eyes of God: just like each flower, each bird, each animal, each sunrise, and every bit of Creation is beautiful, and perfect in its own natural way. But although God made each soul perfect and knows each soul intimately—Can a woman forget her infant, so as not to have pity on the son of her womb? And if she should forget, yet will not I forget thee. Behold, I have graven thee in my hands . . . *(Isa 49:15) and,* Before I formed you in the bowels of thy mother, I knew thee: and before thou camest forth out of the womb, I sanctified thee . . . *(Jer 1:5)—a soul inherits, too, the imperfections of its ancestral spiritual family. As each soul journeys through life, the effect of its inherited soul print, natural weaknesses, life's challenges, and encounters with others may influence a soul to choose to separate itself from Divine Goodness and Light.*

Father Rookey says that understanding one's natural weaknesses and accepting the challenge of overcoming them are defining points of spiritual growth.

Fig. 52. *Soul Steps,* Scelig Mhichíl (Skellig Michael), Kerry, Ireland, 2005. Stone stairs lead to the sixth century monastic settlement on top of the craggy rock island located eight miles off the coast of County Kerry, Ireland.

As a soul acknowledges its weaknesses, its humility becomes its strength in its growing relationship with God and others. Eventually, often by suffering disease and distress, a soul will realize that it needs to stop leaving God and seek to return to Him and its original perfect form: to His Peace, Stability, Strength, and Love. This is the time when a soul faces the source of its suffering and makes amends deep within its most intimate self by repenting from the heart all the transgressions in memory, from the smallest to the most severe. It is the time, also, when Christ is called upon to fill the wounds where human love was absent or betrayed. Through prayer, the Holy Spirit seeps into the interior of the soul, softening the heart until it gives way to the purifying wellspring of God's Love. The soul begins to see from a wider perspective how a path was chosen that led away from God toward spiritual darkness.

As a soul forgives others, often there is a need for it to forgive itself, too, by accepting the Mercy of God and reaffirming its decision to move closer toward Him. Father Rookey often says that the process of returning to God is a beauty treatment. *As a soul begins to mirror God, it begins to radiate its natural beauty as one of God's gifted Creatures doing His Will. It senses its potential for goodness. Then the work of inner fortitude and determination begins as the soul tries to overcome its weaknesses out of love for God, to become perfect in His Sight.*

🐦🐦🐦🐦🐦🐦🐦🐦🐦🐦🐦🐦🐦🐦🐦🐦🐦🐦🐦🐦🐦🐦🐦🐦🐦🐦🐦🐦🐦🐦🐦🐦

Some people want to ask God for help without being willing to make changes in their lives, or recognizing that Jesus said, Your sins are forgiven but sin no more.[1] We receive the Grace of God, but we have to be willing to take on the work required, to change our experience of Him.

Well, if I'm sorry for my sins, I want to make reparation for them by penance. There are lots of examples in the *Old Testament* of people returning to God after the Lord threatened to destroy them and bring their death about. By returning to Him, God lengthened their lives because they did penance in sackcloth and ashes, fasting, and praying. There are lots of examples of that in the *Old* and *New Testaments*. There is a case of justice in my repentance. For example, if I've stolen from a person, I must try to repay them in some way. Prayer and fasting are all part of that process. Our Lady today in Medjugorje, for example, is encouraging us to fast on bread and water on Wednesdays and Fridays, if we can.

What is the importance of fasting? It seems fasting is a natural human inclination as it is an ancient rite, but many people don't fast today.

There must be some power in fasting because our Lord told the disciples about it when a man brought his son to them to be delivered from Satan. Satan was tormenting this young man. Satan was throwing him on the ground, making him foam at the mouth and do all kinds of strange things with him, as usual with those possessed. Jesus took the son, and the man said, I brought him to the disciples, but they could not cast out the demon.[2]

Jesus took his son and commanded the demon out. The demon came out of him, and the son became like a dead person. Jesus lifted him up and restored him to his father. The disciples later asked him, Why couldn't we cast this demon out? And Jesus said, *This kind is only cast out through prayer and fasting.* [3]

This is only one example of the power of fasting. And Mary is always telling us the *Rosary* is the greatest weapon against Satan. Sometimes a healing takes place just by praying a decade or two of the *Rosary*.

The Lord gave us the Sacrament of Confession. He told us, The sins you have forgiven are forgiven; the sins you have retained are retained.[4] He gave His Church the power to forgive sin through His Priests. St. James in his Epistle, in the last paragraph of his letter, suggests to us to confess our sins to one another even. But to obtain the Sacrament of Reconciliation, we must receive absolution from an ordained minister.

Many Catholics don't go to Confession today. Do we need to go to a priest to acknowledge individual acts of sin as opposed to correcting ourselves on our own, through our general acknowledgment of our sinfulness? Is it important for a person to recognize specific acts and to formally ask for Divine Assistance from a priest?

What is so strange in our modern world is that we go to psychiatrists and psychologists who cannot absolve us from

our sins, and we confess our sins to them. They cannot give us absolution, and we pay them for it! *(laughs)* Whereas Jesus made His Sacraments free and gave that power to ordained ministers. We need to make a confession when we have serious sins. Confessing serious sins is the first part of the healing process. This is what actually happens in a healing service.

Often the healing service will be the occasion when a person goes to Confession for the first time in umpteen years—many, many years. That is the beginning of their healing.

We receive many letters telling about the healings of people who have read the books that have been written about the International Compassion Ministry—that they were drawn to go to Confession and back to the practice of their faith.

Dear Father Rookey,

A few weeks ago, I wrote to you and asked for prayers for my family. You wrote me a beautiful letter that first I must get myself right with God and go to Confession before I could ask for help with my family. How right you were, Father! I went to Confession, and now I am going to daily Mass!!

I also told you about a test my sister had from a follow-up of breast cancer. The test showed higher numbers than normal, and I asked for your prayer for her. She had to wait six weeks for a follow-up test. Praise God! Her follow-up test not only showed normal—they were the lowest she's ever had in three years of tests! Thank you so much for your prayers.

Missouri, April 2001

Fig. 53. *Confession,* Father John Struzzo and Father Peter Mary Rookey, Betania, Venezuela, 2006.

Confession is a spiritual method for acknowledging the state of one's soul, of the work we need to do to perfect our spiritual lives. God gives us the free will to act as we do, but when we go against God, in order to come back to Him, He asks that we acknowledge what we did. He wants us to come back in full consciousness.

Oh yes, in Confession, in the Sacrament. There is no substitute for the personal touch. In fact, I am often reminded of the philosophic principle annunciated by the scholastic theologians in the Middle Ages. It is so basic: there is nothing in our intellect that doesn't come first through our five senses. We perceive through our senses. In the Sacraments, like Confession, the Lord Who made us knows that, and that's why He gave us priests. He gave us a mother and father so they could be *God* for us because we can't see God. He knew, if He came to us through our parents, we could see, smell, hear, touch, and experience Him.

With the Sacraments, He gave us signs. The *Baltimore Catechism* calls a Sacrament the outward sign that gives us special Grace.[5] Like the vows, Sacraments are signs. In Confession, we are able to speak our sins vocally. Then we hear the Voice of God through His Priests: "I absolve you from your sins in the Name of the Father, the Son, and the Holy Spirit." We hear and see his hand absolving us. By our sight and our hearing, we feel His Presence, the Presence of God through that confessor, and even maybe perceive His Breath as he speaks. We carry out the Sacraments through the signs. Our Lady, through the apparitions at Medjugorje, is asking us to come to Confession at least once a month.

When people come to the healing Masses, often they come fasting and preparing themselves through prayer. At the healing services, complete rosaries are chanted for over an hour. Is there a link in the ancient tradition of the Church of healing with long periods of fasting and the ritual forms of prayer in the Church?

Yes. It's obvious. The Lord gave us Himself as the example of fasting forty days and forty nights before He entered His Mission. The prophets fasted for very long times and received messages from the Lord with special Graces, and so did all of the Saints down through the centuries. There is no doubt about it—the power of fasting joined with our prayers.

In America today, and even in some parts of Europe, there is an epidemic of obesity. Is there a possibility that overeating, in some cases, is a kind of spiritual illness that masks emotional pain, or long-held hurt, and anger? Is it a way of preventing us from fully developing into the persons God wants us to be? In that sense, is it a form of addiction?

Yes, that is definitely an addiction, overeating. As we all know, it comes from a spiritual inner problem. Overeating and overdrinking are the same thing, really; "I drink to forget my problems." And, "I overeat to forget my problems." In that sense, it's an escape very often, not always, but very often, an escape from my problems.

Is it a way of not dealing with pain in the sense that we want to avoid suffering?

Also. Pain is a problem, of course.

Fasting cleanses our minds as well as our bodies. In fact, I am of the opinion, and it's a medical opinion, also, that we can sometimes overcome some ailments in our physical make-up through fasting—let the body, instead of being overworked with more food, readjust itself, cleanse itself by fasting.

There's a man in Connecticut called Hadam. He was scientifically educated. He got interested in the healing effects of fasting. He read a lot of literature on it. He took an early retirement and started to experiment on himself with fasting. He was able to fast on water for fifty-one and a half days and catalog his experiences. He has done other, shorter-term, fastings. He tells how the Church has always told us, and the Lord has always told us, of the beneficial effects of fasting. He said, Look at our animal friends, what do they do when they get sick? They stop eating, why don't we?

In relation to Christ, though, how do we get ourselves to stop? Is it a lack of trust in Him that causes us to turn away from the pain or from facing our problems? What is it that keeps us from returning to God and to a happy, healthy life?

I think that one thing that helps us is to recognize whatever the challenge I have to face *is*: whether it is a financial challenge, or trouble in my family, bad habits I might have myself, or

whatever—problems with my wife, my husband, or my children—whatever it is. Facing up to those problems is my way of becoming a mature and powerful character. There is no other way. I have to come to terms with problems every day, because it's in beating these problems that I become great, strong in character, that I turn to Christ, if I wish. I'm hopeful we do wish that; otherwise it might be lost energy. We return to the image of Christ by handling our problems.

Are all these things—the eating, the drinking, the not dealing with our problems—delaying tactics?

Exactly. The problems will not go away by my escaping from them. Unless I don't let them form me by committing suicide, or running away from it in some way, or by eating, or drinking too much.

God casts us a certain way. We are a particular kind of person, and we have our weaknesses. But He gives us the power to use our will to overcome them out of love for Him. If we don't accept the trial as presented, it will just happen again.

Right. What I have to finish about St. Monica is that her struggle was her making. That is how *she* became *Saint* Monica. She was the one who was most enriched by her struggle.

So everyone has something he/she needs to deal with.

Everybody has his struggle.

If we can start separating ourselves from our negative behavior and recognizing when we do overeat, or overdrink, overspend or gamble, or whatever we are doing, we can begin to observe what we are doing.

Or even smoking. Any addiction for that matter . . . drugs . . . whatever escape hatch we use to get away—to try to get away—from our problems. When we do recognize our problems, our problems become gold in our hands. That's a great motivation to draw us away from the addiction. I see this as a help to those in

Fig. 54. *Church of the Nativity,* Pilgrimage to the Holy Land, 2005, Father Rookey lies prostrate at the place where it is believed Christ was born in Bethlehem.

institutions for the mentally handicapped, for mental patients. The treatment so often is a palliative treatment that does not touch the basic cause of the mental disturbance that is very often spiritual, or even demonic. I know through experience. Many times we are exposed to mental patients. This is a mental problem to overeat, or to overdrink, or to use drugs. To overcome, we must go to the root of the problem, and it's often a spiritual problem: an unaccepting of our duties, a challenge in our life we must face up to.

ଏଏଏଏଏଏଏଏଏଏଏଏଏଏଏଏଏଏଏଏଏଏଏଏଏଏଏଏଏଏଏଏଏଏ

Dear Father Rookey,

I especially want to thank you for all your prayers for our son's healing. He had suffered all of his adult life with bipolar disorder. He was hospitalized due to medication damaging his kidneys seventy percent. He has come a long way.

He has been home at his own apartment living independently, and his doctors are amazed. Thank you for the continued prayers of you and your staff.

Delaware, February 2001

ଅଅଅଅଅଅଅଅଅଅଅଅଅଅଅଅଅଅଅଅଅଅଅଅଅଅଅଅଅଅଅ

These illnesses could be caused by memories or trauma bonds.

Yes.

Things that happened to us. But maybe, too, it is our self-image, feeling underneath that maybe we just aren't worthy enough to be healed: that the whole distance that leads to Christ, to become like Christ, just seems like such a chasm to cross. Why would we think we can be like Christ? Especially if someone is in the midst of an addiction, a personal crisis, or who has suffered tremendously, or who has hurt a lot of people, they may think, "Why would Christ heal me? Who am I?"

It may be, basically, a case of not having forgiven ourselves or others and not forgetting this memory: trying to forget this memory, instead of facing up to it and trying to forgive, and asking God to give us the Gift of Forgiveness. Christ never preached anything He didn't practice. It's in His famous prayer He gave to us: *Forgive us* our trespasses, as we *forgive those* who trespass against us. We can't receive the Father's Forgiveness unless we forgive others. Even on the Cross, He practiced that and asked, *Father,* forgive them; *for they know not what they do* (Lk 23:34; emphasis added). More practically, He forgave the Good Thief on the cross who asked for His Forgiveness. He said, This day you will be with me in Paradise.[6]

It seems easier not to forgive and to indulge ourselves in the pain. Even though we are not happy in the pain, we perceive it as less painful than having the courage to actually forgive and move on to become closer to God.

That's right. Maybe I don't recognize the problem. It has to be made decisively clear, then I can realize, "Oh, I have not forgiven you." This is my problem. To come to that sometimes takes a long time, and a special Grace that we receive certainly from the Lord, to recognize that my problem is unforgiveness. Or my problem is laziness. Then we can be delivered from the addiction.

Sometimes this unwillingness to move on that, too, comes from fear. We don't want to change our relationships with other people. We are used to a relationship the way it is, and we become fearful of losing that person. As we transition into molding ourselves into the image of Christ, is there a risk involved, or do we just perceive it that way?

Basically, it's a matter of love. Love is demanding. But it is also so rewarding, even if it is demanding. The rewards are greater than the demands. *(laughs)*

Do you think that our motivation needs to be Christ-centered? We can't just do it for ourselves or because someone else wants us to change. Some people feel unloved deep inside. Maybe that's how we got ourselves into that particular situation. But as we feel what Christ's Love is in our lives—that it transcends human love, and only good can come from it—we begin to build trust in Christ and find the courage to change.

Oh yes. Definitely. We're losers if we don't center that love in Christ. Otherwise it's simply an animal love and doesn't receive any reward.

We are not really giving anything up; we are taking the Hand of Christ to lead us through this process.

Oh yes.

We are not losing anything. We are coming into a better stage. We are handing off from one hand to another and accepting the Hand of Christ.

That's a beautiful way of saying it.

Notes

[1] *Neither do I condemn you. Go your way, and from now on do not sin again* (Jn 8:11), Douay.

[2] *. . . I spoke to thy disciples to cast him out, and they could not* (Mk 9:17), Douay.

[3] *Why could we not cast him out? And he said to them: This kind can go out by nothing but prayer and fasting* (Mk 9:27-28), Douay.

[4] *Whose sins you shall forgive, they are forgiven them; and whose sins you shall retain, they are retained* (Jn 20:23), Douay.

[5] "What is a sacrament? A sacrament is an outward sign instituted by Christ to give grace." From: *Baltimore Catechism No. 3*, Third Plenary Council of Baltimore, Imprimatur+Archbishop Patrick Hayes, D.D. (Rockford, IL: Tan Books and Publishers, 1974): Ch.13, "The Sacraments," Q 574, p. 116.

[6] *Amen I say to thee, this day thou shalt be with me in paradise* (Lk 23:43), Douay.

Fig. 55.   *The Risen Christ*, Our Lady's Chapel, St. Ignatius Parish, Chicago, Illinois, 2006.

Spiritual Enslavement and Free Will

St. Michael the Archangel

St. Michael the Archangel,
defend us in battle.
Be our protection against the wickedness and
snares of the devil.
May God rebuke him, we humbly pray.
And do Thou, O Prince of the Heavenly Hosts,
by the Power of God, thrust into Hell Satan,
and all the evil spirits,
who prowl about the world,
seeking the ruin of souls.

Amen

As a soul turns toward God, it experiences resistance from an opposite force called Satan, the most distant point from Him. In the Catholic faith, Satan, a murderer from the beginning . . . and the father of lies *(Jn 8:44), is recognized as a personality: an active, destructive, defiling force operating in the world, attracting, tempting, and maneuvering souls away from God. A fallen Angel, Satan used his free*

Fig. 56.   *Jesus' Hands Bound,* statue, St. John Cantius Parish, Chicago, Illinois, 2006.

will to rebel against Him and is jealous of all of God's Creation and the Love God has for us. He works with his demons to draw souls away from the life-sustaining Love of their Father by attacking the body, mind, spirit, and emotions. Since God created good and evil, even Satan is ultimately under the control of God for he is only a creature of God. God may choose to allow Satan's evil to strengthen a soul or to correct a weakness for the benefit of its sanctification.

Just as the movement from a soul toward God is a process, the movement of a soul away from God's Grace is a process. Although God is his Creator and holds power over him, still Satan tries to compete with God by appealing to a soul's senses through sight, sound, smell, taste, and touch, seeking key entry points to the interior of the soul. With the consent of the soul, a cycle of division, confusion, corruption, chaos, and death follows, spiraling the soul away from God, until it experiences an absence of love and hope. Yet, at every stage, the soul has the option of using its free will to repudiate evil and to accept Christ's Assistance to again seek a pathway toward God.

Process of Departing from God	*Process of Returning to God*
Division	*Unity*
Confusion	*Clarity*
Corruption	*Wholeness*
Chaos	*Order*
Death	*Life*

In Catholic teaching, there are both extraordinary and ordinary forms of evil. According to Father Gabriele Amorth, exorcist and author of An Exorcist Tells His Story, *there are six types of extraordinary possession:*

1.   *External physical pain of the body, not the soul, as experienced by holy people and Saints including St. Padre Pio;*

2. *Demonic possession of the body, not the soul, such as that portrayed in movies like* The Exorcist;
3. *Diabolic oppression, which affects health, work, and relationships;*
4. *Diabolic obsession, which affects the mind leading to feelings of overwhelming depression, desperation, and even suicide;*
5. *Diabolic infestation of places, things, and animals;*
6. *Diabolic subjugation or dependence when people of their own free will surrender themselves to Satan through the act of a blood pact or consecration.*[1]

But by far, the most common form of evil is deemed to be ordinary evil. This includes attacks from familiar demonic spirits who intimately know the weaknesses in a soul's character and inherited traits. By appealing to the senses and by further aggravating soul wounds and fractures, familiar spirits encourage a soul to develop a hardened mentality that justifies taking a path away from God's Grace.

Soul wounds and fractures can be the result of inherited spiritual bondages; rejection by parents and peers; verbal, emotional, physical, sexual, and mental abuse; the absence of proper nurturing or encouragement of Spiritual Gifts; low-level character development; home instability; and occult activity or exposure. Weakened by these spiritual injuries, a soul, by its own free will, may permit demonic spirits to enter.

A path of destruction may follow with the soul abusing itself through low self-esteem, intense anger, despair, and isolation thereby prohibiting itself from feeling the Love of God and others. Instead of drawing closer to God and trusting in Him to heal its wounds, a soul may push further away, believing Satan's lie of its worthlessness and experiencing feelings of self-hatred, mockery, and contempt of self and vulnerable others. This corruption of a soul may make room for the most serious capital sins of pride, avarice, wrath, envy, lust, gluttony, and sloth to take root.

Out of these roots come forth vices including uncontrollable emotions of jealousy, rage, fear, rebelliousness, and murder; the need for power and control of situations and over other people through domination, sometimes through the occult and sexual deviance; addictions; competition as expressed through careerism, fashion, and glamour; excessive ownership through the desire for achievements, resources, and material goods; and other serious character defects may manifest.

Permitting these vices to grow enables the soul to dehumanize and abuse others and self in a cycle of destruction that leads it even further from God, sometimes for decades, a lifetime, or for eternity. Often a soul in this state will enable, not hinder, or even praise others who inflict harm, and thereby further contribute to the damage of itself, its personal relationships, family, and the greater community. Tragically, burdened by this darkness, a soul becomes self-absorbed and may not develop its Spiritual Gifts to serve God and the greater good, thus denying itself the ability to achieve true greatness in the Eyes of God.

To combat the inclination toward evil, a soul must be ever alert to its own vulnerabilities. Through engaging in prayer, forgiveness, and the Sacraments, especially that of Confession, which is considered to be a form of exorcism, a soul can routinely cleanse itself, quickly heal divisions, receive spiritual protection, and return home to the gentle Care of God. By focusing on the cardinal virtues of justice, fortitude, temperance, and prudence, and on the theological virtues of faith, hope, and charity, a soul can begin to experience the healthy benefits of Divine Order: a stable disposition, nurturing relationships, predictability, firm attitudes, self-mastery, joy, compassion, and love.

In time, a soul's spiritual balance will be restored and magnified in the stability and love of its family and larger community. However, depending on its

Fig. 57. *Angel,* statue, St. John Cantius Parish, Chicago, Illinois, 2006.

circumstance, it may be necessary for a soul to re-form its life around others who share the same love of God, adopting spiritual brothers and sisters and parents who can provide the spiritual nurturing needed to live in harmony with Him.

Father Rookey is fully aware of the challenges a soul faces as it turns toward God. A soul's journey toward God cannot be undertaken lightly, for as it progresses, a soul will begin to define itself by what it rejects as much as what it accepts, thereby entering into a mature relationship with others and God. Guided by God's Hand, a soul becomes a cosculptor of its spiritual character. With each decision, a soul can release itself to become closer to God. As Michelangelo described his process, "I saw an Angel in the marble and carved until I set him free."

🐦🐦🐦🐦🐦🐦🐦🐦🐦🐦🐦🐦🐦🐦🐦🐦🐦🐦🐦🐦🐦🐦🐦🐦🐦🐦

What are some of the forms of spiritual enslavement?

Either we are a slave to Satan or we're a slave to Jesus. As the Lord said, *No man can serve two masters* (Mt 6:24); either you obey Satan or you obey God. A conversion is a turning away from serving Satan and turning toward serving God. That's what we are about in the healing ministry. Although some sickness, for example, is allowed by God to purify us and sanctify us because there is no prayer, no sanctifier, like suffering. Jesus Himself proved that by suffering terribly and even dying in agony to open the Gates of Heaven for us. There is nothing compared with suffering to sanctify and to be a power for good in the world.

But a lot of suffering comes from ourselves. I smoke and I end up with cancer of the lungs; or I get ulcers from my attitude, "Don't get in my way"; or, my habit of chewing everybody out comes from my life with anger, impatience, and so on. That is reflected in my body because of the condition of my soul. What affects my body affects my soul and vice versa. What affects my soul affects my body.

Many evils come into our lives through our own doing. Basically, it all comes from Satan. He weakened us through the fall of Adam and Eve, and we are in a weakened position. In that sense all evil comes from Satan in this world. It's our fighting against that, bringing the healing of Jesus that we're about. We're fighting Satan. We're fighting what he brought into the world, seeking deliverance from addictions, for example, addictions to alcohol, perhaps, or drugs, or whatever. In a healing, we're willing to be delivered, which is a deliverance from Satan—from Satan's bondage to that particular addiction.

What role does free will play in the healing process?

I have to will it. We ask, like the Good Thief on the cross did, *Jesus, remember me when you come into your kingdom* (Lk 23:42). We turn toward God. He does the rest, if we are willing. We open ourselves to His Healing Spirit. Jesus rewards immediately: On this day you will be with Me in Paradise.[2]

How are souls wounded today?

One of the great afflictions of our time is depression. I maintain that depression, if psychologists and psychiatrists would hear me out, comes from our fear of one kind or another. Fear also comes from Satan. Jesus came to give us hope and rewards, whereas Satan wants to fill us with fear of him and fear of everything. We become depressed because fear paralyzes. In other words, our life becomes unproductive.

Nonproductivity is a form of fear?

I think so. We're working from a negative: "I can't do anything, and I'm depressed because of that." I always tell people with depression that the Lord in our day sent His servant, Sister Faustina, now Saint Faustina of Poland, to remind us. Are you familiar with the picture He asked her to have painted? The Divine Mercy picture shows His Hands radiating out the rays of His Mercy and His Sacred Heart full of Love. She was given the *Chaplet of Divine Mercy* that she was asked to have us pray at the time of His crucifixion every day at three o'clock. He gave us the great words to find under that picture, *Jesus, I trust in You.* Trust is a positive; trust brings us courage and strength, whereas fear just paralyzes.

What do you think are some of the causes of fear today?

There is the fear of the morrow: "Oh, what am I going to do?" Fearing the future. But Jesus addressed that when He told us, *Sufficient for the day is the evil thereof* (Mt 6:34). Fear not about the morrow, what you are going to eat, how you are going to be clothed,[3] if you are going to drink. The Father knows you need all these things, and He will provide. Consider the lilies of the field, they don't sow, they don't reap.[4] In other words, they don't work . . . *ye of little faith?* (Mt 6:30). Why do you worry?

What forms do spiritual attacks take?

I guess the usual attacks are making you ill. Fear, that's one of Satan's great tools: fear, the shakes, and so on. Just a general malaise, making life very miserable. Not allowing a person to carry on a normal life, thwarting them at every turn, is part of it.

How does the emotion of fear seep in?

It's everywhere. This is the essence of the attack on our country right now—the crashing of airplanes against buildings and putting the fear of more attacks into our hearts and minds. That is all diabolical. These people can only be attacked by Satan to carry out things like that. Man can almost not conjure up by himself the carrying out of these attacks. Who would get a man, for example, the motivation to give his life to kill people like the pilot of the plane did, or the pilots of the planes that crashed into the World Trade Center buildings, killing themselves in the process? That's the suicidal aim. The best example of that is Judas, the betrayer of Christ—he ended up a suicide.

Recognizing evil is the first step in conquering it. It's called Christ's Love. The opposite of all of this hatred. Putting this hatred in our hearts is the opposite of God, because God is Love,[5] as St. John the Evangelist reminds us. One of the expressions of hate is fear, making us fear. It is all tied to bringing us to a sense of utter helplessness. But as often as not, if we are open to it, God again brings good out of that evil. When it gets to a point when we feel entirely helpless, then we turn to God. In suffering, we turn to God—that is the beginning of our healing.

Satan opposes God because his goal is to destroy God's beautiful Creation and a soul's love of Him. By starting cycles of destruction, Satan causes disturbances of individuals, families, communities, and nations. As Father Rookey says, "Individual sin affects everyone." By healing divisions quickly through engaging the therapeutic agents of God's Forgiveness and Love, the cycle of Creation can prevail, and the devastation of destruction can be avoided. At every point of departure of a soul from God, He is there to help the soul return to Him. Through the sacramentals and Sacraments, priestly intervention, the assistance of people in the healing professions, the intercession of His Angels and Saints, and those who love us, and—above all—His steadfast Love, a soul can turn toward Him again.

Christ offers the opposite of the devil's promises. The devil promises only despair, depression, and, eventually, everlasting suffering. Christ promises an eternity of joy and fulfillment in the Presence of God.

Division between people begins the process of destruction.

Divide and conquer. The devil believes in dividing and conquering, whereas Jesus, at the Last Supper, prayed—it's in the account of John the Apostle's Gospel—Father that they may be One, as You, Father, and I are One that they may be One in us.[6] This is a word I often refer to in my own life in regard to our non-Catholic Christians who made all of these rents in the so-called Seamless Garment of Christ that—according to the visions of Maria Valtorta in the *Poem of the Man~God*—was made by Our Lady for Him.[7]

I often think about what the Evangelist tells us happened at the foot of the Cross. The executioners, at the foot of the Cross, were going to follow the custom that allowed them to divide the clothing of the executed among themselves. When they came to the Seamless Garment of Christ, they said, Let's not divide it up, it's so beautiful, this seamless garment. Let's cast lots for it, which they did.

They fulfilled a prophetic word of the *Psalms*, the *Psalm* that speaks of the Passion of the Messiah to come. David said in *Psalm 22:19*: They divide my clothes among themselves, for my clothing they cast lots.[8] That was fulfilled in Matthew 27:35: *And after they had crucified him, they divided his garments, casting lots.*[9] They recognized this wholeness of Christ's Garment, the Church, and they did not divide it. Whereas over the centuries, our nonaccepting Christians divided the community of the Church.

First, Martin Luther renounced his priestly vocation and separated from the Church, then Henry VIII wanted a divorce from his wife and from the Church, too.

Yes. Divorce came in and that was a divisive factor in our faith, also. Now the modern divisive factors are the accepting of the killing of a child in the womb, and the similar acceptance of birth control, and, at the other end of life's pendulum, the killing of those citizens who are considered to be not contributing to the welfare of the country. There is a mentality that we should get rid of them if they are not productive. That was Hitler's thinking, too.

This division in the Church also happens within our families and within our relationships.

Well, we make up the Church, so that is obvious.

ᘓ ᘓ

Dear Father Rookey,

It looked like the enemy got into our daughter's family. After a fight with her husband over the phone, their attendance at your Mass became a lost dream. Those two really needed healing badly; they and their two little girls.

Remembering the power that God has given you, I made a hurry-up call for HELP. It worked! Our son-in-law flew in from Colorado to a cold, nonreceptive wife. Even so, we arrived at church at 9:30 a.m., the

seven of us. My son came along, too, with his little boy who has attention deficit disorder. We all wrote out our petitions. By the end of your meditation on the Rosary, *our feisty daughter and her husband were holding hands. A miracle!*

By 11:00 a.m., my son said that he couldn't stay any longer because his son was having trouble. He had already written his petitions that were now in your hands. You said you would read seven petitions in honor of Our Lady's Seven Sorrows. Out of that huge bundle, you pulled my son's petition for his son's healing. Now, to further confirm that our needs were heard by the Lord, when the volunteers took handfuls of the petitions to pass out for us all to pray for our neighbors—can you believe—two of mine were returned to our pew? On the petitions were written, "Healing for our grandson," and, "Asking God to right the wrong in our lives," which meant to sanctify our marriages and asking God to make the children holy. A miracle! Upon the altar, you so humbly blessed us together as a family.

My daughter, who hadn't spoken to her husband on the way to the service, never stopped talking joyfully to her husband all the way home. A miracle! The two children were thrilled over Mary and the Child Jesus' image on the wall.

Illinois, 2001

Once there is division, confusion settles in. How do we regain the clarity to reverse this process?

This is the *Feast of St. Hilary*. He was a great speaker and defender of the faith against heresy. He tried to clarify the basic dogmas of the Church through his writings. By dwelling on the fundamentals of our faith, the Trinity and the salvation history, especially of Our Lord and the Blessed Lady, we can see our own lives more clearly, and God's Hand working in our lives. Regaining clarity is a process called conversion. Evil makes us

confused. For example, our addictions to drugs, our addictions to alcohol, to pornography, gambling, lust, or whatever our addictions are may confuse our direction, our minds, and the direction of our lives. Whereas the Word of God brings clarity into our lives, turning our lives from the evil, or whatever we've been doing against God. Then we begin to see clearly the direction we should be taking in our lives to overcome the evil and the diseases that come from these behaviors. The misuse of sex brought on the terrible plague of AIDS, for example. Once we turn from those evils in our lives, then we begin to have clearness, and that clearness comes even into our physical makeup.

Turning to God makes us whole in the sense we are complete and perfect.

Right. In the *Bible*, in the *New Testament*, so often the Evangelists prefaced a healing by saying, "Jesus, cast out the devil," and the person was healed and made whole. Diseases they thought of as the devil, which is not theologically incorrect, because the devil started disease. Once he conquered Adam and Eve, made them fall, the whole universe, the whole perfect order that the Lord created in the universe and in our bodies that are little universes, was disturbed. To this day, we call sickness *disease*. We are *not at-ease* when we are sick. "I have a headache." I'm not at ease. "I can't walk properly." I'm ill at ease. *Dis-eased.* Like in the army when they say, "At-ease."*(laughs)*

I always invoke the Power of God to cast out demons, even if a person says he only has a headache, because evil is behind it. The headache wouldn't be there if it weren't for Satan. We should be perfectly healthy. We should never even die, just have a change of residence from an earthly paradise to a celestial one.

Underlying the issue of abortion today is this idea of self-will or self-control.

Yes, I want to control my body.

But at the same time, there may be an unborn person who's going to contribute to the benefit of the world, or to their children in the next generation.

Fig. 58. *Annunciation,* painting, St. John Cantius Parish, Chicago, Illinois, 2006.

Right.

Dear Father Rookey,

I am writing to thank you for praying for my son. In June, 1998, it was discovered that the baby had brain cysts and bilateral rocker bottom feet. His death was predicted at birth or by age one.

I was offered an amniocentesis and an abortion. We prayed about the amniocentesis and felt it wasn't right for our little boy. We asked for and received much prayer including a request from your ministry by my mom. The end result was a healthy, full-term baby boy.

This whole event blessed us in so many ways. God revealed to me how much He loved our child. And while I never felt that God would heal our son, I knew that God loved him immensely, and God would provide for us, whatever happened. I also had such a strong sense of how much God loves all unborn children. God again proves the truth of Romans 8:28: All things work together unto good.

Michigan, 2001

There's also the fear due to emotional and mental confusion stemming from severe financial difficulties and work demands; the opposition of the father to assume responsibilities; family rejection of the relationship, or the absence of support; career and family ambition; and other divisive factors. It is this family and personal chaos that brings about the conditions that lead to death instead of to the acceptance of new life and the willingness to engage in the Mystery of God's Plan for us.

Right, right.

It is a similar experience of confusion and chaos that often precedes divorce, too. It gets back to contemporary bondage today, how people do not serve God but themselves. You are saying it requires spiritual discipline to love a person and God freely.

Right, and in a more practical coming down to earth with that idea, married couples have to realize that their love is centered in their will. The ephemeral kinds of attraction that come from beauty, looks, manners, and so on, are all helps to our free will. But basically, my love must be the love of the will and that's reflected in the marriage vows: In sickness and in health, in good times, bad times, poverty and riches, I take you for myself. It is reflected there that we love from our wills not with a love that is based on passing beauty, or whatever. It is entrenched in my will if I marry, whether a lady or a man. That is really where the love is.

The beautiful marriage of Mary and Joseph is a good example, the mother of Jesus and the foster-father of Jesus. They lived as brother and sister, so their love did not depend on sexual attraction; they offered that to God. God respected that. Joseph was a so-called Nazirite, part of an early religious movement in the Jewish tradition. Young men offered themselves to God, and offered their desires for alcohol, sexual desires, and all to God, usually, however, for a time, not necessarily for life. Joseph was one of those. Mary and Joseph lived as brother and sister. Yet, no couple loved each other like that couple. It was a very superior kind of love because it was not based on sex or beauty but on will: their life of denial to what was normally very appropriate for them.

Dear Father Rookey:

I wrote to you almost eighteen months ago to ask for your prayers because my wife had just left me. Since then, I followed your advice and I maintained a steadfast prayer vigil. Well, a miracle happened. My wife and I are back together again.

During the month of May in 1997, I prayed the Rosary on a daily basis. In the last week of May, a friend suggested that I pray a Novena to Saint Rita.

No sooner was the month of May over than my wife came to me and said she was reassessing her decision to leave me and was open to talking to me again.

I believe this is a true miracle. Bless you for the miracles that you bring to us through the Holy Spirit.

Australia, 1998

We have the free will every moment to love or not love. We are called to take the position that we will love whether or not our love is returned. Is the act of loving then an act of faith? And, out of that love can we return to a sense of order, which is the opposite of chaos, allowing us to heal the cycle of destruction?

Right.

Once a person embarks on a path of destruction, it brings disorder to everyone in his/her life, not just him/herself, whereas God wants us to have order, simplicity, and calmness in our lives. Is that right?

Certainly.

Satan opposes virtue. In the Catholic faith tradition, a virtue, or courage, is the habitual orientation of the soul toward goodness. A soul can choose to move closer to God and away from Satan by living virtuously. However, while a soul may have a high command of one virtue, due to its weaknesses, it may not have command of others, and, as a result, be out of balance with God's Peace. The forces of evil are always working to influence a soul to reject the virtues desired by God and destabilize its peace.

Just as God is opposed by Satan, the virtues are opposed by corresponding sins. According to the

Catholic Catechism, *there are seven Capital Virtues that are opposed by seven Capital Sins.*

Capital Virtue	Opposing Sin
Chastity	Lust
Temperance	Gluttony
Liberality	Avarice
Diligence	Sloth
Meekness	Wrath
Brotherly Love	Envy
Humility	Pride[10]

A soul strengthens as it develops its spiritual character through the development of virtues. Gradually, a soul will grow to prize those characteristics that are most reflective of God and freely choose to emulate those virtues that are most beneficial to itself, its family, and community, thereby strengthening itself in body, mind, and spirit. According to the Catholic Encyclopedia, *there are three main categories of virtues: intellectual, moral, and theological:*

> *The virtues of the intellect include an orientation toward truth as expressed in the speculative intellectual virtues of wisdom, science, and understanding and the practical intellectual virtues of art, including useful and fine art, and prudence, a manner of conduct.[11]*
> *Three moral virtues include justice, of which the virtues of religion, piety, gratitude, liberality or generosity and affability are annexed; fortitude of which the virtues of patience, munificence, and magnanimity and perseverance are associated; and the three virtues of temperance, which include subordinate virtues of abstinence, sobriety,*

Fig. 59. *Altar Crucifix*, St. Ignatius Parish, Chicago, Illinois, 2006.

and chastity, and the annexed virtues of continence, humility, meekness, and modesty.[12] *The great theological virtues are faith, hope, and charity.*[13]

In addition to the spiritual virtues, a soul is assisted by developing the Gifts and Fruits of the Holy Spirit:

Gifts of the Holy Spirit

Wisdom
Understanding
Counsel
Fortitude
Knowledge
Piety
Fear of the Lord[14]

Fruits of the Holy Spirit

Charity
Joy
Peace
Patience
Kindness
Goodness
Generosity
Gentleness
Faithfulness
Modesty
Self-control
Chastity[15]

ৡৡৡৡৡৡৡৡৡৡৡৡৡৡৡৡৡৡৡৡৡৡৡৡৡৡৡৡ

He wants to lead us to peace and happiness. The Catholic Church has given us the Catholic Catechism *that outlines this process of how to perfect our spiritual lives.*

Yes. Perfection *through* the Gifts of the Holy Spirit.

We have the Gifts of the Holy Spirit and the virtues. Those are ideals we should aspire to develop in ourselves. In your life, how do you think about the virtues?

The religious life is an attempt to develop all of the virtues. Some Orders are especially outstanding for certain virtues. For example, St. Francis and the Franciscan Order are associated with the virtue of poverty.

Poverty meaning the poverty of material things, a sense of selflessness.

Yes, selflessness. Well, the best example of that is St. Francis when his father faulted him for giving away so much. The family was fairly wealthy. St. Francis' father brought him before the judge, who was a bishop by the way, as there was no separation of Church and State in those days. *(laughs)* Francis took off his clothes and said, From now on, I'll be like Jesus, without anything, and gave them to his father. Jesus always blessed the poor: Blessed are you who are poor, for yours is the Kingdom of Heaven.[16] And: Whoever gives even a cup of cold water to one of these little ones in the name of a disciple, truly I tell you, none of these will lose their reward.[17]

The poor have always been assisted by the Church and the Saints. The firstfruits of the harvest were given to help feed the poor and vulnerable of the community. Later on during the Reformation, Calvin was critical of the poor. He viewed the accumulation of personal wealth as a sign of God's Blessing. But that was counter to what Jesus taught: the Mercy He showed to the outcast, to those of little means.

In Sirach, Ecclesiasticus, one of the books that was taken out of the Protestant bibles during the Reformation, there are many verses on how to treat the poor: *Despise not the hungry soul : provoke not the poor in his want. Afflict not the heart of the needy, and defer not to give to him that is in distress. Reject not the petition of the afflicted : and turn not away thy face from the needy.*

Turn not away thy eyes from the poor for fear of anger : and leave not to them that ask of thee to curse thee behind thy back . . . Bow down thy ear cheerfully to the poor, and pay what thou owest, and answer him peaceable words with mildness (Sir 4:2-8). *And stretch out thy hand to the poor, that thy expiation and thy blessing may be perfected* (Sir 7:36). So blessed are the poor.

The Poor Clares, St. Clare's Order, is affiliated with the Franciscans.

Yes, the Poor Clares, too.

There are other Orders that focus on education?

Yes. The lifting up, especially the young, to the virtuous life. The Jesuits seem to be known for their education and for teaching the truth of the faith. There are many feminine Orders that have adopted teaching—the School Sisters of Notre Dame and the Sisters of St. Joseph. And there are others who teach the virtue of the Passion and reach out to the sick. St. Camillus founded his Order for the tending of the sick. His original foundation is on an island in the Tiber River in Rome. It is a big hospital.

St. Padre Pio founded a hospital, too.

Yes. He founded a hospital in San Giovanni Rotondo. He reached out in a spiritual as well as a physical way helping the souls.

And Blessed Mother Teresa's Order, the Sisters of Mercy.

Yes. They minister to the poorest of the poor.

Fig. 60. *St. Clare of Assisi*, stained glass window, St. John Cantius Parish, Chicago, Illinois, 2006. St. Clare was a close friend and disciple of St. Francis of Assisi. Like him, she devoted her life to Christ and founded the Order of Poor Ladies (Poor Clares) relying solely on alms and living in seclusion. Once when her convent was besieged, St. Clare held the Blessed Sacrament at the gates and prayed until safety was restored. She is the Patron Saint of needle workers, laundresses, goldsmiths, television writers, and the Santa Clara Pueblo, among others.

O Holy Spirit,

Eternal Spring of joy and peace,
open the hearts of young women,
so that a new flowering of holy vocations
may show forth the fidelity of your love,
and help all people to know Christ,
the true Light come into the world.

Amen

Pope John Paul II

There are the service virtues of providing direct assistance and there are the spiritual virtues that are the charism of the contemplative Orders.

Yes. Praying—the virtue of prayer. The Carthusians are an expression of a contemplative Order.

And the Carmelites?

Yes, although the Carmelites are mixed: active and contemplative.

The Benedictines are known for their spiritual warfare. St. Benedict is the Patron Saint of Exorcists.

Right. And, we'll be celebrating the *Feast of St. Anthony* on the 17th of January. St. Anthony Abbott founded the monastic system in the Eastern part of the Church, the Desert Fathers, and so on. That's a contemplative Order also.

Fig. 61.   *Sisters in Christ*, Ordination Mass, Cathedral of Caracas, Caracas, Venezuela, 2006.

We need to engage this process of seeking a holier life and make a decision to get our lives in order and to have God as our focus followed by our family and our work—all strengthened by a life of prayer. Can we talk about the opposite forces at work as we begin to change our focus? Satan tries to disrupt our process of turning toward God. When you pray, do you become more sensitive to these different forces?

Very much so.

Prayer heightens our sensitivity to the presence of evil. Do you find when you go to certain places, or when you encounter people, or when you are moving around out in the world that you can sense the presence of that opposite force? Do the spirits of mockery, pride, jealously, lust, occultism, and rebellion manifest more frequently?

Yes, very much so. But I'm not as sensitive to it as many people are. Many people sense it. Down in Mexico, for example, we went to a church. We have about thirty-five or so people who travel around the churches, set up everything, and act as catchers for the people who rest in the Spirit, and take up the collection. *(laughs)* As we came to this church, many of them said, Oh, we sense a terrible presence, it's demonic here! Sure enough, when it came to the laying on of hands after Mass, there must have been a good twenty-five to thirty, if not more, people who gave signs of being either possessed or being attacked by Satan. He was throwing them on the floor, speaking obscenities, maybe spitting on me, or telling me to go to the hot place. *(laughs)* The usual signs of being attacked by Satan, if not possessed by him.

There were so many cases that we had to delegate little groups of these people to pray over them and cast out or dispossess the person. I would try to come along and finish it off because the priestly orders are very powerful. That's one of the gifts the Lord gave the Apostles, and, of course, the priests and bishops who follow Our Lord as His successors. They are carrying on, and when they die, we have to continue that work. They have this added power. The power of the priesthood is very powerful against Satan.

Fig. 62.   *El Señor de Los Milagros (Jesus of the Miracles)*, Peruvian mixed-media painting, St. Ignatius Parish, Chicago, Illinois, 2006.

Can there be infestations of spirits in physical buildings or areas as well as in people themselves?

Oh, definitely. We had another case of a lady and her husband in Kentucky where they bought a house that already had been owned, a used house. They went into the house to start preparing to move into it, and she sensed a terrible presence in this house once they moved in. Wow. Their little child, who was only two years old, began to be afflicted by a spirit, by whatever was in that house. She couldn't sleep. She would come out with the words of these devils who would afflict her. She would say, No, we don't say that! The demons wanted her to say obscenities, blasphemous words. She is a very intelligent little girl for her age, a precocious child. They asked if they could come up here. Her mother and the child's godmother came with her and prayed for her here. They came up for Mass.

When she went back, was the child dispossessed?

It was a great help. She's getting over it. They had Masses celebrated in the house and everything. Still it didn't seem to work. But we haven't heard from them in some time, so I guess things are going better. No news is good news. If they were still being afflicted, they would be on the phone for more blessings.

Did you also raise the idea of using blessed salt?

Yes, I told them to use all the sacramentals: blessed salt, sprinkled along the edges of the rooms, holy water, blessed medals, all the blessed objects, crucifixes, and so on.

Did you tell them to have their child drink holy water?

Oh, yes.

And themselves, too?

Yes.

 rece

Blessed Salt

By Rev. John H. Hampsch, C.M.F.

The Vatican II urges us to participate "intelligently and actively" in the use of sacramentals, just as in the use of Sacraments. Salt in the ancient world was a precious commodity that was even monopolized by the royalty in Egypt and Persia. Roman soldiers were partially paid with packets of salt or "sal" in Latin; this was the origin of our word "salary" and of phrases like "worth his salt." Being costly, salt was an appropriate offering to God as a "covenant of salt" *(Lev. 2:13; II Chrn 13:5; Num. 18:19), used in sacrifices by the Israelite (Ek. 43:24), and for the accompanying sacrificial meal (Gen 31:54).*

Belief in salts preservative and healing properties led to its use to dry and harden the skin of newborns (Ezek. 16:4) and to prevent umbilical cord infection. Used for 3500 years to preserve meats from deterioration, it became a symbol of preservation and spiritual incorruptibility that was to characterize anyone offering sacrificial worship. Shared at the sacrificial meal, salt became a symbol of friendship and hospitality, a custom and symbolism still used today in Arab culture. Jesus referred to this salt symbolized friendship covenant in Mark 9:50: "Have salt in yourselves and be at peace with one another"—that is, "preserve that quality (flavor) that makes you a blessing to one another." *Note the double symbol of preservation and flavoring.*

This double primary symbolization is also found in Paul's advice in Col. 4:6: "Let your conversation be always full of grace, seasoned with salt, so that you may know how to answer everyone." That is, let it be wholesome and savory, preserved from the corrupting conversation of worldlings (3:8 and Eph

4:29). His use of the word 'salt' may also have referred to another of its symbols: spiritual wisdom, since the Latin word for savor or taste, "sapientia", is the same as for wisdom.

Some or all of these symbols may have been implied in Jesus' words to his chosen ones, describing them as the "salt of the earth" (Mt. 5:13). He especially indicated that they were to oppose the world's corruption, reminding them that, as salt must preserve its own anticorruptive quality, they too must preserve their anticorruptive influence in a sin-corrupted world (Luke 14:34).

The blessing promised by God on food and water, as well as the prevention of miscarriages and agricultural catastrophes (Ex 23:25-26) was extended by God through Elisha in Jericho (II Kings 2:20-21), when he was inspired to put salt into the contaminated water. Adding salt to already brackish water to decontaminate it made the miracle all the more impressive, since one would expect the opposite effect. This first miracle of Elisha is the primary Scriptural basis for the sacramental use of blessed salt today, as the Roman Ritual indicates.

As a Catholic sacramental, salt blessed by the liturgical prayer of a priest may be used by itself, unmixed, as in exorcisms, and formerly in the exorcistic prayer at baptism, or it may be mixed with water to make holy water, as the Ritual prescribes reminiscent of Elisha's miracle. In whichever form, it is intended to be an instrument of grace to preserve one from the corruption of evil occurring as sin, sickness, demonic influence, or other manifestation. As in the case of all sacramentals, its power comes not from the sign itself, but by means of the Church's official, liturgical, not private, prayer of blessing—a power the Church derives from Christ himself (Matt. 16:19 and 18:18). As the Vatican II document on the Liturgy states (art. 61), both Sacraments and sacramentals sanctify us, not of themselves, but by power flowing from the redemptive act of Jesus, elicited by the Church's intercession to be directed through those external signs and elements. Hence sacramentals like blessed salt and holy water are not to be used superstitiously as having self-contained power, but as "focus-points" funneling one's faith toward Jesus, just as a flag is used as a "focus-point" of patriotism, or as handkerchiefs were used to focus faith for healing and deliverance by Paul (Acts 19:12).

Thus used nonsuperstitiously, modest amounts of blessed salt may be sprinkled in one's bedroom or across thresholds to prevent burglary, in cars for safety, etc. A few grains in drinking water or used in cooking or as food seasoning often bring astonishing spiritual and physical benefits, as I have personally witnessed many times. As with the use of Sacraments, much depends on the faith and devotion of the person using salt or any sacramental. This faith must be Jesus-centered, as was the faith of the blind man in John 9; he had faith in Jesus, not in the mud and spittle used by Jesus to heal him.

In light of this, we can see why Vatican II states that "there is hardly any proper use of material things which cannot thus be directed toward the sanctification of persons and the praise of God" (art. 61 of Liturgy document). Hence new sacramentals may also be added when rituals are revised (art. 79). Blessed salt is certainly not a new sacramental, but the Holy Spirit seems to be leading many to a new interest in its remarkable power as an instrument of grace and healing. Any amount may be presented to a priest for his blessing, using the following official prayer from the Roman Ritual:

"Almighty God, we ask you to bless this salt, as once you blessed the salt scattered over the water by the prophet Elisha. Wherever this salt (and water) is sprinkled, drive away the power of evil, and protect us always by the Presence of your Holy Spirit. Grant this through Christ our Lord. Amen.[18]

(Reprinted with the permission of Rev. John H. Hampsch, C.M.F., Claretian Ministries)

It's interesting because a lot of people either don't know those practices today, or they don't believe in them. During the post-Reformation, the so-called Age of Enlightenment, there was a move to dismiss the existence of the supernatural and our ability to intimately interface with God, especially through the Sacraments. As a result, today there are many people who don't believe in the supernatural because they think humans can understand everything through reason or science. But as human beings, we are limited naturally by our senses; just like other creatures, we simply don't have the ability to completely understand God's Power and Mystery. Does disbelieving in the "super"-natural empower those spirits?

Yes. That's what the devil wants: for us not to believe. Then he can do with us what he wills.

Bill Mea provided the following witness of events that took place at Our Lady of Sorrows Basilica during a healing service:

BILL MEA: *We had a young lady who came to a healing service one time. After Father blessed her, she rested in the Spirit. For some reason, I was glued to her. I knelt down and started praying. The more I prayed for her, the worse her state became. Then she started hissing like a snake. I caught Vicki's eye, Father's secretary, and said, "Get Father." I stayed kneeling and praying, and, in a few minutes, she got worse and started getting agitated and hissing like a snake. When I looked up, there were about six people with me praying. Finally, Father finished with his blessing, and he came over and started praying over this girl. It took about forty-five minutes before she came out of it. I figured she's over it. The devil is gone.*

I was in for a surprise. She told me she had played with an Ouija board. She did belong to a prayer group, praise God. But when she prayed, she felt there was a blockage in her throat. You could hear her, but she

Fig. 63.   *Vicki Guiterrez and Bill Mea,* International Compassion Ministry, Betania, Venezuela, 2006.

said she felt there was something around her throat that kept the prayers from coming out. I saw her later, and she said the same thing happened at her prayer group. There was a priest there, and he prayed for her, and she came out of it. It happened two more times. The last one was at Our Lady of Sorrows. The upshot of it was it took an hour and a half to get rid of that devil. There were at least four devils in that lady that needed to be expelled.

FATHER ROOKEY: *You brought her to the choir chapel. I prayed with her awhile.*

BILL MEA: *I had a bottle of holy water, and when I would throw it on her, her body would jump off the ground. She was cursing in tongues. Remember that? She was cursing in tongues, and you said, "That was right out of Hell." They put on a face straight out of Hell, like a devil. Their eyes roll back in their heads. Their eyes become white. Father took the holy water, unscrewed the cap, and poured the whole bottle down her throat. She never even swallowed. It was like it was going down a sewer. In three minutes it was over with.*

FATHER ROOKEY: *Holy water is a powerful sacramental.*

BILL MEA: *Another time I saw a young lady. I was standing near the altar at the beginning of the service, and there was a young lady standing four or five down from me who was going to be blessed. You threw the holy water, and I was catching someone, and I felt the holy water hit me. For some reason, I turned to the right, and I saw this young lady. And when the holy water hit her, she went back about six feet and fell on the ground. Powerful. The holy water is powerful. She went down like a ton of bricks, then got up.*

FATHER ROOKEY: *My mother used to sprinkle us in our rooms every night—all the rooms.*

Notes

1   Gabriele Amorth, *An Exorcist Tells His Story* (San Francisco, CA: Ignatius Press, 1999), p. 33-36.

2   *Truly I tell you, today you will be with me in Paradise* (Lk 23:43), Douay.

3   *Do not be solicitous for your life, what you shall eat, nor for your body, what you shall put on* (Mt 6:25), Douay.

4   *Your Heavenly Father knows you need all these things. Consider the lilies of the field . . . they labour not, neither do they spin* (Mt 6:28), Douay.

5   *He that loveth not, knoweth not God: for God is charity* (1 John 4:8), Douay.

6   *. . . that they all may be one. As thou, Father, in me, and I in thee; that they also may be one in us . . .* (Jn 17:21), Douay.

7   "Even the mantle woven by His Mother," From: Valtorta, *The Poem of the Man~God*, The Passion, Sec. 599: "The Agony and the Arrest at Gethsemane," Vol. 5, p. 533.

8   *They parted my garments amongst them; and upon my vesture they cast lots* (Ps 22:19), Douay.

9   *And after they had crucified him, they divided his garments, casting lots* (Mt 27:35), Douay.

10   "Vices can be classified according to the virtues they oppose, or also be linked to the capital sins which Christian experience has distinguished, following St. John Cassian and St. Gregory the Great. They are called "capital" because they engender other sins, other vices. They are pride, avarice, envy, wrath, lust, gluttony, and sloth or acedia." From: *Catechism of the Catholic Church*, 2nd ed., "The Proliferation of Sin," Sec. 1866, p. 457.

     "Seven Deadly Sins," *http://www.answers.com/topic/seven-deadly-sinsAurelius Clemens Prudentius, http://www.catholicity. com/encyclopedia/p/prudentius,aurelius_clemens.html.*

     "Aurelius Prudentius (Hymn-Writer)," *http://www.bach-cantatas. com/Lib/Prudentius-Aurelius.htm.*

11   Augustine Waldron, *Virtue*, transcribed by Barbara J. Barrett, *Catholic Encyclopedia*, Vol. XV, *http://www.newadvent.org/ cathen/15472a.htm.*

12   Waldron, ibid.

13   Waldron, ibid.

14   *Catechism of the Catholic Church*, Life in Christ, Part III: "The Gifts and Fruits of the Holy Spirit," Sec. 1830-1832, p. 450.

15   Ibid., p. 451.

16   *Blessed are ye poor, for yours is the kingdom of God* (Lk 6:20), Douay.

17   *And whosoever shall give to drink to one of these little ones a cup of cold water only in the name of a disciple, amen I say to you, he shall not lose his reward* (Mt 10:42), Douay.

18   Rev. John H. Hampsch, C.M.F, *"Blessed Salt"* (Los Angeles, CA: Claretian Tape Ministry), *http://claretiantapeministry.org*.

Praying for the Healing
of the Spiritual Family

A soul is not alone. Each soul is born into a family that is part of a spiritual continuum of the prior generation, part of the great Mystical Body of souls. All departed souls, including those of miscarried and aborted children, all souls of the present generation, and those of future generations form a soul's spiritual family. A living spiritual entity, the strengths and weaknesses of the spiritual family are passed down through the generations. In a biblical manner of expression, the effects of the sins of our ancestors are passed down to the third or fourth generation, but, with God's Great Mercy, blessings are bestowed to the faithful to a thousand generations: I am the Lord thy God, mighty, jealous, visiting the iniquity of the fathers upon the children, unto the third and fourth generation of them that hate me : And shewing mercy unto thousands to them that love me, and keep my commandments *(Ex 20:5-6). For in God's Merciful Justice, He permits parents to see the effects of their sins on their children: allowing them time to repent and return to Him, while showing their children an example of how God can forgive and cleanse souls to grow into a holy way of living through Christ.*

Fig. 64.   *Love One Another*, House of Bethany, Vandalia, Illinois, 2007.

Since Adam and Eve used their free will to turn against God, each soul inherits original sin compounded by the extrinsic effects of ancestral personal sin. But each soul of a generation also has the free will to choose to do the Will of God and be redeemed by Christ, the second Adam: But if he beget a son, who seeing all his father's sins, which he hath done, is afraid, and shall not do the like to them: ... the son shall not bear the iniquity of the father ... *(Ezek 18 14-18). Each soul is aided, too, by the blessings passed down from his/her ancestors' good works:* Therefore, as by the offence of one, unto all men to condemnation; so also by the justice of one, unto all men to justification of life. For as by the disobedience of one man, many were made sinners; so also by the obedience of one, many shall be made just ... where sin abounded, grace did more abound. *(Rom 5:18-20). Whether the family remains intact or the child is adopted into a new spiritual family, the spiritual ties and repercussions between generations and individuals within family units are powerful.*

The souls of the present and future generations are or will be affected, too, not only by their own decisions but also by the spiritual weaknesses and strengths of great-grandparents, grandparents, parents, siblings, aunts, uncles, cousins, and other ancestors. While judgment belongs to God alone, because the souls of the living exist in concert with the souls of the dead, prayers of intercession for the dead will be beneficial both to the living and the dead, through the Mercy of God, in mitigating the effects of sin ... Until they confess their iniquities and the iniquities of their ancestors, whereby they have transgressed against me and walked contrary to me. Therefore I also will walk against them ... : then shall they pray for their sins ... and I will remember my former covenant ... *(Lev 26: 40-45);* (For if he had not hoped that they that were slain should rise again, it would have seemed superfluous and vain to pray for the dead,) And because he considered that they who had fallen asleep with godliness, had great grace laid up for them. It is therefore a holy and wholesome thought to pray for the dead, that they may be loosed from sins *(2 Macc 12:44-45). And so a soul lives: intertwined within the Mystical Body of Christ and its own spiritual history.*

As a soul progresses in its journey toward God, understanding the spiritual profile of its family can be very helpful in fortifying the soul against learned disorders, inherited weaknesses, and inspiring the soul to holiness. For as the soul strengthens in unity with God, not only will this soul be healed but also, at the same time, the beneficial effects of its healing will be extended throughout the mystical family unit from which it comes, back through the generations. Praying for the souls of one's family tree, offering Masses to block the passing on of the effects of sin from the past to present and future generations, in thanksgiving for blessings, and for the intentions of departed souls will help all the souls of a family progress toward God in this world and the next, and for generations to come. Each soul is precious and important. The thoughts, words, and deeds of each soul draw the Communion of Saints closer to, or further from, God.

How do you perceive of the Mystical Body of Christ?

Actually, I taught a course in the seminary on the *Mystical Body*. The Encyclical *Mystici Corporis*, the *Mystical Body of Christ*, by Pope Pius XII, brought this aspect of our faith to the fore for us by reminding us that we are members of His Body.[1] He refers to the texts in St. Paul, where he states definitively we are members of the Body of Christ.[2] Our Lord's Words are often quoted in that respect where He says, *I am the vine, you are the branches* (Jn 15:5). In a lighter tone, we're very serious here, to lighten us up—I think of the little lad whose teacher was telling him about the Mystical Body and quoting this text of Our Lord, and he popped up and said, "Oh, that's easy, Teach. I'm the vine and you're the berries!" *(laughs)*

(laughs) The Mystical Body affirms that we are not only physical descendants but also spiritual descendants.

Yes. That is part of loving our brother. The great Law of Love: of God and love of neighbor. We are all members of His Body. Before St. Paul's conversion, he was named Saul. He was a terrible persecutor of Christians. One day, when he was out looking for Christians to round up to bring back to Jerusalem, he was blinded by a flash of light in the sky and thrown to the ground. Then he heard a voice saying, Saul, Saul, why do you persecute Me?[3] It was Jesus talking to him! He became a Saint, eventually, after that. Jesus let him know that He is present in those who love Him. As John puts it very strongly, He who hates his brother cannot be said to love God. How can I say I love my Father and hate my brother because we are all part of His Body?

We're all going to be together from now until eternity, so we might as well get used to the idea! (laughs)

(laughs) Get used to it!

The Mystical Body goes on forever and ever. In the Mass, the Offertory Prayer *is said for the atonement of sins on behalf of the living and the dead. We pray for intercession for everyone. In the Catholic Church, we don't see any distinction between the living and the dead other than we can't see them; they are separated from us for the moment—just beyond the mystical veil.*

We see now darkly as in a mirror; then clearly face to face.[4] Paul puts it that way.

That's the beautiful teaching of the Church: God knew us before we were born, then we are born or brought into a family He selects for us, we live and will return to Him and join the souls of our family members and the Communion of Saints for eternity.

Fig. 65.   *Gift of Peace,* International Compassion Ministry, Olympia Fields, Illinois, 2005.

God knows all and sees all. He knows all eternity: all things that are in Heaven, for all time.

There is a spiritual concept that conceives of family units as spiritual units, just as communities and countries are types of spiritual units, or principalities, with each unit and each soul existing within the context of a common history *and* common memory.[5] *Spiritual strengths and weaknesses are passed down from one generation to the next, across generations—or* intergenerationally, *as it is contemporaneously called. The Church is the keeper of the* historical memory, *the Church Tradition, from the time of Adam and Eve all the way down to the present. Our religious, national, family, and personal memories can affect how we treat each other. Today, special attention is being given to the idea of the* living memory *of the Church.*[6]

Yes. When Pope Benedict XVI served as Joseph Cardinal Ratzinger, he held the position of Prefect of the Congregation for the Doctrine of Faith and President of the International Theological Commission. He proposed a study on this very subject from 1998 through 1999. As a result, the International Theological Commission prepared the text *Memory and Reconciliation: The Church and the Faults of the Past*[7] in celebration of the Jubilee Year 2000. Cardinal Ratzinger approved its publication. It speaks at great length, from a theological point of view, of the healing of the Church's past and the need for penance to purify historical memory as part of the Church's teachings on forgiveness.

It's a profound document that traces Church teachings on forgiveness, from the Old Testament *through the* New Testament, *and the responsibility of today's generation to atone for the sins of the past.*

Fig. 66.   *Our Lady of Betania, Reconciler of Peoples and Nations,* Betania, Venezuela, 2006. On March 25, 1976, the Feast of the Annunciation, stigmatist and mystic Maria Esperanza Medrano de Bianchini said the Blessed Mother appeared to her calling herself, *Mary, Reconciler of Peoples and Nations.* Other apparitions of the Blessed Mother continued to be seen by Maria Esperanza and many diverse others. The site received official approval from Bishop Pio Bello and thirty-five of thirty-seven other bishops and auxiliary bishops in Venezuela. (Source: Michael Brown and Drew Mariani, *Bridge to Heaven: Interviews with Maria Esperanza of Betania,* Marian Communications, Ltd., Lima, PA, 1993.)

It encourages constant awareness for the need of purification to be in unity with Christ.[8]

Yes. It speaks to the common memory that transcends generations the mystical reality that we are all united, even though we live today in a different historical period from those who lived before us and those who will live after us.[9] In Christ, we are One. It remarks how Pope John Paul II often asked for forgiveness for past mistakes or even faults by some sections of the Church against nations or other faiths. It speaks to the *objective responsibility*[10] we have for atoning for past injustices, infringements of peace, and disrespect for the rights and dignity of others. This needs to be done, not only by the Church but also by governments and other secular organizations as well, to begin developing a new memory based on love and mutual respect.[11] So, there is a lot of precedent for this thinking.

His Holiness Pope John Paul II's public act of penance—going to the Wailing Wall and praying for forgiveness for the hundreds of years of Jewish oppression—seemed to move the heart of the world.

Yes. The Jews have his prayer petition in a museum, so it is preserved there.

Wonderful. It must mean so much to them to finally have their historical suffering addressed by the head of the Church.

I believe he also prayed for the terrible attacks on the Jews throughout the Nazi period.

Some of his friends in Poland were Jews, and he witnessed their suffering during the war years. His Holiness wasn't afraid to face the truth of history, even if it meant public correction of the Church he led in order for the Church to be reconciled with those who were harmed. While he personally wasn't responsible for the oppression of the Jews, he acknowledged that others in his spiritual family were anti-Semitic and may have participated in the atrocities.[12]

Yes. Correct. And he had great trust in the Love and Mercy of God to purify the Church and her members.

His last book was on memory and identity. After a lifetime of study, at the end of his pontificate, this was an extraordinarily important focus.

Yes. He was deeply affected by the regime of the Nazis and the Communist era. In his last book, *Memory and Identity: Conversations at the Dawn of a Millennium*,[13] he reviews the philosophical errors of these ideologies and broadens the conversation to include the importance of cultural memory and identity in guiding the destiny of humankind. The book is updated from the 1993 interviews he had with two Polish philosophers, Jozef Tischner and Krzysztof Michalski, founders of the Vienna-based Institute for Human Sciences (Institut für die Wissenschaften von Menschen).[14]

His Holiness recognized that Jesus understood the Law of Memory.[15]

Of course. Jesus knows us completely as human beings. Memory is part of being human.[16] He said at the Last Supper, *Hoc facite in meam commemorationem*: Do this in memory of me.[17]

The living memory *affects people very profoundly. Atrocities that were done even a thousand years ago are affecting people to this day—all the unhealed soul wounds. We see it all over the world in the sustained conflicts in the North of Ireland and Palestine, and on a smaller scale, in our cities and in our families.*

Yes. Memories have to be healed. We keep saying healing is forgiveness. It's from the heart.

Along with the living memory, you referred to the idea of objective common responsibility.[18]

Yes. The Church asks God's liberation from the consequences of evil committed by prior generations—for those memories and burdens of consciences that extend to her descendants and can continue to fuel hatred and contempt in this generation.[19] While we are not personally responsible for those evil acts, we are responsible for acknowledging that they were evil to atone for the sins of our fathers. In other words, we are responsible for our subjective relationship to those historical events today so they aren't repeated or tolerated in this generation or in the future.[20] So often we are quick to identify with the achievements of our ancestors, but we must also acknowledge where they may have fallen short in living the Loving Way of Christ.

They were just like us—good and bad among them, and good and bad within them.

Correct.

Sometimes we don't understand some of the choices of our ancestors. It takes a certain amount of courage to face the truth and to be honest with ourselves and others.[21] What Pope John Paul II did by going to the Wailing Wall was tremendous. And, he continued to reach out to others who felt alienated by incidences in the Church's history.[22]

It's so beautiful. He even tried to woo the Eastern Rites back to unity by apologizing for the many insulting things that had been done over the centuries. I think that has brought about a unifying effect of healing upon some of the branches of the Eastern Orthodox Church. They are seeking, in fact, unification as well.

That's also mentioned in that theological document on *Memory and Reconciliation.*[23] Certainly Pope John Paul II gave a terrific example of reaching out and humbling himself to the Orthodox Christians in his visit to the Middle East, speaking with the Orthodox Christians, and trying to bring about his dream of reconciliation between the Orthodox and the Roman Church. He begged pardon for all. He not only spoke of it; he practiced what he was speaking of—the asking for forgiveness.

Pope Benedict XVI is also very interested in healing divisions within the Church. Especially the Orthodox Eastern Church and all the different sects within Christianity. Both of these great Popes haven't ignored the divisions. They've acknowledged the divisions and then have tried to make amends.

Exactly.

The thinking of the Church is that there is only one Divine Order.

Of course, the Seamless Garment of Christ. The bottom line in asking for forgiveness is also recalling Christ's Words at the Last Supper, That they may be completely One, so the world may know that You have sent Me and have loved them even as You have loved Me.[24] In other words, not divide ourselves from each other. This is obviously the mind of Christ. We shouldn't be divided in our Christianity: Protestant or Orthodox.[25]

Fig. 67 and 68. Part I and Part II. *A New and Everlasting Covenant: Father Peter Mary Rookey, O.S.M.,* Servite Priory, Berwyn, Illinois, 2006.

Pope Benedict XVI and Pope John Paul II recognized that emotional tensions can linger between generations in the form of feelings attached to memories—feelings of shame, guilt, anger, hatred, or revenge.[26] *You are sensitive to this as well. You participated in a Mass at Holy Name Cathedral in Chicago for the souls of the victims of An Gorta Mor (the Great Hunger in Ireland, 1845-1852), when millions of indigenous Irish people starved to death and suffered terribly with hundreds of thousands evicted from their homes and from their country.*

Yes. That was very touching. Bishop Conway presided in the concelebrated Mass. It was a beautiful Mass. We prayed for those souls and all the souls of the world who have suffered, and continue to suffer, from acts of persecution, artificial famine, and political and social injustice—all forms of violence. We prayed, too, for historical truth to be revealed, because spiritual unity is rooted in Divine Truth. When faults are acknowledged, we can more easily forgive and be healed in the Light and Truth of Christ and be liberated from this separation from one another and God.

Christ calls on us to forgive—even in terrible circumstances. The Church seeks the repudiation of evil in this generation and the opening of hearts of individuals and communities to purify memories so that we can begin anew in the image of Christ.

Irish history of even hundreds of years ago is still a sensitive subject, especially between some Protestants and Catholics. As you said, the Church proposes that, when we begin the process of the purification of memory, we must insist on the acknowledgment of the truth and the need for penance. We ask God to heal the souls of the victims, the persons who inflicted the harm, and the descendants of both.

Yes. This is upstaged very much in our day by the abortion issue. You were just presenting me with a beautiful document *Shepherding the Flock After Abortion* that was written for the Pontifical Council for the Family by Father Pavone, who is head of the organization *Priests for Life.*[27] They have set up programs for post-abortion women and the fathers of their children. Their approach is very touching. They try to help them overcome, come to grips with, the post-abortion syndrome: with the sorrow after the abortion due to their unacceptance of the Gift of Life. Tens of millions of lives have been lost, including all the talents and gifts that belonged to these persons for the benefit of the world.

We spoke earlier about the *Bible* being a call to remember all the great things God has done for us, and how we have very often failed to respond to His Love. We ask Him to heal us because of the sins of our ancestors, and our own failure to return the great manifestations of Love by the Lord, and how He protected us. For example, how God brought the Israelites out of slavery in Egypt through a series of great miracles. The final miracle persuaded Pharoah that all the firstborn of the Egyptians must die—the firstborn of all animals, for that matter. Pharoah finally *begged* them to leave! *(laughs)* The Egyptians even gave their jewelry to them for their journey. *(laughs)*

Many miracles happened during their journey through the desert. God sent food, manna from Heaven. When they were without water, Moses struck the rocks and water rushed forth. God put down nations before them. The Israelites took over lands—other people's fields and cities they had not built. They were given food from the gardens and the farms they had not planted. *(laughs)* He gave them all that, but yet they rebelled. We constantly need to ask God to heal our ungratefulness, our lack of recognition of the great Love God has for us, for all the wonderful things He has done in our lives.

Today, instead of being grateful for God's Love of us, we expect God to love us no matter what. But there is also the idea of Divine Punishment—that we, our family, or our nation may owe a debt for whatever we or other people have done. God permits suffering as a form of justice because He loves us and wants us to learn how to live in the right way. He doesn't want us to benefit from our sin and permits punishment for the sake of the good,[28] as St. Thomas Aquinas says. The sin may be forgiven, but the debt of sin remains.[29]

Yes. Even the powerful are subject to God's Justice. David, for example, whom God had blessed so much. God even turned him from being a servant of King Saul to being Saul's successor, as the next king of Israel. As king, David took another man's wife, Bathsheba. She conceived a child with him. David wanted her for himself and sent her husband Uriah, who was a very honorable man, to the front lines of a battle to get rid of him. Uriah was soon killed, just as David wanted. But God allowed the child of his union with Bathsheba to die. The child suffered

Fig. 69. *King David,* stained glass window, Our Lady of Sorrows Basilica, Chicago, Illinois, 2006.

from a fever for seven days, and David grieved, fasted, and prayed. He came back to God through sorrow and penance, but still the child died.

Eventually, God forgave David and permitted him to have another child, Solomon. He gave him the Gift of Writing, too. David says so beautifully, *Create a clean heart in me, O God, and put a new and right spirit within me.*[30] But God didn't allow David to build the great temple for Him: *Thou hast shed much blood, and fought many battles, so thou canst not build a house to my name, after shedding so much blood before me* (1 Chr 22: 8). He did permit him to store up the materials for it, but He told David that his son Solomon would be the one to build it. God was more concerned about David's heart than He was about his fame. In the end, even the temple was destroyed, but David's beautiful *Psalms* live on.

It seems God holds those in authority to special account. He took Moses to task at Mt. Nebo, after all the work Moses had done trying to keep his people in line with God. God showed him the Promised Land, but told him, Thou shalt see the land before thee, which I will give to the children of Israel, but thou shalt not enter into it *(Deut 32:52).*

Yes. Poor Moses.

Because we are part of a family, a community, and nation, sometimes we bear the suffering and stigma for the sins of other members, the social sins. In contrast, we often recognize good families *and* good communities.

Yes. This is recognized civilly as well. Whole nations can suffer because of the sins of a few. Social sin is made up of many personal sins and causes big disruptions. For example, in Germany after WWI and WWII, all the German people were taxed because of the war atrocities and the Holocaust. Not all the German people were responsible for the crimes against humanity committed by others, but all the Germans were *held* responsible and taxed heavily as an example to all the world of justice.

In the long run, God permits suffering for the good of our souls and for the ultimate good of others. He is more concerned about

Fig. 70.   *Monstrance,* Our Lady of Lourdes, grotto, Chicago, Illinois, 2006.

improving the condition of our souls than our material and temporal, or earthly fulfillment; that's why suffering comes in different forms for different reasons.

Yes, because we are unique persons. As the great St. Thomas Aquinas said, God doesn't will evil, but He permits evil to happen.[31] Our souls belong to God, and He will help us become even more beautiful, even if it involves suffering.

The innocent may suffer because of the sins of others, but if they accept the suffering with patience, they can become holy in the eyes of God.

The innocent may suffer from the effects of the sins of their forefathers as an example to others, or to encourage the children not to repeat the sin. In the case of adultery, for example, a father has an affair and this causes terrible problems in the home, maybe even leading to divorce and feelings of shame and poverty for the children. The children are not guilty of the sin of adultery, but they suffer the consequences. When they marry, they will know what can happen if they commit adultery, and they can choose not to do this.

They have the free will to create their lives in the image of God.

Yes. But many times this will happen again and again, because they also suffer from not knowing how to live in a stable family—the kind of sacrifice and self-control that is involved in having a loving family. So the sin of the father isn't just limited to the sin of adultery; it includes the *effects* of the sin of adultery. God may even permit the father to live long enough to see the effect of his sin on his children as they become adults, and even on his grandchildren.

Fig. 71.   *St. Anthony of Padua and the Child Jesus,* statue, Our Lady's Chapel, St. Ignatius Parish, Chicago, Illinois, 2006. Born into a noble family, St. Anthony joined the Franciscans during the lifetime of St. Francis and, later, the Friars Minor. It is believed the Child Jesus appeared to him in his monastery cell. A quiet man who sought silence in a cave, he was asked one day to preach in the absence of another speaker. His words astounded those who listened. He became known for his Gifts of Teaching and Preaching, and, eventually, was declared a Doctor of the Church. He is the Patron Saint of oppressed and starving people, expectant mothers, animals, and lost articles, among others.

God remembers. He remembers our good deeds and our bad. In Mass and Confession, we testify to God's Power and Love and seek to align our souls within the Divine Order.

Yes. Through Jesus' Blood Sacrifice, we are redeemed. Father Pavone quotes the Holy Father, Pope John Paul II, from *Evangelium Vitae* 99, where he encourages mothers who have had abortions to remember, in the midst of it all, that God is a forgiving God, while not diminishing in any way the seriousness of having had an abortion. Father Pavone suggests that women ask their children for forgiveness for their actions. He reflects the *Bible* in that sense. He also refers to other priests who recommend having Masses said for the child or for a special intention, as part of the penance of the mother, in addition to saying the *Rosary* and other prayers for a period of time, and attending Eucharistic Adoration. All of these acts of repentance help heal the wounds of abortion and separation from God.

I would now like to say a special word to women who have had an abortion. The Church is aware of the many factors which may have influenced your decision, and she does not doubt that in many cases it was a painful and even shattering decision. The wound in your heart may not yet have healed.

Certainly what happened was and remains terribly wrong. But do not give in to discouragement and do not lose hope. Try rather to understand what happened and face it honestly. If you have not already done so, give yourselves over with humility and trust to repentance. The Father of Mercies is ready to give you His Forgiveness and His Peace in the Sacrament of Reconciliation. You will come to understand that nothing is definitively lost and you will also be able to ask forgiveness from your child, who is now living with the Lord.

With the friendly and expert help and advice of other people, and as a result of your own painful experience, you can be among the most eloquent defenders of everyone's right to life. Through your commitment to life, whether by accepting the birth of other children or by welcoming and caring for those most in need of

> *someone to be close to them, you will become promoters of a new way of looking at human life.*[32]
>
> *His Holiness John Paul II*
> Evangelium Vitae

Whenever I can, I go to pro-life Masses. Likely as not, it is led by one of our bishops. Then we pray the *Rosary* in a procession to the nearby abortion clinic. We give the mothers who are going for an abortion a reason to stop and not have the abortion.

Do you support the Priests for Life organization?

Yes. I've had Masses and even healing services in one of the pro-life places that is on the Northwest side of Chicago, on Cicero and the Kennedy Expressway. They have a beautiful facility right around the corner from an abortion clinic. They can direct the expectant mothers to the facility if they can succeed in talking with them to not have an abortion at the doors of the clinic. They send them around the corner to this center, and they are counseled and helped in every way. I've had Masses there. Good Friday is special. I pray the *Rosary* and do the *Stations of the Cross* in front of the clinic on that special day of Good Friday. We try to encourage these pro-life centers in every way we can.

Have you had any of the expectant mothers come to your healing Masses?

I'm sure there have been some of them there.

When you had the Masses, what did you pray for specifically?

Most of the people who come to these Masses are people who are praying for the expectant mothers not to have an abortion and/or that those who have submitted to an abortion will be healed.

Do you also include in your intentions the babies who have been aborted?

Yes. We do pray for all and sundry.

These centers offer practical support services too for these mothers?

They try to help the mothers in every way possible.

That's beautiful. Have you done these Masses only in Chicago?

Oh no, I've been in processions all over the place . . . Texas, Florida. If I'm in a city and they are having a demonstration, I will go—oh, San Francisco. My brother and his wife are very active in the Pro-Life Movement there. We've paraded in front of the clinics in San Francisco.

How long have you been involved in the Pro-Life Movement?

About twenty years.

That's a long time. Do you think we'll ever recover from it as a society?

Oh yes, by all means. I'm sure that good will overcome evil as always. I'm sure the abortion laws will be repealed. There's no doubt in my mind.

We've become such a technology-based society. In the past few decades, there was little meaning given to life in the womb. Now, we are beginning to recognize again the vibrancy of the fetus. From a Catholic point of view, a soul begins at conception. It is a sensitive human being.

Right. That's even a pagan concept. Hippocrates, the Father of Medicine, was a Greek, a pagan. He authored the oath in which he says, I will strive to preserve life from conception to natural death.

That's very interesting.

Since abortion has come of age, they have tried to soften the oath somehow. But a wonderful Catholic doctor here, who came on pilgrimage to the Holy Land with us, has written books in which he speaks very poignantly about the original *Hippocratic Oath*. I wish I had that book here. It is very powerful. His book is directed really to doctors. He tells his fellow doctors who are practicing abortion that they are going against the oath they took.

Fig. 72.   *Good Friday Rosary I*, Albany Clinic, Chicago, Illinois, 2006. Father Rookey prays outside the clinic for an end to abortion with supporters from the Women's Center.

ༀ ༀ

Oath of Hippocrates (circa fourth century BC)

I swear by Apollo Physician and Asclepius and Hygieia and Panaceia and all the gods and goddesses, making them my witnesses, that I will fulfill according to my ability and judgment this oath and this covenant:

> *To hold him who has taught me this art as equal to my parents and to live my life in partnership with him, and if he is in need of money to give him a share of mine, and to regard his offspring as equal to my brothers in male lineage and to teach them this art—if they desire to learn it—without fee and covenant; to give a share of precepts and oral instruction and all the other learning to my sons and to the sons of him who has instructed me and to pupils who have signed the covenant and have taken an oath according to the medical law, but no one else.*
>
> *I will apply dietetic measures for the benefit of the sick according to my ability and judgment; I will keep them from harm and injustice.*
>
> *I will neither give a deadly drug to anybody who asked for it, nor will I make a suggestion to this effect. Similarly I will not give to a woman an abortive remedy. In purity and holiness I will guard my life and my art.*
>
> *I will not use the knife, not even on sufferers from stone, but will withdraw in favor of such men as are engaged in this work.*
>
> *Whatever houses I may visit, I will come for the benefit of the sick, remaining free of all*

Fig. 73.   *Good Friday Rosary II*, Albany Clinic, Chicago, Illinois, 2006. Father Rookey prays outside the abortion clinic with supporters of the Women's Center.

intentional injustice, of all mischief and in particular of sexual relations with both female and male persons, be they free or slaves.

What I may see or hear in the course of the treatment or even outside of the treatment in regard to the life of men, which on no account one must spread abroad, I will keep to myself, holding such things shameful to be spoken about.

If I fulfill this oath and do not violate it, may it be granted to me to enjoy life and art, being honored with fame among all men for all time to come; if I transgress it and swear falsely, may the opposite of all this be my lot.[33]

We've overturned the thinking of thousands of years in a single generation. Of course, it was the message of personal freedom, the fashionable mass marketing of contraceptives, and the historic social/cultural values upheaval, which also complicated the issue, let alone the mothers' and fathers' circumstances, and the loss of the sacred in personal relationships. A terrible mechanistic, utilitarian thinking has been at the fore. It was a convergence of forces that brought abortion into the mainstream culture.

Well, Satan is cunning, a liar and murderer from the beginning.[34] It's always been a conundrum to me how these brilliant minds sitting on that Supreme Court bench could be so erring in their thinking as to think it's all right to kill a child in the womb.

In St. Thomas Aquinas' writings in the Summa Theologica, *he states that infants have what is called* nascent knowledge,[35] *knowledge like Angels.*

Fig. 74. *Cherub*, painting, St. John Cantius Parish, Chicago, Illinois, 2006.

I never read that. I'm pleasantly surprised to hear that. We often call children *little Angels*. One of the proofs the pro-lifers give that the fetus is a real person is because they already respond to the parents' gestures. A mother and child are so closely related. They share life together. The fetus receives his life, receives his food from her; a fetus responds sometimes to a word in some way. They know many things.

St. Thomas talks, too, about the soul having three parts: One part is the nutritive, *the bodily, fleshly development; the other part is the* sensitive *that is able to sense and experience more of the mind; and the other is the* intellect, *or the spirit and soul.*[36] *All three parts develop as the child develops. Each is affected throughout its development.*

Oh yes, of course. Each is an individual soul with a personal history from the moment of conception—a distinct personality. Even souls of the womb are not free of original sin. *Psalm 50* says, *Indeed, I was born guilty, a sinner when my mother conceived me.*[37] These souls are also affected by the personal sins of their parents, including severe emotional disturbance and physical affliction from the use of tobacco, alcohol, and drugs. It's very clear: if the mother uses drugs, the baby may become addicted or deformed—so the innocent unborn child suffers for the sin of its mother. In the case of abortion, although the child is innocent of personal sin, like Jesus, he/she suffered rejection and death.

We're becoming aware that medical science, in the last hundred years, has taught that babies in vitro did not have significant feelings until late in the pregnancy.[38] *This thinking undoubtedly provided a foothold for the abortion era. Abortion didn't matter, partly because it was thought the child was just a lump of unfeeling tissue.*

Very true.

Despite all the great medical advances, the medical community did not have a consensus that even premature babies and full-term infants could feel pain and express emotions until the late 1980s.[39] *It was commonly thought, for example, that when a baby smiled, he was just releasing gas, not expressing happiness.*[40] *Operations were performed on premature babies and circumcisions on infants without anesthetics.*[41] *But new research is showing, even at very early stages in the womb, children have a great capacity to feel pain, share their feelings, and express themselves in very strong ways.*[42] *Twins have been seen kissing and kicking!*[43] *This is similar to what we are told about John and Jesus when they were in their mothers' wombs and how they reacted with joy upon meeting each other.*

You are talking about John the Baptist and his mother, Elizabeth, meeting Mary—the Mystery of the Visitation. Yes. It's beautiful. Incidentally, bringing this down more to our time, I had the experience, unworthy though I am, of expectant mothers when we simply approach them, of their infants in their wombs leaping for joy.

How wonderful.

This has happened a number of times in various places here and overseas. Jesus is in each one of us. Especially after Mass when we have Jesus in us after receiving Communion. Babies often cry during the *Consecration*—they are so sensitive! *(laughs)*

Jesus' chorus! (laughs) Recently in your office, you were praying over an alcoholic and cocaine-using mother and her unborn child, her son, responded to you. She was within days of delivery. She said he woke up while you were praying and went back to sleep when you stopped. Her labor was very easy—she felt like dancing! When the baby was born, he tested "clean"—with no affects from her drinking or drug use.

Praise God!

It was a miracle, really, as she had given birth to another child who had tested positive for fetal alcohol syndrome. Sadly, she is still struggling, but her son has been placed in a foster home. She suffers terribly from the loss—she wants so much to have him.

Maybe in time, because of her love for her child and with God's Grace, she will be healed. She had enough love to bring the child into the world and pray for him.

Yes. She prayed for him to be healthy while she was carrying him and tried to abstain from drinking. She loves him, which science is showing is essential for healthy development. Even the biotechnology community is beginning to acknowledge there is an active sensitive life formed at conception. A baby's heart is the first organ formed, with the heart tube beginning to beat at seventeen-nineteen days.[44] By six to ten weeks, there's movement and the baby has sensitivity to touch.[45] The child can taste and smell by eleven and fifteen weeks, and listen and hear by sixteen weeks.[46] Evidently the womb is a very noisy place—as loud as a dance floor![47]

This whole new area of research is called perinatal and prenatal research.[48] Researchers have affirmed that children in the womb have lots of feelings and expressions—much earlier than we ever thought before. They can cry, play, smile, and learn.[49] They can also feel heat, cold, pressure, and pain, and taste and smell.[50] The personality, intelligence, and body are imprinted in the womb and form the foundation of its being for the rest of its life.[51] Some believe the child can even sense the father's feelings.[52] There is a lot of reciprocal communication going on throughout its time in the womb.[53] It is very important that parents are conscious of their behavior and their child's need for affection.

Right. By all means. This is something I read about years ago, and I have been speaking along those lines. The child in the womb is very sensitive to the feelings and movements of the mother—and of the father, since it is his seed. This is very natural, because the child is part of the mother's body. The intellectual part, the spiritual part of the mother, and the feelings of the mother affect the development of the child. Especially the love of the parents for each other and the child. This helps the child realize from the very beginning it is part of a family. Everybody knows, apart from all the research, perinatal, prenatal, and postnatal, that every child who is neglected, and who does not receive kisses and other marks of love from the parents, especially the mother, can become sick and even die of lack of affection. So even apart from our studies, every nurse and doctor knows that, all the people who work with children.

Biologically, the emotional and psychological state of the mother can be transferred to the child through the umbilical cord and placenta.[54] And, as you are saying, by intellectual, spiritual, and psychological transference. Besides positive emotions, these children feel anger and fear.[55] They react defensively as well. For example, it has been shown when an amniocentesis needle is stuck in the womb, the baby often attacks the needle and can become still for several days.[56] When an abortion is attempted, they resist.[57]

Yes. Right. It is also known that the intellectual qualities as well as the sympathetic qualities of the parents come out in the child. So there is a whole world of interaction beginning in the womb that affects the child and its parents. As the parents grow in love for their child, they often deepen their love for others, too. Family relationships begin in the womb.

Love is so powerful. A favorite theme of mine, not mine, but often repeated is: *Love is the greatest force in the whole universe.* There is no greater force than love. It moves mountains. I just came back from the Holy Land, and I was reminiscing with our group of thirty Polish people about St. Francis who came to the Holy Land when the Crusaders and the Muslims were fighting. He came with a simple approach—a loving approach. The sultan was completely overwhelmed by this man, and even used his resources to release Christian prisoners from his Muslim prisons, and gave them the means to return to their homes. He was completely overwhelmed by the love of this simple Francis. The love of the parents is so important. It is so important.

Love is a human necessity for survival.

Yes. Children die if they don't have that affection, that love.

The children are wounded.

For life.

There is an abortion survivors syndrome *regarding children who have survived a physical abortion, but who are still psychologically aborted by their parents. As a result of these intense and complete feelings of rejection, these people can suffer from significant personality and psychological disorders as adults. John C. Sonne, M.D., has studied this and has found these survivors can exhibit intense self-loathing to the point of being suicidal, frequently abort their own children, have hostility to authority figures, and sometimes murderous sibling rivalry.[58] They may have the need as well to seek attention, engage in risk-taking behavior, and may be out to change the world in a tyrannical way.[59]*

But saddest of all, these survivors can have a very difficult time loving other people or receiving love.[60] They can become almost paralyzed emotionally, but can be volatile, too, so intimate relationships are difficult to maintain.[61] *Understandably, their relationships with God are often affected.*[62] *They often have no belief in God, or have a messianic perception of themselves.*[63] *So it is very important that we love these children from the beginning—that they are conceived in love, not in objectified lust, which interferes with natural loving and bonding.*

Perfectly right.

Dr. Sonne, too, theorizes that much of the violence in the world is rooted in the dehumanization of the child in the womb.[64] *When the parents dehumanize the child, they dehumanize themselves.*[65]

Pope John Paul II refers to *re-humanizing* the parents and the child, if the child has not been aborted, and bringing the humane nature into the parents again. He refers to the "'desacralization' *that often turns into 'dehumanization' of the individual and society."*[66] This is the great theme in his Encyclical *Dives in Misericordia—On the Mercy of God* [67]—the renewal of the sacred.

This need to resurrect a sense of the sacred within ourselves is a very tender subject due to the scale and speed of the abortion movement around the world. The process will require a massive re-examination and redirection of not just individual but world consciousness. There have been tens of millions of children aborted and for every child there are two parents affected. The damage is of epic proportions from the post-abortion syndrome: the guilt, the emotional paralysis, and the inability to go on to trust and form new relationships—to love again. The parents themselves can become disabled by abortion.

Yes. Definitely. I'm glad to see that the churches in the parishes are developing post-abortion syndrome groups to help these mothers who have had the unfortunate experience of an abortion—maybe more than one. They have seen the terrible *effects* on the mother. The child was killed, and the mother is also rendered very ill through it, psychologically—if nothing else—through this terrible experience.

And the fathers of the children, too. Often these relationships don't survive the abortion. The couples feel alienated within themselves and from each other and the Church.

Yes. Abortion leaves very deep wounds. On the healing side of things, expressing love for these parents who have had an abortion is very powerful. When we show them the love they did not show their children, they are overwhelmed and healed. There is no healing like love.

But in order to give love, you need to first feel love.

Yes. That reminds me of a nun in southern Italy who has been very successful with her work in helping those who are involved in drugs. Her approach is to use former drug addicts who have been able to overcome their addictions. They take an addict who is open to being delivered from his addiction into their place and surround him with love: embracing him, showing every kindness, feeding him. They have that type of outreach. Their success is supposed to be ninety percent. So that love approach is very powerful, maybe the most powerful there is.

When people are on drugs, it can be a symptom of having not received enough love, for whatever reason, or that they didn't allow themselves to feel love if love was offered. Even though love is a natural human tendency, if people have become stunted in their ability to love and trust other people, they need to first feel secure, then they need to learn how to love again.

I think we should also point out that this love needs to be spiritually motivated and not be a sensual love that comes and goes. I'm thinking of some of the great lovers like St. Francis, and, now in our time, people like Teresa of Calcutta who saw these people, men especially, and abandoned children living in the streets. She lifted them up and let them know they were loved before they died, for example. Her love was not a sensual type of love, but a spiritual love for these bodies of God. She reached out to these abandoned people to bring this love to them.

She restored their dignity. There is a certain dignity that is affiliated with love.

Yes. Definitely.

It is recognizing the total person—reaffirming the Gift of the Person.

Yes, by having them feel Divine Love, touching their souls with love, then inner healing begins.

Just as hate, an absence of love, affects not just the person bearing the hatred but resounds beyond him, love, as a basic orientation of life, goes beyond the individual and affects the world.

Definitely. I have often spoken about the *effects* of love. You can identify, without being a psychiatrist, a hateful person just by looking at their face. Their countenance identifies a hateful person. In contrast, we are immediately drawn to a person whose countenance shows love. There is a beauty to love. I used to have in our services and our talks a short and incisive one-liner that I thought would teach the people, "Hate and be ugly; love and be beautiful. Hate and be ugly; love and be beautiful." They would come away with that, which is so true, because hatred makes us ugly in our being and our countenance, in our way of life, in how we deal with people and situations.

With hatred, there is a harshness to a person; but with love, the other aspect seems to be compassion.

Yes, very much so.

Pope John Paul II talked about God having tremendous compassion and mercy.

Yes. In his Encyclical *Rich in Mercy* (*Dives in Misericordia*), he used two Hebrew words to describe mercy: *Hesed* and *Rahamim*.[68] He refers to *Hesed* meaning grace, goodness, and love expressed as a faithful, interior commitment between two people, and, more deeply: *Love that gives, love more powerful than betrayal, grace stronger than sin.*[69] He mentions, too, that *Hesed* has a masculine root, emphasizing steadfastness, faithfulness to self, and responsibility for one's own love, whereas *Rahamim*, is the feminine root referring to the womb and a mother's compassion, tenderness, patience, and understanding—her nature to forgive and her perfect unity with her child.[70] It's so beautiful. Both natures of man and woman comprising God and His Merciful Love for us. It's overwhelming.

God loves us like a woman loves the child of her womb, even more so. He has said that *He will always be with us*, even if our own mother fails us: *Can a woman forget her infant, so as not to have pity on the son of her womb? And if she should forget, yet will not I forget thee. Behold, I have graven thee in my hands . . .* (Isa 49:15-16). He knows us intimately and loves us more than our own naturally imperfect parents, because He is our Creator, the One that gave us life. We belong to Him and He is Love. We become more and more like Him as we let His Love come forth through us.

That short phrase that *love makes us beautiful* is also applicable to the case of the mother when she accepts with love her child in her womb, and also her relationship with the father, and all the people around her. It's so powerful. It's personal. We see it in people's eyes. Everybody knows that—we are attracted by the love in the eyes of the beloved.

Love is a transcendent power. To change a hardened mindset requires a transformation of spirit, which you have said is more difficult and more important than a physical healing.

Very much so. For example, if I do not have love, if I have a serious illness, it is very painful. Or, with any painful situation in my life, I tend to be depressed, even suicidal and want to end it all. But when I'm filled with love, that love is helping other people. Then I can see through the pain. When a mother gives birth to a child, the experience is painful. As Jesus Himself put it: *A woman, when she is in labour, hath sorrow, because her hour is come; but when she hath brought forth the child, she remembereth no more the anguish, for joy that a man is born into the world* (Jn 16:21). So we see the good that is coming from our pain. It can become a real joy, a joy that magnifies to those around us.

There can be a sweetness in suffering. We can have faith in our suffering—whether we are suffering for another person, or accepting the difficult life that is before us, or before the mother with her unborn child, or when embracing any long-term suffering or illness—there is a fruit to it, a positive end. That seems to be what Christ is trying to teach us.

It is obvious. Christ redeemed us through His Suffering and Our Lady with her *com-Passion*.

The suffering is based in Love; it is not just suffering to suffer.

Exactly. He didn't relish it. In the garden in the Holy Land, where we were just a few weeks ago, as He was prostrate on the ground, He said, *Father, if thou wilt, remove this chalice from me : but yet not my will, but thine be done* (Lk 22:42). He didn't relish the suffering, but He knew what this loving gesture was going to bring about. He did it willingly.

It may be that the suffering these aborted children have endured, through the affects of the suffering on their parents, in the long-term, may lead their parents to a form of redemption.

Exactly. The parents can recover their mistakes, if they have had an abortion, by offering their sufferings to cover their sin. Our Lady, in her apparitions at Medjugorje, has said that especially mothers who have had abortions must do much penance so they can offer their suffering that came from the abortion, or lack of love, to cover their sins.

In the end, the result, or the goal of penance, is to be reunited with God—to feel love within and for others.

Very true. We all have Jesus in us. Of course, it's easier to love Him in some more than others. *(laughs)* We need to grow the Jesus in us, love the Jesus in each other.

It's all the same process. No matter what it takes or what form it comes in, it's all about love.

Right. It's all about love.

Father Frank Pavone, M.E.V., Moderator General, Missionaries of the Gospel of Life, and who also heads the Priests for Life organization,[71] and Father Robert T. Sears, S.J., Ph.D.,[72] who is in the healing and deliverance ministry, have both posited the question of whether baptism

Fig. 75.   *Guardian Angel,* altar, Our Lady of Sorrows Basilica, Chicago, Illinois, 2006.

of vicarious desire is possibly applicable to aborted souls. Since there is a rupture of the relationship between the parents and the child, there is need for reconciliation of some kind. Father Sears believes that some of the souls of aborted children are not at peace but alienated and hurt because they did not experience love but murder.

Just like children who encounter abuse and go into adulthood full of rage and pain, Father Sears has discerned that some of these aborted souls internalize the pain inflicted on them—for the Love of God is obscured to them. Although the children desired to live according to God's Will for them, through no fault of their own, they were deprived of His Gift of Life. They are in need of affirmation by their parents that they are loved and innocent, and they are in need of Divine Healing as well. Part of the process of reconciliation that seems to be effective is having the parents recognize the human dignity of the child by naming the child, and, through prayer, welcoming the child into their hearts. Sometimes, when a Mass is offered as an intercessory prayer, peace prevails.

These children are part of our human family and united mystically to us and Christ Who calls us to all be at One with God. Baptism of children by water is the traditional way of uniting souls with Christ. It was commonly thought that unbaptized babies went to Limbo. But that was never Church doctrine and has been discounted in our time. Masses now are mostly held for the benefit of the grieving parents. We are taught, through faith, these children are at peace with God. Of course, we are not theologians. But Pope Benedict XVI and Pope John Paul II have recognized the importance of these questions and have asked the *International Theological Commission* to undertake this very subject, as it is at the heart of several dogmas. In the meantime, we can hope that through the Mercy and Compassion of Christ these little ones will be healed through His Tender Care and, through His Mercy, attain unity with Him.

Fig. 76.　*Jesus Crowned with Thorns*, stained glass, Our Lady of Sorrows Basilica, Chicago, Illinois, 2008.

Created for the Mystical Body of Christ, unborn children are distinct persons with the potential to fully develop their bodies, minds, and spirits as willed by God. These precious souls belong to our spiritual community and need to be recognized as members of their families, cared for, and loved. As Jesus said, See that you despise not one of these little ones : for I say to you, that their Angels in heaven always see the face of my Father who is in heaven . . . it is not the will of your Father, who is in heaven, that one of these little ones should perish *(Mt 18:10-14).*

Stillbirths, abortions, and miscarriages can be the source of much painful suffering within families and can even lead to damaging emotional effects with extended family members. According to Rev. Robert T. Sears, Ph.D., S.J., the act of abortion and the disappointment of miscarriage is often accompanied by feelings of deep hurt, guilt, and shame. When silence, denial, or anger prevails, the reconciliation process is sometimes delayed for decades.

The Gifts of Repentance and Forgiveness are the first actions of healing. In the case of abortion, the mother and father need to repent of having used their free will to reject the Will of God and the child He ordained for them: By thee have I been confirmed from the womb : from my mother's womb thou art my protector *(Ps 70:6). The parents may also need to ask for forgiveness from God for the failure of their relationship to welcome God's Will for them and from each other, and for any abuse suffered or exchanged that led to the decision to abort their child. They may also need to reconcile the contributing actions of family members, friends, doctors, and aides who encouraged the choice for abortion, or who did not help them cope with financial, health care, and basic life necessities. And, perhaps, they will need to search deep within their souls to become reconciled with God for creating the baby at what seemed to them to be an inopportune time.*

Often an abortion occurs when there is an absence of family support; excessive financial strain; or an unconsecrated, unstable, immature relationship between the mother and the father; and other similar challenges. The parents may need to ask for forgiveness for their fearful desperation and lack of trust in God to provide for them. Importantly, because their baby suffered the pain of death and rejection, they need to ask for forgiveness from the baby's soul, for like Jesus, the Saints, and other deceased family members, the baby's soul lives in constant community with the living.

The restoration of love for the child, through Our Lord, can enable the parents to release their pain and accept God's Eternal Care of the child in love and in peace. The parents can also ask Jesus to name the child to remember him/her as a full family member: The Lord hath called me from the womb, from the bowels of my mother he hath been mindful of my name *(Is 49:1). Through the Mystical Body of Christ, we believe that the child can be united in love with its parents for Jesus has said,* Suffer the little children, and forbid them not to come to me *(Mt 19:13).*

In instances of miscarriage and stillbirths, a similar reconciliation process can be followed, with the mother and father forgiving each other for each other's failings, anger, or nonacceptance of God's Will for their family and their child. It is the opening up of the hearts of all to the tender process of healing with compassion, dignity, forgiveness, and love that leads to reunion with God and all members of the spiritual family. With healing, hearts can be receptive to welcoming new life with the birth of other children, or taking care of children in need in the spirit of redemption, in complete unity with God.

It is the memory of the early loss of a parent, a divorce, an abortion, or any other significant life experience that we can carry with us. Part of the power of these memories depends on how we choose to relate to them because memories and the emotions they inspire can form strong roots in our hearts. Some people never get over a severe pain in their lives. It can take over their entire personality. They become so identified with the pain that they never allow Christ in to heal it. In the worst cases, the pain turns into sustained anger and bitterness.

Very true.

Sometimes events and encounters happen to us that we don't feel we are capable of forgiving.

Yes. That's an old story. Even if a person can forgive others, very often, the biggest hurdle is for them to forgive themselves. But with Christ's Help, forgiveness is possible if we open our hearts and let Him in—if we surrender our pain to Him. He suffers for us today, just as He did nearly two thousand years ago.

There are calamities or tragedies that happen in our lives, too, whether it is a war, a famine, a disfiguring accident, or a life-changing illness, like cancer or a heart attack. These events form the facts of our lives. Like a tree trunk that has a branch lopped off, our souls are marked by these events. We probably didn't anticipate these terrible incidences when we were young, but these are the facts of our lives—part of our individual history and memory.

And with the Help of God, we can accept them and move forward with forgiveness and love. I often remark when Jesus gave the *Our Father* to the people, this perfect prayer of His, the only phrase He felt necessary to comment on, after He had prayed with them, was the phrase about forgiveness. At the end, He says, *For if you will forgive men their offenses, your heavenly Father will forgive you your offenses. But if you will not forgive men, neither will your Father forgive you your offenses* (Mt 6:14-15). That was very important for Him. Through the Eucharistic Celebration, we can ask Him to intercede for us—to heal our souls of our most difficult challenges. He wants us to come to Him. He said, *Do this for a commemoration of me* (Lk 22:19). In memory of His Sacrifice for us—that He still offers for us.

God won't forgive us, if we can't forgive each other. This is similar to Christ's Instruction: Amen I say to you, whatsoever you shall bind upon earth, shall be bound also in heaven; and whatsoever you shall loose upon earth, shall be loosed also in heaven *(Mt 18:18). We need to forgive and ask forgiveness of people even if they are no longer physically with us.*

That's our out! *(laughs)* They may have mentioned that in the theological work. We have this release from Our Lord through the Sacraments of Holy Orders and the Sacrament of Reconciliation. He gave us an out—the option of forgiveness!

God offers us a way to free ourselves from the bondage of sin and from the memory of the sin.

Yes. Right. Of course, the reconciliation, the absolution, that is given depends on my forgiveness, my letting go, if you will; otherwise, God cannot heal us perfectly. Again, He says, *For if you will forgive men their offenses, your heavenly Father will forgive you also your offenses. But if you will not forgive men, neither will your Father forgive you your offenses* (Mt 6:14-15). So it depends on our own willingness to forgive in order for us to be forgiven, to be absolved.

He also talked a lot about the weeds and the wheat. Good resides alongside evil.

That's right. The *Memory and Reconciliation* document also brings out how the Church must be discerned. It is not the entire Church that has sinned. The Church is holy and is divinely ordained, but the Church will always have the *weeds*—the sinners; it is made up of many sinners. From the beginning, it has always been that way. The Church has not only good fruits but also has weeds among the good seeds. The Church is called the *Mother of Sorrows* because of the suffering inflicted on her from outside the Church, and the suffering she endures because of sins committed by those inside the Church—past and present.

Because the Church, like our families, is composed of all of us and all our imperfect ancestors.

Yes. That's right. So, although the Church is holy, individuals in the Church are not always holy. They are striving for holiness, maybe, but they are not perfect. So that leaves us with many faults, mistakes, for want of a better word, in our history.

When the Church acknowledges these unfortunate histories, it brings the Mystical Body back into alignment with the Divine Order.

Yes. Right

It is the honest consciousness of the memory that exposes what is good and what is not.

Right.

You've talked often about looking at someone's good points. It's the same idea. If we can be vigilant in pulling these weeds out of the gardens of our own hearts and recognizing our own errors, we can more easily grow the portion of Christ within us. As you say, we are trying to become more beautiful. When we don't acknowledge the failures and pain of our memories and those of others, people can get stuck, even whole nations can get stuck in their thinking about other people, other nations, or other religions.

They stop growing in love and increase their pain—many wars are the result of pent-up pain and anger. Animosity is created unless these points of separation with the Divine Order are identified and addressed. We need to live in concert with God—eliminate divisions and behaviors that disrupt harmony. This applies to persons as well. For example, in the instance of divorce, the Church must say no because divorce is a violation of Divine Law as expressed through the Sacrament of Marriage. If the Divine Law is broken, imbalance will occur that will affect future generations.

God wants us to direct our wills to be holy and does not want us to break down His Divine Order. God gave us the Mosaic Law through Moses, the prophet. He gave the commandment of *Thou shalt not commit adultery* (Ex 20:13)—the basic breakup of the family. If adultery has happened often in the family history, it is obvious that much healing has to be done within the family.

The Ten Commandments seem to be directed to those areas in our life that can cause us the most harm.

Of course. Well, actually, I see the Commandments as a perfect pattern of life that will give complete fulfillment. Instead of being prohibitive, I see them, and so many others too, not myself only, as directives to a most fulfilled, perfect life. If I keep those Commandments, my life is fulfilled completely. In the case of adultery, the man, it seems, is often the one who does the adultery. If a number of people have done this in the history of the human family, it is obvious that a lot of healing has to take place *because* of these adulterous unions. Guided by God's Law, the members of the present generation can freely choose to cooperate with God's Call for redemption, live in a sacramental marriage, and free themselves from this terrible past.

The Commandments are directions to a path of peace?

Yes, like directions on the highway of life. If we follow those, we'll reach our goal.

They act as warning signs, too.

Right. *Thou shalt not commit adultery* (Ex 20:13). But we know better. That causes divorce. We cheat on one another, as many times as we want, and then our selfishness can create criminal children. The children have no father or mother, no family life. That is the seed for evil—just as one example.

Or if we want something that doesn't belong to us.

Yes. *Thou shalt not steal* (Ex 20:15). I crave your possessions, and I end up robbing you, or take from you in some way. Damage your reputation—*take* from your good name. Then those cravings cause me harm instead of good, and I end up in Hell, if nothing else.

These violations of the Commandments can start in very subtle ways and grow.

Correct.

In the instance of the father and adultery, the sin itself can multiply in ways we didn't imagine.

Oh yes. Again, it comes in a word, in an urge. The dictum says, *there is nothing like a solitary sin.* A sin affects the whole universe.

In ways we never considered.

Yes. In ways, we never considered.

It may be the disrespect of the son for his father or his mother, the deep anger—the fracturing of relationships. There is some thought, too, that a way of healing is to do the opposite of the sin—that the opposite is the cure. If it's overdrinking, the cure is not drinking. Engaging the opposite creates wholeness, leading back to a balance.

Even the pagan Romans had a beautiful Latin expression, *In Medio Stat Virtus*—virtue stands in the middle between two extremes.

That's where we find peace. We try to have balance.

Correct.

When people sense they are getting out of balance, do you find they become more susceptible to different sins? Maybe they are overtired, overstressed, or worried, and become irritable.

Oh yes. It is a basic in our life, our soul; our intellect is part of the soul. If we don't follow the beautiful directives of the Commandments, then the body is affected. We can encounter all kinds of troubles in our makeup—in our body, mind, and spirit.

The one affects the other, or leads to the damage in the other.

Sure. It's all joined together.

It can come from any direction. Something can affect our body, which then affects our mind, or our mind can affect our body.

Correct.

We have to be vigilant as to what we expose ourselves.

Exactly.

It's the idea that we are all connected to each other. When someone offends us, we react in one way or another, and how we choose to react affects him/her and other people. And vice versa. But it's always a choice. Everybody is free to do whatever he/she wants. It's just that God would like all of us to want to do the same thing and act with consideration and love. That's why we need guideposts to help us recognize what causes disturbance and what doesn't. Today, we are taught to accept disturbance as normal behavior; but it is disorienting for us and can be destructive for society as a whole.

Yes. An example is the huge new juvenile detention place on Ogden Avenue by the Eisenhower Expressway, part of the Rush Hospital plan there. I was remarking, "Instead of building bigger and bigger prisons and detention places, we should be working on the causes of why they were built." Building up the families, taking away those elements in our legislation and in our lives that destroy a family, like divorce, and all of the lack of surveillance over the children on the part of the parents, which, in effect, amounts to a lack of love for them, and working on the causes of those youths being sent to those detention places rather than working on the other end making bigger and bigger prisons and detention places. In medicine, they put it this way, *preventive medicine.* Instead of making more hospitals, which take care of us after the fact, after the diseases come, we should put our efforts and energies on the preventive—to prevent us from going to the hospital—diet, exercise, proper attitude, and so on.

Today, the art of creating a healthy spiritual family is being lost. There are certain structures in a family that are conducive to creating emotional stability, predictability, and the spiritual strength and character that need to be developed for the benefit of the individual and everyone else as well—the healthy personalities and disciplines needed for long-term stable relationships.

Correct.

The Church strongly supports the family unit as the foundation of society.

Of course. It is part of the Gospel. Again, it is the love of God, love of neighbor. Our closest neighbors are our parents and children.

There is considerable social pressure to focus on what we think we need instead of on the essentials of the basic elements of a strong family. We are slow to realize that it is the simple things that can keep a family strong. It's not how big the house is or what clothes we wear, but the simple respect of a father for his wife, the mother, and showing, by example to the children, how to communicate, how to resolve problems, how to forgive, even in this very basic unit.

Yes. Blessed Teresa said, *Love begins by taking care of the closest ones—the ones at home.*[73] Start with the fundamentals.

Every family has problems. But if our family has the same trouble generation after generation, we need to find out why.

Yes. We need to find the source of our problem and face it—root it out. Sometimes an exorcism of the evil spirits affecting the family tree has to take place in order to remove this terrible series of evil events; for example, the spirit of alcoholism, the spirit of anger, etc. Then the family can begin again with a clean slate. That's the history not only of families but also of individuals as well. There was a great British person in the literary tradition, G. K. Chesterton, who became a convert. He said he wanted to join a Church that was always beginning. This is basic. The generation healing can begin now by asking the Lord to heal the past so we can begin anew.

Do spiritual bondages cross generations?

It's obvious. Just like we mentioned the breakup of the family through adultery or similar things, so it's the same as the breaking of the bond of alcoholic addiction or drug addiction from a family tree, or a gambling addiction, perhaps. Or, maybe there is a suicidal tendency. I'm not into the healing of the family tree too much, but I do pray for people for that. I guess that's really where it is, the *praying* for the healing of the family tree.

What about mental illness?

Mental illness also can be prayed for and healed, through the Healing Power of Christ.

Vicki Gutierrez is Father Rookey's secretary at the International Compassion Ministry. She shared some of her many experiences of the Love and Mercy of God:

I was in business for myself selling meat to Chinese restaurants. I really loved it, but I had two partners who took over and I lost everything. I went to Queen of Heaven cemetery and stood in front of the Cross. I said, "Blessed Mother, Jesus, I don't know where I have to go, but point me in the right direction and help me find a job, not just any job, but one that I will like." The next day, I had an International Compassion Ministry newsletter in the mail, so I volunteered. I was a volunteer from 1992 to 1993. The secretary who was here, her name is Marge Ward, decided she wanted to stay home with her kids. She said, "Why don't you be Father's secretary? You belong here."

I asked Jim Hrechko if I could have the secretary's job, and he said they would try to work it out. Ever since then I've been with Father. It's not a job to me; it's a blessing: the healings that I hear about, all the miracles that happen are all blessings from Heaven, and just being around Father. In my eyes, he's so saintly. I've learned so much from him.

One time I was at a dinner, and he had a bunch of priests around him, and I happened to glance up. Father Rookey had a white light like a light bulb inside of him and it protruded all around him. I looked at

the other priests, and they looked like ordinary men. I looked at Father, and he was glowing. (laughs) It's so hard to explain! I said, "Wow, Father truly is a Saint, how could that happen?" Another time at Mass, he held up the Host, and he looked at it, and I could see a light come from his eyes to the Host. He was looking at the Lord.

To be here for people is so rewarding and such a blessing. When people receive miracles, I am in such awe that the Lord is so wonderful, so giving. One day in the morning, the phone rang. Father was out of the office. A young girl said, "My sister is all rolled up in a fetal position on the sofa. I don't know what to do." I said, "Let's say a prayer for her, and I'll put the prayer on the altar." I said a prayer with her sister, and I wrote the girl's name down, and put it on the altar. Later, the phone rang. It was about a quarter to four in the evening. A girl says, "Are you Vicki?" I said, "Yes." She was from Ireland. She said, "My sister called and I was in a fetal position. After my sister hung up, I felt a warmth go through my body. I felt I was healed. I already went to the doctor, and he can't get over it." I said, "That's so wonderful! I'm going to put your name down for thanksgiving and continue to thank the Lord for His Healing." She was crying because she was overjoyed. She had had mental illness.

I put the book on the altar, and I said a prayer, then thought, "Whoa, Father is all the way in England, and he's praying for these people. These prayers are so powerful!" I was flabbergasted at the thought. All of sudden, the Lord spoke to me through my heart. He said, "Don't you know the book is on My Altar, under the feet of My Cross, and I'm answering every intention?" The phone rang, and I said, "Whoever you are give me your intention, the Lord is answering prayers and answering them powerfully." After that, every time the phone rang, there was a healing.

Fig. 77.   *Vicki Gutierrez,* International Compassion Ministry, Olympia Fields, Illinois, 2006.

But it's by working with Father that I'm learning so much about God's Love and Mercy, how He uses everybody as tools, and about praying with the heart and trusting the Lord to answer those prayers. Every day is different. It's just a lot of fun. To help people is so, so rewarding. Today we got a letter, and they said the minute they put their letter in the mail box they were healed. They said, "How can I explain this to you, Father? How can I explain this?" It's hearing stories like that. A lot of people would say, "Oh, yeah, sure." But I've learned that you have to be open to the Lord, because there is nothing that is impossible for Him. Just like the person who put the letter in the mail. It's wonderful that ocean of mercy. He's begging people to come to Him through their faith and trust. A lot of people don't understand why some people are not healed, but you have to trust. He has His reasons and something good is going to come out of it for those who love the Lord.

Today I heard Father talking to someone on the phone, and she was complaining about the pain she was going through. He said, "Pain is the most powerful prayer there is." I thought about that, and it's true: through suffering, you are suffering like the Lord is suffering. A lot of things are profound that come through Father. He's a Saint to me. One time he said, "When we receive the Lord, we also receive Mary because He is part of her." A lot of those things are profound to me.

ˌ♫

An important part of the healing process is recognizing the person and the family as a continuum between the generations and the responsibility each soul has for affecting others. Also having an understanding that spiritual illnesses can manifest in a physical way.

Yes, one of the desperate feelings of people concerning their family tree is feeling so helpless. But these bonds can be broken in a kind of exorcism or deliverance. Some priests have been working on intergenerational healing of the family more than others. Father Robert De Grandis, S.S.J.[74] is one; Father Robert Sears, S.J., Ph.D.,[75] another. And there is one out in California, Father John Hampsch, C.M.F.[76] He's done a great deal on that, so this is all a very important chapter in healing. Father Sears puts it beautifully. He says, "Jesus is the source of healing for all past generations as well as present and future generations; all souls Jesus has chosen to redeem: the living, the dead, and those yet to be born. Through His Resurrection, He enters into God's Eternity, and becomes a new Adam, or the new graced foundation for humanity. So all our prayers for healing are in and through Jesus' mediation."

Jesus reorders the disorder caused by Adam throughout the Mystical Body?

Yes.

We can ask for His Redemption of the Divine Order through prayer and the Mass?

Yes, through the Mass and intercessory prayers.

The purpose of the Mass is to give praise to God and to bring ourselves into order with Him.

Yes. In the Mass, we can throw our troubles onto the Lord. He constantly intercedes for us, takes on our sins, through the Sacrifice of the Eucharist. We can ask Him to forgive us for not being faithful to His Commands, His Laws. All those things that cause disorder of His Perfect Love and Order.

Even illness can be thought of as a disorder—a departure from the complete wholeness and Perfect Order of God. Often in the healing process, first there is a recognition or naming of the illness, then acknowledging that we need Divine Intercession: we are powerless to these forces, or at least we are weak, or susceptible, to them.

Right.

Science is discovering that in our DNA there are the genes for alcoholism, depression, and adultery, even our personality.

We all have weaknesses that affect our body, mind, and spirit. But it is our will to overcome them that decides how we live. We can overcome them with the Help of God—*everything is possible with God* (Mt 19:26).

That gets back to Confession, constant purification, and new beginnings: constantly accepting responsibility and renewing ourselves, thereby helping our families. The Church helps us regularly maintain a spiritual discipline and experience deep communication with God by offering the Sacraments.

Yes. So much in ministry can be attributed to the Grace of turning to God through a good Confession and a resumption of the practices of our faith. That happens so often at our healing services. It is a very important, the most important, product of the healing services. Much more important than a physical healing that may be more impressive but is not as important as the inner healing. There can be aggressive external forces at work, too, preventing our healing and that take perseverance to overcome.

For example, the Lord rewarded the tenacity of this Canaanite woman. He threw all kinds of curves at her, and still she stuck with it, and He gave in. And here yesterday, just before Mass, this mother and her daughter came all the way here. She feels, and her daughter also feels, that the daughter is possessed. They are looking for an exorcist. But I told them that I am not an exorcist, so I cannot make an appointment. If you are possessed and want to make an appointment, I'm not allowed to do that. I tried to get a hold of the exorcist, but he is also a military man, and he's engaged until the end of September. I said, "I'll give you the names of the variety of dioceses that surround Chicago like Rockford, Peoria, the *suffragan* diocese." That's Latin for a diocese attached to an archdiocese.

If you ever read Gabriel Amorth's book *An Exorcist Tells His Story*—he's the famous exorcist in Rome—you'll find in his book a constant appeal to the bishops to appoint an exorcist in their dioceses. They don't believe that the devil is that strong. The constant theme in this book is why don't the bishops appoint an exorcist? They are supposed to according to Canon Law. I read another book when I was a student, it's called *Begone, Satan!* It was about an exorcism of a young person in Iowa, if I'm not mistaken.

That's part of the resistance. If all of that information is away from people, they don't hear about it. They don't understand what's happening to them. A lot of it is diagnosed as mental illness. For people who do recognize these forces, there is the practice of the Three Family Mass. A special Mass is said three times to ask for the deliverance from illnesses within the family tree. The names of all of the family members for generations are listed, and their souls prayed for during the Mass.

Right. They pray for all the different types of attacks on the family tree, from adultery to addictions, all the behaviors that harm the family. They go through a whole litany of *attacks*, in lieu of a better word, on the family through the history of that family. If the family has a family history buff, then they can identify some of those things. That is part of the grace of getting a history of the family.

Prayer for the Healing of the Family Tree

by Rev John H. Hampsch, C.M.F.

Heavenly Father, I come before you as your child, in great need of your help; I have physical health needs, emotional needs, spiritual needs, and interpersonal needs. Many of my problems have been caused by my own failures, neglect, and sinfulness, for which I humbly beg your forgiveness, Lord. But I also ask you to forgive the sins of my ancestors whose failures have left their effects on me in the form of unwanted tendencies, behavior patterns and defects in body, mind, and spirit. Heal me, Lord, of all these disorders.

With your help I sincerely forgive everyone, especially living or dead members of my family tree, who have directly offended me or my loved ones in any way, or those whose sins have resulted in our present sufferings and disorders. In the name of your divine Son, Jesus, and in the power of his

Holy Spirit, I ask you, Father, to deliver me and my entire family tree from the influence of the evil one. Free all living and dead members of my family tree, including those in adoptive relationships, and those in extended family relationships, from every hindrance to receiving the fullness of Your love. By your loving concern for us, Heavenly Father, and by the shedding of the blood of your Precious Son Jesus, I beg you to extend your blessing to me and all my living and deceased relatives. Heal every negative effect transmitted through all past generations, and prevent such negative effects in future generations of my family tree.

I symbolically place the cross of Jesus over the head of each person in my family tree, and between each generation; I ask you to let the cleansing blood of Jesus purify the blood lines in my family lineage. Set your protective angels to encamp around us, and permit Archangel Raphael, the patron of healing, to administer your divine healing power to all of us, even in areas of genetic disability. Give special power to our family members' Guardian Angels to heal, protect, guide and encourage each of us in all our needs. Let your healing power be released at this very moment, and let it continue as long as your sovereignty permits.

In our family tree, Lord, replace all bondage with a holy bonding in family love. And let there be an ever deeper bonding with you, Lord, by the Holy Spirit, to your Son Jesus. Let the family of the Holy Trinity pervade our family with its tender, warm, loving Presence, so that our family may recognize and manifest that love in all our relationships. All of our unknown needs we include with this petition that we pray in Jesus' precious Name. Amen.[77]

(Reprinted with the permission of Rev. John H. Hampsch, C.M.F., Claretian Ministries)

Interesting.

Finding the horse thieves!

Right! Skeletons in the closet!

Finding the things that need to be healed. Doing a history of the family is not all bad.

It gets back to what we were talking about very early on about Divine Law and Natural Law. We are created to operate in a certain way. And if we decide to ignore that reality, then we suffer and others do, too. It matters what we do, because we are all connected.

Actually, this is really again our doing, going against the directives, the Commandments, He gave us to avoid the evils in our society. We then bring those evils on ourselves. A simple example, when I use drugs in an abusive way. The drugs are not evil. God made them. But it is my misuse of them, abuse of them that makes them evil. When I abuse drugs, I'm going to have all of the consequences that come from the use of drugs: the change of personality leading to other types of evil besides—destroying my family, perhaps my marriage, or even stealing, or fighting, or anger. All the things that come with it. That's a simple example of what happens when I go against these beautiful directives. I'll have to come to terms with the evils that come upon me by not observing them. I bring suffering on innocent others because of my sins. It's very simple.

Yes. But God may permit suffering, especially if we bring it upon ourselves.

It's the old story of I'm an alcoholic, and I can't overcome the addiction until I find myself in the gutter without my wife, family, job. Nothing. Then I reach the bottom, and I have only one way to go—and that's up! *(laughs)* And that's my healing. That's God bringing good out of evil. He doesn't want evil, even if we fell and caused the evil. We're the ones who caused the evil by not obeying His Perfect Laws. That's what makes disorder in our lives: the sickness and the disorder in the world—war, evil of every kind.

Of course, tragedies happen to people who have not sinned as well. There is the instance where God permits suffering to strengthen our souls in the virtues of faith and perseverance.

Of course . . . Job lost everything. He suffered tremendously. He loved God, and even offered prayers just in case his children offended Him: *Lest perhaps my sons have sinned . . .* (Job 1:5). But God allowed Satan to test this innocent, holy man.

Job was very wealthy, and he lost even his children. He suffered terribly with sores all over his body. Even his friends had given up on him. But God didn't. Because of Job's faithfulness, God rewarded him with twice as much as he had before, and he lived to one-hundred forty years of age, and had ten more children. This, too, made a big impression on those who knew him. He made Job even greater in the end. This is our challenge, despite everything, to choose to be One with God, to accept our suffering, to do His Will.

Sometimes it's a Mystery why God allows this suffering to happen. It can be for us, like it was for Job, for the strengthening or purification of our souls or others.

Yes.

Notes

[1] His Holiness Pope Pius XII, *Encyclical of Pope Pius XII on the Mistical Body of Christ to Our Venerable Brethren, Patriarchs, Primates, Archbishops, Bishops, and Other Local Ordinaries Enjoying Peace and Communion with the Apostolic See* (Citta del Vaticano: Libreria Editrice Vaticana, 1943), *http://www.vatican.va/holy_father/pius_xii/encyclicals/documents/hf_p-xii_enc_29061943_mystici-corporis-christi_en.html.*

[2] "That this Mystical Body which is the Church should be called Christ's is proved in the second place from the fact that He must be universally acknowledged as its actual Head. 'He,' as St. Paul says, 'is the Head of the Body, the Church.' [43] He is the Head from

Fig. 78. *The Prodigal Son,* sculpture, St. John Cantius Parish, Chicago, Illinois, 2006.

whom the whole body perfectly organized, 'groweth and maketh increase unto the edifying of itself.' From: His Holiness Pope Pius XII, *MYSTICI CORPORIS CHRISTI*, Sec. 34.

3   *Saul, Saul, why persecutest thou me?* (Acts 22:7), Douay.

4   *We see now through a glass in a dark manner; but then face to face* (1 Cor 13:12), Douay.

5   "This memory of the redemption and divinization of man, so profound and so universal, also triggers many other dimensions of memory, both personal and collective. It allows man to understand himself deeply, within the definitive perspective of his humanity. It allows him to understand the different communities in which his history evolves the family, the clan, the nation. Finally, it allows him to understand the history of language and culture, the history of all that is true, good, and beautiful." From: Pope John Paul II, *Memory and Identity: Conversations at the Dawn of a Millennium* (New York, NY: Rizzoli International Publications, 2005), p. 144-145.

6   "Memory evokes recollections. The Church is, in a certain sense, the 'living memory' of Christ; of the mystery of Christ, of his Passion, death, and Resurrection, of his Body and Blood. This 'memory' is accomplished through the Eucharist." Ibid., p.144.

7   President Joseph Cardinal Ratzinger [Pope Benedict XVI], Rev. Sebastian Karotemprel, S.D.B., Msgr. Roland Minnerath, Rev. Thomas Norris, Rev. Rafael Salazar Cardenas, M.Sp.S., and Msgr. Anton Strukelj, *Memory and Reconciliation: The Church and the Faults of the Past* (Citta del Vaticano: International Theological Commission, 1999), "Introduction."

8   ". . . the Church knows that she is not only a community of the elect, but one which in her very bosom includes both righteous and sinners, of the present as well as the past, in unity of the mystery which constitutes her. Indeed, in grace and in the woundedness of sin, the baptized today are close to, and in solidarity with, those of yesterday. For this reason one can say that the Church—one in time and space in Christ and in the Spirit—is truly 'at the same time holy and ever in need of purification.' It is from this paradox, which is characteristic of the mystery of the Church, that the questions arise as to how one can reconcile the two aspects: on one hand, the Church's affirmation in faith of her holiness, and on the other hand, her unceasing need for penance and purification." From: Ratzinger, et al., *Memory and Reconciliation*, Sec. 3, "Theological Foundations."

9   ". . . one can speak of a solidarity that unites the past and the present in a relationship of reciprocity. In certain situations, the burden that weighs on conscience can be so heavy as to constitute a kind of

moral and religious memory of evil done, which is by its nature a common memory. This common memory gives eloquent testimony to the solidarity objectively existing between those who committed the evil in the past and their heirs in the present. It is then that it becomes possible to speak of an objective common responsibility. Liberation from the weight of this responsibility comes above all through imploring God's forgiveness for the wrongs of the past, and then, where appropriate, through the 'purification of memory' culminating in a mutual pardoning of sins and offenses in the present." From: Ratzinger, et al., *Memory and Reconciliation*, Sec. 5.1, "Some Ethical Criteria."

[10] "Objective responsibility refers to the moral value of the act in itself, insofar as it is good or evil, and thus refers to the imputability of the action. Subjective responsibility concerns the effective perception by individual conscience of the goodness or evil of the act performed. Subjective responsibility ceases with the death of the one who performed the act; it is not transmitted through generation; the descendants do not inherit (subjective) responsibility for the acts of their ancestors. In this sense, asking for forgiveness presupposes a contemporaneity between those who are hurt by an action and those who committed it. The only responsibility capable of continuing in history can be the objective kind, to which one may freely adhere subjectively or not. Thus, the evil done often out lives the one who did it through the consequences of behaviors that can become a heavy burden on the consciences and memories of descendants." From: Ratzinger, et al., *Memory and Reconciliation*, "Some Ethical Criteria."

[11] "Purifying the memory means eliminating from personal and collective conscience all forms of resentment of violence left by the inheritance of the past, on the basis of a new and rigorous historical-theological judgment, which becomes the foundation for a renewed moral way of acting. This occurs whenever it becomes possible to attribute to past historical deeds a different quality, having a new and different effect on the present in view of progress in reconciliation in truth, justice, and charity among human beings, in particular the Church and the different religious, cultural and civil communities with whom she is related." From: Ratzinger, et al., *Memory and Reconciliation*, Sec. 5.1, "Some Ethical Criteria."

[12] "The Shoah was certainly the result of the pagan ideology that was Nazism, animated by a merciless anti-Semitism that not only despised the faith of the Jewish people, but also denied their very human dignity. Nevertheless, 'it may be asked whether the Nazi

persecution of the Jews was not made easier by the anti-Jewish prejudices imbedded in some Christian minds and hearts . . . Did Christians give every possible assistance to those being persecuted, and in particular to the persecuted Jews?' There is no doubt that there were many Christians who risked their lives to save and to help their Jewish neighbors. It seems, however, also true that 'alongside such courageous men and women, the spiritual resistance and concrete action of other Christians was not that which might have been expected from Christ's followers.' This fact constitutes a call to the consciences of all Christians today, so as to require 'an act of repentance (tushuva),' and to be a stimulus to increase efforts to be 'transformed by renewal of your mind' (Rom 12:2) as well as to keep a 'moral and religious memory' of the injury inflicted on the Jews. In this area, much has already been done, but this should be confirmed and deepened." From: Ratzinger, et al., *Memory and Reconciliation*, Sec. 5.4. "Christians and Jews."

[13] Pope John Paul II, *Memory and Identity: Conversations at the Dawn of a Millennium.*

[14] Ibid., "Editor's Note," p. xi.

[15] "Memory is the faculty which models the identity of human beings at both a personal and a collective level. In fact, it is through memory that our sense of identity forms and defines itself in the personal psyche. Among the many interesting things I heard on that occasion, this struck me particularly. Christ was acquainted with this law of memory and he invoked it at the key moment of his mission. When he was instituting the Eucharist during the Last Supper, he said: 'Do this in memory of me (Hoc facite in meam commemorationem,' Lk 22:19)," ibid., p. 144.

[16] ". . . Paul Ricoeur spoke of remembering and forgetting as two important and mutually opposed forces that operate in human and social history. Memory is the faculty which models the identity of human beings at both a personal and collective level. In fact, it is through memory that our sense of identity forms and defines itself in the personal psyche," ibid.

[17] Ibid.

[18] Ratzinger, et al., *Memory and Reconciliation*, Sec. 5.1., "Some Ethical Criteria."

[19] Ibid.

[20] Ratzinger, et al., *Memory and Reconciliation*, ref: objective responsibility, etc., and "Introduction."

[21] "The purification of memory is thus 'an act of courage and humility in recognizing the wrongs done by those who have borne or bear the

name of Christian.' It is based on the conviction that because of 'the bond which unites us to one another in the Mystical Body, all of us, though not personally responsible and without encroaching on the judgment of God, who alone knows every heart, bear the burden of the errors and faults of those who have gone before us.' John Paul II adds: 'As the successor of Peter, I ask that in this year of mercy the Church, strong in holiness which she receives from her Lord, should kneel before God and implore forgiveness for the past and present sins of her sons and daughters.' In reiterating that 'Christians are invited to acknowledge, before God and before those offended by their actions, the faults which they have committed,' the Pope concludes, 'Let them do so without seeking anything in return, but strengthened only by 'the love of God which has been poured into our hearts (Rom 5:5).'" From: Ratzinger, et al., *Memory and Reconciliation*, "Introduction."

22 "... the Holy Father [Pope John Paul II] also states, 'Love of the truth, sought with humility, is one of the great values capable of reuniting the men of today through the various cultures.' Because of her responsibility to Truth, the Church 'cannot cross the threshold of the new millennium without encouraging her children to purify themselves, through repentance, of past errors and instances of infidelity, inconsistency and slowness to act. Acknowledging the weaknesses of the past is an act of honesty and courage . . .' It opens a new tomorrow for everyone." From: Ratzinger, et al., *Memory and Reconciliation*, "Conclusion."

23 "The basis of this new memory cannot be other than mutual love or, better, the renewed commitment to live it. This is the commandment ante omnia (1 Pt 4:8) for the Church in the East and in the West. In such a way, memory frees us from the prison of the past and calls Catholics and Orthodox, as well as Catholics and Protestants, to be the architects of a future more in conformity with the new commandment. Pope Paul VI's and Patriarch Athenagoras' testimony to this new memory is in this sense exemplary. Particularly problematic for the path toward the unity of Christians is the temptation to be guided—or even determined—by cultural factors, historical conditioning, and those prejudices which feed the separation and mutual distrust among Christians, even though they do not have anything to do with matters of faith." From: Ratzinger, et al., *Memory and Reconciliation*, Sec. 5.2, "The Divisions of Christians."

24 *And the glory which thou hast given me, I have given to them; that they may be one, as we also are one : I in them, and thou in me; that they may be made perfect in one : and the world may know that thou hast sent me, and hast loved them, as thou hast also loved me* (Jn 17:22-23), Douay.

25 "The principal divisions during the past millennium which 'affect the seamless garment of Christ' are the schism between the Eastern and Western Churches at the beginning of this millennium, and in the West—four centuries later—the laceration caused by those events 'commonly referred to as the Reformation.' It is true that 'these various divisions differ greatly from one another not only by reason of their origin, place, and time, but above all by reason of the nature and gravity of questions concerning faith and the structure of the Church.' In the schism of the of eleventh century, cultural and historical factors played an important role, while the doctrinal dimension concerned the authority of the Church and the Bishop of Rome, a topic which at that time had not reached the clarity it has today, thanks to the doctrinal development in this millennium. In the case of the Reformation, however, other areas of revelation and doctrine were objects of controversy." From: Ratzinger, et al., *Memory and Reconciliation*, Sec. 5.2, "The Divisions of Christians."

26 "Lastly, in relation to civil society, consideration must be given to the difference between the Church as a mystery of grace and every human society in time. Emphasis must also be given, however, to the character of exemplarity of the Church's requests for forgiveness, as well as to the consequent stimulus this may offer for undertaking similar steps for purification of memory and reconciliation in other situations where it might be urgent. John Paul II states: 'The request for forgiveness . . . primarily concerns the life of the Church, her mission of proclaiming salvation, her witness to Christ, her commitment to unity, in a word, the consistency which should distinguish Christian life. But the light and strength of the Gospel, by which the Church lives, also have the capacity in a certain sense, to overflow as illumination and support for the decisions and actions of civil society, with full respect for their autonomy . . . On the threshold of the third millennium, we may rightly hope that political leaders and peoples, especially those involved in tragic conflicts fuelled by hatred and memory of often ancient wounds, will be guided by the spirit of forgiveness and reconciliation exemplified by the Church and will make every effort to resolve their differences through open and honest dialogue.'" From: Ratzinger, et al., *Memory and Reconciliation*, Sec. 6.3, "The Implications for Dialogue and Mission."

27 Rev. Frank Pavone, *Shepherding the Flock After Abortion* (Staten Island, NY: Pontifical Council for the Family, Priests for Life), *http://www.seminarianlifelink.org/postabortion/shepherdingflock.htm*, *www.priestsforlife.org*.

[28] "Evil of fault must not be done that good may ensue; but evil of punishment must be inflicted for the sake of the good." From: Pegis, *Basic Writings of St. Thomas Aquinas*, Aquinas, ST II, Q, 79, ART. 4: "The Will of God, Fourth Article, Whether Blindness and Hardness of Hearts Are Directed to the Salvation of Those Who Are Blinded and Hardened," Vol. II, p. 656-657.

[29] This restoration of the equality of justice by penal compensation is also to be observed in injuries done to one's fellow man. Consequently, it is evident that when the sinful or injurious act has ceased, there still remains the debt of punishment." From: Pegis, *Basic Writings of St. Thomas Aquinas*, Aquinas, ST II, Q, 87, ART 6: "Whether the Debt of Punishment Remains After Sin?" Vol. II, p. 715.

[30] *Create a clean heart in me, O God : and renew a right spirit within my bowels* (Ps 50:12), Douay.

[31] Pegis, *Basic Writings of St. Thomas Aquinas*, Aquinas, ST I, Q, 19: "The Will of God, Ninth Article, Whether God Wills Evils," Vol. I, p. 209.

[32] Joannes Paulus P. II, *Evangelium vitae, To the Bishops, Priests and Deacons, Men and Women religious lay Faithful and all People of Good Will on the Value and Inviolability of Human Life* (Citta del Vaticano: Libreria Editrice Vaticana, 1995), *http://www.vatican.va/holy_father/john_paul_ii/ encyclicals/documents/hf_jpii_enc_25031995_evangelium-vitae_en.html.*

[33] Hippocrates, "The Hippocratic Oath," *From The Hippocratic Oath: Text, Translation, and Interpretation,* translated from the Greek by Ludwig Edelstein (Baltimore, MD: Johns Hopkins Press, 1943).

[34] *He was a murderer from the beginning, and he stood not in the truth; because the truth is not in him. When he speaketh a lie, he speaketh of his own : for he is a liar, and the father thereof* (Jn 8:44), Douay.

[35] "Ignorance is a privation of knowledge due at some particular time. This would not have been in children from their birth, for they would have possessed the knowledge due to them at that time. Hence, no ignorance would have been in them, but only nescience in regard to certain matters. Such nescience was even in the holy angels, according to Dionysius." From: Pegis, *Basic Writings of St. Thomas Aquinas,* Aquinas, ST I, CI, ART. 1. Q101: "Whether in the State of Innocence Children Would Have Been Born with Perfect Knowledge," Vol. I, p. 941.

[36] Aquinas, ST I, Q. 118, ART. 2: "Whether the Intellectual Soul is Produced from the Semen?" Vol. I.; p.1085-1086; ST I, Q. 76, ART. 3: Whether Besides the Intellectual Soul There Are in Man Other Souls Essentially Different From One Another?" Vol. I. p. 704-707.

37 *For behold I was conceived in iniquity; and in sins did my mother conceive me* (Ps 50:7), Douay.

38 David B. Chamberlain, Historical perspectives on pain: experiments in infant pain," *Life Before Birth,* Association for Pre-Natal and Perinatal Psychology and Health (APPPAH), excerpts from "Babies Don't Feel Pain: A Century of Denial in Medicine," *www.birthpsychology. com.* For full text of this article, see: Robbie Davis-Floyd & Joseph Dumit, editors, "Cyborg Babies: From Techno-Sex to Techno Tots" (NewYork and London: Routledge, 1998).

39 Ibid.

40 Ibid.

41 Ibid.

42 Ibid.

43 David B. Chamberlain, Ph.D., Communication before language, *Life Before Birth,* Association for Pre- and Perinatal Psychology and Health (APPPAH), *www.birthpsychology.com*

44 Enid Gilbert-Barness, Diane Debich-Spicer, *Embryo and Fetal Pathology: Color Atlas with Ultrasound Correlation* (West Nyack, NY: Cambridge University Press 2006).

45 David B. Chamberlain, The fetal senses, *Life Before Birth,* Association for Pre- and Perinatal Psychology and Health (APPPAH), *www. birthpsychology.com.*

46 Ibid.

47 Fred J. Schwartz, M.D., Music and perinatal stress reduction, *Life Before Birth,* Association for Pre- and Perinatal Psychology and Health (APPPAH), *www.birthpsychology.com.*

48 *Journal of Prenatal & Perinatal Psychology & Health* (Forestville, CA: Association for Pre- and Perinatal Psychology and Health), *www. birthpsychology.com.*

49 Dr. Carlo Bellieni, "What the Unborn Sense in the Womb,' Zenit.org, Rome, Oct. 4, 2005.

50 David B. Chamberlain, The fetal senses.

51 Allan N. Schore, Ph.D., The neurobiology of attachment and early personality organization, Historical perspectives, *The Birth Scene,* Association for Pre- and Perinatal Psychology and Health (APPPAH), *www.birthpsychology.com.*

52 John C. Sonne, M.D., The varying behaviors of fathers in the prenatal experience of the unborn: protecting, loving and 'welcoming with arms wide open,' vs. ignoring, unloving, competitive, abusive, abortion minded or aborting. *Journal of Prenatal and Perinatal Psychology and Health,* 19(4) (Summer, 2005),*www.birthpsychology.com;*

http://apt.allenpress.com/aptonline/?request=get-abstract&issn=1097-8003&Vol.ume=019&issue=04&page=0319.

[53] Bellieni, "What the Unborn Sense in the Womb," and David B. Chamberlain, Ph.D., Communication before language," *Life Before Birth,* Association of Pre- and Perinatal Psychology and Health (APPPAH), *www.birthpsychology.com.*

[54] Bruce H. Lipton, Ph.D., Maternal emotions and human development, *Early and Very Early Parenting, Life Before Birth,* Association for Pre- and Perinatal Psychology and Health (APPPAH), *www.birthpsychology. com.* And, Paul Thomson, Psy.D., The impact of trauma on the embryo and fetus: an application of the diathesis-stress model and the neurovulnerability-neurotoxicity model, *Journal of Prenatal and Perinatal Psychology and Health,* 19(1), Fall 2004.

[55] Chamberlain, Historical perspectives.

[56] Chamberlain, The fetal senses."

[57] "The Truth about Fetal Pain," Physicians for Life, *http://www. physiciansforlife.org/content/view/921/43/.*

[58] John C. Sonne, M.D., The varying behaviors of fathers in the prenatal experience of the unborn: protecting, loving and 'welcoming with arms wide open,' vs. ignoring, unloving, competitive, abusive, abortion minded or aborting.

[59] Ibid.

[60] Ibid.

[61] Ibid.

[62] Ibid.

[63] Ibid.

[64] Ibid.

[65] Ibid.

[66] "Finally, there is the 'desacralization' that often turns into 'dehumanization': the individual and the society for whom nothing is 'sacred' suffer moral decay, in spite of appearances." From: His Holiness Pope John Paul II, *Dives in Misericordia—On the Mercy of God* (Citta del Vaticano: Libreria Editrice Vaticana, 1980), Sec. 12. "Is Justice Enough?"

[67] His Holiness Pope John Paul II, *Dives in Misericordia—On the Mercy of God.*

[68] His Holiness Pope John Paul II, *Dives in Misericordia—On the Mercy of God,* Footnote 52.

[69] "But precisely at this point, hesed, in ceasing to be a juridical obligation, revealed its deeper aspect: it showed itself as what it was at the beginning, that is, as love that gives, love more powerful than

betrayal, grace stronger than sin." From: His Holiness Pope John Paul II, *Dives in Misericordia—On the Mercy of God*, Footnote 52.

[70] "While hesed highlights the marks of fidelity to self and of 'responsibility for one's own love' (which are in a certain sense masculine characteristics), rahamim, in its very root, denotes the love of a mother (rehem, mother's womb). From the deep and original bond—indeed the unity—that links a mother to her child there springs a particular relationship to the child, a particular love. Of this love one can say that it is completely gratuitous, not merited, and that in this aspect it constitutes an interior necessity: an exigency of the heart. It is, as it were, a 'feminine' variation of the masculine fidelity to self expressed by hesed. Against this psychological background, rahamin generates a whole range of feelings, including goodness and tenderness, patience and understanding, that is, readiness to forgive." From: His Holiness Pope John Paul II, *Dives in Misericordia—On the Mercy of God*, Footnote 52.

[71] Rev. Frank Pavone, MEV, *http://priestsforlife.org*.

[72] Rev. Robert T. Sears, S.J., Ph.D, *http://www.familytreehealing.com*.

[73] "Love begins by taking care of the closest ones—the ones at home. Let us ask ourselves if we are aware that maybe our husband, our wife, our children, or our parents live isolated from others, do not feel loved enough, even though they may live with us. Do we realize this? Where are the old people today? They are in nursing homes (if there are any). Why? Because they are not wanted, because they are too much trouble, because . . ." From: José Luis González-Balado, *Mother Teresa In My Own Words 1910-1997* (New York, NY: Gramercy Books, 1997), p.52.

[74] Rev. Robert De Grandis, S.S.J., *http://www.degrandisssj.com*.

[75] Rev. Robert T. Sears, S.J., Ph.D., *http://www.familytreehealing.com*.

[76] Rev. John H. Hampsch, C.M.F., *http://claretiantapeministry.org*.

[77] Rev. John H. Hampsch, "Praying for Healing of the Family Tree" (Los Angeles, CA: Claretian Tape Ministry).

Reaching for God

Each person, composed of body, soul, and spirit, is called by God to live in Perfect Peace as a creature within His harmonious Divine Order. Blessed by free will, each soul may choose to rush to Him with love, like a child joyfully reunited with its mother, or a soul may choose to turn away from Him. Seemingly deaf to His Call, a soul may choose to follow a path of disorder bringing destruction upon itself and others. Other souls dawdle through life, distracted by the world's lure of excitement, power, and pleasure, prolonging the journey to Him. Still others, filled with pride, rebellion, jealousy, and anger, deliberately depart from His Healing Light, becoming darkened for eternity, choosing to live in permanent disorder and aggressively destroying His Perfect Creation by bringing chaos and death to themselves and others.

Through God's Great Mercy, the suffering encountered upon a soul's life journey is experienced in many ways for the benefit of each soul. For those who have chosen to live apart from His Divine Order but who also choose to love Him, suffering can be remedial for itself, its family, and community, helping the soul and others understand the boundaries of His Order. Gradually, through painful life encounters experienced away from His Perfect Ways,

Fig. 79. *Eucharistic Celebration: Father Peter Mary Rookey, O.S.M.,* Friars' Chapel, Our Lady of Sorrows Basilica Chapel, Chicago, Illinois, 2005.

these souls begin to recognize and amend the thoughts, words, and actions that are disruptive to His Divine Creation and their own peace.

For others, suffering is a path for rediscovering God by ultimately surrendering worldly concerns, and even the body of the soul, to His Care. Sometimes these souls, who have opened wide their hearts to His endless Love and Mercy, are purified and healed in body, mind, and spirit as a testimony to His Power and Glory.

Others, who have chosen to live in union with His Love, and who continually seek purification, are strengthened through His patient Guidance, choosing to take on the suffering of others to draw souls to Him. For frightened, despairing, and discouraged souls, these suffering souls gracefully bring renewed pathways to the restorative virtues of Faith, Hope, and Love. Beautiful souls extend Christ's redemptive Mercy and Love into the deepest recesses of hearts throughout the whole world, releasing bondages to sin, and healing the precious souls of God's Creation, bringing them into joyous reunion with Him.

God sometimes permits suffering to demonstrate His own Power and Mercy, too; for example, when He permits spontaneous healings to happen in your Masses and healing services.

Yes. At our Mass and healing services, we have been blessed with thousands of healings. We always ask for people to write to give witness to the Glory of God. It is often through their suffering and healing that others are brought back to the Church. Their family and friends can't deny what has happened to this person they know very well. When Jesus was asked about the man who was born blind, *Rabbi, who hath sinned, this*

Fig. 80.   *St. Thérèse of Lisieux,* Our Lady's Chapel, St. Ignatius Parish, Chicago, Illinois, 2006. St. Thérèse (1873-1897) entered the Carmelites at the age of fifteen and became a suffering soul. Her autobiography, *The Story of a Soul,* led to her being named a Doctor of the Church. Many miracles are attributed to her. She is the Patron Saint of missionaries, aircraft pilots, and those with illness.

man, or his parents, that he should be born blind? (Jn 9:2). He said, *Neither hath this man sinned, nor his parents; but that the works of God should be made manifest in him* (Jn 9:3). His blindness was healed to show glory to God.

Like the suffering souls.

Right. God also permits the Holy Souls like St. Thérèse of Lisieux, who was bedridden, to suffer for the sanctity of others—just like Christ suffered for us. Many souls are saved this way.

This happens in your healing Masses, too. Someone will pray for another and they will suffer from headaches or have other trouble in their lives for awhile, and then they learn that the person they had been praying for has been healed or has come back to the Church. At one Mass, you were praying for a woman whose arm was hurting, and, after the Mass, your own arm was sore.

We can only try to do what Christ did for us. He suffered for us in every way. Through our own suffering and intercessory prayers, others are healed through His Power.

When you pray your intercessory prayer, you invoke Jesus, the Blessed Mother, the Angels, and the Saints to help this suffering person.

Normally, I pray according to the way Jesus did it, as far as I have figured out from Mark in the *New Testament*. Jesus seemed to cast out the demon first, then He healed. So that's what I do. I invite St. Michael the Archangel to cast out the demons into Hell through the Power of God and even say, "Be gone, Satan!" from this holy daughter or holy son. Then I invoke the blessing of healing upon them and the Holy Spirit.

It's a two-step process?

Yes.

You rebuke the demons. When you are praying, do you feel as though you push them out?

I take a very respectful attitude and let Jesus take all of the credit. I just do what He told us to do, and the people are delivered and healed. I think if He gave me a lot of, oh, insights into these things, I might get proud and think I did it.

Yes. But you do think of it as a one-two punch? Banish and bless through the Authority and Power of Christ?

Yes. When Jesus sent His Apostles out, it says He gave the Apostles power over unclean spirits and to heal the sick, so I think they go together.

Do you consider that too, when you pray for people who have passed on?

Well, those who have passed on, they are hopefully in Purgatory, and you can't do much about them except pray for them and ask the Lord to be merciful to them. We can't directly alter their situation. That's up to the Lord. But it seems that our praying for them, which is the Tradition of the Church, does shorten their stay; it delivers them into Heaven more quickly. Servite-wise, there is a very interesting wall painting in the sacristy in the church in Todi, Italy, where St. Philip Benizi died, where he is laid out. The painting shows interestingly, unbelievably, Purgatory and Heaven. In the painting, there is St. Philip Benizi, and who else? St. Patrick! They are shown helping Mary deliver the souls out of Purgatory, and she is slipping them through to Heaven. It is so interesting.

Does it depict the levels of Purgatory?

Yes. There are those who are nearly liberated for Heaven, then the middle, then one that is tantamount to Hell. The only difference is they have assurance they are going to Heaven.

Their suffering can be relieved through our intercession. We need to pray for them.

If they are in Heaven, we don't need to pray for them; then we ask for their assistance. That's part of the Mystery of Purgatory that helps us to understand it.

But the souls in Purgatory can help us?

Yes. We should pray for them and their intentions. They are being purified by suffering, and so are we, except they have an

advantage because they cannot sin any more. Eventually, we hope we will join them in Heaven with the purified souls, the Saints, in complete union with God.

ผผผผผผผผผผผผผผผผผผผผผผผผผผผผผผผผผผผผผ

All souls are called to become holy. Through its natural gifts, a soul allows God's Love to illuminate its way and take its rightful place in the Mystical Order. Throughout the life of a soul, it is challenged to become ever more beautiful by opening its most intimate being to God's sanctifying Grace. As a soul follows its destiny, it goes through a process of on-going purification until it transitions into a state of full purity, shining with sustained love until it is totally consumed with love for God.

For most souls, this perfecting process includes periods of trials and tribulations that challenge the body, mind, and spirit. Many times, a soul will falter by succumbing to sin through weakness to temptation, pride, and fear, or hardening itself to God's Call. Each time a soul darkens by choosing to distance itself from God's Loving Light, it can also choose to turn again toward Him by asking for forgiveness, expressing sorrow, and making acts of restitution to reorder itself within His Divine Plan. As a soul becomes habituated to living with Grace, it will eventually experience the joy of Heaven and live peacefully in the Presence of the Trinity.

When its earthly journey is over, souls are bound for Heaven, Hell, or Purgatory. Only those rare souls who have attained spiritual perfection while living on earth are transitioned into the state of Heaven. For those souls that did not use their earthly life to perfect their beings in service to God through selfless service to others, but who have remained open to His Call, upon physical death, their lives will be judged by Jesus Christ. These souls enter into a state of further purification where they can be cleansed of the remnants of sin.

Fig. 81. *Prayer Intention Candles and the Infant Jesus of Prague,* St. John Cantius Parish, Chicago, Illinois, 2006.

Divine Justice demands that, while sins may be forgiven, each soul must provide satisfactory restoration for all violations of His Laws, including the suffering it has caused others directly or indirectly, known or unknown to the soul, all sins of commission and omission. This remedial spiritual state is called Purgatory. Mystics throughout the centuries have implored others to pray for the souls undergoing tribulation. Images of souls enduring purifying Divine Fires are common. As a soul is purified, it becomes transformed by God's Grace and Knowledge.

As members of Christ's Mystical Body, souls in the state of purgation can be assisted by the intercession of souls on earth through offerings of Masses, private prayers, fasting, acts of charity, good works, alms giving, and similar pious acts, as well as prayers for intercession by the Angels and Heavenly Souls. These acts of love and sympathy are offered to speed the process of purification directed to perfect, eternal union with God. In turn, earthbound souls can ask for the effective intercession of souls in Purgatory, for, despite their trials, they are close to the Heart of God.

But for those souls who have chosen to persistently reject God's Love and live separately from Him while on earth, the consequence of their obstinate sin is to live in a state of Hell, a condition that is far distant from God's Presence and precludes the Presence of His Grace. Through Divine Providence, the choice of a soul's ultimate state—Heaven, Hell, or Purgatory—is selected by the soul itself through God's Gift of Free Will.

The vibrant relationship between the living and departed souls is an integral part of Church teachings rooted in the penitential traditions of the ancient Church, which were based on the inherited practices of the Orthodox Jews and pagan cultural traditions. Prayers for the dead were inscribed in the catacombs, included in liturgies, and addressed in literature. An island retreat for penitents, St. Patrick's Purgatory, Lough Derg, Ireland, was established by the sixth century attracting pilgrims throughout the centuries through today.

In the tenth century, St. Dunstan described the practice of commemorating the dead on the third, seventh, and thirtieth day of departure. During this period, too, beautifully inscribed rolls listing the names of the living departed souls, commemorated with verses of praise, were circulated among religious houses. Also in the Middle Ages, guilds organized burial services and gave alms to poor people to pray for the departed, as the poor are believed to be under the special care of Christ and their prayers especially effective. Memorial donations to churches, the sick, and the elderly were notable practices, with the wealthy endowing universities and willing land to the Church to ensure that Masses were said on their death anniversaries.

Clement of Alexandria (d. prior to 215) and Origen (d. 253/254) advanced the early Christian philosophy that God uses punishment beneficially to educate and redeem souls, a belief later confirmed by St. Thomas Aquinas (d.1274). The spiritual state of Purgatory was first confirmed as a dogma at the Second Council of Lyons (1274), expressed by the Council of Florence (1438-1439), and decreed by the Council of Trent (1563). Eventually, a special Mass, originating at the monastery at Cluny, France, for the souls of the departed, became part of the liturgical calendar as the Feast of All Souls, November 2, immediately following the Feast of All Saints, November 1. These feast days offer a special time to remember loved ones and to remind ourselves of the need to embrace a selfless life of continual purification.

The Church today continues to support the ancient traditions that assist the Poor Souls of Purgatory and aid the purification of those still on earth through the soul strengthening practices of Mass offerings, fasting, prayer, alms giving, and good works. Just as Jesus Christ constantly offers Himself for the redemption of all souls, earthly souls can also open themselves to God's Grace by offering physical and spiritual sacrifices for Divine Intercession for themselves, family members, and whoever is in need of prayer to become more quickly united in a common spiritual union of Perfect Light, Peace, and Love.

Father Rookey and other religious who have devoted their lives to the selfless service of God, and who are trained in the art of directing souls, help guide souls in their journeys to God. For those recently departed souls,

Father Rookey says there should be no fear of what is before them, for all attention will be on God. [1]

Eternal Rest Grant Unto Them O Lord and May Perpetual Light Shine Upon Them.

🐦🐦🐦🐦🐦🐦🐦🐦🐦🐦🐦🐦🐦🐦🐦🐦🐦🐦🐦🐦🐦🐦🐦🐦🐦🐦🐦

Suffering occurs in the living, as well as in those souls in Purgatory, for their correction and purification. But we can always pray to ask for them and ourselves to be released from suffering through Christ's Mercy.

Yes. The souls in Purgatory are close to God, even though they are suffering the challenge of spiritual purification. Often people call because they are under stress, under trials of many kinds of sickness, marriage problems, and so on. I tell them, "In the end, these diseases are not from God, but the Lord brings good out of them for us. He brings good out of evil." And then I tell them, "There is no other way of becoming great persons, recovering the image and likeness of God, which we lost in Adam's sin, except through struggles, through challenges like this—whatever the trouble they are experiencing. Coming to grips with these troubles is the making of ourselves back into that image and likeness that we lost." There is no other way.

Just think of any *greats* in history. You can see if they didn't have challenges, or if they had walked away from the challenges they faced, they wouldn't have become great. St. Monica is the great example. These trials and struggles are the stuff that make us great, and, in that sense, they are a great boon to us. Our Lord was maybe referring to that when He said, The Kingdom of Heaven suffers violence.[2] There is violence—we have to fight to gain the Kingdom of Heaven.

Fig. 82.   *Do This in Memory of Me: Eucharistic Celebration and Father Peter Mary Rookey, O.S.M.*, International Compassion Ministry, Olympia Fields, Illinois, 2005.

Fig. 83.   *Blessed Mother*, stained glass window, St. John Cantius Parish, Chicago, Illinois, 2006.

We have to fight for it.

Yes. Fight for it.

Suffering comes for different reasons, but we have a choice in how we respond. We can either take it on as a challenge, or we can become angry and resist it.

Yes. Exactly. Then it doesn't do us any good.

It just makes us bad to be around! (laughs)

Exactly. And it makes us suffer the more.

We need to find a purpose for our suffering.

Right. That's it. Offer ourselves with Christ. As Paul puts it, Filling up in the sufferings in Christ.[3]

Many of the Saints rejoiced in their suffering and trials because they saw them as a way of becoming closer to God by continually purifying their souls.

Yes. St. Padre Pio suffered the bleeding wounds of the stigmata, shedding blood for decades to save souls. St. Faustina Kowalska also desired to be a living sacrifice for the intercession of souls. Jesus gave her the beautiful *Divine Mercy Chaplet* that we pray every day at three o'clock: *For atonement of our sins and those of the whole world.*

The Blessed Mother is warning us to return to a life of prayer centered on God: to fast and pray for our sins and the sins of others. Many believe the world is in a bad way and there will be repercussions for our sins.

Of course. There's bound to be. The result of evil brings on evil consequences.

Whether it's in the weather, earthquakes, famine, or wars?

Everything was in order before we fell. Man was the head of the universe. The Lord had made him governor of all Creation, and, when he fell, all Creation fell and went into disorder.

Do you see that within our societies there are disorders we don't even recognize—that we have normalized disorders?

Yes. But the effects of the sins remain. It's obvious.

The law is the law. For example, slavery; people thought that was normal. Slave owners were people who went to church, and some were high in the community—even some of the American presidents owned slaves. It took time and the suffering of millions of people for generations for us to understand that it was wrong. Sometimes we can't even see what we are doing because sin is normalized.

Well, there was slavery in the *Old Testament*. But Jesus came to deliver the prisoners, deliver the slaves, that's the *"New"* Testament. A new Covenant of Love.

Over time, we begin to recognize the precious dignity of persons through the suffering of others. God's Time is not our time. He seems to teach us over time.

Like Peter said, One day is a thousand years for Him.[4]

We need to address, as completely as possible, our family's spiritual history and ask for forgiveness and Divine Intercession to help the family back to a healthy way of being. It's similar to when we go to a doctor and he wants to know about all the physical illnesses and problems that are passed down, but these are spiritual problems.

Right.

It's a physical, emotional, spiritual, and psychological profile of our family.

Right.

In very serious family situations like a pattern of attempted suicide or other intractable problems, if people don't want to change, is that part of it? Their free will? Even though you pray and hold up your end of the bargain, that person still has the free will to not change. You are not trying to control them through prayer, but there is a relationship with Christ, through prayer, to help the other person.

We have to consider how Christ would handle that. In the *Poem of the Man~God*, according to the visions of Maria Valtorta, one of

Satan's great temptations to Jesus was why go along with all this suffering and death because comparatively few people will benefit from all your suffering in the whole world?[5] But Jesus didn't accept that. He went on and prayed and offered Himself for us. It's like His Law: Love your enemies, do good to those who persecute you.[6] This is just the opposite of what the world would preach: What greater love than this no man has except to lay down his life for his brother.[7] What we forget is this is the ultimate in the perfect person.

We recognize this civilly, for example, when you are made a hero because you saved me from drowning, or you're a fireman and you saved my life and got me out of the burning building, and so on. This is the same way in a marriage. Our praying and sacrificing for the person, even if our love is not returned; that is the maker of great people—to love even when they are not loved in return.

That's how God loves, too.

That's the way God loves us. That's the way Christ loves us. They say that Christ's religion is the only one that tells us to love our enemies, do good to those who persecute us.

Be steadfast in that love because that's the only thing that will bring them back.

That's a real Divine Love. The kind of love God has for us.

And the kind of love a parent has for a child.

Yes.

When a person is entering a marriage, they are marrying all the spiritual history of their proposed spouses' family, too, the potential ancestral predispositions to good and evil?

Yes. But it is the person's free will that determines whether good or evil will prevail. That is the great salvation history of Christ: *But when it pleased him, who separated me from my mother's womb, and called me by his grace, to reveal his Son in me* (Gal 1:15). Each soul has a choice to follow Christ.

But even though, if baptized, the soul may be relieved of the inherited punishment for the sins of its ancestors, it may be susceptible to

the effects of the sins of its ancestors: the temporal consequences that manifest in illness, suffering, and death, and the weaknesses of character that are part of the concupiscence *of its family history, or the inclination to sin in a certain way.*

In marriage, a spouse is called to assist in the intercessional healing and strengthening of the other toward holiness. Marriage is a sacred union of the spirits of the husband and wife. Co-joined, the challenges and blessings of one become the challenges and blessings of the other and those of their children.

Most people don't think of that today. We think more about personal attraction and the character of the individual, but not the potential spiritual influences of the family on the individual, and, possibly, on the marriage.

Again. Even if these influences manifest, we need to handle the challenge, realizing how enriched I will become by handling my problem with my spouse, for example. That when I walk away from it, cut myself off from it, it doesn't do me any good. It's our handling of the challenges that makes us the great persons we become. A good example is Blessed Teresa of Calcutta. She saw these people on the streets. She belonged to a comfortable teaching congregation in India for upper class Indian children, but she saw these people dying on the streets, of hunger or of distress of some kind, and all of the abandoned children. Instead of walking away from it, she came to terms with the suffering and thought she was called by the Lord to start a new congregation to care for these people. That's what made her so great.

Should we consider the things we complain about or are concerned about as a calling to meet the challenge?

Right. And then there are the political fields. For example, Winston Churchill. They called him a bulldog because he stood up to the Nazis. He was the strength of the opposition to the Nazis who wanted to take over England. One of my favorite

Fig. 84. *Jesus, I Trust in You,* House of Bethany, Vandalia, Illinois, 2007.

quotes about him is the commencement speech he gave at a university there. Bombs were falling all over England during the war, and he gave this talk that consisted of just never, never, never, never—about ten times—give-up! That was his total speech! *(laughs)*

We need to look beyond the immediate situation and persevere over the long term.

Yes. That's right. This is the way we are in this ministry. We've been stopped over the years and told to close down and everything, and yet the ministry has gone on.

That's how you know it's blessed by Christ.

Yes, with Jesus' Help. My meditation is on the Way of the Cross, the three falls. He kept His goal in mind and went on up, up, and away—in the way TWA [airlines] used to advertise! We know that God is with us, and He will see us through every difficulty. He never allows any difficulty to come into our lives that He and we cannot handle.

In this ministry, like Blessed Mother Teresa's ministry, it is the idea of seeing ourselves within a greater Mystery and within a greater community. She didn't identify herself only with her family, or within her own religious community, but with her local community in India, and then she had a bigger impact on the whole world.

She was very concerned about the spiritual desolation of families today. She said, "Peace and war begin at home."[8] Today, the divorce rate is so high. Now we have a generation of children of divorce causing much confusion for themselves and others. There is the phenomenon of starter marriages. Children of divorce often will marry for a short period of time just because they are replicating what their parents did by recreating the pain and anger of rejection experienced when the marriage broke up. Later, they get married again, but this time it's outside the Church. It's so sad.

That's why divorce is directly opposed to what Christ is telling us: What God has joined, let no man put asunder.[9] But we know better, and so we have divorce. If we only realized that staying together or at least not divorcing is a means of our becoming holy. This made a Saint out of Monica, the mother of Augustine. She today with her pagan husband, who treated her like a pagan, would have gone to an attorney and paid a couple of hundred dollars to be divorced. But no, she stayed with him and prayed for him. For forty years she suffered with this pagan husband and errant son Augustine. And her husband finally became a Christian, and, of course, Augustine also. But if she hadn't stayed with them both and had gone off and run away from this challenge to her faith and to her life, she would never have had S-A-I-N-T in front of her name. That was her making and that is the history of fallen man: taking on the challenge or refusing the challenge.

God brings good even through our falls, through our sins and overcoming them. Let's say, I'm addicted to alcohol. It's my fighting my addiction that makes me an outstanding person. I remember a priest in our Order who was an alcoholic, and he overcame his addiction. When he walked down the street standing tall, his victory came out in his personality, in his gait, in his whole way of living, because here was a man who had conquered.

There is a spiritual concept, too, of the virtue of steadfastness. If you are married to someone who is breaking down the family, or if your children go in a direction that seems so awful, one person in your family can help be strong and that will affect everyone else.

That's right, it only takes one. One of our promoters in the South, in Charlotte, North Carolina, is an outstanding counselor, Phil DeLuca, MSW. He has written a book that is very popular called *Solo Partner*[10] in which he helps and directs just one partner to heal the marriage. Even if the other partner doesn't go along, that person can bring about a healing in the marriage—going solo. One partner alone. He lectures all over the United States.

Since we were created by God, and He knew us before we were born, and the family unit into which we were born, and the particular circumstances that we were born into, we need to stay together.

Well, St. Monica was a solo partner. She prayed. She didn't have all this psychological, psychiatry language to go by, but she simply prayed at it with marvelous results!

She must have been praying pretty hard!

ʗ ʗ

Dear Father Rookey,

The following has happened to our family, through your prayers. You are miles away, but these miracles have taken place:

1. *The reunion of my sister with her husband after twenty-five years;*
2. *The cure of knee pain, from which my youngest sister was suffering;*
3. *The cure of my mother's heart ailment;*
4. *My nephew, who was refusing to attend school, goes now.*

I will remember you as a priest, praying for an unknown person like me.

Africa, 1999

ʃ ʃ

What would you say to the children of divorce today when they reach out; when they aren't sure what to do because they haven't had the modeling of a secure marriage? What is the child supposed to do when their parents are electing to be divorced?

I would say maybe the child will be the one to stop the divorce. As a prophet told of Jesus: *And a little child shall lead them* (Isa 11:6). Jesus came to us as a little child. So often a marriage is cemented by the child. Children start coming and the parents forget themselves and start concentrating on the child. That's what I would say to a person whose parents are thinking of divorce.

I'm thinking of the innocent. Among all this confusion today are these innocents who are hurt by all this. Where do they get their strength

for overcoming and creating a new model for themselves? How do they reach beyond that?

Number one is Christ's Word: What God has joined let no man put asunder[11]—if they value marriage. First, we have so many cases when people call and ask about reconciliation, and we find out the marriage is invalid. They have been already married two or three times. You have to dig a little bit. Then I tell them, "You're asking me to pray for something that is against God's Law!"

A man called, oh, it must be several years ago now. I was right here at the phone, and he was crying mercilessly because his wife had left him, and he wanted prayers that they would be back together again. I find out he was married before, she was married before—maybe several times—and he wanted me to pray for reconciliation for an invalid union. I said "You're asking me to pray to God for something that He's against." How silly can you be?! Some people don't realize the source of their problem is that they are not following the perfect rules that the Lord gave us to live by. We know better. We go our own way.

You are saying that divorce is a kind of betrayal and abuse of children?

Yes.

ϾϾϾϾϾϾϾϾϾϾϾϾϾϾϾϾϾϾϾϾϾϾϾϾϾϾϾϾϾϾϾϾϾϾϾϾϾϾϾ

Dear Father Rookey,

In the summer of 1999, I had been praying intently for a man who was in a coma, and he passed away. At the September service when it was over, I was feeling empty, and I said, "Lord, I need someone to pray for," as I began to exit the church out through the sacristy. There at the top of the sacristy stairs was a lady with sorrow on her face and a small boy in her arms. And she said to me, "Will you pray for this boy?" I was stunned that He might answer me this quickly.

It seems the lady was the grandmother of this boy, her daughter's child born out of wedlock, and his father wanted nothing to do with him. Grandma said it was a desperate situation, and the boy seemed to be greatly disturbed, even going so far as to take a small knife and stab at the flowers when she had him in the garden. Why wouldn't he act this way being deprived of the love he needed desperately? I asked her to let me have him, even though I didn't know what to expect. He came in my arms as a gentle lamb, and I carried him over to Father Rookey and explained the child was being tortured. He blessed him with great love.

I then had the notion to bring him in the chapel. I continued to hold him in my arms, and he never moved. Grandma and I prayed intently at the foot of the altar. Finally I laid him down, and he never moved as though dead. We offered up the sufferings of this child to the Lord, as he was too young to understand. Finally I picked him up and returned him to Grandma. She left the church, and I had not seen her since November 3rd when I met her at another service.

She told me the situation had greatly improved, and the father was even providing financial support. Grandma had a smile on her face and a sparkle in her eyes. Praise and glory to you, Holy Spirit.

Again, several months passed before I saw her again. She said one day the little boy told her he loved Jesus and began to pray for her. Now when they are together, he prays for her, and she for him.

Thank You, Jesus, for a loving Grandma, Your Holy Priest, and Your many wonders.

In divorce, we tend to focus on the impairment of the relationship of the spouses, but, while they are impaired, they are manipulating the children because the children are subject to their will. In the marriage, what is the duty of the spouses? Isn't there a duty to the children?

They are depriving their children of the basic things—a father and a mother.

They are giving a bad example?

Yes. They are giving them a bad example. Jesus said that if you break up a marriage and marry somebody else you are living in adultery. That's why the so-called annulment means there was no marriage to begin with. But still, I think, and the Holy Father is trying to bring this out also, that even though there was no marriage to begin with because there was no intention of making a marriage forever, or whatever the reasons for the annulment, if we wanted to think of those poor children, we would suffer as Saint Monica did and not run away from it and let it sanctify us. Difficult as that might be.

But you wouldn't recommend putting children in danger if someone was threatening them physically.

That's true. That's true. If it's a case of life and death, then that's different, of course. Then there is no question, we should try to save them. But that's not the situation in the majority of cases.

But it's this contributing to the confusion of the children that's an abuse.

That's the worse thing. Nowadays we see that sign, *Divorce $250 and up*. Almost anything goes.

It's easy to get divorced. It's accepted today. But we don't realize that the price that's really paid isn't the money; it's years of confusion for the children, their struggles with feelings of anger and rejection, and, as they grow up, often experiencing a series of broken relationships and passing this emotional damage on to future generations.

Right.

It's setting in motion a cycle of confusion for ourselves, too, with the disruption of the whole family and extended family members questioning how they should relate to each other. It's complicated for everyone.

The *Catholic Catechism* is the directive on this. It's powerful. One of the greatest gifts Pope John Paul II gave us in his pontificate is the *universal catechism.*

It gives direction on marriage, parenting, and all of these things?

It treats the basics of our faith so beautifully. His other works *Love and Responsibility*[12] and *The Theology of the Body*[13] are also wonderful expressions of the Sacrament of Marriage.

Marriage, as a Sacrament, is an eternal joining. Is divorce really a delusion? Can there be any such thing if two people are truly spiritually joined? Is divorce similar to what we were discussing regarding addictions: that divorce can be a mask, a temporary way out of a deeper spiritual problem?

Particularly with people who just go from one spouse to another. Sometimes we have these people who are married and then try, try again.

It's because they don't get to the original source of the pain. Is that right?

Well, I think it is because they don't realize that love, true love, is not a matter of flesh but rather the spirit and the will. It's centered in the will. If it weren't centered in the will, Jesus could never have offered Himself. Fleshly speaking, we flagellated Him, spat on Him, betrayed Him, and so on, through our representatives there in Jerusalem at the time. Even the Apostles ran away after He was apprehended—except John, he came back and stayed with Our Lady.

Fleshly speaking, Jesus could not love us or love those who represented us. His Love was in His Will—in His Will to love us. For example, "I love you, maybe as my wife. But you have stepped out on me," as we say, gone to another man, or vice versa. Or, a wife loves the husband despite of his having betrayed her. Look at the love. How can we say "No" when Jesus loved even Judas who betrayed Him? St. Peter denied Him three times in the midst of His Passion. But yet He accepted Peter, and Peter didn't give up on the Love of God as did Judas. St. Peter asked for His Pardon, and Jesus not only pardoned him, but He let him make up through his three gestations of love. After the Resurrection when He appeared to the Apostles, He asked Peter three times if he loved Him. Even made him, in spite of his betrayals, the rock upon which He built His Church. Peter became the first representative of Jesus, after He went up to Heaven.

We don't realize in marriage that our love has to be a love of the will. God makes us attractive to each other to help us marry. The attraction only lasts for a short time, so the continuation of the marriage must be in the will: "I love you in spite of everything." That's why we need to reach an understanding in another sense that we elect to love each other, that's really the basic thing.

I often tell people that the beauty of the attraction is toward the spirit within the person. If the person is beautiful inside that person will always be attractive. I always think back to Teresa of Calcutta who was not a movie star. To the contrary, she would have never been made a star in Hollywood because she had big lines on her face, a big nose; she was not a beauty in that sense.

But every year, Teresa of Calcutta was chosen as one of the most admired women in the whole world, wasn't she, because her beauty was from within? She showed this love to the abandoned in the streets. She washed them, fed them, and listened to them. At least, she said that they would know they were loved before they died. Love is in the will. It's in the heart. That's what I must understand when I marry: that my love must be a love of the will, of the heart, not simply an attraction of the flesh.

When people are getting married, they may not want to think about the vows when they are saying, for richer or poorer, in sickness or in health . . .

Yes.

'Til death do we part. *This is the Church's way of reminding people that this isn't just for today, this is long term, and how they love each other will affect future generations in this world and the next. When we are talking about using our free will, it applies to this Sacrament too. The marriage vows are just as serious as the vows of a priest. Marriage is a chosen life path, a way of experiencing life on earth. It is a long, unpredictable journey, and, like going into the forest, we don't know what we are going to experience in a marriage, but whatever it is . . .*

Yes.

You emphasize that there is a constant need for forgiveness. Part of the process of asking for forgiveness is demonstrating acts of atonement. Today, we use the word reparation *to describe the process of coming back into unity or repairing the damage of what's been done. It's not just saying, "I'm sorry." There are different steps involved. The first part is acknowledging what I've done; and the second part is making reparation, or making that person whole whom I've sinned against—giving back what I have stolen, or apologizing for something I've done or not done with the commitment not to do it again. Then there is forgiveness. There is a preamble to forgiveness. It isn't just, "Please, forgive me." There is a consciousness involved in the process.*

Yes. We need to reorder ourselves to become One with God and the person we offended. But also, we so often find it difficult to forgive, so we need a softening up process to bring us to that point. I think one of the strongest helps to my forgiving (for example: if someone tried to murder me, or my husband has walked out on me and committed adultery), and one of the strongest motivations, in fact, it is very basic, is that it is only by my *forgiving* that I can be healed and make my life useful again. Because as long as I cannot forgive, I'm rendered less productive.

Less whole.

Fig. 85. *Mother Teresa,* courtesy of Seattle University Calcutta Club.

Yes. And in fact, this wound in me can produce all kinds of disturbances in my mental and physical health.

To stop the hemorrhaging, or the damage, the multiplication of the effects of the wound from the sin, is forgiveness that step?

It could easily be.

Do you find that forgiveness is often the turning point or re-direction of the relationship back to unity again.

Of course. Not only that, but the returning of health. I've seen it. My attitude changes. My whole life. Today, there is so much talk of abuse. My father or mother abused me, or my teachers.

We can hold onto hurt feelings for our whole life, letting them keep us from doing what God wants us to do. But we can't turn back to wholeness until we forgive—even if that person never apologizes or won't recognize what they have done. God can make up for their hurt by filling our wounds with Christ's Love.

Unforgiveness can bring on depression—all kinds of evils in our lives. It's obvious. It's part of the basic Commandment. Again: love of God, love of neighbor. Love your enemies! Do good to those who injure you, calumniate you.[14]

Because they are still part of us in the Mystical Body. Even though they hurt us, they are still part of us.

That's true.

We can decide for ourselves how far we're going to take this: whether we are going to carry this wound for our entire lives and into other relationships with people. If we decide to let the wound go deeper and deeper, the damage becomes worse.

It affects all of our relationships.

But that is our responsibility.

Yes.

Not the person who inflicted the original wound. It is our responsibility to heal the wound.

Correct. We can gain the strongest motivation to obtain forgiveness and get rid of unforgiveness, which is, basically, hatred. That is: "Hey, who's winning here? I'm losing! This is making me unhappy and feel depressed." My healing can only come from complete forgiveness: Love your enemy, do good to those who calumniate you, who speak all evil against you.[15] This is the revolution of Christianity. Somebody said—I'm not sure it's true—that Christ's Word is the only religion that commands us to love our enemies.

On our end of it, we can make the decision in an instant or in years that we're going to create healthiness in our own lives—that we are going to be healthy people, even if that other person never changes. That other person may choose to be evil and destructive for his/her whole life.

That's their problem; yours it is to engage in forgiveness, no matter what happens on their part.

And to recognize they may have caused disorder in your life, but you are responsible for re-ordering your life through healing and the Grace of God.

Asking Our Lord, like Our Lord's Words on the Cross. Archbishop Fulton Sheen formed the expression—or maybe it was someone else—that Christ taught forgiveness in the beatitudes with His Word, Blessed are you when men speak ill of you and do all evil against you. Rejoice and be glad. That's the way they treated the prophets before them. Do good to them. Do good to those who do evil against you.[16] He *preached* forgiveness on the Hill of Beatitudes, and He *practiced* it on the Hill of Calvary by saying, Father forgive them, they know not what they do.[17] And to the Good Thief, *This day thou shalt be with me in Paradise* (Lk 23:43).

Do you find that part of maintaining order is not allowing the wound to take root in you in the first place; that the moment a person hurts you, you try to forgive them as quickly as possible.

Oh yes. Before the wound becomes intolerable.

So you push it back if someone hurts you or offends you, because people do offend you at times.

Get rid of it.

You push it back and you don't let it penetrate. Is that it?

Otherwise, you're in trouble. It came to me that it is the most powerful motivation you can have.

If somebody offends you—you are human, so your feelings can get hurt—do you immediately ask God to forgive them?

Oh yes. Sure. Destroy that temptation immediately.

The temptation to go for it . . . become angry?

Yes, "You punch me in my eye; I'll punch you right back." The first impulse.

St. Patrick had a prayer protection song called the Deer's Cry: Christ before me, Christ above me, Christ to my right, Christ to my left—*a spiritual shield. Is what you're describing similar to that?*

Yes. It definitely is. It is Christ's Word. It has to be right.

Fig. 86.   *St. Patrick,* Our Lady's Chapel, St. Ignatius Parish, Chicago, Illinois, 2006. A Romanized Celt, St. Patrick was born into a Christian family; his grandfather was a priest and his father a deacon. In his mid-teens, he was abducted by slave traders and sold to a master in Ireland where he tended sheep for six years and learned the ways of the Irish people. At the time, Ireland was in a stage of very early Christian development. Alone, his spirituality deepened. Through prayer, he encountered Christ and had visions and dreams, one of which encouraged him to escape and return to his homeland. Once reunited with his family, he had a dream in which he heard the voices of the Irish people calling him back. He, eventually, returned to Ireland as a bishop. Noted for his spiritual powers, perseverance, penitential purgations, and political acumen, he firmly established the Church amidst the pagan stronghold. He died circa 461.

The idea is that we live in constant unity within the Order of God the best that we can. We consciously try to keep returning to unity. It is interesting this idea of order and the responsibility to keep order in our own lives, no matter what happens, because we are always encountering disturbances.

Yes. But it's God's Grace that keeps us whole.

ଔ ଔ

Patrick's Hymn

Patrick made this hymn. It was made in the time of Laoghaire son of Niall. The cause of its composition, however, was to protect him and his monks against deadly enemies that lay in wait for the clerics. This is a corselet of faith for the protection of body and soul against devils and men and vices. When anyone shall repeat it every day with diligent intentness on God, devils shall not dare to face him, it shall be a protection to him against every poison and envy, it shall be a defense to him against sudden death, it shall be a corselet to his soul after his death. Patrick sang this when the ambuscades were laid against his coming by Laoghaire, that he might not go to Tara to sow the faith. It appeared before those lying in ambush that they (Patrick and his monks) were wild deer with a fawn (Benen) following them. Its name is 'Deer's Cry'.

St. Patrick's Breastplate
(circa 432 AD, translated by J. Ryan, S.J.)

I arise to-day
 through a mighty strength, the invocation of the Trinity,
 through belief in the threeness,
 through confession of the oneness
 of the Creator of creation.

I arise to-day
 through the strength of Christ with His baptism,
 through the strength of His crucifixion and His burial,

*through the strength of His Resurrection with His
ascension,
through the strength of His descent for the Judgment
of Doom.*

I arise to-day
*through the strength of the love of the Cherubim,
in obedience of angels,
in the service of the archangels,
in hope of resurrection to meet with reward,
in prayers of Patriarchs,
in predictions of Prophets,
in preachings of Apostles,
in faiths of Confessors,
in innocence of holy Virgins,
in deeds of righteous men.*

I arise to-day
*through the strength of Heaven:
light of sun,
brilliance of moon,
splendor of fire,
speed of lightening,
swiftness of wind,
depth of sea,
stability of earth,
firmness of rock.*

I arise to-day
*through God's strength to pilot me:
God's might to uphold me,
God's wisdom to guide me,
God's eye to look before me,
God's ear to hear me,
God's word to speak for me,
God's hand to guard me,
God's shield to protect me,
God's host to secure me,*
*against snares of devils,
against temptations of vices,
against inclinations of nature,
against every one who shall wish me ill,*
*afar and anear,
alone and in a multitude.*

I summon to-day all those powers between me (and these evils)
     against every cruel merciless power that may oppose
     my body and soul,
     against incantations of false prophets,
     against black laws of heathenry,
     against false laws of heretics,
     against craft of idolatry,
     against spells of women and smiths and wizards,
     against every knowledge . . . man's body and soul.
     Christ to protect me to-day
          against poison, against burning,
          against drowning, against wounding,
          so that there may come to me abundance of reward.
     Christ with me, Christ before me, Christ behind me,
     Christ in me, Christ beneath me, Christ above me,
     Christ on my right, Christ on my left.
     Christ in breadth, Christ in length, Christ in height.
     Christ in the heart of every man who thinks of me,
     Christ in the mouth of everyone who speaks of me,
     Christ in every eye that sees me,
     Christ in every ear that hears me.

I arise to-day
     through a mighty strength, the invocation of the Trinity,
     through belief in the threeness,
     through confession of the oneness,
     of the Creator of creation. [18]

(Source: The Miracle of Ireland, *Daniel-Rops, ed., Earl of Wicklow, trans., Dublin: Clonmore & Reynolds Ltd., 1959, p. 28-30)*

🐿🐿🐿🐿🐿🐿🐿🐿🐿🐿🐿🐿🐿🐿🐿🐿🐿🐿🐿🐿🐿🐿🐿🐿🐿🐿🐿🐿🐿🐿🐿

When we ask God to help us forgive a person quickly, this helps to create a shield of protection, the shield of God's Presence.

Good point.

Is this an idea that we can bring into our own family: that we can protect our family spiritually from disorders by creating this shield of protection? If all the people in our family know they need to forgive, that helps keep the disorders outside the family, so they don't take root within the family.

That reminds me of St. Augustine, whose feast was just a few days ago on the 28th of August. He established a community, and wrote a governing rule: *The Rule of St. Augustine.* [19] Many Orders adopted the rule. It is quite a generic rule, so it is adaptable to many spiritual, or religious, congregations. We, the Servites, follow that rule. Anyway, in the chapter on forgiveness, he says either do not have quarrels, or, if you do, get rid of them as quickly as possible; if you have a difference with your brother, or sister for that matter, forgive as soon as possible so that the wound does not fester and become greater.

That's interesting.

You reminded me there of that provision. It is a wonderful rule.

There is the idea of contagion, too, that spiritual illness can spread.

Contagion. Oh, yes. You're dead right. It is very, very dangerous. Everybody knows that. Wars start because the hatred spreads.

Forgiveness is a preventive measure, too. If you have forgiveness as a constant in your life, it helps prevent these illnesses; it becomes a way of conditioning the spirit.

Yes, correct.

We don't need to spend so much time on negative thoughts, we can spend more time on healthy things.

I thank the Lord. I think He has been very gracious to me, because, in almost ninety years of life, He has helped me many times recognize the importance of forgiving and forgetting. He gave me that as a wonderful gift. I don't take any credit for it myself. That gift has helped me not have ulcers *(laughs)*, or inner lack of peace. When there's peace, the mind and soul are at peace and the body runs more smoothly.

There is a calmness that it brings about.

Yes.

A calmness that comes from within us and can extend into the family, as far as it is allowed.

Also. There is no doubt about it.

But there is the other side of it, too. Jesus said that when He enters into a family there could be a breaking up of two against three.

That doesn't have to mean hatred on the part of the person who has embraced Christianity. For example, I, as your son, embrace Christ, but you are still a pagan, my father. There will be division there if they cannot accept my embracing Christ: loving my neighbor, loving my enemy, and so on. Often those who embraced Christianity in the first three hundred years ended up decapitated, thrown to the lions, or put into slavery. I think He was thinking or warning us about that: that the father would be against the son, and the mother-in-law against the daughter-in-law, and so on.

Then the question becomes, in the face of all that, what is a person willing to suffer to follow this way?

Yes. No doubt. Because my forgiveness of you doesn't mean that you forgive me, and you continue to speak ill of me, abuse me verbally, and by your actions, and so on.

But that may be the instance where God uses our suffering not only for the good of our own souls but also for the good of other souls through sacrificial suffering.

Yes.

That's what you do when you pray. You have the power to pray for intercession for our souls.

We all do. The Lord put that into His Perfect Prayer, the *Our Father: Forgive us our trespasses as we forgive those who trespass against us.*

Do you see this transference at your Masses: that part of healing can include suffering?

Fig. 87.   *Carved-Rock Cross,* Scelig Mhichíl (Skellig Michael), Kerry, Ireland, 2005. Ireland's westernmost monastic settlement predating the sixth century. A cross was carved into the sheer rock face marking the site as Christian.

Also. Very much so.

Have you experienced that yourself?

Yes. I experience it every day on the telephone, for example. All the people calling every day, and so often their problem is unforgiveness. It is very distressing to hear that and try to bring them around. They are the ones who are losing by not forgiving. They have no peace. *(laughs)*

I can hear my Grandmother O'Brien saying, "You're not put on this earth to be happy; you're put on this earth to be holy!"

(laughs) That's beautiful. Yes. Sometimes we suffer terrible things in this life, war, sickness, all kinds of problems for many different reasons. But in the end, it's all for the glory of God.

We are only creatures of God with limited knowledge of why suffering occurs. God knows why, but we may not live to see the benefit.

Yes.

In your family, did your mother demonstrate forgiveness? You grew up in a big family.

You brought up a good point there. I believe this is one of the great graces and merits of a big family: that we are schooled in the school of mutual relationships. We are living so close together, we have to get on. That's one of the beautiful by-products of having a large family.

Of course when we lived in more of an agricultural society, when most people lived on farms, if people didn't get going they didn't eat! (laughs) It became a matter of survival.

Right. *(laughs)* Work together, eat together . . .

Suffer together! (laughs)

Fig. 88. *This Is the Cup of My Blood: Eucharistic Celebration and Father Peter Mary Rookey, O.S.M.,* International Compassion Ministry, Olympia Fields, Illinois, 2006.

(laughs) Forgive together.

(laughs) Yes. That's interesting. Parents have the opportunity to set the example in their families. This is something that needs to be taught. Today, we have such little families, people don't know these basic things.

Every other family is a one parent, thanks to the sin against the sixth Commandment: *Thou shalt not commit adultery* (Ex 20:13).

It all comes down to living within this perfect union and having a sense of what it is. Instead of reacting to the disorder, we are creating a sense of order.

You're just emphasizing the old proverb: *That's more powerful than words.* On the lighter side, I often think back on our days in the Ozarks, and my friends would see me drive around about two hundred miles around those missions. They were wanting me to get a better vehicle, and I said if I got an expensive car, when I drive up to the little missions and preach on the altar where they live modestly, the people would say, "Your actions speak so loudly I can't hear a word you are saying." *(laughs)* That's an old one.

That's true. Maybe you don't even realize this yourself because you live this day-to-day. You have a structure in your life that permits order. But there are a lot of people who don't have structure in their lives, so they don't interface with the world from a point of strength, centered and secure in the Love and Authority of God. Instead, they are constantly reacting. But with you, you have enough spiritual strength that you can fend disturbance off—you can see it coming.

Again, all by the Grace of God; it's none of my doing. It's all a special Grace. Of course He gives us the Grace when we are open to it and ask. The Apostle says if we ask for the Holy Spirit to fill us, He will.

And choose to create order out of disorder, if we so choose. Keep disorder outside the door. Have peace.

Yes. With God's Help.

Notes

1   *Catechism of the Catholic Church*, The Profession of Faith, Part III: "The Final Purification, or Purgatory," Sec. 1030-1032, p. 268-269; Michael J. Taylor, S.J., *Purgatory* (Huntington, Indiana: Our Sunday Visitor Publishing Division, 1998); Jacques Le Goff, *The Birth of Purgatory* (Chicago, Illinois: University of Chicago Press, 1981); Fr. F. X. Schouppe S.J., *Purgatory Explained* (Rockford, Illinois: Tan Books & Publishers, 2003), *http://www.tanbooks.com/index.php/page/shop: flypage/product_id/694/*; Edward J. Hanna, *Purgatory*, transcribed by William G. Bilton, Ph.D., *Catholic Encyclopedia* (New York, NY: Robert Appleton Company, 1911), Vol. XII, *http://www.newadvent. org/cathen/12575a.htm*; Eileen Good, *Places Apart: Lough Derg* (Dublin, Ireland: Veritas Publications, 2003), *www.veritas.ie*; W.H. Grattan-Flood, *St. Patrick's Purgatory*, transcribed by Mary Thomas, *Catholic Encyclopedia* (New York, NY: Robert Appleton Company, 1911), Vol. XII, *http://www.newadvent.org/cathen/12575a.htm*; P.J. Toner, *Prayers for the Dead*, transcribed by Michael T. Barrett, *Catholic Encyclopedia* (New York, NY: Robert Appleton Company, 1908), Vol. IV, *http:// www.newadvent.org/cathen/04653a.htm*; Joseph Pohle, *Justification*, transcribed by Terry Wilkinson, *Catholic Encyclopedia* (New York, NY: Robert Appleton Company, 1910), Vol. VIII, *http://www.newadvent. org/cathen/08573a.htm*; J. Pohle, *Sanctifying Grace*, transcribed by Scott Anthony Hibbs and Wendy Lorraine Hoffman, *Catholic Encyclopedia* (New York, NY: Robert Appleton Company, 1909), Vol. VI, *http://www. newadvent.org/cathen/06701a.htm*; Pope John Paul II, *Heaven, Heaven and Purgatory, L'Osservatore Romano* (Citta del Vaticano: Heaven: 28 July 1999, 7, Heaven: 4 August 1999, 7, Purgatory: 11/18 August, 7, 1999), *http://www.ewtn.org/library/PAPALDOC/JP2HEAVN.HTM*; Pegis, *Basic Writings of Aquinas*, Aquinas, ST II, Q, 87. ART. 8: "Whether Anyone is Punished for Another's Sins?" Vol. II, p.718; Pegis, *Basic Writings of St. Thomas Aquinas*, Aquinas, ST II, Q. 87, ART. 7: "Whether Every Punishment is Inflicted for a Sin?" Vol. II, p. 716; Pegis, *Basic Writings of St. Thomas Aquinas*, Aquinas, ST II, Q, 79, ART. 4: "The Will of God, Fourth Article, Whether Blindness and Hardness of Heart are Directed to the Salvation of Those Who are Blinded and Hardened," Vol. II, p. 656-657.

2   *... the kingdom of Heaven has suffereth violence, and the violent bear it away* (Mt 11:12), Douay.

3   *Yet now he hath reconciled in the body of his flesh through death, to present you holy and unspotted, and blameless before him : If so ye continue in the faith, grounded and settled, and immoveable from the hope of the gospel*

which you have heard, which is preached in all the creation that is under Heaven, whereof I am Paul am made a minister. Who now rejoice in my sufferings for you, and fill up those things that are wanting of the sufferings of Christ, in my flesh, for his body, which is the church (Col 1:23-24), Douay.

4   *But of this one thing be not ignorant, my beloved, that one day with the Lord is as a thousand years, and a thousand years as one day* (2 Pet 3:8), Douay.

5   "He [Lucifer]showed Me the uselessness of My death, and the usefulness of living for My own sake, without worrying Myself about ungrateful men, leading a rich happy life full of love. Living for My Mother, ensuring that She did not suffer. Living so that by means of a long apostolate I could take back to God many men, who, if I had died, would forget Me, whereas, if I had been their Master not for three years, but for many, many years, would end up becoming one with My doctrine." From: Valtorta, *The Poem of the Man~God*, The Passion, Sec. 599: "The Agony and the Arrest at Gethsemane," Vol. 5, p. 542.

6   *Love your enemies, do good to them that who hate you* (Lk 6:27), Douay.

7   *Greater love than this no man hath, that a man lay down his life for his friends* (Jn 15:13), Douay.

8   "Peace and war begin at home. If we truly want peace in the world, let us begin by loving one another in our own families. If we want to spread joy, we need for every family to have joy." From: José Luis González-Balado, *Mother Teresa In My Own Words 1910-1997* (New York, NY: Gramercy Books, 1997), p. 48.

9   *What therefore God hath joined together, let no man put asunder* (Mt 19:6), Douay.

10   Phil DeLuca, MSW, *The Solo Partner: repairing your relationship on your own* (Point Roberts, WA: Harley and Marks Publishers Inc., 1996).

11   *What therefore God hath joined together, let no man put asunder* (Mt 19:6), Douay.

12   John Paul II, *Love and Responsibility*, rev. ed. (San Francisco, CA: Ignatius Press, 1993).

13   John Paul II, *The Theology of the Body: Human Love in the Divine Plan* (Boston, MA: Pauline Books and Media, 1997).

14   *Love your enemies, do good to them that hate you. Bless them that curse you, and pray for them that calumniate you* (Lk 6:27-28), Douay.

15   Ibid.

16   *Blessed shall you be when men shall hate you, and when they shall separate you, and shall reproach you, and cast out your name as evil, for the Son of man's sake. Be glad in that day and rejoice; for behold your reward is great*

in Heaven. For according to these things did their fathers to the prophets (Lk 6:22-23), Douay.

17   *Father, forgive them; for they know not what they do* (Lk 23:34), Douay.

18   Daniel-Rops, editor, *The Miracle of Ireland, Patrick's Hymn,* translated from the French by The Earl of Wicklow (Dublin, Ireland: Clonmore and Reynolds, Ltd., 1959): p. 28-30.

19   The Dominican Family, the *Rule of St. Augustine, http://www. op.org/international/english/Documents/general_docs/augustin.htm.*

Seeking the Character of Christ

For a soul who has chosen to be distant from God, or who has lived in a place of prolonged trauma, or stress, for an extended period, it may take time to become comfortable with the peace, predictability, and security of living with God. Like a child, the soul needs to become familiar to the Voice, Ways, and Love of its Father. Father Rookey emphasizes the need for studying the Word of God, the works of the mystics, the lives of the Saints, and interfacing with people who live a spiritual life. As a soul learns the Ways of God and increases its spiritual intelligence, the soul begins to relax soothed by His Grace and Peace. Slowly it strengthens its resolve to choose to live in the Way of God for longer periods of time. This refinement of the integrity of the soul leads to its ability to more frequently feel the Love of Christ in its heart. With the ability to more fully trust God, the soul will eventually be able to magnify the Love of God beyond itself.

Father Rookey is an example of a soul who has achieved the balance of living a holy life strengthened by a spiritual discipline. He is able to gently love those who are the most unlovable and teaches us to love those who do not love us without losing the firmness of faith and Mystery of God's Love for all.

Fig. 89.   *Christ Teaching*, stained glass window, St. Ignatius Parish, Chicago, Illinois, 2006.

Part of the process of returning to God is getting to know Christ. How is Christ revealed to us? What are the characteristics He brings to us so we will know how to love? Even if we are born with a natural understanding of how to love, we often become separated from this loving feeling in our lives due to all kinds of external and internal conditions and experiences. When we return to God and start taking Christ into our hearts, how do we get to know Him little by little again?

Well, immediately through the *Bible*, the Word of God comes to mind; it directs us through His Word. That's why He gave us the *Bible* to give us the direction.

He has certain characteristics that He chose to show us in the Bible.

That's right. That's where we find these characteristics. The mystic writers also describe them; those who have proven to be real mystics, legitimate mystics. They can enlighten us, also.

You are especially fond of two books: Mystical City of God *and the* Poem of the Man~God. *How have they taught you about the Ways of Christ?*

Just as an example, yesterday was the Feast of the Transfiguration. I cheated a bit. And instead of reading a whole volume of the *Poem of the Man~God*, the night before, I read the section pertaining to the Mass for the following day. I slept over it and let it sink in a little to prepare for the Mass of the following morning. I tried to find in the *Poem of the Man~God* the vision she's had of that particular episode in the *Bible*, in the *New Testament*. It's just very uplifting. According to Maria Valtorta, who was given visions, the Lord told her to write out the visions, and, often as not, He gave an explanation to her about some of them.[1] That is very comforting also.

By reading, do you understand more about the personality of Christ?

I understand the *Bible* a lot better because she throws in many details that invariably the accounts of the Evangelists do not. They are brief. St. Mark doesn't waste a lot of time. He comes right to the point in his account, the shortest account. Our Lord, in the *Poem of the Man~God*, goes into detail explaining all of this or that part of the vision she has been given. Scripture scholars like Cardinal Bea, a Jesuit, who was head of the big Gregorianum University in Rome, has reviewed her work. He was a professor at this big university in the scripture division. He headed that up. He was amazed how she describes the terrain of the Holy Land, and she never left Italy. She never traveled anywhere except in Italy. That made him a believer in the authenticity of this work. He praised it very highly, as did Pope Paul VI. He ordered a copy of the books. There are ten volumes in Italian, which are condensed into five volumes in the English editions.

Was she a nun?

No, but she did have the vows. A lay religious, she did not marry. That's what makes it so tremendous. A former Baptist preacher in Cleveland wrote to me. Somehow he had heard about my interest in Maria Valtorta. He said he read the five volumes five times. I'm not so good at those thick books. My eyes don't hold out that long, I have so much reading to do. Just trying to get through my daily log of correspondence is enough.

He said through reading that work, he and all of his household and some of his parishioners became Catholic. Now he's pushing this. He's very well educated. The last time I was in Cleveland, he came to the services, and he introduced me to a brother preacher friend. And he's coming into the Church also after reading the *Poem of the Man~God*. It is a powerful, powerful work.

Does it also help understand Christ more? What He intended? It must strengthen your point of view as a representative of Christ, as a priest.

Oh yes. I use this to help me in explaining the Gospel because He goes into detail, providing the context of His Words and the occasion of having a miracle or whatever it is. It is a great help to me for sharing with the people during a homily. I use it very often First Saturdays. I even read a little section of the work.

Is there any similarity in what is portrayed in the Voice of Christ and in Our Lady's appearances and the messages she's been giving?

Yes. She reflects Jesus' Words always. Very much so. I was re-reading an Italian magazine, and they were retelling about the apparition in Fatima on May 13th. I was smiling again at Our Lady's answer to Lucy, who is the oldest one of the visionaries. She told Lucy they would be going to Heaven in the not too distant future. She said they would die or pass on. Lucy asked, Will Jacinta go to Heaven? She said, Yes. And, Francesco? Our Lady said, Yes, Francesco will go to Heaven, but he has to pray a lot of rosaries first! *(laughs)* I said to myself, maybe she's talking to me. Pray a lot of rosaries! So that's what I'm doing.

What is it that comes through the strongest in the Poem of the Man~God *in terms of the Voice of Christ? What is it that He's trying to bring to us? What is His main message? Is it simple? Is it consistent?*

For example, during Holy Week, I read a lot of the Passion. It's so touching, it brings tears to my eyes—all of these details about how Mary suffered and how Jesus suffered about Judas. What struck me was the time He took, the trouble, and the patience He had with Judas. He talked to him, one of intimate intimates, the one who betrayed Him. I was just reading a *Psalm* this morning. It is a prophecy about His Passion regarding Judas. What it brought up was how, here it is . . . *Psalm 54.* It begins: *Hear, O God, my prayer, and despise not my supplication : be attentive to me and hear me* (Ps 54:1-2). Then the second section begins: *For if my enemy had reviled me, I would verily have borne with it. And if he that hated me had spoken great things against me, I would perhaps have hidden myself from him. But thou a man of one mind, my guide and my familiar. Who didst take sweetmeats together with me : in the house of God we walked with consent* (Ps 54:13-15).

What was Christ's reaction to Judas? He didn't voice anger? How did He deal with the betrayal?

No, He forgave him just like He forgives us. He made excuses for him, even when the other Apostles saw through Judas. Jesus

Fig. 90. *Our Lady of Fatima,* statue, Our Lady of Sorrows Basilica, Chicago, Illinois, 2006.

said we should pray for him. That's one of the things that strikes me, for all the time, for nothing. It didn't do any good. Judas ended up in Hell. Still Christ reaches out to us no matter how great of a sinner we may be.

The Passion is so gripping. Then with the Feast of the Assumption coming, I'll be reading again, for the umpteenth time, Mary's passing. That's at the end of the book, the last volume, number five in the *Poem of the Man~God*. How she's with John, and Jesus put her into his hands. John took care of her until she died. He was at her bedside when she was dying. It's just a tiny thing that has made me pray the *Hail Mary* with so much more fervor. She prayed various *Psalms*, too, as she was preparing to go to Heaven.

Also, the words of the Angel, Gabriel, and Mary's cousin, Elizabeth, that form the first part of the *Hail Mary*. When I pray the *Hail Mary*, I think, "Wow, these are the words of Gabriel—the Holy Spirit induced it!" It makes me pray with all the more meaning. That is what Mary asked John to pray while she was preparing to go to Heaven.

When you pray, the particular incident is present to you?

Yes, well the whole volumes are tremendous.

Many believe that Christ worked through Maria Valtorta in the 1940s to write this book, which indicates that the spiritual aspect of Christ is transcendent of time. Even though Christ lived here in human form over two thousand years ago, He is present immediately supernaturally to anyone if they choose and He chooses to make Himself known.

It makes Mass more alive. His coming to us in the Presence of the Eucharist is an overwhelming Mystery! It's so . . . it shakes me up so much to see a priest just go through the routine when there is so much there. Of course, I don't realize it either. We are human, so we are not always a hundred percent attentive. It's part of our human nature. Often when a priest goes through

Fig. 91.   *This Is My Body: Eucharistic Celebration and Father Peter Mary Rookey, O.S.M.*, International Compassion Ministry, Olympia Fields, Illinois, 2006.

the Mass, he goes through the motions obviously not lifted up too much.

But it is part of the Mystery of the Mass to be engaged. It's necessary to educate ourselves and to have enough of a discipline to become aware that we are constantly in communication with God. It doesn't just end with the Mass but continues.

It's an ongoing thing. The Lord reminds us of that with His mystics like Louisa, the great divine-wound mystic of the 1800s, and—more recently—Teresa Neumann. When Teresa received the Host, it remained in her. She was a *living tabernacle.* The Host remained in her mouth until the next time she received a Host. She didn't eat anything.

There have been a few of the Saints who just existed on Communion. It's the mystical part that is important.

Definitely. Obviously. He tells us that even a glass of cold water given in My Name will be rewarded.[2] We revere other people as other Christs in a mystical way. Whatever we do for that person(s) is done to Christ Himself, so we get the reward of having administered to Christ Himself.

Today we had the reading at Mass about a woman who wasn't part of Christ's group, a foreigner, insisting that she be healed. What was the teaching from your point of view, a Christ point of view?

Well, He was testing her faith. I was thinking about that text in a more humorous way. That was the coarsest thing Jesus said, It's not good to throw the food to the dogs.[3] It was the closest thing He came to calling her an S.O.B. *(laughs)* Yet she was equal to that and said, Even the dogs eat the crumbs that fall from the tables of their masters.[4] Then Jesus said, O woman how great is your faith.[5]

You often refer to healing as a beauty treatment. You understand that Jesus wasn't seeing people only as good. He did recognize the ugliness in a person, the part of the person that was unloving, for example, in

Fig. 92. *A Cup of Water,* Convent of St. Augustine, Los Teques, Venezuela, 2006.

how He regarded Judas. He accepted people as they were, but wanted them to become more loving, more beautiful by overcoming those traits that caused them to become separated from God.

Judas was supposed to be a handsome man, but it was all exterior, a veneer.

Like this lady asking to be healed. Jesus didn't just say, I'm going to heal you. He knew that she had to engage in the process from her heart. She had to find the courage to ask Him.

Right.

The woman overcame her fears and—despite opposition—opened her heart and asked Jesus to heal her. Judas decided not to open his heart. He drew distant from Him and did not overcome his fear until his fear manifested itself in jealousy and despair and destroyed him.

Perhaps that's a lesson in perseverance, the lady going after Jesus.

So even in the case of Judas, Christ would see him in what way? Did He look beyond the surface and speak to the goodness within Judas' soul?

Well, he was trying to dwell on his good points. He had his good points.

Are you saying that we first need to make the decision to start searching for Christ, no matter what our circumstance? We need to overcome our fears, open our hearts, and start searching for God?

Definitely. We realize our need first—and then start searching.

One Hundred Facets of Christ

While Christ is indefinable, the following words begin to express attributes associated with Him:

Abstinence	Encouragement	Justice	Reason
Adoration	Endurance	Kindness	Religion
Affability	Faith	Language	Respect
Art	Focus	Leadership	Responsibility
Balance	Forgiveness	Liberality	Rest
Celebration	Fortitude	Light	Right conduct
Charity	Friendliness	Love	Scholarship
Chastity	Generosity	Loyalty	Security
Cheerfulness	Gentleness	Magnanimity	Self-control
Cleanliness	Goodness	Meditation	Sensitivity
Communication	Good will	Meekness	Sentiment
Compassion	Grace	Miraculous	Silence
Concentration	Gratitude	Modesty	Sincerity
Constancy	Healthfulness	Munificence	Sobriety
Contentment	Holiness	Mystery	Stability
Continence	Honesty	Order	Steadfastness
Courtesy	Honor	Patience	Surrender
Courage	Hope	Perseverance	Temperance
Decorum	Hospitality	Piety	Tranquility
Deliverance	Humility	Practicality	Truth
Diligence	Imagination	Prayerfulness	Understanding
Discipline	Impeccability	Predictability	Valor
Docility	Inclusion	Prescience	Virtue
Duty	Integrity	Promptness	Warmth
Ease	Joy	Prudence	Wisdom

When someone comes out of a period of confusion in their lives, sometimes he/she can't understand what is from Christ and what isn't. Is it a process of educating ourselves?

There again in our healing services, we implore the Power of the Spirit upon us. Just as St. Teresa of Avila experienced the purgative, illuminative, and unitive progression of prayer, one of the beautiful works of the healing services is when we are finally overcome by the Spirit, and we feel this great Love and are illuminated. Love enlightens. The Holy Spirit is the Spirit of Love. Many people are just so overcome they continually like to rest in the Spirit, as we say, because it brings them this wonderful knowledge of the Holy Spirit and Christ's Gentle Love. Really, the great knowledge is the *knowledge of the heart.* Because the knowledge of the head is very often kind of cold *(laughs)*, whereas the heart makes everything warm and easy. That's part of the way of knowing, understanding our humanity, our limitations, and understanding each other; Love brings us all these gifts.

The searching and the reading begin the process. But what we are really after is an experience *of Christ?*

An experience. Yes. We have to experience this more from the heart.

Words are just a description, the entryway, and then we need to open our hearts.

Those words are part of the meaning, like when we say, *Your words are life, Lord.*[6] In the Liturgy, we pray for the meaning of the Gospel and *celebrate* the *Good News. May our sins be blotted out.*[7] There is a power in even reading those Words of the Lord.

And the idea of blotting out *meaning separating ourselves from anything in the past and having the understanding that God only wants for us goodness and life. We choose that every moment.*

It's choosing life. As Moses told the people, choose life and not death. In Deuteronomy 30:19, it is said: *I call heaven and earth to witness this day, that I have set before you life and death, blessing and cursing. Choose therefore life, that both thou and thy seed may live.* That's what we are faced with today: choosing life rather than the culture of death.

It's rather simple. You are saying we should use our free will, open our hearts, and choose to know Christ and understand that every minute He's with us. We must choose to know Him.

Oh, definitely. Definitely.

As we strengthen ourselves that helps people around us by providing clarity.

Yes. We try to. Of course it takes years and years sometimes to let the Lord do this to us—let the Spirit of Love in—and it then comes out from us onto people without our really realizing it. As an example, Sabina came in a couple of mornings ago, and she said she felt this powerful Spirit as we came together and greeted each other for the morning. Everybody can have this, if we let the Spirit take over in our lives.

And feel God's Love in our hearts.

Yes. It's powerful. Another example comes to mind in this same vein. Jim comes into the office here, as we're talking and I'm praying with people on the phone, and he has to step back because the Power of the Spirit is affecting him. He might rest in the Spirit! *(laughs)* He is very sensitive to the Spirit, and many of our others, also. And Marge, well you've been here at Mass when she receives Communion, and she rests in the Spirit. I see this as a terrific experience for all of us that she has this wonderful *rendez-vous* with the Lord.

As people learn more and educate themselves, once they begin to open their hearts to Christ, a transition occurs. It's like anything else we learn—we receive a heightened sensitivity and deeper understanding. On the surface, when we consider Blessed Mother Teresa, we might say how could anybody do what she did dealing daily with the poorest of the poor—especially considering the conditions in which she was living. Yet, she had such a high sensitivity to Christ that everywhere she went, she could see God. She lived a mystical life.

Well, she was open to the Spirit. He took over in her life and was able to work all these wonderful things. She was recognized even by the Popes, like John Paul II, as a person in our times mirroring Christ.

The magnification of Christ . . . people like Blessed Mother Teresa and methods such as your healing services provide a different way of looking at the world, of seeing through Christ's Eyes, or letting Christ be with us so we begin to see the world in a shift from how we may have seen it before. As we begin to see through Christ's Eyes, we are giving Christ permission to come into our lives and act through us.

That's where it is. Once we let that happen. We are all a little bit hesitant because we feel it's going to cost. Cost us our bad habits *(laughs)*, or it's going to be a change.

We see it as a sacrifice instead of a reward.

Yes. A reward! *(laughs)*

A retired teamster, Joseph Molloy serves in the office of the International Compassion Ministry. His encounter with the Holy Spirit through Father Rookey changed his life.

My first experience with Father Rookey was when some women from my parish wanted to go see him and they said, "You've got to get there early. You've got to be there by six o'clock." I said, "O.K., I'll drive you." They didn't want to drive at night. Of course, some of them were up in age. When we got there, we were sitting down, and we started to pray the Rosary, the mysteries, and I started looking at my watch thinking, "Where is this guy?"

They started on another Mystery again, and, finally, about 9:30, he walked in. His hair was messed up, he had a beard, and he had this robe on that looked like he had slept in it—kind of nonchalant. And I thought, "Where did they pick him up? Madison street?" Everyone went up there to get a blessing, and I went up there. I hadn't known anything about this healing service. So I went to see him three more times.

Fig. 93. *Joe Molloy Receiving Communion,* International Compassion Ministry, Olympia Fields, Illinois, 2005.

*One day, he was at Holy Redeemer in Evergreen
Park, and it was on a Sunday afternoon. This woman
said she'd like to go but had no way of getting there. I
said, "I'll take you." They were all getting up to the
altar. She convinced me to go up, and Father came over,
I don't know why. He stopped right in front of me, took
two steps backward and said, "God Bless this . . ."—and
I went flying. The next thing I knew, I bounced off the
pew. Ever since then, he puts me down.*

*I see him from my desk. He'll be talking to someone
on the phone. He'll look like he's sleeping, but he's
praying. I believe he's a living Saint. I really do. He said,
"I'm nothing but a sinner." I said, "Aren't we all?"*

*But I love the man. I came to work one day. I've
been here three years going on four.*

I made a prayer card Cleanse Me Lord. *Already,
50,000 prayer cards have been printed. I wrote it
about two years ago. It's printed in Spanish, Polish,
and Croatian. Vicki and I had a call from a lady on
the North Side. This gentleman in her building, he
must have been getting up in age, dying, and he didn't
want a doctor, priest—nothing. She took that card and
started praying. The next day, he got up, and he was
well. Other people use it too. I was amazed. I feel it
was the Holy Spirit leading me.*

Cleanse Me Lord

*May the most Precious Blood,
which flowed from
the most Holy wounds
of our loving Lord Jesus,
pour over me,
to wash, cleanse, purify,
heal, guide and protect me
from all evil,
harm, sickness and bless
and make me
as Holy as I can be.
I ask this in the Holy Name of Jesus*

*and through His most Precious Blood
and His most Holy wounds.*

May the Most Precious Blood of Jesus, Save Us,

Amen.

Notes

1. "Jesus orders me: Take a completely new notebook. Write down on the first page what I dictated on August the 16th. She will be spokein of in this book." From: Valtorta, *The Poem of the Man~God*, The Hidden Life, Sec. 1, "Introduction," p. 7; "I can affirm"—one of Valtorta's declarations reads—"that I have had no human source to be able to know what I write, and what, even while writing, I often do not understand." From: Valtorta, *The Poem of the Man~God*, "The Person and Works of Maria Valtorta," Vol. 1, p. X.

2. *For whosoever shall give you to drink a cup of water in my name, because you belong to Christ : amen I say to you, he shall not lose his reward* (Mk 9:41), Douay.

3. *It is not good to take the bread of the children, and to cast it to the dogs* (Mt 15:26), Douay.

4. *Yea Lord; for the whelps also eat of the crumbs that fall from the table of their masters* (Mt 15:27), Douay.

5. *O woman, great is thy faith!* (Mt 15:28), Douay.

6. *And Simon Peter answered him : Lord, to whom shall we go? Thou hast the words of eternal life* (Jn 6:69), Douay.

7. *Turn away thy face from my sins, and blot out all my iniquities* (Ps 50:11), Douay.

Sharing Christ's Healing

All souls are from God, and God wants them all to come home, no matter what they have done or how hardened their hearts. God works through our bodies, minds, and spirits to touch our hearts and to penetrate the interior of our souls. Father Rookey understands the Mystery that the health of the body, mind, and spirit are all connected and offers to share Christ's Healing Powers and Love with people from all over the world without question. He delights in the Good Thief turnaround, even if it happens in the final moments of a soul's life on earth. Often as a soul seeks reunion with God, other ailments are healed, or are seen in a new light as a magnification of God—a soul suffering on behalf of others. God and His Angels accompany each soul along its journey waiting anxiously for the soul to invite Him into its heart. No matter how often a soul falls away from God, still they wait, always listening for the first quiet "Yes" to do God's Will again.

It is important that a person is consistent in Christ. As one becomes closer to Christ, meditations, prayer, learning about Christ, and

Fig. 94. *Jesus and His Sacred Heart,* statue, Our Lady of Sorrows Basilica, Chicago, Illinois, 2008.

participating in the Sacraments, all provide an anchor for extending His Message to the world. We begin to have a certain orientation toward people that isn't from our own point of view, as an individual human being, but more from Christ's point of view.

Well, I'm trying. We try to seek Christ in others. I don't think I'd be in this healing ministry if I didn't see Christ in all people. I wouldn't answer the phone and pray with them, for example, and lay hands on them in our healing services. It's too much strain. You're up to the wee hours every night, and you're hearing these tales of woe all day long. *(laughs)* We wouldn't do that unless we could see Christ in those people.

You must hear a lot of the same things from people when they call you.

It's always suffering of one kind or another. But we get a lot of reports of healings, also. Somebody called today, a lady who stood in proxy for her mother, and her mother was completely healed. She was supposed to have had a toe removed due to diabetes, but now the toe will not be amputated. We get a lot of cheerful reports, as well as the difficult ones.

By contrast, one of the volunteers here in the office was standing in proxy for a long time for her son-in-law who was given to drugs and all. Certainly, he was taken over by the devil. Every time she stood in proxy, the devil would attack her. He would make this holy daughter of Christ go through all the sufferings of the possessed: throwing her down on the floor, flapping her body against the hard floor, vomiting, spitting at us, speaking terrible words through her against Christ. But with much praying, and the use of sacramentals and holy water, she would come around again. But that was when she was standing in for this relative. It brushed off on her. That's in contrast with the woman standing in proxy for her mother, and she was healed. That happens very often in the services, and on the telephone. People are healed by the intercession of people who pray in proxy for them.

In her case, does the devil not want her to stand in proxy? Is this a manifestation of resistance?

Of course. He doesn't want to lose this man.

His Holiness John Paul II has requested that we become dedicated to a culture of life instead of a culture of death. Moving out of spiritual darkness brings us light, and a love of life, and a deep appreciation for the Mystery of all Creation.

Jesus said, I've come to bring you life. I am the Resurrection and the life. He who believes in Me will never die. He will have life everlasting.[1]

You've prayed for gangsters, including the Kray brothers.

They were twins: the two worst gangsters in Britain. We went to see one in prison. He died last year of cancer. I have a tape of the interview. They allowed him to come out of the hospital.

He took the step first. He invited you in?

Yes. His brother, who was in the mental institution part of the prison, was more remarkable with his conversion. He had never admitted to his misdeeds. I talked to him shortly before he died, it must have been three to four years ago. He called on the phone the evening before I was to come back to the United States from England. He wanted me to pray with him. We had a kind of a Good Thief turnaround. He prayed from the heart, very devoutly, the *Lord's Prayer* and everything, and the *Miracle Prayer*, and I gave him God's blessing. It would have been great, but I never heard if he had asked for a priest before he died. He probably belonged to the Anglican Church, the Church of England.

How did he get in touch with you?

I got a phone call here, right on this phone, from him in prison. The good guy had had a conversion in prison before that. Our Mass and healing service was advertised in England in the newspaper. He probably got the number from that. He telephoned me here. He said, I see you're coming to England. Then he telephoned Bernie Ellis and asked if we would kindly come to see him in prison. Bernie Ellis is also a convert and received a big triple healing.

He was very insistent then.

Actually, he called me on behalf of a brother gangster, a friend gangster. He wanted me to go see the family because his friend had a son, about eight years old, who was very ill. Bernie and Martin Duggan found the man's address and took me there. We went up to the house and blessed this gangster's son. Later I was told that his father had gone to prison.

Did he ever convert?

The father? I don't know. I couldn't follow. The mother was Catholic. But the father being a gangster . . . I don't know if he allowed her to practice her faith, but he was very touched. We blessed the house, and blessed the child, and he was there. I guess the child was healed. I never heard much about it after that. Kray would have told me if he hadn't gotten healed. He would have told me for sure.

And Kray kept wanting to see you?

Yes. He was the converted brother. I wish I could say once and for all "You are converted" and that's it. But Jesus told His sleeping Apostles at Gethsemane: *The spirit indeed is willing, but the flesh is weak* (Mt 26:41). He also came out with: For a just man shall fall seven times a day.[2] We always need conversion. Those are the words of our Lord.

Dear Father Rookey,

A long-time friend called in the middle of the night asking me to bring him some fresh orange juice. He was in the hospital, dying of cirrhosis of the liver and hepatitis C. I hadn't talked with him in about four years. He had had a difficult life. He was an American Indian and had been orphaned as a child and adopted into a family where his stepfather was a Freemason. He felt like he never fit in and was anguished by the suffering of his native people and the state of the world.

He grew up during the 1960s and 1970s, the turbulent era of the American Indian and the civil-rights movements. Despite the confusion of the time, he did much humanitarian service, including working on environmental and indigenous rights issues and serving the elders of the community by working for the archdiocese. He was a poet and musician, too. Though a friendly person, he suffered from bouts of anger, depression, alcoholism, drug abuse, and relationship troubles most of his adult life, and confused his spiritual direction by dabbling in the New Age.

We talked about God now and then over the next few days. He said that he had no one left to be angry with anymore. I offered him the rosary beads you had prayed with, and this big man grabbed them and put them around his neck like a child. I asked him if he wanted to pray with you, and—to my great surprise—he said, "Yes." You answered my phone call and prayed with him. He rested in the Spirit! He woke up a few minutes later and said, "He hung up on me!" I explained that he had rested in the Spirit, and he said, "That felt great!" He was all smiles!

A few days later, I visited him with his brother. He couldn't talk, but we told him we loved him, thanked him for all of the things he had taught us, and for the good moments we had shared together. We turned him over to God, the Creator. He looked at me with a sparkle in his eyes. He struggled a few more days; it wasn't an easy death, but when he passed, he looked peaceful and serene. You said he had had a Good Thief turnaround. Thank you, Father Rookey, for caring and praying. And, thank God for touching his heart. After all, in the end, he just wanted to be loved. May he rest in peace.

Chicago, February 2003

You were speaking about this constant regimen for keeping oneself pure. But have you noticed someone you've healed, and he/she came back again worse?

Of course.

We still face a battle for control of us. Part of it is our own will, but are forces opposing us in the world too?

Yes. The Heavenly Father made us whole. Again, after the fall of Adam, as quoted here in Jesus' Words: The Spirit is willing, but the flesh is weak.[3] Our flesh became weak. We were weakened by that fall and all falls since Adam. That's why maybe Jesus told us through St. Peter who asked, How many times must I forgive my brother, seven times? Jesus said, No, seventy times seven times.[4] That is a way of saying *always*.

God takes our weaknesses into consideration, as He did with St. Peter at the Last Supper when Jesus said, One of you is about to betray me.[5] In the end, Peter said, Even if they all betray you, Lord, I'll never forsake you. Jesus said, Oh, you'll never forsake me, Peter? Before the cock crows twice, you will have betrayed me thrice.[6] God foresees, because of our weakness, that we may again fall, but we must pick ourselves up as He did on the way to Calvary when He fell.

We need to understand our humanity and have compassion for ourselves and for others. This isn't an easy way to live! It's very challenging.

Again, that's basic in our healing: to forgive *ourselves*. Some people say, how can God forgive me, I killed my child in the womb?—when a mother has an abortion, for example. How can God ever forgive me for that? But we mustn't put limits on Divine Providence.

That was a joke with Pope Leo XIII. He was one of the longest reigning Popes. He died in 1902. Somebody in an audience was supposed to have said, I think the Lord will give you a year or two or more of reign. He said, Let's not put limits on Divine Providence! *(laughs)* We limit Divine Providence

Fig. 95. *Sharing Christ's Peace*, Basilica of the Annunciation in Nazareth, Pilgrimage to the Holy Land, 2005.

when we don't accept the forgiveness of God. That is one of the bases of suicide. It was the motivation for Judas. He felt Jesus could never forgive him, so he committed suicide.

If we can see ourselves as being able to be forgiven within this idea of Divine Providence that goes beyond our human understanding and extend it beyond ourselves to our relationships with others, then we won't put limits on our own ability to forgive.

Yes. We have also to accept *forgetfulness*, you know. We often hear people say, "I forgive, but I can't forget." You have to also forget. The psalmist repeats that God removes our sins to the East farthest from the West.[7] That is as far as the Lord has forgiven and forgotten our sins. There you have it. I mean, it's the Word of God.

In your Mass and healing services, you often quote the passage that our sins are blotted out. Even God doesn't hold us to that memory.

Yes. He forgets them. Correct. The *Psalm 50* is full of that; the *Miserere Psalm:* Have mercy on me, O God, according to your steadfast love, according to your abundant mercy blot out all my transgressions.[8] The *Miserere Psalm.*

    The Scripture scholars inform us that it was probably after David lost his child born out of wedlock, his child of adultery, that he wrote this beautiful *Psalm:* O purify me and then I shall be clean . . . wash me and I shall be whiter than snow . . . from my sins turn away your face, blot out all my guilt . . . a pure heart create for me, O God, a steadfast spirit within me.[9]

Forgiveness requires a complete healing process wherein we are sharing our healing and freeing others from the memory. We need to blot out other people's sins.

I can't forgive without the Grace of God. That's the healing of hatred. Because if I don't love and forgive, I really hate you. The opposite of forgiveness is hatred. Forgiveness is love. Unforgiveness is hatred. If I don't forgive you, I am really hating you.

And restricting that person's ability and the ability of ourselves to grow?

The Grace, of course.

We are withholding the Gift of Grace?

I can't love if I'm a hateful person. I limit my life.

When we keep reminding people of how they have hurt us, that's a way of being hateful?

Love makes us live to the hilt. Hatred just takes the life out of us, really. According to medics even, it is the source of illness that is obvious, because the body and soul are so united. What affects the soul affects the body. Everybody knows that. It's very simple.

It seems when we can get to the point of forgetting the hurt and forgiving the other person—that's when these miracles start to happen for ourselves, too.

Right.

That's why people say, I have to forgive you because I have to go on.

Yes, definitely.

You are saying that we need to go on living in the present, continuing to encounter, accept, and overcome our weaknesses, and—bit by bit—refine our spirits by receiving the Gifts of the Sacraments, and, through the Graces bestowed by God, move closer toward Him. We need to constantly forgive others and ourselves for the weaknesses in our souls that cause suffering and encourage each other, through prayer and actions, to keep persevering to the end. We're all on the same path of spiritual enlightenment, whether we realize it or not. The key obstacle is surrendering our wills and then using our Spiritual Gifts to be in alignment with Divine Will: for that is where we find our purpose and God's Peace.

Yes. And Christ is there to help us through it all. He loves us so much that He is willing to take on our suffering, as we try to become more and more like Him.

ᏉᏉᏉᏉᏉᏉᏉᏉᏉᏉᏉᏉᏉᏉᏉᏉᏉᏉᏉᏉᏉᏉᏉᏉᏉᏉᏉᏉᏉᏉᏉᏉᏉᏉ

"Tony Brown's Miracle," by Tony Brown

I first met Father Rookey in 1993 when Margaret Trosclair brought him to WTX radio for Mary's Helpers News Program. He was a most likable individual who possessed a sense of humor, as well as a warmth, that generated good feelings among those in his midst.

Being in the presence of Father has lifted any doubts about the existence of God in my mind. It has been said many times that he has the power to heal through Christ. Even though I had heard him recite the Healing Prayer on Mary's Helpers News Program, I was about to see him in action. Because of a very generous individual, I was able to be a part of the twenty-four pilgrims who traveled to Medjugorje from New Orleans to celebrate the 13th Anniversary of the first apparition. Father was our spiritual director during this pilgrimage.

On June 24, 1994, we were on Apparition Hill when Father rose from the spot where he had been meditating and walked over to where a young man from France was lying on a stretcher unable to walk. Father asked him if he wanted him to pray for him. The young man said, "Yes," and Father Rookey began the prayer. People crowded around as Father continued to pray over the young Frenchman. Father asked the young man if he would like to try to get up.

At first, the young man was unable to do so. At that point, I noticed Father Rookey was reaching into his breast pocket. From his pocket, he took out his Servite crucifix. He began praying over the French fellow more intensely. A swell of people began to crowd

Fig. 96. *Mary, My Mother, Queen of Peace*, International Compassion Ministry, Olympia Fields, Illinois, 2006. This image of the Blessed Mother is affiliated with Medjugorje, Bosnia & Herzegovina, where it is believed she has been appearing since 1981 sharing messages of love and peace. Father Rookey has been on over twenty-five pilgrimages to Medjugorje.

around, and I was pushed further away from Father. Because of my location, I was unable to hear Father ask the young man to rise, but I could see him reach out his hand. As the young man began to get up, the shouts of praises to God, as well as the Hail Mary could be heard everywhere. This Frenchman, who just one hour before had to be carried up Apparition Hill on a stretcher by his four friends, stood up, bent over, and touched his toes. He also raised his arms above his head and began to walk around.

Father Rookey, through prayer, faith, and Jesus Christ, had performed a miracle on the site of the first apparition on Apparition Hill. I had been blessed by God, Jesus, Mary, and my sponsor. Because of this very generous person, I was able to witness with my own eyes this miracle. For had I not known the circumstances around the event, I would have doubted it.

The people on Apparition Hill began to cheer, cry, and sing the Ave Maria. They began to surge in on Father Rookey, and it was at this time that I remember thinking how drained he appeared after this healing. It seemed to me that people were coming out of nowhere asking Father to heal this one and that one. It reminded me of one of the biblical stories of Christ being overwhelmed by people wanting Him to heal them.[10]

(Reprinted with the permission of Margaret Trosclair, O.S.S.M., Mary's Helpers)

᠍ᠥᠥᠥᠥᠥᠥᠥᠥᠥᠥᠥᠥᠥᠥᠥᠥᠥᠥᠥᠥᠥᠥᠥᠥᠥᠥᠥᠥᠥᠥᠥ

Father, I think I'm done.

You're Dunne? I'm Rookey! *(laughs)*

Deo Gratias!

Notes

1   *I am the Resurrection and the life; he that believeth in me, although he be
    dead, shall live : And everyone that liveth, and believeth in me, shall not
    die for ever* (Jn 11 25:26), Douay.

2   *For a just man shall fall seven times and rise again : but the wicked shall
    fall down into evil* (Prov 24:16), Douay.

3   *. . . the spirit indeed is willing, but the flesh is weak* (Mt 26:41), Douay.

4   *Lord, how often shall my brother offend against me, and I forgive him? Till
    seven times? Jesus saith to him I say not to thee, till seven times; but till
    seventy times seven times* (Mt 18:21-22), Douay.

5   *Amen I say to you, one of you that eateth with me shall betray me* (Mk
    26:21), Douay.

6   *Although all shall be scandalized in thee, yet not I. And Jesus saith to him
    : Amen I say to thee, to day, even in this night, before the cock crow twice,
    thou shalt deny me thrice* (Mk 14:29-30), Douay.

7   *As far as the east is from the west, so far hath he removed our iniquities
    from us* (Ps 103:12), Douay.

8   *Have mercy on me, O God, according to thy great mercy. And according
    to the multitude of thy tender mercies blot out my iniquity* (Ps 50:3),
    Douay.

9   *Thou shalt sprinkle me with hyssop, and I shall be cleansed : thou shalt wash
    me, and I shall be made whiter than snow . . . Create a clean heart in me,
    O God, and renew a right spirit within my bowels* (Ps 50:9-12), Douay.

10 Tony Brown, "Tony Brown's Miracle," *The Mary's Healers Newsletter*
    (Marrero, LA: Mary's Helpers Inc., June 1994-March 1995).

Christ's Healings of Body, Mind, and Spirit

The International Compassion Ministry has received beautiful testimonies of healings of body, mind, and spirit from all over the world. Following are excerpts from some of the many letters filled with the love and joy of the experience of Christ. The letters were originally edited by Sister Mary Caran Hart, S.S.N.D., who provides editing and archival services for the International Compassion Ministry. The excerpts are presented without names to ensure the privacy of those who have shared their experiences.

Christ's Healings of Body

Dear Father Rookey,

Last November, you prayed over the phone for a twenty-four-year-old man who had been in a coma for two weeks after a serious truck accident. He flew out [of the vehicle] and had severe head trauma. The doctors told the family he would most likely be in an institution for the rest of his life.

I took blessed oil and a prayer card to the hospital and called you, holding the phone to his ear. As you prayed over him, he started to

Fig. 97. *Father Peter Mary Rookey, O.S.M., in Rome,* oil on canvas by Andre Durand, London, England, 1991.

cry—even though his teeth were clenched in a large head brace. I blessed him with your oil and talked to him about healing and what Jesus wants him to do yet.

A week later, I went back to the hospital and was told he was on the rehab floor. As I came around the corner to his room, I saw his dad and another guy talking to a nurse in the hallway. I said, "Hello," to his dad and the other guy standing there said, "Hi!" It was him. His nurses said they usually see one miracle a year in their department and in 2004 it was him.

Praise to our dear Lord Jesus, and thank you again, Father, from the bottom of my heart.

Wisconsin, April 2005

℧ ℧ ℧ ℧ ℧ ℧

Dear Father Rookey,

A miracle truly took place after my phone call to you and your prayers for my sister-in-law who was told she had two to three days to live.

I called you on Monday. Wednesday, I went to see her in intensive care. They took her off life support on Tuesday afternoon and Wednesday she looked as if she had never been sick. Doctors, nurses, dieticians, and priests at the hospital looked at her chart and could not believe what they read.

It is Friday, July 1st, a week since this happened, and she is going home today looking better than I have seen her in years. May God bless you a hundredfold for all you do for so many.

New York, July 2005

℧ ℧ ℧ ℧ ℧ ℧

Dear Father Rookey,

I am writing with great joy and thanksgiving. I called several weeks ago to ask for prayers for my husband's grandmother, who is now eighty-eight and has survived diabetes for forty years and cancer for over twenty years.

The day you began to pray for her, her condition stabilized and began to reverse. She is now at home. Praise and thanks to the beloved Holy Trinity!

You have also healed me of many fears. When I asked your intercession for this, about two minutes later, I felt a tingling warmth from my toes on up and a great peace! I have not been burdened by that sense of spiritual or physical fear since that night.

I hope you don't mind if I pray for your presence and that of Granny for a bit longer. Thank you so much for showing me how to be cheerful, firm in my faith, and trusting.

Washington D.C., October 2001

ভ ভ ভ ভ ভ ভ

Dear Father Rookey,

Your praying with myself and my family over the phone gave us such hope and strength. That was the day my brother opened his eyes for the first time since in the coma. Thank you and God bless you for the work you do.

Ohio, February 2001

ভ ভ ভ ভ ভ ভ

Dear Father Rookey,

I first attended your Mass in August 2000 and have continued every since. In October 2000, I went to your healing Mass and I felt a power that was really strong. Because I was still on dialysis, I was afraid to fall. I kept saying, I can't fall, but then I heard a voice and the voice said, "Don't be afraid, just pray," and I fell. The following Monday, I was told I would be taken off the dialysis machine. I know the doctor didn't believe me when I told him about you, and I also told the techs, but I know it was the Holy Spirit who helped me. Today, I am still off of dialysis.

Thank you for giving so much to the world.

Illinois, June 2001

ℭ ℭ ℭ ℭ ℭ ℭ

Dear Father Rookey,

Thank you for your prayers for my nephew. During heart surgery, the doctor came out and told the family to call a priest. He didn't think he could save him.

I'm sure your prayers helped save his life.

Michigan, August 2005

ℭ ℭ ℭ ℭ ℭ ℭ

Dear Father Rookey,

I called you because I was diagnosed with severe anemia. After my call to you, I could see a little pink coloring in my finger nails. Monday, I had another blood test and yesterday I was told that my blood count was much better. Thank you, Jesus, and thank you, Father. Thanks for all the work you do for everyone.

Missouri, July 2002

Christ's Healings of Cancers

Dear Father Rookey,

My husband was diagnosed with pancreatic cancer and was given six months to live. We learned, after our visit with you, the cancer was contained.

We learned our daughter was having health problems consisting of masses in her two ovaries. An ultrasound was done and there were no masses. My husband knows he would never live this long with his illness without continued prayer and faith in our Lord.

May God continue to bless you and your ministry.

Kentucky, July 2005

cccccc

Dear Father Rookey,

I would like to say a very special thanks to you for your visit to Ireland last July, 2001. My sister had been told that she had a month left to live, due to cancer. She had become so weak she was unable to move or do anything for herself. I asked for a healing blessing for her.

At the same time that you prayed your healing prayer over me for her, she felt a change come over her and felt movement in her body. From then on she has improved so much she is able to help herself and is feeling stronger every day.

Thank God! Oh yes, Father Rookey, it's a definite miracle, no doubt about it.

I pray that God keeps you healthy, happy, and passionate in serving Him.

Thanks again.

Ireland, October 2001

ℭ ℭ ℭ ℭ ℭ ℭ

Dear Father Rookey,

Shortly prior to attending your wonderful Mass and healing service, a bone scan showed five lesions scattered about my body that were considered to be stemming from one of the three different types of cancer, which have plagued me for over the past nine years.

As I watched in awe the many sickly people approach you for your blessing and seeming to fall back to rest in the Spirit, I earnestly prayed to Jesus and His Blessed Mother that I too might be one of the fortunate ones, and it did happen to me. When I came to, I had the most wonderfully peaceful feeling and actually felt that everything was being lifted from my body.

I told several people about it and they were rather incredulous, but I kept it all in my heart, thanking Jesus for the very special experience.

Last month, I went for a follow-up scan, and, to the doctor's amazement, all the lesions had disappeared! He had no explanation except that it was the hand of God.

Michigan, October 2001

ℭ ℭ ℭ ℭ ℭ ℭ

Dear Father Rookey,

My family and I had the beautiful experience of attending your healing Mass in March. What a wonderful evening—it was so special. The next day I had to see my oncologist. He took all the usual blood profiles that had been going up and up—over 900 markers. When I went in for my next appointment, my tumor markers had dropped to 300.

I didn't write right away—I wanted to make sure there was not a mistake as I just could not believe what had happened so quickly. Thanks so much for the blessing you have given to me and my family.

Florida, April 2001

C C C C C C

Dear Father Rookey,

My father attended one of your healing services nearly five years ago. At the time he had been diagnosed with cancer and was in the process of chemotherapy and radiation treatment.

Through all of his cancer treatment, my father would always openly express exactly what was on his mind. One of the comments I will always remember is what he retold each time after radiation treatment, "Now I know how Christ suffered." During those treatments, I tried to tell my dad that there was merit to redemptive suffering, and that he could use his pain to join with the sufferings of Christ for the salvation of souls.

Somehow I know he got the message, for every now and then he will repeat the story of his experiences during treatment. He talks also about why the good Lord allowed him to recover from this third bout with cancer and says that the Lord still had one more thing for him to do before he died. The job was, very simply, to care for my mother who has Alzheimer's. The difficulties that we had during his cancer treatment only served to reconcile each and every one in our family.

As difficult as the days of intense treatment were for all of us, I would not give them back, for they allowed me to realize just how very blessed we are to have my father with us. It all puts such a very different slant on things in one's life. Thank you for being open to the Spirit and praying for my father.

Illinois, May 2001

ଔ ଔ ଔ ଔ ଔ ଔ

Dear Father Rookey,

I had two surgeries this past year to remove lesions from my left temple. The surgeon told me that my lesions may reappear, and last week, another one started to develop. I immediately applied the St. Peregrine oil and prayed the *Miracle Prayer,* as well as the beautiful prayer on the back of the holy oil leaflets, which can be obtained at your gift shop. I did this three or four times per day, and, by the third day, it was completely healed. No sign whatsoever. Praise to God and St. Peregrine for my healing.

At one of your healing Masses, I picked up some of your blessed healing cloths and I gave one to a friend whose wife was having circulation problems in her legs. She had to use a machine that vibrated, after which she had tremendous tremors. Then her husband handed her the blessed cloth; she touched the cloth and the tremors stopped.

Praise God and all His holy Saints and Angels.

Illinois, February 2001

ଔ ଔ

In his Masses and healing services, Father Rookey uses blessed oil. The anointing of the sick with oil is part of the ancient tradition of the Church.

Blessed Oil
By Abbot Andrew Miles, O.S.B.

"They shall come streaming to the Lord's blessings: the grain, the wine, and the oil" (Jer.31:12). In these words the prophet Jeremiah foretells the

blessings that God would one day pour out upon his people.

Oil in particular was a special sign of God's blessing. Among the many beautiful provisions of the Good Shepherd is his anointing: "You anoint my head with oil" (Ps. 23:5). The tribe of Asher was especially blessed among all the tribes of Israel (the word "asher" means "happy" or "blessed") because, as Moses said, "the oil of his olive trees runs over his feet" (Dt. 33:24).

It is no wonder then, that oil became a symbol of the fullness of God's blessings poured out through his Holy Spirit, and that the expected savior would be the Anointed One (the Messiah of Christ). Thus oil has become a rich symbol of our life in Jesus, of our sharing in his anointing and in the outpouring of his Holy Spirit.

Using oil can be a beautiful and powerful way of renewing our life in Jesus, especially when this oil has been "made holy by God's word and by prayer" (1Tim 4:5).

Oil in the Bible

Perhaps no other element in the bible was used for such a wide variety of purposes as was oil. Listed below are only some of them.

Oil was used in cooking and baking. In particular, the loaves offered in sacrifice were to be made with oil (Ex. 29:2). Oil was often mixed with perfumes and used to make oneself more beautiful and attractive (Ruth 3:3; Jdt. 16:7). As such it was also used to honor guests. Anointing them with perfumed oil was a sign of great honor and respect, as well as a way of offering refreshment after a journey (Lk. 7:37-38, 46; Ps. 23:5). Perhaps for this same reason it was often referred to as an "oil of gladness, bringing joy to the heart" (Ps. 45:8; Is. 61:3; Heb. 1:9).

Oil too was a source of light, being used in lamps both in homes and in the temple (Ex. 27:20; Mt. 25:3).

The flame thus kindled likewise became a symbol of the Holy Spirit, whose fire purifies and enflames us with love and zeal (Acts 2:3). The healing properties of oil were also recognized (Ex. 16:9; Lk. 10:34). The apostles used it for healing, apparently at the instruction of Jesus himself (Mk. 6:13), and this practice was continued in the early Church (Jas. 5:14).

Moses gave instructions for the making of a sacred anointing oil (Ex. 30: 22-25). With this oil the Israelites were to consecrate the priests (Ex. 29:7; Lev. 8:12). Even the meeting tent and the objects of worship were to be anointed with this oil, and thus consecrated to God (Ex. 30:26-29; Lev. 8:10-11).

The kings of Israel were also anointed with oil (I Kgs. 1:39; II Kgs. 9:6). Furthermore, we read that when Samuel anointed David as king "from that day on, the spirit of the Lord rushed upon David" (I Sam. 16:13). From this experience, and perhaps others like it, oil became a symbol of the Holy Spirit. The prophets therefore who spoke under the influence of the Spirit were considered to be anointed by God (Is. 61:1), and were sometimes even anointed with oil (I Kgs. 19:16).

Jesus, the Anointed One

The expected savior of Israel, being the Anointed One, was to receive the full and complete anointing of God's Spirit. Every blessing given through oil in the Old Testament was to be poured out in fullness upon the Messiah, and through him upon all God's people.

Throughout his entire life, Jesus showed himself to be the Anointed One. At his baptism in particular, he received a powerful anointing of the Spirit, as Peter later bore witness: "God anointed him with the Holy Spirit and power. He went about doing good works and healing all who were in the grip of the devil" (Acts 10:38).

Fig. 98. *St. Peregrine the Cancer Saint,* statue, International Compassion Ministry, Olympia Fields, Illinois, 2005.

The New Testament witnesses also to Jesus' threefold anointing as King (Lk. 1:33), Prophet (Lk. 4:18), and Priest (Heb. 7:17), and to his being anointed with the oil of gladness (Heb. 1:9). In short, the fullness of anointing, the fullness of God's Spirit, is to be found in Jesus. It is to him that we must go to receive of that anointing.

"The Disciples were called Christians" (Acts 11:26)

Since Jesus is the Christ, the Anointed One, it is not surprising that his followers soon came to be called "Christians," "anointed ones." To be a Christian means to share in the anointing of Jesus, to receive his Holy Spirit and the blessings the Spirit imparts.

How do we do this? How do we receive Jesus' anointing? Scripture mentions three initial steps: repentance, faith, and baptism (Acts 2:38). But there was also, in addition to baptism, even in apostolic times, the laying on of hands with prayer for the gift of the Holy Spirit (Acts 8:15-17). By at least the second century, this was accompanied by an anointing with oil. Oil was no doubt used together with the laying on of hands because it signified becoming a sharer in the anointing of Jesus through the gift of the Holy Spirit. In the course of time, this came to be called the Sacrament of Confirmation, and the oil used was called "chrism."

To this anointing there was later added a pre-baptismal anointing to prepare catechumens for baptism. This oil came to be called the "oil of catechumens." A third oil mentioned in the letter of James (5:14) is the "oil of the sick." Until at least the ninth century, lay people as well as clergy could use oil in praying for the sick. For example, Pope Innocent I in 416 wrote: "Not only priests but all Christians may use this oil for anointing, when either they or members of their household have need of it" (Letters 35:8).

The first oil, chrism, is also used in baptism, when for some reason confirmation does not follow immediately, and it is used as well in the ordination of bishops and priests. These three oils are blessed each year by the bishop during Holy Week. Together, they signify in various ways our full sharing in the anointing of Jesus. By using all these oils we give outward expression to our faith in Jesus as God's anointed, and thereby share more deeply in his anointing.

Blessed Oil for all Christians

Besides the three oils which the Church now reserves for use in the sacraments, the Church also recognizes the use of blessed oil for use by all Christians (See Roman Ritual, p. 393, no 3.). We find, for example, in the Roman Ritual a special prayer for the blessing of oil. In this prayer the priest prays:

> Let it (the oil) bring health in body and mind to all who use it . . . You have ordained it for anointing the sick . . . We pray, that those who will use this oil, which we are blessing in your name, may be delivered from all suffering, all infirmity, and all wiles of the enemy.

The purpose of this oil as stated in the prayer is primarily for healing and protection from harm; but the oil can also be used to pray for all the blessings which the oil represents, that is, all the riches which are ours through the three sacramental anointings. We can use the oil in this way because the Church sees the blessed oil, as well as other blessed objects (such as holy water), as "extensions and radiations of the sacraments" (Roman Ritual, p. 387). In this sense, just as holy water can be used to renew our baptismal commitment to Jesus, so blessed oil can be used to renew the anointings received in the sacraments. (Using blessed oil with prayer for blessings, should *be distinguished from the Sacrament of Anointing of the Sick which is administered by a priest, often in conjunction with the Sacrament of Penance and the Holy Eucharist, to the elderly and those who are seriously ill.)*

Using Blessed Oil

Although any vegetable oil may be used, it is best to obtain olive oil because of its rich biblical significance. You may wish to add a small amount of perfume to the oil to give it a pleasing fragrance.

If possible, have the oil blessed according to the blessing in the Roman Ritual. If this is not possible, another prayer of blessing could be used, inviting others to join in the prayer. Through this prayer, the faith of others is joined to the faith of the one using the oil or being anointed. This combined prayer can be especially powerful (See Mt. 18:19; Acts 19:12).

The oil can be used in praying for oneself or in praying for others. The simplest way of anointing is to make the sign of the cross on the forehead while saying the prayer (See Ex. 9:3; Rev 7:3). But other parts of the body can also be anointed, especially when the need for healing may be localized in one or several parts of the body. But various parts of the body can also be anointed to consecrate them to the Lord—even as parts of the temples were once consecrated with oil. (See Rom. 6:13)

When praying for others it would be advisable to inform them that you are using blessed oil, and are not administering a sacrament of the Church. It is also advisable to keep the oil in a special and safe place, setting it aside as something holy.

A Prayer for using Blessed Oil

(Although a prayer from the heart is always preferable, the prayer given below might serve as a pattern in formulating your own. You may wish to choose one or

the other parts of the prayer according to your needs, developing it in your own words. You may, also wish to precede this prayer by a prayer of repentance and a renewal of faith in Jesus.)

Father, by this holy oil, consecrate me to yourself, to belong entirely to you.

Consecrate me, Father, in your Son, Jesus, your Beloved and your Anointed, that I might share in his perfect anointing, living fully in him, "not having a justice of my own" (Phil. 3:9), but sharing in his holiness and in his consecration to you.

Through this oil, Father, consecrate me by your Spirit "to a life of obedience to Jesus Christ and purification with his blood" (I Pt. 1:2).

Consecrate me, Father, to share in the royal priesthood of your Son, that I may offer "spiritual sacrifices acceptable" to you "through Jesus Christ" (I Pet. 2:15).

Anoint me, Father to share in the "kingly reign" (Rev. 1:9) of your Son. Let no sin reign in me, but only your divine Spirit of holiness.

Anoint me, Father, to share in the prophetic ministry of Jesus, "to bring glad tidings to the poor" (Lk. 4:18), to bear witness, in the power of your Holy Spirit, to the salvation you offer us in Jesus.

May this oil be for me, Father, an oil of gladness, lifting every depression and sadness, and filling me with the joy of your Spirit.

Through this oil may Your Spirit fashion me in the image of Jesus, to reflect his beauty and attractiveness (Ps. 45:3), and to spread abroad the fragrance of his all embracing love (I Cor. 2:14; Song 1:3,12).

May it be within me the source of Your eternal light, burning brightly until the coming of Your Son in the full splendor of Your kingdom.

May the fire of your Spirit be kindled within me to purify my mind and my heart and to set me aflame with your divine love.

Consecrate me, Father, by this oil as your holy temple, your "dwelling place in the Spirit" (Eph. 2:21-22). Consecrate and make holy each member of my body to serve you in holiness and honor (I Thes. 4:4). [In your prayer, you may wish to mention specific members of your body, as well as your mind, will, emotions, feelings, etc.]

[When praying for healing for yourself:]
Father, I anoint myself with this oil
in the name of Jesus, Your Son.
He is your healing remedy for all my illnesses.
Through this holy oil may I experience the
healing power of Your Spirit flowing out to me
through the death and Resurrection of Jesus.

As this oil penetrates and heals, may Your Divine Spirit penetrate my whole being and drive out all darkness, sin and evil, and fill me completely with your healing light.

Father, may I be restored, for Your honor and glory, to full health of body, mind, and spirit.

Amen.[1]

(Reprinted with permission)

ﭏﭏﭏﭏﭏﭏﭏﭏﭏﭏﭏﭏﭏﭏﭏﭏﭏﭏﭏﭏﭏﭏﭏﭏﭏﭏﭏﭏ

Dear Father Rookey,

This is a testimonial of the Lord's Healing Grace. In August 1999, my mother was stricken with cancer of the esophagus. She started the treatments of chemotherapy and thirty treatments of radiation. In November of 1999, she went for the surgery but was told that they could not do it because the cancer had spread to a lymph node that attached to the aorta valve of the heart. She was sent home, basically to die.

We started going to the healing Masses and saying the *Miracle Prayer* every night. She was on all different kinds of medicine, morphine, and a feeding tube because they said that she would not eat regular food again.

By the Grace of God and through you, Father, my mom is off the feeding tube, went from eight prescriptions down to three, and has no pain. She is going on two years of surviving. She eats like a government mule, and the hospice kicked her out last August. Her nurse told her she didn't die quick enough. She started driving again and is now taking Communion to the sick of our Church. I feel that a miracle has taken place and that the Lord is watching over us. We have a bumper sticker in our car window that says, "Miracles Happen," and, believe me, I know they do. I am living with one.

Illinois, June 2001

ℂ ℂ ℂ ℂ ℂ ℂ

Dear Father Rookey,

I am writing to you to thank you and to let you know that I am doing very well. At Christmas, 1998, I called you from Stockholm (you said I was your first caller from Sweden!) to ask for your help and told you about my rather aggressive kidney cancer. We had heard of your good work from friends in New York who gave us your telephone number. Thank you so much for taking time for me, talking to me, and praying with me! You then sent me the *Miracle Prayer* and blessed cloth.

You can't imagine how much comfort this all gave me. I said the prayer over and over again and held my prayer card and cloth close to me all the time and, praise God, the cancer had not spread. After an operation, over one and a half years ago, I am still free of cancer! May the Lord continue to bless you and your work.

Sweden, Easter 2000

Christ's Healings of Brain Tumors and Brain Injuries

Dear Father Rookey,

My husband was diagnosed with a malignant brain tumor and had surgery, but the doctor was not encouraging in his prognosis for this type of tumor.

My husband and I attended your healing Mass during this time even though he was not Catholic and we were both rather skeptical. However, we went forward for your laying on of hands and my husband found himself on the floor.

That was almost nine years ago. He has had good MRIs on a regular basis. He has joined the Catholic Church, is a St. Vincent de Paul caseworker, and continues to instruct pilots for a major airline.

We give thanks to God for guiding us and our doctors, but something special happened to my husband at that service that went beyond what we or they could do. We believe God blessed him with a Gift of Health.

Georgia, March 2001

✧ ✧ ✧ ✧ ✧ ✧

Dear Father Rookey,

When you came to our church to conduct a healing service, I invited a young girl, fourteen years old, who was battling an incurable, inoperable, brain tumor. I would like to add that this girl and her family had no faith foundation.

She and her mother came to the service, despite some very grueling and debilitating chemotherapy. She literally dragged herself up to the altar where you prayed over her.

Father, I would like to tell you that today this young lady's incurable, inoperable tumor is completely gone! I truly believe that our Lord worked through you that day at the healing service. Thanks must also go to the doctors who are also His Instruments.

Most especially—this family has found the Lord!!! They go to church and she goes to a Catholic College. Praise be to God. Thank you for your prayers, Father.

Indiana, October 2004

℧ ℧ ℧ ℧ ℧ ℧

Dear Father Rookey,

I was diagnosed with lymphoma and told that I had a tumor. Before the surgery, my daughter called you and asked you for prayers and blessings. It was to be a major surgery. During the surgery, no tumor was found. It has been five years since then. I have blood tests every six months. All is clear.

When you were at church, my daughter and I came to see you. When you prayed over me, God's Healing was present through you. I felt a surge of something like electricity wave through me, starting at my head, all the way to my feet. I felt heat where the surgery was performed. Yes, I did fall and rest in the Holy Spirit.

Thank you for coming. May Our Lord Jesus, Our Blessed Mother, and all the Angels keep you well and in their loving care for many years to come.

Australia, November 2004

℃℃℃℃℃℃

Dear Father Rookey,

We attended three of your wonderful Masses and healing services, and, YES, we experienced two miracles with two of our daughters who were not supposed to live.

The first was our eldest daughter who was diagnosed with a malignant brain tumor four years ago. Doctors told her it would come back (wrong). After attending three of your services, she had an MRI last year and the results show no sign of cancer.

The other daughter was doomed for destruction as she was a drug addict. Before moving, she came with us to attend your services at our parish. That was the beginning. After you touched her, she laid down for a long time. She went to a 90-day Christian rehab and is doing great.

Louisiana, December 2000

℃℃℃℃℃℃

Dear Father Rookey,

Last April, my mother suffered from a brain aneurysm and she was comatose for two weeks after surgery. Then she was paralyzed with no speech or response to stimulation. The doctors said that she would never get any better.

I celebrated the Feast of Mercy for her and attended your healing Mass. While I was at your Mass, she started moving her left leg. The next day, she began speaking. This was miraculous to all working in the hospital and her family. Today, she is home and eighty percent recovered. She has her speech back, all mobility, and her memory. If you were to meet her today, you would never know anything had happened.

This has been a profoundly moving experience for her and she prays constantly. She and her entire family thank you for the healing Mass and the special blessing in the Holy Spirit you bestowed.

Praise the Lord God Almighty in Heaven and on earth. He Lives!

Missouri, August 2001

℃℃℃℃℃℃

Dear Father Rookey,

At your healing service, I asked for a healing for my nephew who had a condition that could cause partial paralysis. It was suggested that his head be cut open and a pad be put in so that the brain would not touch the nerves. After your healing service, he has not had any more problems with this. It will be one year in August.

I brought my son to your service. He was in need of a healing from an addiction and depression. I feel that he is getting a gradual healing.

Thank you so much for coming to us.

Michigan, July 2000

Christ's Healings of the Nervous System

Dear Father Rookey,

I have wonderful news to tell you. I have received an almost instantaneous healing. For almost four years, I suffered with a very painful affliction called trigeminal neuralgia. Three nerves around my cheek, eye, and forehead were damaged, causing pain like electric shocks continuously. I could eat only soft foods because anything touching the roof of my mouth triggered the pain. I had been to three doctors and had an MRI, but the problem did not originate there. I faithfully took the two prescribed pills daily for all those years. I lost fourteen pounds and kept getting weaker.

One day in the mail, I received a copy of the International Compassion Ministry newsletter and after reading about the many miracles of healing, I felt impelled to call you.

My pain was so severe that I could hardly stop crying as I spoke to you. Later at bedtime as I was reaching to take the usual medicine, I heard a loud voice inwardly say, "No—don't take the medicine." I put the pill back in the bottle. The following day, and each day after, I did not take any pills. I could not believe that I was without any sign of pain. I was so afraid it would recur. It has been thirty-five days now, and I have no pain—no problem eating.

I thank God daily and ask Him to bless you, and I ask Jesus to guide me so I can best do His will to help others.

Illinois, February 2001

ℭ ℭ ℭ ℭ ℭ ℭ

Dear Father Rookey,

In August of 1999, with prompting from my mother, I came to your healing Mass. I had been diagnosed with severe carpal tunnel syndrome in both wrists and wore metal braces to sleep at night. Within two weeks and very much to my utter surprise, the carpal tunnel had been cured by the Holy Spirit I experienced through you.

Michigan, June 2000

ℭ₎ℭ₎ℭ₎ℭ₎ℭ₎ℭ₎

Dear Father Rookey,

About twelve years ago, I phoned to see what city you would be in to heal me. I was told of a little city in Florida that I had never heard of. I flew there as I was to have an operation on Wednesday and it was now Saturday. I stood in line and when you saw me you asked, "What are you doing here?" I told you that I was to be operated on Wednesday. You said, "Come here," and you put your hands on my head.

On Monday, I got x-rays again and my carpal tunnel on both hands was Gone! I have never had any pain since.

Thanks a lot—twelve years late.

Louisiana, November 2004

ℭ₎ℭ₎ℭ₎ℭ₎ℭ₎ℭ₎

Dear Father Rookey,

At your healing services, I stood behind a child in a wheelchair. You anointed him, and he got up and walked. Tears of joy streamed down my face. I thanked God for him, even if I couldn't be helped. You blessed me, and I walked back to the wall that I had leaned against for almost five hours.

Two friends rubbed all up and down my spine, my neck, and my right arm, and prayed so hard for me. After about twenty minutes, I moved my head to the left and right and up and down. I hadn't been able to do this since my accident. It's been a whirlwind of events ever since. I prayed to God, and I just never gave up. You just gave Him a little boost. I am forever, from the bottom of my heart, thankful to you, Father. I attend Mass and adoration. I keep working on this right arm, and

I know with the *Miracle Prayer,* it's just a matter of time.

Thank you, Jesus, Mary, and Joseph, and thank you, Father Rookey.

Missouri, April 2000

℃ ℃ ℃ ℃ ℃ ℃

Dear Father Rookey:

In 1989, I had a successful laminectomy. In March 1999, I was hit bodily by a moving dumpster, thrown eight-twelve feet, and knocked against a brick wall. As a result of the accident, the doctors told me I tore everything apart. If they operated, I would be a paralyzed for the rest of my life. I would have to learn to live with the pain that was continuous day and night. I was declared physically disabled, as I could no longer work, sit, stand, or walk or perform any normal activity more than twenty minutes at a time.

In July 2001, I read in the *St. Louis Review* that you came to St. Louis once a month for a healing service. On Saturday, August 4, 2001, I attended your healing service. Nothing happened. But on Monday, August 6, 2001, I was without pain and have been pain free ever since. I can sleep, walk, sit, stand, whatever I want—PAIN FREE. It's like this sixty-eight-year-old woman has a new body. Now I live in continual amazement of what all I can do. Not only am I amazed but so is everyone I know, including those who only know me by sight. My life now is a prayer of thanks to Almighty God for His Goodness and Mercy to me and for giving all of us you.

May God reward you.

Missouri, December 2001

Christ Healings of Sight and Hearing

Dear Father Rookey,

I can't thank you enough for the nice words in that beautiful card you sent me. I had put it under my pillow, and the next day my hearing was restored. It is a true miracle through your miraculous prayers. I am very grateful for all you've done for me.

Arizona, July 2001

☙ ☙ ☙ ☙ ☙ ☙

Dear Father Rookey,

You've blessed us with many healings, Father. We first saw you in London when I first rested in the Spirit. I prayed for one thing: that my son's partial deafness would be cured.

Within hours of leaving the service, my backache stopped, my severe depression lifted, and then we discovered that the perforation in my son's left ear was healed.

The consultant said that in the thirty years he had practiced, he had never known a perforation of that size to even start to heal. My son often quotes St. Padre Pio, "Pray, hope, and don't worry."

England, September 2004

☙ ☙ ☙ ☙ ☙ ☙

Dear Father Rookey,

In the past, I have witnessed many miracles our Lord has performed through you. In my own family there have been a few. After attending your Mass and healing service, my oldest daughter was cured of glaucoma and of cervical dysplasia so severe that she has had multiple surgeries for it. In both cases, her doctors were astounded.

My youngest daughter had been so depressed. After attending your Masses, she was diagnosed with polycystic ovary disease that was treated successfully.

Thank you and God bless you.

Florida, May 2000

༒ ༒ ༒ ༒ ༒

Dear Father Rookey,

I was diagnosed with MS (multiple sclerosis) in March of this year. That was one of my darkest hours. My dear friend reached out to me and offered to take me to see you. We traveled together with our four young children. After being touched by you the first time, I felt joyous. I had some improvement of my symptoms, and my vision cleared. My healing was gradual, but I did have a recurrence of some symptoms.

I received such a peace from you and—by resting in the Spirit—I knew I could deal with whatever God's plan was for me. We had all smelled roses, and my daughter found a Miraculous Medal at the foot of Mary's statue. My six-year-old daughter was also touched by you and no longer has to wear glasses.

After seeing you again, I again rested in the Spirit. I now have had a complete remission of my symptoms. I have such an inner peace and greater love for Jesus and Mary. I am able to see this disease as a blessing because it's brought me closer to God. Praise God for His Goodness and you, Father, for being His Instrument.

North Carolina, September 2000

༒ ༒ ༒ ༒ ༒

Dear Father Rookey,

I've known this lady for about three years.

She told me for years she lived in emotional and physical turmoil. It became so bad one day she said she decided to turn her life over to Jesus as she could not deal with it any longer.

Fifteen years ago, she lost sight in her left eye. Her daughter decided to be a stand-in at healing services for her. After five years, the mother received her sight back. Then she lost about fifty percent of the sight in her right eye ten years ago. When a doctor did tests, a blood vessel was found to have broken behind the right eye, and also one of her carotid arteries was found to be blocked. About that time, Father Rookey had prayed for and blessed her, and now her vision is perfect and the blockage of the carotid artery has disappeared.

The doctors are mystified and don't understand how all of this could have happened. Do you?

Chicago, Illinois, April 2000

Christ's Healings of Autoimmune Diseases

Dear Father Rookey,

I attended your healing Mass in the year 2000. I had lupus for three or four years. Two weeks after the healing service, I had a doctor's appointment. He had taken a blood test, and he said, "Your lupus is gone, no signs of lupus."

I'm so thankful and grateful for the prayers and the miracle that you and the Lord Jesus made possible in my life. When I went to your Mass on February 11, 2000, I had a very good feeling, but I find it hard to explain. I never had it before. I thank you so much.

Hawaii, March 2001

ଔଔଔଔଔଔଔଔଔଔଔଔଔଔଔଔଔଔଔଔଔଔଔଔଔଔଔଔଔଔଔଔ

"My Healing through Fr. Rookey" by Elson Legendre

I was diagnosed with Rheumatoid Arthritis in 1980. I feel confident that many of you, reading this, will be able to relate to the pain and misery that arthritis can cause. The first five years of my illness were very difficult. It was an effort to button my shirt; to start my car, I had to use both hands to turn the ignition key. There were many other simple tasks that, someone without arthritis could do easily, were monumental for me to do.

As the years went by, to maintain a fair standard of life with this illness, I would, on six week intervals, receive cortisone injections in my hands and my knees, plus fluid had to be removed from my knees at each visit.

On August 15, 1994, the Feast of the Assumption, I attended a Healing Service conducted by Father Peter Mary Rookey, OSM, held at Immaculate Conception Church in Marrero. As I was in line approaching the altar, I was placed to the extreme right. For some reason I was asked to move more to the center of the altar where the Blessed Sacrament was exposed. As I waited for Father to come and give his blessing, I looked up at the Blessed Sacrament and asked Jesus to grant me His peace and love. I did not ask for a healing. Father came, blessed me and I rested in the Spirit.

That night, as I laid down, I felt this heat come over my body. My initial reaction was that I was having a *flare up* which happens, at times, to people suffering with Rheumatoid Arthritis. I then realized this heat was not the same; and I must say, it made me restless and I could not go to sleep while this sensation was happening, which lasted for over an hour.

Fig. 99.   *Mother of Sorrows*, painting by Ferdinand Roccanti, 2006. Inscribed: *Dear Father Rookey, May Mother Mary who is the spotless image of the adorer of God, continue to fill you with grace and wisdom. May God bless you and keep you safe all the days of your life.*

A few days passed and I had put this out of my mind. I went to Mary's Helpers center and the conversation of the Healing Service came up. I them told them about this feeling I had the night of the Service. Someone told me it was possible that I could have received a healing, as this is one of the signs that a healing has occurred. I then started noticing that I was feeling better, walking up stairs without difficulty and a feeling of just feeling great. I then proceeded to discontinue some of my medication and this great feeling continued. I said to myself, "Could I have really been healed?"

On September 7th, 1994, the opening day of Our Lady of Sorrows Novena at Immaculate Conception Church in Marrero, I had a doctor's appointment. As usual, he examined my hands and knees. No inflammation, no fluid in the knees, no cortisone injection needed. I then related the story about the Healing Service. He looked at me kind of funny. His response was he had watched healing services on TV. I then requested that he give me a blood test which would confirm whether I have rheumatoid factor in my blood or not. On September 11th, I received a call from his office advising me that the result was negative—no rheumatoid factor in my blood. I could not believe this. I was truly HEALED of the illness! To confirm this healing, it is documented in my records that I had blood work done in 1992 and the results were positive.

I wish to take this opportunity to publicly thank Jesus for this healing. I would also like to honor His Blessed Mother for all the wonderful graces I have received through her intercession. To you, Fr. Rookey, I thank God for sending you to us.[2]

September 1994

(Reprinted with the permission of Margaret Trosclair, O.S.S.M., Mary's Helpers)

Dear Father Rookey,

I am long overdue in writing and thanking you for your prayers over the phone for a dear friend who had liver cancer. You prayed with me over the phone for him, and after surgery six months later, he was cancer free. He did not have to take the last two months of chemo. He is doing great today.

In 1997, I attended your Mass. I had lupus for twelve years, and I was healed. No more pain and suffering. I am thankful for the power of Jesus in healing bodies. God bless and keep you and your ministry.

Wisconsin, July 2004

๏ ๏ ๏ ๏ ๏ ๏

Dear Father Rookey,

Your visit to our parish and our dinner with us was a miracle for me.

I first saw you in 1994, at the onset of my illness. I was the *victim* looking for an end to Wegener's disease attacking my body. As the days passed, I came to slowly realize my healing was in the acceptance of my illness.

When I saw you again last year, I came to know how much I really had not fully accepted this cross. Jesus said to me, "In My time, not yours." We had started praying the *Miracle Prayer* at our prayer meeting on Fridays. When I saw your calendar this past February, I thought, "this is really going to be the 'healing.'" I went around for a week telling people I would be healed. This was very hard for me as I was reading Sister Faustina's Diary weekly to the prayer group. For nearly six years, I had tried to think as she did, asking God for crosses to bear.

I was experiencing many assaults, and I came to realize through intense prayer that my way of thinking was wrong for me. So I began to go back thinking about the cross I must continue to bear and live only the Will of God, not my own.

When I saw you sitting over the organ on Thursday, I was overcome with the mere fact you were here physically in my church. As the church started to fill up, I was in awe. I began to see the works of the Holy Spirit in getting the word out that you were coming with basically no advertisement and in less than two weeks.

As I was sitting there during the *Rosary*, I looked around to all the people there, over a thousand, and realized at that moment there in my midst were souls hungering for healing of every kind. I began praying for all of their healing, and asked God to forget mine, which I began to feel insignificant compared to theirs. A smile spread across my face as I was feeling this, and I could hardly contain myself with joy. When I told you this in the car as we were driving to my house for dinner, you said to me, "You have received great Graces."

I felt immediately your words were my healing that night. Father, three of my co-workers have gone back to the Church! I began to realize then that faith ritual is not enough. Until I could have full forgiveness and love in my heart for everyone, and look upon all as children of God, then I really had nothing. I know now this is what I must attain for myself before I can be ever physically healed.

My husband of twenty-nine years was a reluctant catcher that evening, and, as you know, did not share dinner with us. Jesus has given him to me for my first lesson in forgiveness and love. I placed the *Bible* across my chest the night after you left and randomly opened to Matthew where he speaks of divorce and knew immediately this was not an option for me, dispelling all previous thoughts. I know now he will come back through me!

Thank you for your presence in my life. I will keep you in constant prayer.

Florida, March 2001

Christ's Healings of Back Injuries and Pain

Dear Father Rookey,

I believe in your power to help people by your intercession on their behalf to the Lord Jesus Christ. I know this because I wrote to you for my mother who also was in so much back pain she was in tears. She received a miraculous healing.

I, with the help of my mother, have raised my son ourselves after his father left when I was five months pregnant because I would not have an abortion. I cannot say that it has been easy, but it has been rewarding, and the decision to have him was the best and smartest one I ever made.

New York, February 2001

❧ ❧ ❧ ❧ ❧ ❧

Dear Father Rookey,

From the spring through early October of 2001, I had been suffering from increasing shoulder and neck pain. I could not lift a suit of clothing onto its hanger without wincing in pain. I found it impossible to write on a chalk board with any kind of reasonable speed.

I noticed an announcement for a healing service in my parish church bulletin. I had never been to such an event, but I knew that prayer could help me. Father, you led the Servite Rosary at the service, and, during the *Rosary*, I smelled the flowers you said had been promised by Our Lady. I came up at the end of the service to be anointed, and I began to feel improvement in my shoulder immediately. Within one or two days, I knew that I had been miraculously cured, because suddenly I was able to do my customary activities without pain.

I attended at least two more prayer services, which you held during that school year, and I again experienced a cure of lower back and sciatic pain that I had had for some time, as well as a strange infection of the sinuses. I am happy to report that there has been no recurrence of my shoulder pain or the other related areas. Now, I'm finally expressing my thanks to you for your ministry, Father. It has changed my life. May God bless and protect you and all the members of your ministry.

Illinois, February 2005

ʊ̌ ʊ̌ ʊ̌ ʊ̌ ʊ̌ ʊ̌

Dear Father Rookey,

On May 27, 2001, you did a healing Mass that my mum-in-law attended. She had previously phoned me at six o'clock to say a prayer to heal my back and she said she would do the same at your Mass.

When I went to bed that night, I could feel a Presence, so I opened my eyes and I saw what looked like a negative of a photograph with heat waves through it and a figure wearing a long flowing gown. I could see a face with dark circles where the eyes should be and arms were moving up and down my torso. I didn't feel scared. When I reached out my hands, the arms reached out to mine.

The next morning, I woke and told my husband because I thought I was imagining things, and he told me what it was. My mum-in-law told me it was real, and my back was feeling great. My family has benefited from this as I can spend a longer time with my daughter

Fig. 100. *Eucharistic Celebration: Father Peter Mary Rookey, O.S.M.,* Friars' Chapel, Our Lady of Sorrows Basilica, Chicago, Illinois, 2005.

without having to rest as much, and my mood had lightened because the pain isn't getting me down as much as it used to.

I would like to thank you and my mum-in-law for taking the time to help me.

England, July 2001

ᚳ ᚳ ᚳ ᚳ ᚳ

Dear Father Rookey,

God's blessing on you and all the people who help you with your ministry! It will be four years, on the 21st of this month, since I was healed at this very church. I have given a testimony, but was told to say it briefly so I could not say all that happened on that blessed day.

I went to the hospital to have a needle put into my spine. The doctor told me he was not going to do it at that time. He then told me I would have to return on the 11th after taking the medication.

On the same day, two priests took me to your healing service and I was healed. My life is completely changed. On that blessed night, I went down and heard a voice asking me, "Do you believe?" Such a powerful voice! The pain was so severe, I thought I was dying. I begged God to take the pain away. I was then brought in front of the church.

On the ground was something like snow— very fine but pale blue and glistening. Then I saw a blue revolving light over me going from my head to my feet. Then I felt a calm I cannot describe. I don't know how long I remained there. The voice came and commanded me to get up and go to my mother. When she saw me coming, she held up her hands and I went on my knees and told her that I was better. All pain had gone!

When I went to see my doctor, he said if he had not seen me before, he would not have believed. I wanted to be the leper that returned to give thanks. I come back to give thanks at this church on the 21st every year.

London, May 2001

❧ ❧ ❧ ❧ ❧ ❧

Dear Father Rookey:

Since age twenty-five, each morning my first thought on waking was "I wonder how bad the pain will be?" and, "will I be able to go to work?"

On June 13th, my cousin called me up and said, "You have been healed of the back pain you had for the last forty-four years." I was surprised and then realized the pain I usually had was gone. She said she had been at a healing service the previous night and it was announced that people were being healed of bone and back problems. My cousin said my face came into her mind. She said this happened on the feast of the Sacred Heart of Jesus. I found myself telling her when I pray for the spiritually and physically injured it is always to the Sacred Heart.

Now, days later, I'm still in a state of shock. I carried the pain for so long it was part of my everyday life, and now it is gone and I have a strange feeling within. I recalled later that I was lying in bed that night when I suddenly felt very warm and said to myself, "I wonder if I'm being healed of something," and then I forgot all about it and went to sleep. I now recall when I could hardly walk from the pain a month ago, I said, "Jesus, I need help with this if I am to be any kind of useful servant."

Chicago, Illinois

Christ's Healings of Lungs

Dear Father Rookey,

Our family appreciates your work so much. In April, you called my nephew during his stay in the hospital where he had had a special surgery on his lung. He was having fluid removed every five days from his lung and it had collapsed two times. Since you prayed for him on the phone, he has had no fluid building in the lungs. Praise the Lord! I want to tell of God's wonders and love and of my nephew's healing all the days of my life.

Florida, June 2001

✝ ✝ ✝ ✝ ✝ ✝

Dear Father Rookey,

About six years ago, I went to your healing Mass. When I went to my doctor after that he said, "If I hadn't been taking care of you, I would not believe you ever had pneumonia."

Thank you, thank you.

California, July 2004

✝ ✝ ✝ ✝ ✝ ✝

Dear Father Rookey,

My doctor sent me for an x-ray of my chest. But before I went, I phoned you and explained that I had a tumor on my lung. I felt reassured by your prayers.

My x-rays came back clear of cancer.

England, 2003

c̡ c̡ c̡ c̡ c̡ c̡

Dear Father Rookey,

One of my co-workers' brothers became seriously ill about a week and a half ago. On a Saturday night, about midnight, he woke up in excruciating pain, grabbed his scapular, and drove himself to the emergency room. The attending physician told him that he had most likely ruptured his aorta and would probably not survive. He is only about thirty-eight-years old. He was transferred to another hospital and began undergoing extensive testing, including x-rays, a CAT scan, and a MRI.

Over the course of a few days, they advised that he had a large mass on his lung, in addition to a blood clot on the same lung. He was also told he had bacterial pneumonia. Needless to say, he was in very bad shape. Several specialists were called in, including an oncologist.

I spoke with my co-worker and suggested that we call your prayer line and storm Heaven. She, her brother, and myself believe in the power of prayer.

I called your ministry number about 4:00 P.M. on Tuesday afternoon, hoping to get him on your prayer list. Much to my surprise and delight, you answered the phone, Father! I asked that you please pray for my friend, thinking that you would add him to your prayer list the next day. You asked me to pray with you, and you began praying for him right then. I had also started saying the *Rosary* for him (and you) and others here at work started praying for him.

By that very same evening, he began to show improvement. On Wednesday, his sister received a call saying that all the tests showed that there was no cancer, and apparently no blood clot. He did have bacterial pneumonia, would require some surgery and would have a long recovery.

Well, I am excited to tell you that he is being released from the hospital today! Three of the specialists who were called in, including the oncologist and a pulmonary specialist, are just amazed at his recovery. They just cannot believe it—but we can. We had the Divine Healer working with us!

Father, thank you for all of your prayers and for having your members pray for him. It looks like he is on the road to recovery. We will be forever indebted to the Mercy of Jesus. God bless you and the work that you do in His Name.

Missouri, February 2003

❦ ❦ ❦ ❦ ❦ ❦

Dear Father Rookey,

I just wanted to thank you for taking the time to pray over the phone with me.

My neighbor and her daughter were both killed in a car accident in July 2002. The son, twelve-years-old, was my son's best friend and was hurt severely. He spent six weeks in the ICU in Children's Hospital and then started having complications. There was some sort of fungus growing on his lungs from pneumonia, which he had contracted. The fungus was taking over his lungs, and the doctors didn't think he would overcome this obstacle. Because of his labored breathing, his other organs were shutting down.

This is when I called you. You prayed with me, and then I went to the hospital to see him, and, rubbing his legs, told him about your praying for him. I also taped the *Miracle Prayer* on his bed near his head. I had also been praying the *Miracle Prayer* for him. I lit my candle that I had received from you. The very next day, he began to improve! A chest x-ray showed his lungs to be completely clear of the fungus. For the first time in six weeks, he was able to be taken off the ventilator! I was so happy, so were my children and everyone.

Within the week, he was released from the hospital and he continues to progress. What a miracle! The doctors said he was a miracle child. He had had so many injuries that no one thought he'd recover.

I just want to thank you again. My girlfriend had cancer in her breast. I prayed the *Miracle Prayer* for her. They got all the cancer and her lymph nodes were clear!

Also, my brother had a lump in his neck, and I gave him the *Miracle Prayer* and lit my candle for him. At first the doctors said it was cancer. Then they rechecked it and it was benign!

I have told so many people about these miracles and about you, Father. I will be forever grateful that I found out about you and your power through Jesus Christ our Lord.

Michigan, January 2003

ℭ ℭ ℭ ℭ ℭ ℭ

Dear Father Rookey,

Thank you for your wonderful ministry to the people of the world. You are a blessing to many lives.

You called my nephew at the hospital and the fluid stopped building in his lungs. He was released to go home two days later. Praise the Lord for the miracle!

He had already experienced a miracle in 2000 as the doctors gave him only four months in June of that year. Then we went to your healing Mass. Praise the Lord. It is August 2001. To the doctors who do not really understand, he says, "Jesus is my best doctor."

May God's blessings shine on you.

Florida, August 2001

Christ's Healings of Hearts

Dear Father Rookey,

Here are copies of before and after medical records of my son. Thank you for your prayers for the healing of his heart defect. We thank God every day for His Loving Touch. We also thank God for you—a messenger of His Kindness and Love. God bless you.

Statement from Doctor:
N.B. Statements before prayer:

He is a nearly seven-month-old child who has a small-to-moderate-sized secundum, ASD [atrial septal defect]. Due to increased flow across the pulmonary valve (possibly very mild pulmonary stenosis), SBE [subacute bacterial endocarditis] prophylaxis is recommended. I discussed with his parents the importance of cardiac follow-up and possible need for closure of the ASD in a number of years; both surgery and transcatheter procedures were discussed. I would like to reevaluate him in the Cardiology Clinic in one year, obtaining a chest x-ray.

Statement from Doctor after prayer:

This is a three-and-a-half-year-old child who had a small secundum atrial septal defect and mild pulmonary valve stenosis. The ASD has closed spontaneously.

Texas, April 2001

❦ ❦ ❦ ❦ ❦ ❦

Dear Father Rookey,

Two years ago, we were invited to a Mass with you. A week before your Mass, my husband was diagnosed with a heart problem and he was scheduled for a serious test. As soon as we knew of your Mass, he canceled the test. We prayed and asked the Lord to heal him if He wished.

The whole family and friends went to your Mass, and all of us were blessed that day when you touched us. We rested in the Spirit. A few days later, my husband went to the hospital for the test, and you can see on the other side of this letter, his arteries and his heart were and are healthy. Praise the Lord!! Thanks for our intercession.

We received another blessing that day. My son filled out the paper to get your monthly letters. All of them are a ray of hope in our lives. When we received your newsletter, we hardly believed that you will be coming to a place near us. Thanks a lot for all you have done for us and for Our Lord's Kingdom.

Florida, February 2001

ℭℭℭℭℭℭ

Dear Father Rookey,

In December, I sent you an emergency fax requesting your prayers for my mother. Here is what I sent:

Nine days ago my mom had quadruple bypass surgery. But now it appears that complications are setting in due to her diabetes. Both of her feet are turning black due to poor circulation or blood clots. If you could possibly call her and pray with her, our family would be forever grateful.

You called her the same day and prayed with her. Within 12 hours, both of her feet were fully healed and returned to a healthy pink color. The nurses, who were concerned about the possibility of her losing her limbs, were amazed. She is now fully recovered.

We are eternally grateful!

Georgia, June 2000

Dear Father Rookey,

Early in July of this year, my mother was hospitalized for numerous in-patient tests and examinations due to her recurrent syncopal episodes, coronary artery disease, and hypertension. The test results regarding her syncopal episodes were inconclusive. However, one of the tests, magnetic resonance angiography (MRA) of the neck revealed a "marked (90%-95%) stenosis in the right external carotid artery" [quotation form her Diagnostic Reports of July 2, 2004—copy enclosed]. Although not directly related to or causing her syncopal episodes, her newly diagnosed condition was a serious one—a greater than 90% occlusion in the external carotid significantly impairs blood supply and distribution to the extracranial (facial) parts of the head. It usually requires a surgical operation as a treatment modality. In my mother's case, however, surgical procedure was contraindicated due to an age-related high risk (she is 86-years-old). So she was released from the hospital on her routine antihypertension treatment regimen she has been on for many years.

A week later, she saw her eye doctor for her yearly check-up and, during an opthalmological examination, the doctor noticed some changes in her right eye caused by eye-nerve damage. He was informed about my mother's newest MRA results, and he referred her for an additional test—bilateral extracranial carotid ultrasound with color Doppler technique, which was scheduled for July 26.

You, Father, prayed over my mother on July 18. As scheduled, my mother underwent the ultrasound with Doppler test on July 26. In her Diagnostic Report (please see the enclosed copy), the "Findings" section stated, "No hemodynamically significant stenosis is seen in either extracranial carotid artery distribution; stenosis from 30%-49%." To close the story, let me add that during a follow-up visit, the eye doctor, after re-examination of my mom's eyes, said that her right eye condition improved.

Even for such a skeptic as I am by habit—by a nature of such drastic reduction in stenosis ratio (from 95% to 49%), which is now not 'hemodynamically significant', without any medical treatment prescribed or procedure performed, and during such a short time—there is no other explanation but a sincere belief that your intercessory prayer had led to that amazing outcome in my mother's case.

Thanks be to Jesus Christ and His Mother for granting my mother their graces through Father Peter's prayers. May God bless you, Father—a great laborer for the Harvest in Our Lord's Vineyard—with His incessant Graces for all you do to others, and may God allow you to do more and more for many years to come.

With all due respect, gratitude, and with Love and Peace in Jesus Christ and Mary.

Barbara Wojtowicz

(Reprinted with the permission of Barbara Wojtowicz)

Chicago, October 2004

೫೫೫೫೫೫೫೫೫೫೫೫೫೫೫೫೫೫೫೫೫೫೫೫೫೫೫೫೫೫೫೫

Dear Father Rookey,

After going to my doctor, you prayed for God's Intercession for me after having a mild heart attack; one artery was blocked fifty percent and the other ninety percent. I remember you said you would join your rosary with mine as you said good-bye. Since then, I have said the *Rosary* every day.

On February 6th, I went for a stress test and evaluation by my doctor. I was told I did fifty percent better than the average for my category.

When I went to the doctor's office, he said that he and his assistant had just come back from looking at the test pictures and results. He said the second and third arteries showed *normal* and he patted the papers that showed this and put them aside!! He said they would treat the stinted artery.

My husband and our daughter were with me and thinking I would now get scheduled for surgery, but our prayers were answered!! I find that some people have difficulty believing this miracle, but I have a sketch the doctor drew for us while I was in the hospital. I will make a copy for you.

We are elated! We thank you for your prayers. Also, the swelling from my eyelid allergy has not come back for five weeks. I have had it four times at regular intervals of eighteen-twenty-one days. Thank you for those prayers, too.

Praise God and many thanks to you, Father.

Pennsylvania, February 2003

Christ's Blessings of Babies

Dear Father Rookey,

You prayed with me for my daughter who was in her fifth month of pregnancy and was having early labor. She carried the child full term—and delivered a healthy daughter on February 1, 2000. Thanks to God! Your ministry has made a change in our lives.

Wisconsin, July 2000

ℭℭℭℭℭℭ

Dear Father Rookey,

Our twin little girls are doing very well now. You helped pray them into existence.
Many thanks.

Illinois, April 2001

ℭℭℭℭℭℭ

Dear Father Rookey,

Thank you for your blessing in February. By the way, our daughter was pregnant and at that point the baby was breach. After you blessed her, she said the baby turned around and she had a normal birth.

Kansas, July, 2001

ℭℭℭℭℭℭ

Dear Father Rookey,

I am writing to express my gratitude for your help and prayers during a very difficult time.

I called your office and told you of my desire to have a baby. I cried as you prayed over me and said, "We'll ask God to send you as many children as you can handle." A new sense of relief came over me.

Well, after many tears, I miraculously conceived a few weeks after I talked with you! I was so happy, especially because the doctors were recommending in-vitro fertilization as our last option. We had already decided we would not do that as a means to conceive.

During my somewhat difficult pregnancy, I again called and asked for prayers, Happily, I delivered a healthy baby boy on September 8th, our Blessed Mother's birthday, and I don't think it was coincidence.

Thank you, Father for your prayers and for the hope and inspiration you provide through your ministry to all who come to you.

Illinois, November 2004

Christ's Gifts of Multiple Healings

Dear Father Rookey,

I spoke to you on the phone about our dire need for a suitable location for our business—and in God's own and right time we found one. Thank you for praying with me for this favor. We are indeed grateful to Our dear Lord and the Blessed Mother and the Saints for this and many favors received through your prayers and the *Miracle Prayer.*

A friend was so distraught that one of her friends was dying in the hospital of a sickness that couldn't be diagnosed. She was not Catholic. I promptly shared some of the St. Peregrine oil and prayer with them. They used it everyday on the patient and she took a great turn for the better. She attended your healing service last October with the family to give thanks and gratitude. Father, I would like to add that the patient was from Turkey.

A young boy had an accident and the doctors were about to amputate his leg. I shared some of the St. Peregrine oil with him and within a few days the doctors ruled out amputation. The boy is a non-Catholic, but he's so thankful for the oil and grateful for this great miracle from the Lord. He's well, able to walk, and is back to normal.

Texas, July 2001

ℭℭℭℭℭℭ

Dear Father Rookey,

I thank you for your many prayers. I want to update you on some of the people I have asked you to pray for:

I asked you to pray for my brother who had lung cancer. He has been cured. Thanks be to God!

The four-year-old son of a friend broke his arm and had a very successful surgery. The mother had great peace when you prayed with me for them.

I called to ask you to remember another friend who was having difficulty with his lungs. The doctors could not find a diagnosis. On Tuesday, they had found the cause. He has a certain kind of pneumonia, but his recovery looks favorable.

Thank you.

North Carolina, April 2001

ℭℭℭℭℭℭ

Dear Father Rookey,

Just before your visit this year, my mother was rushed to the hospital—part of her heart had stopped! She attended your healing Mass, and she now seems fighting fit.

I brought my twelve-year-old daughter to your healing Mass at least twice. She suffered from Photosensitive Epilepsy. On a recent brain scan they said there was hardly anything (abnormal patterns) to pick-up. In about a week, they are reducing her epilepsy tablets!

I know you are encouraged when people tell of their experiences. This is one reason I am writing this. I am certain there are many, many people who have never come forward at your

Masses to give witness. I myself would find it difficult. I am certain a lot of people have had healings that they are too shy to talk about. May God bless you and may you still be visiting England when you are over a 100.

England, September 2001

ℭ ℭ ℭ ℭ ℭ

Dear Father Rookey,

Thank you for everything. You must have guessed I needed a lot of healing. My eyes and ears have leveled off. I'm so grateful to you! The reason I healed so slowly was that I was literally dying. I had encephalitis in 1979 (twenty-two years). This week it totally went out of my system. Thanks be to God. Praise to Him and thanks to you. I can see to take care of my home. What a blessing!

My husband has been healed, too. I prayed for him, and anointed him, and now he hears no voices and some of the frightening visions went away. We owe it all to you. You have indeed blessed our marriage. We sent a picture of two friends to you. They have received healings, too. I told the gentleman he would walk again. You must have been praying for him at the time as two days later he got out of his chair and walked with a cane to the bathroom. He hasn't stopped walking now. Thank you. Now his wife has faith and hope. She was almost a hunchback with much pain. She is now able to stand straight and the hump has gone.

I am Jewish. I am indeed fond of you for all the healings. I declare you a Saint.

May 2001

Christ's Healings of Prisoners

Dear Father Rookey,

I am retired from twenty years of service with the New York Police Department where I worked both as a police officer and a detective. I now own a private investigation company located in New York. I am writing this letter to tell you how grateful I am for you, Father Rookey. In 1994, I was diagnosed with prostate cancer. I went to a doctor who presented me with your *Miracle Prayer*. The physician told me to say this prayer daily and the Good Lord would change my whole life in a special way.

Well, I've been saying the prayer every day since then. I said this prayer and began feeling better immediately. I called your number to request more prayer cards. When I called, I was able to speak with an elderly gentleman. I asked this gentleman for additional *Miracle Prayer* cards and he said there would be no problem and no cost. As the conversation went on, I began to realize that the person I was speaking with was you. I told you my plight, and you suggested that we pray together over the telephone. After praying for a short period of time, you assured me that everything would be fine. Two days later, I underwent massive prostate surgery. The doctor told me that my cancer was a C-grade cancer. Note: Cancer runs in A, B, C and D grades; D being the worst.

Some eight-plus years later, my cancer is still gone and my P.S.A. (Prostrate Specific Antigen) is 0. After my surgery and the continual saying of the *Miracle Prayer*, my life began to change drastically. I became involved in the Cursillo Movement for approximately one year. The Cursillo Movement led me to The Kairos Interdenominational Christian Prison Ministry in a federal prison. Kairos is a four-day retreat where the volunteers sleep in the prison with the prisoners and have a follow up program, in this case every Wednesday. For a year we were going every Wednesday when we realized there was no Catholic program in this facility. We then started a Catholic program on a Thursday.

For approximately five years, I have been going to the prison two days a week. While in this prison ministry, I have spoken about the *Miracle Prayer* and the love God has for us, and—to my amazement—there have been numerous healings. People who have been diagnosed with medical problems have gone for testing and their illnesses have mysteriously disappeared. Inmates with broken families, because of the their illegal activities, have been saying the prayer together with their families at the same time every day. This seems to heal their family situation. Some men are from different countries, and they say this prayer the same time every day with their family, taking into account the time differences so the inmate and his family are on their knees the same time every day. Some men, who are very violent and hostile, say this prayer daily and now are involved in art classes where they display their love of God in their artwork.

I give these cards to my business clients whom I feel are in need. These people generally have marital problems or criminal cases. The results of these individuals saying this prayer and asking Our Lord and Savior for forgiveness are unbelievable.

In conclusion, I would like to say that one of my favorite analogies that I tell the inmates, in federal prison, is that life is like a fifteen round professional fight. When the fighter is beaten, cut, exhausted, and knocked to the ground, he knows that if he stays down for just ten seconds it will all be over and there will be no more pain, yet the fighter gets up. He gets up because he wants to win and such is life. And I also tell them that when a fighter gets up off the canvas, he immediately looks to his corner for advice and help. When the bell rings and he goes back into the corner, these corner men begin to work on him physically, to heal his pain and to stop the bleeding; emotionally, to calm him down; and psychologically, to give him instructions. I tell these men that it is up to them to surround themselves with a good corner, and I also tell them that I would be proud to work their corner under the condition that they work mine too.

I cannot only speak for myself but also for my clients and the inmates in prison that they are proud to have you in their corner. The results of your compassion ministry speak for themselves. And once again, I am proud to have you in my corner.

New York, September 2002

℘ ℘ ℘ ℘ ℘ ℘

Dear Father Rookey,

On your last visit to our church, you prayed with me for my son who was in prison. I sent him the *Miracle Prayer,* that he prayed and shared with some of the other inmates. He asked for more cards and gave them to those who asked. This went on for many months.

Just recently, my son heard from the parole board that he was being released eight months early. Another inmate who was saying the prayer, also heard of his early release. One of the young men cannot read or write, so my son and he said the prayer together. He had been in prison for twenty years and had twenty more years, which meant a life sentence. The twenty year sentence has been dropped recently, and he will be released next June. Praise the Lord!

More inmates wanted more *Miracle Prayer* cards and are praying and believing for a miracle. None of them are Catholic, and now, one of them wishes to become a Catholic. Praise God! Your ministry gives much hope and strength from Jesus and Our Blessed Mother Mary. May Our Lord continue to bless and strengthen you when you travel.

Georgia, January 2001

ℭ ℭ ℭ ℭ ℭ ℭ

Dear Father Rookey,

I am writing to thank you for your prayers of intercession for my son. I wrote to you very recently about him. He is the young man who, while at a party with friends and while drinking, took a flashlight from the belt of a police officer. He was charged with a felony and obstructing government operations. Things were looking very bleak, and the trial date was set for September.

The lawyer called and said he could not explain it, but that the DA (District Attorney) had dropped the felony charges, and after some negotiations with a colleague of the DA, the other charge was dropped as well. My son had to plead guilty to a very minor charge of harassment. His lawyer and his colleagues informed us that this whole turn of events was a miracle in their words. They said this DA never does this and that they were stunned and shocked.

Thank you for this miracle in the life of my son.

Michigan, August 2005

ℭ ℭ ℭ ℭ ℭ ℭ

Dear Father Rookey,

Presently, I'm incarcerated in jail on drug charges. My mother has talked to me about you for years. She gave me your *Miracle Prayer* and said if I read it every day, something good would happen to me. Despite my outlaw attitude, I decided to give it a try.

Every day for the last two months, I have said the prayer no matter how I felt. Not much happened. Then one night about ten days ago, for some reason, I opened up the *Bible* and the page happened to be Romans 10:9-10. It said if I believed that God raised Jesus from the dead, I would be saved!

At first I said, "Saved from what?" Then I said, "It must mean saved from Hell." I believe I've been living in Hell most of my life. Nevertheless, I read the *Miracle Prayer* card and went to sleep. I usually never dream, or at least I don't recall my dreams, That night I had a dream I shall never forget!

I was taken to a cave-like place, and on a stone-like slab, there lay Jesus Christ. He was dead, and then His Eyes opened up. I was afraid, then filled with awe. He looked at me and said, "Now you know, and you know now what to do!" I have been wondering if I'm going crazy or something. I was compelled to tell other inmates about the prayer I have, and many are reading it right now.

A miracle seems to be happening, as my attorney says he believes the police broke the law with my search warrant, and I may have my charges dismissed. No matter what happens, I will do what I've been told to do!

If somehow I get free, I will travel the four corners of the earth to meet you personally, if I may. Thank you for all.

Wisconsin, September 2004

Christ's Healings of Addictions

Dear Father Rookey,

A twenty-seven-year-old practiced homosexuality, and, after awhile, turned to drugs. He became a target for male prostitution, organized crime, and the occult. Finally, almost losing his life, he also contracted HIV.

He said his loving mother and sister continued to pray. His sister gave him a rosary and a book about the *Rosary*. Then his sister had a locution and heard a feminine voice saying, "Tell your brother to 'Hail Mary'." His mother kept reminding him he was born on a special day, August 15th (The Feast of the Assumption).

Finally, when he became frightened, he started to say the *Rosary*. Later, somehow he ended up at a church where Father Rookey was having a service. He was begging God to save him. When Father touched him, he rested in the Spirit and received the fragrance of roses. The Lord has released him from the drugs and sex addiction. He said, "I firmly believe the *Rosary* was instrumental in saving my life." There follows a full page thanking Our Lord for the beautiful things that have taken place, how he now is a servant of God and longs for the ability to be a charismatic leader and bring others to the Lord.

❥ ❥ ❥ ❥ ❥ ❥

Dear Father Rookey,

Though I was brought up Catholic, my childhood was in a family that was cursed and possessed and I never felt safe. I was put into state custody because my father could not afford to raise me and my mother was too mentally ill to raise me. So I was led into different homes and different religions.

Satan brought me into drugs, sex, and alcoholism. After seven years of marriage to a very abusive man, I got a divorce. Then an ex-boyfriend told me about the healing services, and on March 12, 1996, I saw you, and I knew there was something special about you, Father. When you walked into the hall, I saw Jesus and Mary walking behind you. After I was anointed by you, I rested for the first time in the Holy

Spirit. Ever since then I was healed of alcoholism. During your homily, you said how much Mother Mary loves us and that she forgave all for what they had done to her loving Son. If she could forgive, surely I could. That was the first day of my conversion.

Since then, I am married to a most holy and loving Catholic husband. We never miss a First Saturday healing service. I have been healed of fear, anger, unforgiveness, resentment and smoking. I am so grateful to you for loving others equally, like Jesus.

Thank you for loving me.

Wisconsin, May 2001

Christ's Healings of Mental Disorders

Dear Father Rookey,

A few weeks ago, I called you and asked for prayers. I was very depressed and frightened as I couldn't seem to pull out of it. I dreaded getting up in the morning as everything seemed to close in on me. I blamed it on major and minor problems in 2004.

I called you on Monday, and you told me fear was from the devil. You then prayed with me. When I woke up Tuesday, I was back to normal. The fear and depression were gone.

I thank you for your prayers. It is so good to know you are there with prayer support.

Florida, February 2005

ଓ ଓ ଓ ଓ ଓ ଓ

Dear Father Rookey,

I was little prepared for the incredibly beautiful sermon you preached at our church. The *Rosary* came alive, and it was if we were *pushed back in time* and actually stood before the bleeding Body of Christ. My friend and I were dumbstruck and felt the Presence of the Holy Spirit using you as a vehicle to come to us.

I am a bipolar person and my friend has a schizoid personality. Miraculously, immediately my Catholic psychiatrist found a new medicine that straightened my ups and downs so that I can control them and I am symptom free!

The *voices* my friend used to hear have left her. We could never thank you enough!

California, July 2001

ᏉᏉᏉᏉᏉᏉ

Dear Father Rookey,

About one month ago, I called and asked for prayers for my seventeen-year-old son who was suffering from excessive anxiety, worries and going into depression. He felt as if he were going insane and he was losing weight from having no appetite. Thank you for praying for him with me on the phone. One of your prayers asked for the intercession of St. Michael the Archangel (my son's middle name is Michael).

When my son got home from school that day, he was singing and whistling. He said that he felt much better. I asked him when he had started feeling better. He said it was around lunch time. It was 12:15 P.M. when you prayed for him on the phone.

Father, thank you for your love and prayers. I have heard that St. Francis De Sales said that one prayer of an obedient man is worth more than a thousand prayers of a disobedient man. Thank you for your obedience to God. My son thanks you for praying for him.

Ohio, June 2005

℃℃℃℃℃℃

Dear Father Rookey,

This is a letter of thanks and a testimony to a true miracle that was given to me through you and your wonderful healing gift.

From the time I was ten-years-old, I had the uncontrollable habit of pulling hair out. I started with my eyelashes then went on to my head. The last several years, I pulled hair for a half to a full hour every day. My husband was fed up with my promises to stop. It pained him to watch as I disfigured my looks and wasted time.

When I attended your healing Mass, I smelled something like sandalwood. After you blessed me, I touched the oil to my fingers that you had put on my forehead, and it was the same smell. I knew then that I had received a healing. I have not pulled one hair since. My new hairs—literally thousands of them—are now about two to three inches long. My husband who has had a hard time believing in God, knows something mighty has happened.

Thank you from the bottom of my heart.

North Carolina, January 2001

℃℃℃℃℃℃

Dear Father Rookey,

My cousin had a dream that her husband was going to try to kill himself. About a week later, I received the call that he was in intensive care, fighting for his life after ingesting anti-freeze. The next day, I felt a powerful urge to give him your tape on *The Seven Sorrows of Our Lady*. He listened to the tape and then gave it to his wife.

Within a few days, he wanted to live, to see his kids, and to change his life! The doctor told his wife it was a miracle, that in all his years of being a physician he had never seen anyone live with toxin levels that high.

Praise God forever; His Mercy is so great! Thank you so much for your prayers.

Illinois, February 2001

Christ's Healings of Headaches

Dear Father Rookey,

My wife and I attended your healing Mass in July, 2000. My wife had been suffering for many months with daily intense headaches, for which no cause nor cure could be found. After you anointed her forehead with holy oil and blessed her, her headaches simply vanished and she hasn't had any since. A year earlier, when you prayed for me, I was healed of colon cancer.

Thank you, Jesus and Father Rookey.

New Jersey, March 2001

℗ ℗ ℗ ℗ ℗ ℗

Dear Father Rookey,

As the healing portion of your Mass began, you called out for volunteer catchers. Being an able-bodied, young, twenty-nine-year-old, 6'1", two-hundred-sixty-pound, guy, I quickly volunteered. I was touched spiritually each time you laid hands on one of these people that I was prepared to catch. At the end, you prayed for the catchers and I was slain in the Spirit.

Upon leaving the Church, I had the strangest burning sensation in my forehead and the feeling of throbbing waves of heat. I prayed, "God, I believe that You are healing me and I believe." The next morning, I needed to refill my prescription for my headache, but in faith I did not do it, and have not done it for two years.

Through your intercession and the Power of God, I was delivered from the horrible and crippling pain of these migraine headaches.

Florida, July 2001

Christ's Healings of Autism

Dear Father Rookey,

I would like to thank you for praying for a three-year-old boy the doctors said was autistic. He is now doing beautifully and in a regular classroom, functioning normally! Thanks be to God!

Thank you for all you help and prayers.

Florida, April 2001

❧ ❧ ❧ ❧ ❧ ❧

Dear Father Rookey,

Several weeks ago, we brought our two grandsons to receive your blessing. The one who is ten-years-old suffers from autism. Since your blessing, he has improved greatly. He has made the high honor roll in school, has gotten off all medication, and his behavior has improved. The eight-year-old who had severe surgeries, is doing well and holding his own. God bless you.

Wisconsin, August 2000

❧ ❧ ❧ ❧ ❧ ❧

Dear Father Rookey.

My niece was diagnosed with Selective Mutism. While a beautiful, strong girl, she had great difficulty speaking aloud and could only whisper what she needed at school. When you called her, she listened but could not speak to you. Later, her mother asked her what you had said and she responded, "He said Jesus loves me!"

Since that time, she has gradually gained in confidence and has progressed strongly in her ability to speak aloud. When she made her first Confession, the priest told her parents that she was a chatterbox!

Thank you, Jesus, for speaking to her heart. Thank you, Father Rookey, for having the gift to say the healing words that brought Christ's Light to her soul.

Pennsylvania, 2005

Christ's Healings of the Spirit

Dear Father Rookey,

After I was introduced to the *Miracle Prayer* in 1995, I began praying it for consolation. I especially remembered the phrase, *Jesus will change your life in a very special way. You will see.* Well, I had a deep and overwhelming dream of conversion where I was plunged into the Sacred Heart of Jesus and awoke full of love for God. I had no previous devotion to the Sacred Heart, and although I believed in God and prayed often, I did not know what it felt like specifically to love God. I had wanted to feel it, but I didn't. I imagined just being respectful was enough.

From that day on, I have loved God as sincerely and concretely as I loved my newborn babies or my husband, only more. It has totally changed my life. From then on, I understood that everything we long to receive in this world from another human being can never be satisfied, and that is no longer distressing or grieving, since we are meant to discover and experience perfect love in the next.

Illinois, August 2001

℃ ℃ ℃ ℃ ℃ ℃

Dear Father Rookey,

I want to let you know that at your healing Mass, I asked for better health and the ability to let go of all emotional sickness. Upon receiving your letter, I became more aware of offering my crosses united with the Lord. My blood pressure has come down to normal, though I've had high blood pressure for thirty-eight years. My heart test and blood work all came back good. My nephew, three years after attending the healing service, still has not had to have surgery on his head. I thank you so much.

Michigan, July 2001

℃ ℃ ℃ ℃ ℃ ℃

Dear Father Rookey,

My mother has a great devotion to Our Lady of Sorrows and the Sacred Heart of Jesus. She has prayed that all her children (eight all together) come back to the Church, and we are, one by one.

I know now I can never be happy or live a good life without the Church and the Sacraments. I thank God for you and your brother priests for helping me to come back to the Church. In June, 1999, I attended the first of many of your healing Masses.

Thank you for your dedication to Our Lady and for your awesome example of a brother priest of Jesus Christ.

Illinois, June 2000

℃, ℃, ℃, ℃, ℃, ℃,

Dear Father Rookey,

When you went to Hawaii, I called all our friends where we used to live and asked them to be sure to attend the evening Mass. Even though they're not Catholic, they promised they would go. The next day, they called me and relayed to me the feeling of the Holy Spirit resting on and in them. They were touched in a deep place.

These people come from the orientation of the New Age attitude where God is not acknowledged in full as the prime and final reference whereby all things are measured. They refer to God now!

They also told me of a woman who was cured of nine tumors that were gone the next day, and another woman who received complete remission from her cancer. They were wonderfully accepting about the Holy Spirit and overwhelmingly embraced what happened.

New York, May, 2001

Christ's Gifts of Mysticism

Dear Father Rookey,

I experienced some incredible things at your healing service in 1999. Many times during the readings as you spoke, you moved back and forth toward the Gospel lectern. Two or three times during this part of the Mass, I was pulled briefly into a trance and felt my soul being stirred (envisioned in my mind) by an old-fashioned laundry stick. I also sensed a huge power ball the full height of the basilica. It rolled starting from the front left side of the church to the back and swept across the back and up the right to the front. I sensed this several times.

When I again focused on you, I noticed a white light that was bouncing off the left rounded wall behind you under the sconce. I kept watching this light to see if it was the *white shadow* you were casting, or if it was a spotlight from somewhere being deflected.

I watched intensely, then I saw the most wondrous sight. The entire sea of the congregation was outlined in pure-white light. It outlined their shoulders and heads. It was incredible! After the Mass, you asked the congregation if anyone had smelled roses. I looked at my friend and negated any chance of that since I said I was wearing perfume. She said she was smelling it, too. You then asked if anyone had seen Mary, or had seen Jesus in the Host. Some raised their hands.

Not wishing to brag about my experience, I said to my friend, "It makes you feel inferior, doesn't it?" "No," she said slowly, "I got other things. During the beginning part of the Mass, when Father Rookey was speaking on the left side of the altar, I saw a white light bouncing off the wall behind him under the sconce. Then a strong white light began to emanate from the center of his body and then obliterated his figure." I then told her of my similar experience.

May the light of the Holy Spirit be with you, Father Rookey, and in you and through you always and for a very long time.

Illinois, July 2001

ℭ ℭ ℭ ℭ ℭ ℭ

Dear Father Rookey,

I will never forget when Sister told me I could still receive Communion, but *spiritually* and not through the Host. With that strong message, I now continue to receive the Body of Christ spiritually through my prayers during Communion. While at times it has been difficult, I know I must abide by the Church rules as we ask our own children to abide by the rules set by us as parents.

Now, to share my miracle during your healing Mass. When it came time for Communion, I was thinking the Lord might not mind if I received Him through the Host because this was such a powerful holy service. I was strongly tempted when I remembered the Vatican II rules. It was then that I decided I would stay in my seat and receive the way I've been receiving the Lord for the past few years. While everyone was going to Communion, I closed my eyes as I always do for my silent prayer and blessing, when I received the most powerful fragrance of roses. It was so strong it caused me to immediately open my eyes and look around to see who was there.

I was amazed and pleased to see that I was all alone—figuratively speaking that is—and I remembered you saying some would receive that gift. I thanked and praised the Lord and the Blessed Mother for this beautiful gift. It confirmed and reassured me that my decision was the right one, and the Lord was with me no matter what. I thank the Holy Spirit for giving me another zap of Christian energy to keep me moving forward in life with increased faith and love.

Michigan, July 2001

❧ ❧ ❧ ❧ ❧ ❧

Dear Father Rookey,

At your healing services and Masses, I've had many mystical experiences. As you suggested, I would come early and go to Confession, participate in saying the *Rosary,* and in the Mass, and then the laying on of hands. Often, when I came home, I would sleep for hours. One day, I slept so long, that a friend came to check on me, but at the time I remember I was talking to

Jesus—I can't remember what He was saying to me. I would experience headaches, too, after standing in proxy for someone else's healing. Another time, while laying down, I prayed about a relationship that was causing me great sorrow. I felt the fluttering of a bird's wings burst from my heart and felt very calm afterwards. Often, I could smell the scent of roses at the Masses, and one time, when I didn't smell them at the Mass, the fragrance filled my car on the way home!

At one Mass, when you touched me, I felt heat go down the side of head to my ears. I had a vision of Christ pulling His Cross but could not see His Face. He fell and He felt white with extreme pain. I could hear the sound of the Cross as it slowly dragged across fine gravel stones. At another service, after you blessed me, I saw a middle-aged woman dressed in a long blue dress in a market buying groceries—it must have been for the Sabbath. I couldn't see her face, but she was round in figure and in a hurry. She looked at Christ, who was nailed to the Cross across the way. I remember understanding how many people looked at Him and didn't pay any attention because they thought He was just another criminal getting his due. Even in the crowds, He was alone in His Suffering.

Last year, in December at your Mass, I had a vision that I was somewhere in the universe above the Earth and Christ was below me but above the earth, nailed to His Cross. Just the top of His thorn crowned Head and the edges of His Hands were visible. All of sudden, He cried out, "Eloi, Eloi," and lightening came from both of His Hands and cracked the universe in two from top to bottom. Because I'm not a bible scholar, I had to look the crucifixion up and then asked you how to say the words—they sounded just as I had heard them said.

My feeling is that Christ is in agony these days because of the condition of the world. There could be great suffering ahead for all of us if we do not turn back to the Ways of God. We need to change ourselves and help to change others through prayer and teaching. Praise to Jesus Christ, Our Lord and King, and thanksgiving for His Blessings to us through you.

Chicago, Illinois 2002

℃℃℃℃℃℃

Dear Father Rookey,

Almost every day I hear about someone who is beginning to shed tears as they pray, particularly while praying the *Rosary*. Father calls it the Gift of Tears.

Saturday, November 3rd, I was praying in the chapel at Our Lady of Sorrows. I had been saying the *Rosary* in reparation for the sins of abortion. I came out to the rectory where Father Rookey was with the lady from Oshkosh, Wisconsin who had given me the rosary I had been using. I had the rosary in my hands as I walked up to her to thank her again. She looked down at it and said, "Oh look, some of the links have turned to gold." I turned to Father and showed him. As the three of us looked, all the large links between the decades turned gold also.

Talk about timing! I remembered what I had just been praying about. Our Blessed Lady told me, not by words, but by the tears. She is asking us to join her army to defeat the great evil we have unchained. The army will be one of tears and remorse praying the *Rosary*. She is asking for volunteers. Where would we be if she had said, "No?"

Later, as I passed a little girl in a wheelchair who seems to have no control over her body, I stopped, said a brief prayer, and put this rosary on her shoulder. She said a few words, and they were muffled. The instant I touched her with the rosary, she cried out with a clear and loud voice, "Glory to God."

The next day, which was Sunday, I awoke pain-free from the neck and shoulder pain I had had for the last nine months or so. As I prayed the *Rosary*, the small links turned gold also, but then turned back to silver. The same thing happened Tuesday during and after adoration. A lady who works for Father said eventually they will all remain gold.

Our Lady is gently calling her children. All Praise and Glory to you Heavenly Father for Your Guidance.

In my heart the Blessed Mother is saying keep connected and linked to My Son in adoration of the Eucharist and your spiritual life will be filled with golden gifts.

Christ's Granting of Peaceful Deaths

Dear Father Rookey,

My wife and I attended several of your healing Masses and saw many miracles in our life. As you know, she passed away on April 1, 2001.

If her passing sounds like the healing didn't work, nothing could be further from the truth. She was supposed to have three months of suffering. Instead she had eighteen months of quality life. She was able to pray constantly and became very close to God and Mother Mary. She brought many others along in faith by her witness and service as a Eucharistic minister up until the week before she left to be with God. She brought me closer to God. She said, "Daddy, I will win either way. If I am cured, I will win. If I go to be with God, I win."

I could go on and on about all of the miracles we were privileged to see during these past two years. One of the bigger ones is that she was able to spread her faith to her son and me. We miss her terribly, but at the same time, we have peace and joy knowing that she is with God. Your prayers and healing have sustained us through some tough times.

Thank you,

California, July 2001

᪥ ᪥ ᪥ ᪥ ᪥ ᪥

Dear Father Rookey,

My beloved, gentle, caring daughter, forty-eight-years-old, died on March 14, 2000. She had been diagnosed with cancer three years previously. A few weeks after the diagnosis, she was speaking with a priest friend of many years when their telephone conversation was interrupted by a stranger who asked Father if our daughter knew of your healing ministry. He gave the location and date of your healing service. Father turned to speak with the stranger, but he was gone. Father had never seen him before nor since.

Our daughter came to you many times during those three years and left with peace and a quiet happiness. I prayed she would be able to go on a pilgrimage to Fatima and to Lourdes. She was well enough to go and returned with joy and even stronger in faith.

I thank you, Father, for each time you blessed her and for helping my husband and me to find the strength to care for her. I once thought that should this ever happen to her, I would be destroyed in body, mind, and soul. Once more our dear Lord has been with me with the miracle of His Comfort, because I mourn, just as He said He would. My own faith has grown beyond the tragedy of this terrible disease as I experience acceptance and peace and am able to pray that God's Will be done. I know she has found eternal life, peace, and joy.

Illinois, April 2001

℃ ℃ ℃ ℃ ℃ ℃

Dear Father Rookey,

Last May, I called and spoke to you on the phone while I held a picture of my eighty-one-year-old father who was dying. You prayed for him. My father and my family experienced God's Grace and protection during his last days and well into the future. While we were praying the *Rosary* at his bedside, I smelled roses. When I tried to brush it off, the smell increased, and then in my mind's eye, I saw the deepest red roses.

Dad died a little after one in the morning. At the moment of his death, his best friend felt a Presence at her bedside and saw someone sitting on her bed. She nearly broke down crying when we told her the time of his death, because it was the exact time of the incident.

We also prayed the *Chaplet of Divine Mercy* for our Dad and prayers from the little blue *Pieta* prayer book. I'm so glad you were able to send out another newsletter. I really treasure them.

March, Michigan 2003

℃ ℃ ℃ ℃ ℃ ℃

Dear Father Rookey:

One evening, I received the sad phone call that my father had suffered a massive brain hemorrhage while fishing with my brothers in Canada. He was on a remote island and had to be brought by boat, ambulances, and planes to two hospitals. My friends called you, and you prayed for our family that night. I flew in tears to be with him. He was given last rites and disconnected from life support.

For hours, he breathed relatively gently. Because his body was in great physical condition, the doctors said he could linger for a day to up to four days. I didn't want him to suffer any longer. Later, I anointed him with St. Peregrine's oil and holy water in the places of the Five Wounds of Christ: on his forehead, palms, feet, and side, then knelt to say the *Rosary*. On the third prayer, he stopped breathing! I got the nurses and they were astonished.

They left me alone with him, and I finished the *Rosary*. When I finished, I could hear loons calling back and forth for about five minutes. They were the birds he loved. I pulled back the curtain of the window and the sky was bursting with stars. Just as the curtain came back, one fell from the sky. My cousin called from Ireland and told me, "When a star falls from the sky, a soul goes to Heaven." That night, my father and God taught me one more lesson: that death can be beautiful and I didn't need to grieve. While there have been many moments of sadness, I have not suffered terrible grief.

Thanks be to God, and thank you for your prayers that held us up through that beautiful night.

Chicago 2003

Notes

1   Abbot Andrew Miles, O.S.B., "Blessed Oil," Pecos Benedictine Community, Pecos, New Mexico. Dove Publications, *http://www. pecosmonastery.org*.

2   Elson Legendre, "My Healing through Fr. Rookey," *The Mary's Healers Newsletter* (Marrero, LA: Mary's Helpers Inc., September, 1994).

Hymn to Father Peter Mary Rookey on the Occasion of the Celebration of the 65th Anniversary of His Blessed Ordination

꽃 꽃

The following Hymn to Father Peter Mary Rookey is written in a genre reminiscent of the praise poems of Ancient Ireland. In that time, it was the practice of poets to capture the greatness of their Chieftains in songs that were passed down through the generations. In keeping with the Irish indigenous tradition, Secundinus, one of three bishops who assisted St. Patrick in Ireland, wrote the Hymn of St. Patrick *to record the spiritual legacy of his master. The* Hymn of St. Patrick *is the inspiration for the following work.*

Written in an alphabetical acrostic style, each stanza begins with a Latin word, although several Greek words are also included. This hymn is offered with deep love and thanksgiving for the precious spiritual lessons shared and the miraculous Gifts of the Holy Spirit bestowed through the person of Father Peter Mary Rookey to souls throughout the world.

Fig. 101. *A Priest Forever, Father Peter Mary Rookey*: Ordination Anniversary, Servite Priory, Berwyn, Illinois, 2008.

May God bless him and keep him,
May God let His Face shine upon him,
and have mercy on him,
May God show His Face to him,
and bring him peace,
all the days of his life.

Kathleen E. Quasey, May 7, 2006

Hymn for Father Peter Mary Rookey
On the Occasion of the Celebration of the 65th Anniversary of His Blessed Ordination

Audite (Listen)
Listen, O' you people of Our Lord,
All suffering souls both far and near.
All you Angels singing sacred chords,
Listen, a servant of God is here.

Benignus (Good-Hearted)
He is of good heart and is most kind,
A peaceful spirit flows forth from him.
He widely shares gentleness of mind,
To calm many whose spirits are dim.

Consecratus (Dedicated to the Service of God)
The Holy Spirit streams through his hands,
The Light of Christ shines about his head.
Multitudes gather throughout the lands,
For at Christ's table, all are well fed.

Disciplina (Disciplined)
He submits to long prayer and fasting,
To consume Christ's Power day and night.
With warrior strength for forceful casting,
He fights the damned demons of false light.

Exorcista (Exorcizer)
Through Christ's Grace, he mightily prevails,
Blessed words split hard chaff from tender wheat.
Hurtling Satan to the lowest Hell,
He re-claims souls from the darkest heat.

Fidelis (Faithful)
Faithful, he kneels before Christ the King,
Proclaiming His Glory for good deeds.
A soldier, he presents souls and sings,
Praising his Master, who rules and leads.

Gaudium (Joy)
Young with joy, he shares with great vigor,
Good News and Grace from Heaven above.
He amazes all with his rigor,
Tamed by the humility of love.

Hilarus (Cheerful)
Knowing well fickle human nature,
A big heart, a loving ear he lends.
With a smile, a heart becomes more pure,
With laughter, a clever story ends.

Intelligens (Intelligent)

Learned in Your Word and Great Wisdom,
With open mind, he discerns Your Will.
He speaks seven tongues for Your Kingdom,
Making known Your Mercy to the ill.

Legitimus (Lawful)

Through God's Law, he holds Your Holy Wood,
Carving forgiveness to order hearts,
With each cut, Your Rule is understood.
Freed from frightful bondage, souls depart.

Kyrie (O Lord)

O' Lord, he proclaims Your Holy Name,
A high pitched voice he boldly raises.
Imploring mercy to help the lame,
He rends his heart to sing Your Praises.

Mystagogus (Conductor to Sacred Places)

In sacrifice, the sublime is sensed,
As he inhales Mysterious Grace.
In sacred exchange, a soul is cleansed,
Grateful tears fall from a joyful face.

Nobilis (Well-known)

Throughout the world, holiness abounds,
Beyond the pale, Your Beneficence
Pours through his hands, Your Graces profound,
Throngs witness to Your Munificence.

Odorus (Fragrant)

Our Lady's perfume wafts the masses,
As his touch warms cold hearts before him.
Sleeping souls awake as he passes,
While she is lauded by cherubim.

Potens (Powerful)

Your power he demonstrates to all,
Demons are vanquished at his command.
St. Michael comes at his earnest call,
To Your Cross they flee at his remand.

Quietus (Peaceful)

In battle or prayer, he is at peace,
Offering intentions to Your Care.
Resting in Your Grace, his worries cease,
His deep love shows as his soul lays bare.

Restitutor (Restorer)

He restores Your Truth by word and deed,
Confessing and cleansing unclean souls.
His soft touch sows many sacred seeds,
Spirits bloom within the mystic whole.

Sanctus (Holy)

Holy is this chosen one so true,
Filled with pure grace in Your Tender Heart.
Consumed with chaste thoughts of love for You,
He seeks Your Face, never to depart.

Transcendens (Transcendent)

Bounded not by time or earthly space,
Or human thoughts or Satan's strong hold.
Free, he moves swiftly from place to place,
On wings of prayers, with light hands of gold.

Unitas (Oneness)

Immersed in Your Thoughts he deeply dwells,
Breath by breath You penetrate his soul.
Your Heart embraces as his heart swells,
Your captive won, rests completely whole.

Veritas (Truthfulness)

On Your rock he plants his sturdy foot,
Your lawful Truth is clearly proclaimed.
Your tremendous Word is the firm root,
Despite the vexed clamor of the
shamed.

Xenium (Gift)

Your precious gift by souls is measured,
By those he brings to Thy loving care.
Souls rejoice and Your Love is
treasured,
As Your Light bursts forth beyond
compare.

Ymnos (Hymn)

He sings out to You in glorious praise,
And plays the piano keys with might.
Praying loudly twice then thrice to
raise,
Body and soul to Your Holy Sight.

Zona (Territory)

He claims the earth, below and above,
For Your Divine and Mystic Realm.
He conquers hard souls with gentle
love,
Bidding blessed Angels to come and
dwell.

Bibliography

Papal Addresses, Books, Encyclicals, Homilies, and Letters:

His Holiness Pope Benedict XVI:

—Ratzinger, Joseph Cardinal [Pope Benedict XVI]. *God in the World: Believing and Living in Our Time: A Conversation with Peter Seewald.* Translated by Henry Taylor. San Francisco, CA: Ignatius Press, 2002.

—Ratzinger, Joseph Cardinal [Pope Benedict XVI]. *Salt of the Earth: The Church at the End of the Millennium: An Interview with Peter Seewald.* Translated by Adrian Walker. San Francisco, CA: Ignatius Press, 1997.

—Ratzinger, President Joseph Cardinal Ratzinger [Pope Benedict XVI], Rev. Sebastian Karotemprel, S.D.B., Msgr. Roland Minnerath, Rev. Thomas Norris, Rev. Rafael Salazar Cardenas, M.Sp.S., and Msgr. Anton Strukelj. *Memory and Reconciliation: The Church and the Faults of the Past.* Citta del Vaticano: International Theological Commission, 1999.

His Holiness John Paul II:

—*Apostolic Letter Mulieris Dignitatem: On the Dignity and Vocation of Women on the Occasion of the Marian Year.* Citta del Vaticano: Libreria Editrice Vaticana, 1988. *http://www.vatican.va/holy_father/john_paul_ii/apost_letters/documents/hf_jp-ii_apl_15081988_mulieris-dignitatem_en.html.*

—*Apostolic Letter ROSARIUM VIRGINIS MARIAE of the Supreme Pontiff John Paul II to the Bishops, Clergy and Faithful of the Most Holy Rosary.* Citta del Vaticano: Libreria Editrice Vaticana, 2002. *http:// www.vatican.va/holy_father/john_paul_ii/apost_letters/documents/ hf_jp-ii_apl_20021016_rosarium-virginis-mariae_en.html.*

—*Crossing the Threshold of Hope.* Edited by Vittorio Messor. New York, NY: Alfred A. Knopf, 1994.

—*Encyclical Dives in Misericordia—On the Mercy of God.* Citta del Vaticano: Libreria Editrice Vaticana, 1980. *http://www.vatican. va/edocs/ENG0215/_INDEX.HTM.*

—*Encyclical Evangelium Vitae, To the Bishops, Priests and Deacons, Men and Women Religious, Lay Faithful and all People of Good Will on the Value and Inviolability of Human Life.* Citta del Vaticano: Libreria Editrice Vaticana, 1995. *http://www.vatican. va/edocs/ENG0141/_INDEX.HTM.*

—*Encyclical Redemptor Hominis, To His Venerable Brothers in the Episcopate The Priests, the Religious Families, the Sons and Daughters of the Church and to all Men and Women of Good Will At the Beginning of His Papal Ministry.* Citta del Vaticano: Libreria Editrice Vaticana, 1979. *http://www.vatican.va/edocs/ENG0218/_INDEX.HTM.*

—*Heaven, Hell and Purgatory. L'Osservatore Romano,* Citta del Vaticano. Heaven: 28 July 1999, 7, Hell: 4 August 1999, 7, Purgatory: 11/18 August, 7, 1999. *http://www.ewtn.org/library/ PAPALDOC/JP2HEAVN.HTM.*

—*Love and Responsibility,* revised edition. San Francisco, CA: Ignatius Press, 1993.

—*Memory and Identity: Conversations at the Dawn of a Millennium.* New York, NY: Rizzoli International Publications, 2005.

—*The Pope in Ireland: Addresses and Homilies,* "Address of Pope John Paul II at Drogheda, 29 September, 1979." Dublin, Ireland: Veritas Publications/Catholic Communications Office, 1979, p.19.

—*The Theology of the Body: Human Love in the Divine Plan.* Boston, MA: Pauline Books and Media, 1997.

His Holiness Paul VI:

—*Homily of the Holy Father Paul VI, "Canonization of Oliver Plunkett."* Citta del Vaticano: Libreria Editrice Vaticana, 1975. *http://www.vatican.va/holy_father/paul_vi/homilies/1975/documents/hf_p-vi_hom_19751012_en.html.*

His Holiness Pope Pius XII:

—*Encyclical of Pope Pius XII on the Mistical Body of Christ* to Our Venerable Brethren, Patriarchs, Primates, Archbishops, Bishops, and Other Local Ordinaries Enjoying Peace and Communion with the Apostolic See. Citta del Vaticano: Libreria Editrice Vaticana, 1943. *http://www.vatican.va/holy_father/pius_xii/encyclicals/documents/hf_p-xii_enc_29061943_mystici-corporis-christi_en.html.*

Books:

Agreda, Venerable Mary. *City of God: Popular Abridgement of The Divine History and Life of the Virgin Mother of God (Manifested to Mary of Agreda for the Encouragement of Men).* Translated by Rev. George J. Blatter. Rockford, IL: Tan Books and Publishers, Inc., 1978.

Amorth, Gabriele. *An Exorcist: More Stories.* Translated by Nicoletta V. MacKenzie. San Francisco, CA: Ignatius Press, 2002.

Amorth, Gabriele. *An Exorcist Tells His Story.* Translated by Nicoletta V. MacKenzie. San Francisco, CA: Ignatius Press, 2002, p. 33-36.

Augustine, St. *The City of God.* Translated by Gerald Walsh, S.J., Demetrius B. Zema, S.J., Grace Monahan, O.S.U., and Daniel J. Honan. Imprimi Potests, John J. McMahon, S.J., Provincial, New York. Nihil Obstat, John M.A. Fearns, S.T.D., Censor Librorum. Imprimatur+Francis Cardinal Spellman, Archbishop of New York. New York: NY: Image Books, 1958.

Avila, St.Teresa. *Teresa of Avila: The Interior Castle.* Translated by Kieran Kavanaugh, O.C.D., and Otilio Rodriguez, O.C.D. Mahwah, New Jersey: Paulist Press, 1979.

Gilbert-Barness, Enid and Diane Debich-Spicer. *Embryo and Fetal Pathology: Color Atlas with Ultrasound Correlation.* West Nyack, NY: Cambridge University Press, 2006.

Beevers, John. *The Autobiography of Saint Therese of Lisieux: The Story of a Soul.* New York, NY: Image Books, 1989.

Broderick, James, S.J. *The Origin of the Jesuits.* Chicago, IL: Loyola Press, 1997.

Brown, Michael H. and Mariani, Drew J. *The Bridge to Heaven: Interviews with Maria Esperanza of Betania.* Lima, PA: Marian Communications, Ltd. 1993.

Butler, W.F.T. *Confiscation in Irish History.* Dublin: Talbot Press, Ltd., 1918.

Carrico, James A. *Life of Venerable Mary of Agreda: Author of The Mystical City of God Autobiography of the Virgin Mary.* Nihil Obstat, Nicolaus Ferraro, T.K.T. Adsessor. Imprimatur+Most. Rev. Leo A. Pursley. Fort Wayne, IN: Alex J. Fiato and Leonard M. Sieradski, 2002.

Carty, Fr. Charles Mortimer. *Padre Pio: The Stigmatist.* Imprimatur+John Gregory Murray, Archbishop of St. Paul. Rockford, IL: Tan and Books Publishers, 1973.

Catechism of the Catholic Church, 2nd ed. Interdicasterial Commission for the Catechism of the Catholic Church. Imprimi Potest+Joseph Cardinal Ratzinger. Citta del Vaticano: Libreria Editrice, 1997.

—The Profession of Faith, Part I, Article 12: "I Believe in Life Everlasting," Sec. 1020-1060, p. 266-275.

—The Profession of Faith, Part II: "The Communion of the Church of Heaven and Earth," Sec. 960-962, p. 250.

—The Profession of Faith, Part III: "The Final Purification, or Purgatory," Sec. 1030-1032, p. 268-269.

—Life in Christ, Part III: "The Gifts and Fruits of the Holy Spirit," Sec. 1830-1832, p. 450-451.

—Life in Christ, Part V: "The Proliferation of Sin," Sec. 1866, p. 457.

The Catholic Encyclopedia: An International Work of Reference on the Constitution, Doctrine, Discipline and History of the Catholic Church, Vol. XV. Edited by Charles G. Herbermann~Edward A. Pace~Conde B. Pallen~Thomas J. Shahan and John J. Wynn. Nihil Obstat, Remy Lafort, S.T.D., Censor. Imprimatur+John Cardinal Farley, Archbishop of New York. New York, NY: *Catholic Encyclopedia*, imprint, Robert Appleton Company, 1907-1912. New York, NY: Encyclopedia Press, Inc., 1913. Online edition: New Advent, Inc., 2003. *www.newadvent.org*.

—Grattan-Flood, W.H. Vol. XII. *St. Patrick's Purgatory*. Transcribed by Mary Thomas. New York, NY: Robert Appleton Company, 1911. *http://www.newadvent.org/cathen/12575a.htm*.

—Hanna, Edward J. Vol. XII. *Purgatory*. Transcribed by William G. Bilton, Ph.D. New York, NY: Robert Appleton Company, 1911. *http://www.newadvent.org/cathen/12575a.htm*.

—Hilgers, Joseph. Vol. XI. *Novenas, Ad honorem Sanctae Dei Genetricis, Rosarii sacratissimi Reginae*. Transcribed by Herman R. Holbrook. New York, NY: Robert Appleton Company, 1911. *http://www.newadvent.org/cathen/11141b.htm*.

—Moran, Patrick Francis Cardinal. Vol. XII. *Blessed Oliver Plunkett*. Transcribed by Marie Jutras. New York, NY: Robert Appleton Company, 1911. *http://www.newadvent.org/cathen/12169b.htm*.

—Pohle, Joseph. Vol. VIII. *Justification*. Transcribed by Terry Wilkinson. New York, NY: Robert Appleton Company, 1910. *http://www.newadvent.org/cathen/08573a.htm*.

—Pohle, Joseph. Vol. VI. *Sanctifying Grace*. Transcribed by Scott Anthony Hibbs and Wendy Lorraine Hoffman. New York, NY: Robert Appleton Company, 1909. *http://www.newadvent.org/cathen/06701a.htm*.

—Reid, George J. Vol. III. *Canon of the Old Testament*. Translated by Ernie Stefanick. New York, NY: Robert Appleton Company, 1908. *http://www.newadvent.org/cathen/03267a.htm*.

—Toner, P.J. Vol. IV. *Prayers for the Dead*. Transcribed by Michael T. Barrett. New York, NY: Robert Appleton Company, 1908. *http://www.newadvent.org/cathen/04653a.htm*.

—Waldron, Augustine. Vol. XV. *Virtue*. Transcribed by Barbara J. Barrett. New York, NY: Robert Appleton Company, 1912. *http://www.newadvent.org/cathen/15472a.htm*.

Chamberlain, Ph.D., David B. *The Mind of Your Newborn Baby*, 3rd Ed. Berkeley, CA: North Atlantic Books, 1998.

Chearbhaill, Máire Ní. *Saints and Blesseds of the Servite Order*. Chicago, IL: Friar Servants of Mary, 1988.

Cobett, William. *A History of the Protestant Reformation in England and Ireland*. Rockford, Il: Tan Books and Publishers, 1988.

Cruz, Joan Carroll. *Eucharistic Miracles and Eucharistic Phenomena in the Lives of the Saints*. Nihil Obstat, Rev. John H. Miller, C.SC., Censor Librorum. Imprimatur+Philip M. Hannan, Archbishop of New Orleans, 1986. Rockford, Illinois: Tan Books and Publishers, Inc., 1986. Ch. 1, p. 3-7.

DeLuca MSW, Phil. *The Solo Partner: Repairing Your Relationship on Your Own*. Point Roberts, WA: Harley and Marks Publishers Inc., 1996.

DeMontfort, St. Louis.*The Secret of the Rosary*. Translated by Mary Barbour, T.O.P. Nihil Obstat, Gulielmus F. Hughes, S.T.L., Censor Libororum. Imprimatur +Thomas Edmundus Molloy, S.T.D., Archiepiscopus-Episcopus Brooklyniensis. Bay Shore, NY: Monfort Publications, 1954.

De'Pazzi, Saint Maria Maddalena. *Maria Maddalena de'Pazzi (Selected Revelations)*. Translated by Armando Maggi. Mahwah, New Jersey: Paulist Press, 2000.

Diamond, Eugene F., MD. *This Curette for Hire*. Chicago, IL: ACTA Foundation, 1977.

Donaghy, Rev. Thomas J. and Lawrence G. Lovasik. *Lives of the Saints*,Vol. 1-2. Totowa, NJ: Catholic Book Publishing Co., 1997.

Donnelly, Frank. *Until the Storm Passes: St. Oliver Plunkett, the Archbishop of Armagh Who Refused to Go Away.* Drogheda, Ireland: St. Peter's Roman Catholic Church, 2000.

Douay Rheims Version. *The Holy Bible,* revised by Bishop Richard Challoner, A.D. 1749-1752. Imprimatur+J. Cardinal Gibbons, Archbishop of Baltimore. Rockford, Illinois: Tan Books and Publishers, Inc., 1971.

Duffy, Eamon. *The Stripping of the Altars: Traditional Religion in England 1400-1580.* New Haven, CT: Yale University Press, 1992.

Fickett, Harold. *The Living Christ: The Extraordinary Lives of Today's Spiritual Heroes.* New York, NY: Doubleday, 2002. Ch. 2, "In Mexico City: The Healer."

Forristal, Rev. Desmond. *Oliver Plunkett in his own words.* Nihil Obstat, Kevin Kennedy, D.D., Imprimatur+Dermot, Archbishop of Dublin. Dublin, Ireland: Veritas Publications, 1975.

Freeman, Philip. *St. Patrick of Ireland.* New York, NY: Simon and Schuster Paperbacks, 2004.

Gibler, Rocheavene M. *The Power of Miracles: The Truth Behind Spiritual Healing.* London: Headline Book Publishing, 1998.

Good, Eileen. *Places Apart: Lough Derg.* Dublin, Ireland: Veritas Publications, 2003. *www.veritas.ie.*

Goodenough, Erwin R. *The Church in the Roman Empire.* New York, NY: Henry Holt Company, 1931.

Graham, The Right Reverend Henry G. *Where We Got the Bible: Our Debt to the Catholic Church.* Imprimatur+Johannes Ritchie, Vicar General, Glasguae 1911. Rockford, IL: Tan Books and Publishers, 1977.

Hampsch, Rev. John, C.M.F. *Healing Your Family Tree.* Huntington, Indiana: Our Sunday Visitor Publications Division, 1989.

Hippocrates, "The Hippocratic Oath." From *The Hippocratic Oath.* Translated from the Greek by Ludwig Edelstein. Baltimore, MD: Johns Hopkins Press, 1943.

James, E.O. *Seasonal Feasts and Festivals*. New York, NY: Barnes and Noble, 1961.

Keane, O.S.M. Very Reverend James Mary, editor. "Queen of Martyrs: Pray for Us." Chicago, Illinois: Servite Fathers, 1987.

Le Goff, Jacques. *The Birth of Purgatory*. Chicago, Illinois: University of Chicago Press, Chicago, 1981.

Linn, Dennis and Matthew Linn. *Healings of Memories: Prayer and Confession Steps to Inner Healing*. Imprimatur +Leo F. Weber S.J. Ramsey, New Jersey: Paulist Press, 1974.

—*Healing Life's Hurts: Healing Memories Through the Five Stages of Forgiveness*. Imprimi Potest+Bruce F. Biever, S.J., Provincial, Wisconsin Province Society of Jesus. Ramsey, New Jersey: Paulist Press, 1978.

Linn, Matthew, Shiela Fabricant, and Dennis Linn. *Healing the Eight Stages of Life*. Imprimatur+Patrick J. Burns, S.J. Ramsey. New Jersey: Paulist Press, 1988.

—*Healing the Greatest Hurt*. Imprimatur+Patrick J. Burns, S.J. Ramsey, New Jersey: Paulist Press, 1985.

Linn, Shiela Fabricant, William Emerson, Dennis Linn, and Matthew Linn. *Remembering Our Home: Healing Hurts and Receiving Gifts from Conception to Birth*. Imprimatur+D. Edward Mathie, S.J. Ramsey. New Jersey: Paulist Press, 1999.

Loyola, Ignatius. *The Spiritual Exercises of St. Ignatius of Loyola*. Edited by Susan B. Varenne. Translated by Louis J. Puhl. New York, NY: Knopf Publishing Group, 2000.

MacNutt, Francis. *Deliverance from Evil Spirits: A Practical Manual*. Grand Rapids, MI: Chosen Books, 2001.

Marnell, William H. *Light from the West: The Irish Mission and the Emergence of Modern Europe*. New York, NY: The Seabury Press, 1978.

McAll, Kenneth. *Healing the Family Tree*. London: Sheldon Press, 1982.

McCarthy, C.S.V., Fr. Thomas P., and Cynthia Nicolosi. *Forever a Priest*. Oak Lawn, IL: CMJ Marian Publishers/Soul Assurance Prayer Plan, 2004.

Metress, Ph.D., Seamus P. *Outlines in Irish History: Eight Hundred Years of Struggle*. Detroit, MI: Connolly Press, 1995. p. 27-28.

Michalenko, C.M.G.T., Sister. *The Life of Faustina Kowalska: The Authorized Biography*. Nihil Obstat, Rev. Joseph J. Sielski, M.I.C. Imprimatur, Most Rev. Richard J. Drabik, M.I.C., Provincial Stockbridge, MA. Nihil Obstat, Most Rev. George H. Pearce, S.M. Imprimatur+Most Rev. Joseph F. Maguire, Bishop of Springfield, MA. Ann Arbor, MI: Servant Publications, 1999.

Mould, B.T., Doctor C. Pochin-Mould. *Ireland of the Saints*. London: Batsford Ltd., 1953.

Mullan, Don. *Eyewitness Bloody Sunday: The Truth*. Dublin, Ireland: Merlin Publishing, 2002. *www.merlinwolfhound.com*.

Murray, David D. *A Pilgrim's Guide to Maria Valtorta's The Poem of the Man~God*, 3rd edition. Ringwood,Vic. 3795 Australia: Maria Valtorta Reader's Group, 2002. *www.valtorta.alphalink. com.au*.

O'Callaghan, Sean. *To Hell or Barbados: The Ethnic Cleansing of Ireland*. Kerry, Ireland: Mount Eagle Publications, 2000.

O'Carroll, C.S. Sp, Michael. *Theotokos: A Theological Encyclopedia of the Blessed Virgin Mary*. Wilmington, DE: Michael Glazier, Inc., 1983.

Parsons, Heather. *Father Peter Mary Rookey: Man of Miracles*. Dublin, Ireland: Robert Andrew Press, 1994.

Peck, M. Scott Peck, M.D. *People of the Lie: The Hope for Healing Human Evil*. New York, NY: Touchstone, 1983.

Pegis, Anton C., editor. *Basic Writings of St. Thomas Aquinas*. Vol. I. and II. Nihil Obstat, Arthur J. Scanlan, S.T.D., Censor Librorum. Imprimatur+Francis J. Spellman, D.D., Archbishop, New York. New York, NY: Random House, 1945.

—Aquinas, ST I, Q. 19, ART. 9: "The Will of God, Ninth Article, Whether God Wills Evils," Vol. I., p. 209.

—Aquinas, ST I, Q. 76, ART. 3: "Whether Besides the Intellectual Soul There Are in Man Other Souls Essentially Different From One Another?" Vol. I. p. 704-707.

—Aquinas, ST I, Q. CI, ART. 1: "Whether in the State of Innocence Children Would Have Been Born with Perfect Knowledge," Vol. I., p. 941.

—Aquinas, ST I, Q. 118, ART. 2: "Whether the Intellectual Soul Is Produced from the Semen?" Vol. I., p. 1085-1086.

—Aquinas, ST II, Q. 79, ART. 4: "The Will of God, Fourth Article, Whether Blindness and Hardness of Heart Are Directed to the Salvation of Those Who are Blinded and Hardened," Vol. II., p. 656-657.

—Aquinas, ST II, Q. 87, ART 6: "Whether the Debt of Punishment Remains After Sin?" Vol. II., p. 715.

—Aquinas, ST II, Q. 87, ART. 7: "Whether Every Punishment Is Inflicted for a Sin?" Vol. II., p. 716.

—Aquinas, ST II, Q. 87. ART. 8: "Whether Anyone Is Punished for Another's Sins?" Vol. II., p. 718.

—Aquinas, ST II, Q. 91, ART. 4: "On the Various Kinds of Law, Whether There Was Any Need for a Divine Law?" Vol. II., p. 753.

—Aquinas, ST II, Q. 94, ART. 6: "Whether The Natural Law Can Be Abolished From The Heart of Man?" Vol. II., p. 781.

Rees, Elizabeth. *Celtic Saints: Passionate Wanderers*. London: Thames and Hudson, 2000.

Rengers, OFM, Cap., Rev. Christopher. *The 33 Doctors of the Church*. Nihil Obstat, Rev. Isidore Dixon, Censor Deputatus. Imprimatur+Most. Rev. William E. Lori. Rockford, Il: Tan Books and Publishers Inc., 2000.

Rookey, O.S.M., Father Peter M. Rookey. *Shepherd of Souls: The Virtuous Life of Saint Anthony Pucci.* Oak Lawn, Illinois: CMJ Marian Publishers, 2002.

Daniel-Rops, editor. *The Miracle of Ireland.* Translated from the French by The Earl of Wicklow. "Patrick's Hymn." Translated by J. Ryan, S.J. Nihil Obstat, Joannes O'Donoghue, Censor. Imprimi Potest+Joannes Carolus Archidep. Dublinen, Hiberniae Primas, Dublini. Dublin, Ireland: Clonmore and Reynolds, Ltd., 1959, p. 28-30.

Schouppe S.J., Fr. F. X. *Purgatory Explained.* Rockford, Illinois: Tan Books & Publishers, 2003-2005. *http://www.tanbooks. com/index.php/page/shop:flypage/product_id/694/.*

Spink, Kathryn. *Mother Teresa: A Complete Authorized Biography.* New York, NY: Harper Collins Publishers, 1998.

Staniforth, Maxwell and Andrew Louth, translators. *Early Christian Writings: The Apostolic Fathers.* New York, NY: Penguin Books, 1968.

Taylor, S.J., Michael J. *Purgatory.* Huntington, Indiana: Our Sunday Visitor Publishing Division, 1998.

Teresa, Mother. *In the Heart of the World: Thoughts, Stories, & Prayers.* Edited by Beck Beneate. Novato, CA: New World Library, 1997.

Teresa, Mother. *Mother Teresa: In My Own Words, 1910-1997.* Edited by José Luis González-Balado. New York, NY: Gramercy Books, 1996.

Teresa, Mother. *Mother Teresa's Reaching Out in Love: Stories Told by Mother Teresa.* Compiled and edited by Edward Le Joly and Jaya Chaliha. New York, NY: Barnes and Noble Books, 2002.

Third Plenary Council of Baltimore. *Baltimore Catechism No. 3.* Imprimatur+Archbishop Patrick Hayes, D.D., 1921. Rockford, IL: Tan Books and Publishers, 1974. Ch.13, "The Sacraments," Q 574.

Timmermans, Felix. *The Perfect Joy of St. Francis.* Translated by Raphael Brown. Garden City, NY: Image Books, 1955.

Tobin, Greg. *The Wisdom of St. Patrick: Inspirations from the Patron Saint of Ireland*. New York, NY: Barnes and Noble, 2004.

Trosclair, S.O.S.M., Margaret M. *Do You Believe Jesus Can Heal You?* Marrero, LA: Mary's Helpers Inc., 1996.

Valtorta, Maria. *The Poem of the Man~God*. Vol. 1-5. Translated from the Italian by Nicandro Picozzi, M.A., D.D. Revised by Patrick McLaughlin, M.A. Valtortiano srl, Isola de Liri (FR) Italy: Centro Editoriale, Valtortiano, 1990:

—The Hidden Life, "The Person and Works of Maria Valtorta," Vol. 1, p. X.
—The Hidden Life, Sec. 1: "Introduction," Vol. 1, p. 7.
—The Hidden Life, Sec. 12: "Joseph is Appointed Husband of the Virgin," Vol. 1, p. 65-66.
—The Second Year of Public Life, Sec. 178: "Jesus Meets Three Men Who Want to Follow Him," Vol. 2, p. 191.
—The Second Year of Public Life, Sec. 199: "Jesus Goes to the Lepers of Siloam and Ben Hinnom, The Power of Mary's Word," Vol. 2, p. 307-309.
—The Passion, Sec. 598: "The Passover Supper," Vol. 5, p. 518.
—The Passion, Sec. 599: "The Agony and the Arrest at Gethsemane," Vol. 5, p. 533.
—The Passion, Sec. 599: "The Agony and the Arrest at Gethsemane," Vol. 5, p. 542.
—The Glorification, Sec: 616: "Comment on the Resurrection," Vol. 5, p. 712.

Walsh, Dermot P.J. *Bloody Sunday and the Rule of Law in Northern Ireland*. Dublin, Ireland: Gill & MacMillan, 2000.

Willis, S.J., John R., editor. *The Teachings of the Church Fathers*. San Francisco, CA: Ignatius Press, 2002.

Woods, O.P., Richard J. *The Spirituality of the Celtic Saints*. Mary Knoll, New York: Orbis Books, 2000.

Abstracts and Articles:

Bellieni, Dr. Carlo. "What the Unborn Sense in the Womb." Zenit.org. Rome, Oct. 4, 2005.

Brennan, Malcolm. "English martyrs," *The Angelus,* December, Vol., Number 12 (1978). *http://www.angeluspress.org/angelus/1978_December/Saint_Oliver_Plunkett.htm.*

Brown, Tony. "Tony Brown's Miracle," *The Mary's Healers Newsletter.* Marrero, LA: Mary's Helpers Inc. (June 1994-March 1995).

Caplan, Robert J., Kim O'Neil, and Kimberly A. Arbeau. Maternal anxiety during and after pregnancy and infant temperament at three months of age. *Journal of Prenatal & Perinatal Psychology & Health,* 19(3) (Spring, 2005)

Chamberlain, Ph.D., David B. Historical perspectives on pain: experiments in infant pain, excerpts from: Babies don't feel pain: a century of denial in medicine. Association for Pre- and Perinatal Psychology and Health (APPPAH). *http://ww.birthpsychology.com.* For full text of this article, see: Robbie Davis-Floyd & Joseph Dumit, editors. "Cyborg Babies: From Techno-Sex to Techno Tots." NewYork and London: Routledge (1998).

—The fetal senses. Association for Pre- and Perinatal Psychology and Health (APPPAH). *http://www.birthpsychology. com/lifebefore/fetalsense.html.*

—Communication before language. Association for Pre- and Perinatal Psychology and Health (APPPAH). 1995. *http://birthpsychology.com/lifebefore/comm.html.*

—Prenatal memory and learning. Association for Pre- and Perinatal Psychology and Health (APPPAH). *http://www. birthpsychology.com.*

De Grandis, S.S.J., Rev. Robert. *Healing the Broken Heart.* *http://www.degrandisssj.com.*

Dietzen, Rev. John. "Church never said 'limbo' was fate of unbaptized." *The Catholic New World,* Chicago, Illinois (September 25-October 8, 2005).

Hampsch, C.M.F, Rev. John H. "Blessed Salt." Claretian Tape Ministry. *http://claretiantapeministry.org.*

—*Praying for Healings* of the Family Tree. Claretian Tape Ministry. *http://claretiantapeministry.org.*

Legendre, Elson. "My Healing through Fr. Rookey," *The Mary's Healers Newsletter.* Marrero, LA: Mary's Helpers Inc. (September, 1994).

Lewis, Ph.D, Marilyn W., Barbara L. Lanzara, M.D., Janet L. Stein, M.D., and Deborah S. Hasin, Ph.D. Maternal drinking patterns and drug use increase impact of terrorism among pregnant women attending prenatal care. *Journal of Prenatal & Perinatal Psychology & Health* 19(4) (Summer, 2005).

Lipton, Ph.D., Bruce H. Maternal emotions and human development. *Early and Very Early Parenting, Life Before Birth.* Association for Pre- and Perinatal Psychology and Health (APPPAH). *www.birthpsychology.com.*

Miles, O.S.B., Abbot Andrew. "Blessed Oil." Pecos Benedictine Community, Pecos, New Mexico. Dove Publications. *http://www. pecosmonastery.org.*

Paci, Stephano Maria. "Vatican exorcist Amorth speaks on Satan's smoke." *Spero News,* March 16, 2006. *http://www. speroforum.com/site/article.asp?id=2879.*

Pavone, Rev. Frank. *Shepherding the Flock After Abortion.* Pontifical Council for the Family, Priests for Life. *http://www.seminarianlifelink. org/postabortion/shepherdingflock.htm; www.priestsforlife.org.*

Reardon, David C. The character of post-abortion syndrome: a list of major psychological sequaelae of abortion. Elliot Institute (1997). *http://www.abortionfacts.com/reardon/post_abortion_ syndrome_character.asp.*

Rhodes, Jeane M., Ph.D. Historical perspectives. *Journal of Prenatal & Perinatal Psychology & Health. http://birthpsychology. com/birthscene/ppic3.html.*

Schore, Ph.D, Allan N. The neurobiology of attachment and early personality organization. *Journal of Prenatal and*

Perinatal Psychology and Health, Vol. 16(3) (Spring 2002). *http://birthpsychology.com/birthscene/ppic3.html.*

Schwartz, M.D., Fred J. Music and prenatal stress reduction. *Journal of Prenatal and Perinatal Psychology and Health,* Vol. 16(3), (Fall, 1997). *http://www.birthpsychology.com/lifebefore/sound3.html.*

Sears, Ph.D., S.J., Robert T. The background of satanism today. Unpublished.

—A Christian approach to discerning spiritualities. *Journal of Christian Healing,* Vol. 21, no. 1 (Spring, 1999) p. 15-34. *http://www.familytreehealing.com.*

—Healing and family spiritual/emotional systems. *Journal of Christian Healing,* Vol. 5, no. 1 (1983) p. 10-23. *http://www. familytreehealing.com.*

—Healing the gender wars: a scriptural view. *http://www. familytreehealing.com.*

—Into the heart of God: John's Gospel and spiritual development (2004). *http://www.familytreehealing.com.*

—Jung and Christianity: an interpersonal perspective. *Journal of Christian Healing,* Vol. 12, no. 2. (Summer, 1990) p. 11-19. *http://www.familytreehealing.com.*

—Model for spiritual development. *http://www.familytreehealing. com.*

—Praying for the departed: theological reflection. *The Journal of Christian Healing,* Vol. 7, Number 2. *http://www.familytreehealing.com.*

—Trinitarian love as ground of the Church, with critique by Roger Haight, SJ. *Theological Studies,* Vol. 37 (Dec. 1976) p. 652-679. *http://www.familytreehealing.com.*

—Trinitarian love and male-female community. *Journal of Christian Healing,* Vol. 6, no. 1 (1984) p. 32-39. *http://www. familytreehealing.com.*

—Resurrecting the wounded community. *Journal of Christian Healing*, Vol. 16, no. 4. (Winter, 1994) p. 3-15. *http://www.familytreehealing.com.*

Sodergan, M.S., Andrew J. Hope for healing: miscarriage and the dignity of the human body (2005). *http://www.christendom-awake.org/pages/may/hopeforhealing.htm.*

Sonne, M.D., John C. On tyrants as abortion survivors. *Journal of Prenatal & Perinatal Psychology & Health,* Vol. 19, No. 2, (2002), pp 149-14. *http://apt.allenpress.com/aptonline/?request=get-abstract&issn=1097-8003&volume=019&issue=02&page=0149 www.birthpsychology.com.*

—The varying behaviors of fathers in the prenatal experience of the unborn: protecting, loving and 'welcoming with arms wide open,' vs. ignoring, unloving, competitive, abusive, abortion minded or aborting. *Journal of Prenatal and Perinatal Psychology and Health,* 19(4) (Summer, 2005). *http://apt.allenpress. com/aptonline/?request=get-abstract&issn=1097-8003&Vol. ume=019&issue=04&page=0319.*

Speckhard, Ph.D., Anne, and Natlia Mufel 2005. Transitioning to the west: gender attitudes about contraception and pregnancy in a former Soviet Union country. *Journal of Prenatal & Perinatal Psychology & Health,* 19(4).

Thomson, Psy.D., Paul. The impact of trauma on the embryo and fetus: an application of the diathesis-stress model and the neurovulnerability-neurotoxicity model. *Journal of Prenatal and Perinatal Psychology and Health,* 19(1), (Fall 2004).

Verny, M.D., D. Psych, F.R.C.P.(C), Thomas R. 1996. Perspectives on violence. *Journal of Prenatal & Perinatal Psychology & Health. http://www.birthpsychology.com/violence/verny.html.*

Vitz, Paul C. and Philip Mango. Kerrnbergian psychodynamics and religious aspects of the forgiveness process. *Journal of Psychology and Theology.* Rosemead School of Psychology Biola University, 0091-6471/410-730 1997, Vol. 25, No.1. *http://www.saintmichael.net/articles/articles_forgiveness.htm.*

"What the Church Has Said About Children Who Die Without Baptism: Father Peter Gumpel Gives an Overview." *Zenit—The World Seen from Rome,* December 12, 2004. *http://www.zenit. org/english/visualizza.phtml?sid=63609.*

"What the Unborn Sense in the Womb: Interview with Dr. Carlo Bellieni." *Zenit—The World Seen from Rome,* October 4, 2005. *http://www.zenit.org/english/visualizza.phtml?sid=63609.*

On-Line Articles

"Aurelius Prudentius (Hymn-Writer)." *http://www.bach-cantatas. com/Lib/Prudentius-Aurelius.htm.*

"Cathedral Tour: Chapel of St. Patrick and the Saints of Ireland." Westminster Cathedral. *http://www.westminstercathedral.org. uk/art/art_chsp.html.*

"Does a Fetus Feel Pain?" Abort 73.com. *http://www.abort73. com/HTML/I-A-2a-pain.html.*

"The Rule of St. Augustine." The Dominican Family. *http://www. op.org/international/english/Documents/general_dox/augustin. htm.*

"Fetal Pain: Unborn Babies Suffer Pain While They Are Being Killed by Abortion." Minnesota Citizens Concerned for Life. April 20, 2004. *http://66.102.7.104/search?q=cache: OmVS_AdLXnIJ: www.mccl.org/fp_news/fetal_pain.htmfetalmove mentdurinabortion&hl=en&gl=us&ct=clnk&cd=3&ie=UTF-8.*

"Oliver Plunkett." *Patron Saint Index. http://www.catholic-forum. com/saints/sainto13.htm.*

"Praying for Peace." *An Phoblacht Republican News,* Thursday, 22 April, 1999. *http://republican-news.org/archive/1999/April22/22lett.html.*

"Profile: Cardinal William Conway." *BBC News World Edition,* Friday, December 20, 2002. *http://news.bbc.co.uk/2/hi/uk_news/ northern_ireland/2594079.stm.*

"Seven Deadly Sins." *http://www.answers.com/topic/seven-deadly-sinsAureliusClemensPrudentius.*

"Saints & Angels, St. Oliver Plunkett." *Catholic Online. http://www.catholic.org/saints/saint.php?saint_id=372.*

"The Truth about Fetal Pain." Physicians for Life. *http://www.physiciansforlife.org/content/view/921/43/.*

Audio Tapes:

Rookey, O.S.M, Father Peter Mary. *Canticle of Love.* Olympia Fields, IL: International Compassion Ministry.

Rookey, O.S.M., Father Peter Mary. *Seven Sorrows Scriptural Rosary.* Olympia Fields, IL: International Compassion Ministry.

International Compassion Ministry

Letters and calls can be directed to:

International Compassion Ministry
20180 Governors Highway Suite 203
Olympia Fields, IL 60461-1067
708.748.MARY (6279)
Father Peter Mary Rookey, O.S.M

List of Illustrations

Cover Photographs

Servite Reliquary Crucifix and Father Peter Mary Rookey, O.S.M., Chicago, Illinois, 2005. Photograph by John Sundlof.

Rosary Meditation I, Father Peter Mary Rookey, O.S.M., International Compassion Ministry, Chicago, Illinois, 2005. Photograph by John Sundlof.

The Miracle Prayer

Fig. 1. *The Risen Christ,* stained glass window, St. Ignatius Parish, Chicago, Illinois, 2006. p. ii

Chapter One: Those Who Believe

Fig. 2. *Father Peter Mary Rookey, O.S.M.,* International Compassion Ministry, Olympia Fields, Illinois, 2005. Photograph by John Sundlof. p. xii.

Fig. 3. *Father Peter Mary Rookey Preparing for Mass I,* International Compassion Ministry, Olympia Fields, Illinois, 2005. Photograph by John Sundlof. p. 2.

Fig. 4. *Touched by the Spirit,* Our Lady of Sorrows Basilica, 2002. p. 4.

God Calls

Fig. 18. *Seeking the Sacred: Father Peter Mary Rookey, O.S.M.,* Pilgrimage to the Holy Land, 2005. Photograph by Robert A. Benson. p. 72.

The Journey Continues

Fig. 19. *Servite Mosaic Emblem,* altar, Our Lady of Sorrows Basilica, Chicago, Illinois, 2006. p. 78.

Fig. 20. *Pietà,* original sculpture by Michelangelo Buonarroti (1499); marble reproduction carved in Pietrasanta, Italy, by Spartaco Palla, Our Lady of Sorrows Basilica, Chicago, Illinois, 2005. Photograph by John Sundlof. p. 82.

Fig. 21 and 22. *Our Lady of Sorrows,* altar and statue, Our Lady of Sorrows Basilica, Chicago, Illinois, 2006. p. 84-85.

Fig. 23. *Crozier,* Ordination Mass at the Cathedral of Caracas, Caracas, Venezuela, 2006. p. 92.

The Gift of Healing

Fig. 24. *From the Remains of St. Philip Benizi, O.S.M.,* relic, Friars' Chapel, Our Lady of Sorrows Basilica, Chicago, Illinois, 2006. p. 96.

Fig. 25. *Filled with Laughter, Father Peter Mary Rookey, O.S.M.,* International Compassion Ministry, Olympia Fields, Illinois, 2004. Photograph by Robert A. Benson. p. 104.

In the Service of Souls

Fig. 26. *Crucifix,* St. John Cantius Parish, Chicago, Illinois, 2006. p. 110.

Fig. 27. *Father Peter Mary Rookey Playing the Organ,* organ loft, Our Lady of Sorrows Basilica, Chicago, Illinois, 2006. p. 118.

Fig. 28. *St. Cecilia: Patron Saint of Musicians, Poets, and Singers,* stained glass window, Our Lady of Sorrows Basilica, Chicago, Illinois, 2006. p. 119.

God's Gift of Peace

The Power of Saints and Relics

Fig. 39. *Blessed Mother and the Infant Jesus,* Our Lady's Chapel, St. Ignatius Parish, Chicago, IL, 2006. p. 174.

Fig. 40. *Reliquary of St. Ambrose, Father and Doctor of the Church,* St. John Cantius Parish, Chicago, Illinois, 2006. p. 178.

Praise, Invoke, Petition

Fig. 41. *Intercession: Eucharistic Celebration and Father Peter Mary Rookey, O.S.M.,* International Compassion Ministry, Olympia Fields, Illinois, 2005. Photograph by John Sundlof. p. 186.

Fig. 42. *Phone Prayer: Father Peter Mary Rookey, O.S.M.,* International Compassion Ministry, Olympia Fields, Illinois, 2005. Photograph by John Sundlof. p. 190.

Fig. 43. *Blessed Mother,* Italian wood-carved statue, Chicago, Illinois, 2006. p. 196.

Pray, Pray, Pray

Fig. 44. *Father Peter Mary Rookey, O.S.M.,* Chicago, Illinois, 2005. Photograph by John Sundlof. p. 200.

Fig. 45. *Jesus Christ Baptized by St. John the Baptist,* stained glass window, Our Lady of Sorrows Basilica, Chicago, Illinois, 2006. p. 208.

Giving Gifts to God

Fig. 46. *Our Lady of Czestochowa, the Black Madonna,* altar, St. John Cantius Parish, Chicago, Illinois, 2006. p. 214.

Fig. 47. *Father Peter Mary Rookey, O.S.M.,* Chicago, Illinois, 2005. Photograph by John Sundlof. p. 216.

Fig. 48. *Peace: Father Mary Rookey in Petra, Jordan,* Pilgrimage to the Holy Land, 2005. Photograph by Robert A. Benson. p. 222.

Freely Aligning with God

Turning Toward God

Spiritual Enslavement and Free Will

Fig. 60. *St. Clare of Assisi,* stained glass window, St. John Cantius Parish, Chicago, Illinois, 2006. p. 274.

Fig. 61. *Sisters in Christ,* Ordination Mass, Cathedral of Caracas, Caracas, Venezuela, 2006. p. 276.

Fig. 62. *El Señor de Los Milagros (Jesus of the Miracles),* Peruvian painting, St. Ignatius Parish, Chicago, Illinois, 2006. p. 278.

Fig. 63. *Vicki Guiterrez and Bill Mea,* International Compassion Ministry, Betania, Venezuela, 2006. p. 284.

Praying for the Healing of the Spiritual Family

Fig. 64. *Love One Another,* House of Bethany, Vandalia, Illinois, 2007. p. 290.

Fig. 65. *Gift of Peace,* International Compassion Ministry, Olympia Fields, Illinois, 2005. p. 294.

Fig. 66. *Our Lady of Betania, Reconciler of Peoples and Nations,* Betania, Venezuela, 2006. p. 296.

Fig. 67. and 68. Parts I and II. *A New and Everlasting Covenant: Father Peter Mary Rookey, O.S.M.,* Servite Priory, Berwyn, Illinois, 2006. p. 300-301.

Fig. 69. *King David,* stained glass window, Our Lady of Sorrows Basilica, Chicago, Illinois, 2006. p. 304.

Fig. 70. *Monstrance,* Our Lady of Lourdes, grotto, Chicago, Illinois, 2006. p. 306.

Fig. 71. *St. Anthony of Padua and the Child Jesus,* statue, Our Lady's Chapel, St. Ignatius Parish, Chicago, Illinois, 2006. p. 308.

Fig. 72. *Good Friday Rosary I,* Albany Clinic, Chicago, Illinois, 2006. p. 312.

Reaching Out to God

Fig. 85. *Mother Teresa,* courtesy of Seattle University Calcutta Club. p. 386.

Fig. 86. *St. Patrick,* Our Lady's Chapel, St. Ignatius Parish, Chicago, Illinois, 2006. p. 390.

Fig. 87. *Carved-Rock Cross,* Scelig Mhichíl (Skellig Michael), Kerry, Ireland, 2005. p. 396.

Fig. 88. *This Is The Cup of My Blood: Eucharistic Celebration and Father Peter Mary Rookey, O.S.M.,* International Compassion Ministry, Olympia Fields, Illinois, 2006. p. 398.

Seeking the Character of Christ

Fig. 89. *Christ Teaching,* stained glass window, St. Ignatius Parish, Chicago, Illinois, 2006. p. 404.

Fig. 90. *Our Lady of Fatima,* statue, Our Lady of Sorrows Basilica, Chicago, Illinois, 2006. p. 408.

Fig. 91. *This Is My Body: Eucharistic Celebration and Father Peter Mary Rookey, O.S.M.,* International Compassion Ministry, Olympia Fields, Illinois, 2006. p. 410.

Fig. 92. *A Cup of Water,* Convent of St. Augustine, Los Teques, Venezuela, 2006. p. 412.

Fig. 93. *Joe Molloy Receiving Communion,* International Compassion Ministry, Olympia Fields, Illinois, 2005. Photograph by John Sundlof. p. 418.

Sharing Christ's Healing

Fig. 94. *Jesus and His Sacred Heart,* statue, Our Lady of Sorrows Basilica, Chicago, Illinois, 2008. p. 422.

Fig. 95. *Sharing Christ's Peace,* Basilica of the Annunciation in Nazareth, Pilgrimage to the Holy Land, 2005. Photograph by Robert A. Benson. p. 428.

Index

Q

R

Edwards Brothers Malloy
Oxnard, CA USA
October 16, 2013